Labour and the Free Churches, 1918–1939

Labour and the Free Churches, 1918–1939

Radicalism, Righteousness and Religion

Peter Catterall

BLOOMSBURY ACADEMIC
LONDON • NEW YORK • OXFORD • NEW DELHI • SYDNEY

BLOOMSBURY ACADEMIC
Bloomsbury Publishing Plc
50 Bedford Square, London, WC1B 3DP, UK

BLOOMSBURY, BLOOMSBURY ACADEMIC and the Diana logo
are trademarks of Bloomsbury Publishing Plc

First published in Great Britain 2016
Paperback edition first published 2018

A catalogue record for this book is available from the British Library.

ISBN: HB: 978-1-4411-1589-8
PB: 978-1-3500-6726-4
ePDF: 978-1-4411-0160-0
ePub: 978-1-4411-2599-6

A catalog record for this book is available from the Library of Congress.

Typeset by Newgen Knowledge Works (P) Ltd., Chennai, India

To find out more about our authors and books visit
www.bloomsbury.com and sign up for our newsletters.

To my Nonconformist forebears and relatives, who saw in their efforts to make the world a better place a humble expression of their faith.

Contents

Illustrations

Tables

Figure

Preface

This study originated from conversations with my father about the changing nature and ideals of the Labour Party during the course of the twentieth century. Two research issues to be investigated were established. The first was the commonplace view widely expressed in the literature until the 1960s that Nonconformity had somehow made an as yet unexplored and unquantified contribution to the rise of the Labour Party. The second was that, by the late twentieth century, this contribution had largely disappeared, taking with it something of the spirit and ideals that had turned Labour into a crusade and leaving it instead simply a political organization. To address these issues, I embarked upon a PhD, generously funded by the British Academy, under the always thought-provoking and much-missed guidance of the late lamented John Ramsden at Queen Mary University of London, more years ago than I care to remember. Unlike the modern doctoral student, I then had the luxury of gradually marinating the ideas I had tried to develop over a wide-ranging career. Having to think through related questions, such as the role of religion in the politics of the Conservative Party or of the contemporary Middle East has, I hope, over the years resulted in a deeper and more nuanced understanding of the issues addressed herein.

The result is a work which can be seen narrowly as a contribution to the history of the Labour Party and an attempt to explain the peculiarities of its development in the unusual social and ideational setting in which it found itself, not least because of the prominence of Nonconformity, in early twentieth-century Britain. It can also be seen, equally narrowly, as a contribution to the history of the Free Churches, attempting in the process to explain their social role, their relations with the Liberal and Labour parties and their decline in the twentieth century. This, however, is not an institutional biography of either set of organizations, though there are such elements in particular chapters. It might be more accurate to describe it as a comparative history, though this would also be misleading. It is more nearly seen as an attempt to examine the complex interplay between religious and political organizations, and to conceive of how such a research project can be realized, with the peculiar relationship between Labour and Nonconformity as a case study.

Both religion and politics attempt to speak to truths about the human condition, and how to improve it. This study examines their interaction in the distinctive political, social, economic and intellectual setting of England and Wales during the interwar years. It is a relationship explored through four distinct prisms: at the organizational level of the Free Church leadership; at the level of electoral sociology through looking at responses to the rise of Labour in the chapels; in terms of the impact individual Nonconformists had on Labour, its politics and its policies; and the extent to which this shaped a moral economy of ideas about society, the State and the role of individuals in building a better life for all. This means that it does not fall neatly into the hermetically sealed pigeonholes through which historical practice is customarily (though regrettably in my view) exercised at present. It is not simply an intellectual, political, social or economic history. Instead it has elements of all of these, and attempts to place each in context.

Necessarily, many debts have been incurred in the course of this research. I gratefully acknowledge the assistance of the staff of the following libraries and archives for their assistance: Bolton Central Library and Archives; Bradford Central Library; Bradford Heritage Recording Unit (now part of Bradford Museums collections); the British Library; Cambridge University Library; Churchill College, Cambridge; Hope UK (formerly the Band of Hope Union); Hull History Centre; the Institute of Historical Research, London; John Rylands Library, Manchester; Lambeth Palace Library; Liverpool Record Office; London Metropolitan Archives; the National Archives; Norfolk Record Office and Norwich Central Library (which I was lucky enough to consult before the disastrous fire of 1 August 1994); the Parliamentary Record Office; Stockport Central Library; the University of London Library; and West Yorkshire Archives, Bradford. Special thanks must also go to the many staff of Dr Williams's Library and Friends House Library who helped me over the years. I should particularly mention three former staff at the Institute of Alcohol Studies: Derek Rutherford, for his insights and enthusiasm; Lois Brown, who guided me through their rich holdings of temperance-related material; and Andrew McNeil who, by commissioning me to write *Labour and the Politics of Alcohol: The Decline of a Cause*, required me to think through an important aspect of this research. Stephen Bird, the former archivist of the Labour Party, was most helpful in guiding me through the papers now at the People's History Museum, Manchester. The late Rev. Richard Hamper was equally kind in allowing me to examine archives formerly in the possession of the Free Church Federal Council (and now at Dr Williams's Library).

I have benefited greatly from the warm interest many have taken in this research. To all those who have shown me around chapels, who have written to me or have consented to be interviewed, I owe a great debt. I would particularly like to thank Joyce Jewson for making available various material in the possession of St Mary's Baptist Church, Norwich; the staff of Eastbrook Hall, Bradford (now, sadly, demolished), for all the assistance they afforded me; and Frank Pogson and Gordon Woodhead for their advice and for permission to consult material in their respective possession.

Emma Goode and Claire Lipscomb at Bloomsbury have been helpful, encouraging and very patient editors. I am most grateful to them for their support and chivvying throughout the completion of this manuscript.

Finally, the advice, insights and guidance provided by one's peers on both general context and elusive references are always invaluable. In this regard I would like in particular to thank Clyde Binfield, Robert Pope and Andrew Thorpe, all of whom kindly read the manuscript in its entirety and whose extensive comments have no doubt helped me avoid a number of errors. In addition, I must thank Stuart Ball, David Bebbington, Mark Clapson, James Dingley, Stephen Donoughue, Clive Field, Mark Freeman, Jason Frost, Hugh Gault, Robin Gill, Michael Hughes, Lesley Husselbee,

Mel Johnson, Michael John Law, Jon Lawrence, Hugh McLeod, Sue Morgan, James Obelkevich, Jonathan Parry, Martin Pugh, Keith Robbins, Chris Stevens, Willie Thompson, Alan Wilkinson, Philip Williamson and Matthew Worley. I also acknowledge with gratitude the assistance of those now regrettably deceased: Philip S. Bagwell, Ben Pimlott and Duncan Tanner. To these debts to the departed I must add one to my father, Alfred. I owe him so much, and conversations with him greatly helped me to hone my ideas.

It is all too probable I would never have finished this endeavour without the love and support of Caroline Watkinson and the thought-provoking comparisons she raised about the relationship between religion and politics elsewhere and in earlier eras. To the history of that relationship I offer here this modest contribution.

Peter Catterall
Bexley, February 2016

Abbreviations

AP	Charles G. Ammon Papers (Hull History Centre)
AYB	*Alliance Year Book and Temperance Reformers' Handbook*
BCA	Bradford Congregational Association
BCBRTOA	Bolton Card, Blowing, Ring and Throstle Room Operatives' Association
BDFCC	Bolton & District Evangelical Free Church Council
BHRU	Bradford Heritage Recording Unit
BMA	Bolton Metropolitan Archives
BOCSPA	Bolton Operative Cotton Spinners Provincial Association
BSSLH	*Bulletin of the Society for the Study of Labour History*
BTCYB	*Bradford Trades Council Year Book*
CAPR	Council of Action for Peace and Reconstruction
CLCB	Central Liquor Control Board
CIU	Club and Institute Union
COPEC	Christian Order in Politics, Economics and Citizenship
CPGB	Communist Party of Great Britain
CSL	Christian Socialist League
CYB	*Congregational Year Book*
DLGP	David Lloyd George Papers (PROL)
DORA	Defence of the Realm Act 1914
FCYB	*Free Church Year Book*
FHL	Friends House Library
FTU	Friends Temperance Union
GEP	Sir George Edwards Papers (NRO)
IAS	Institute of Alcohol Studies
ILP	Independent Labour Party
JURCHS	*Journal of the United Reformed Church History Society*
LCA	Liverpool City Archives
LCC	London County Council
LFCC	Liverpool Free Church Council
LMA	London Metropolitan Archives
LN	Liberal National (Party)
LNU	League of Nations Union
LPA	Labour Party Archives (People's History Museum, Manchester)
LYB	*Labour Year Book*
LYM	*Minutes and Proceedings of the London Yearly Meeting of the Society of Friends*
MFGB	Miners' Federation of Great Britain
MSF	Methodist Sacramental Fellowship

NCEFC	National Council of the Evangelical Free Churches
NCEFCP	National Council of the Evangelical Free Churches Papers
NCF	No-Conscription Fellowship
NDP	National Democratic Party
NEC	National Executive Committee (Labour)
NECCC	National Emergency Committee of Christian Citizens
NMWM	No More War Movement
NRO	Norfolk Record Office
NUWM	National Unemployed Workers Movement
PLP	Parliamentary Labour Party
PPU	Peace Pledge Union
PROL	Parliamentary Record Office, London
PWHS	*Proceedings of the Wesley Historical Society*
RFS	Religious Film Society
SCCCCD	Standing Committee of the Christian Churches on the Coal Dispute
SPD	Sozialdemokratische partie Deutschland
SSC	Society of Socialist Christians
SSS	Socialist Sunday Schools
STV	Single Transferable Vote
TCCC	Temperance Council of the Christian Churches
TNA	The National Archives, London
TUC	Trades Union Congress
UDC	Union of Democratic Control
UKA	United Kingdom Alliance
UKBHAR	*United Kingdom Band of Hope Annual Report*
WSC	Sir Winston S. Churchill Papers (Churchill College, Cambridge)
WSOC	War and Social Order Committee (Quaker)
WTL	Workers' Temperance League
WYAB	West Yorkshire Archives, Bradford
YMCA	Young Men's Christian Association

Introduction

Nonconformity has trained our speakers in its pulpits and fashioned our devoted workers in its Sunday Schools.

J. Ramsay MacDonald[1]

It was reading the Gospels and studying the story of the life of Jesus Christ and his spirit and teaching, that brought me into the labour movement. I tell you brothers of the Continental Countries that without the spirit and teaching of Jesus Christ you will fail to realise your ideal of the reconstruction of society on a juster and more human basis.

J. Keir Hardie[2]

The distinctiveness of British Socialism

Alan Bullock claimed in 1960 that 'the contribution of Nonconformity to the British Labour movement is a commonplace: a chapel upbringing has been as characteristic of British trade union leadership, for instance, as a public school education of the leaders of the ruling class'. As the son of a (Unitarian) manse,[3] Bullock was perhaps more inclined than other historians of his generation to spot this connection. He was, however, in good company with many leading figures of the Labour Party itself. The commonplace Bullock pointed to was cited by a range of Labour figures, including those like Clement Attlee of Anglican rather than Nonconformist heritage, during the interwar years and beyond.[4] Then, in 1964, the leader of the Labour Party, the Congregationalist Harold Wilson, observed of the distinctiveness of British Socialism:

> It was the late Secretary of the Labour Party, Mr. Morgan Phillips, who said that Socialism in Britain owed far more to Methodism than to Marx. If he had forgotten his alliteration and said 'Nonconformity', he would have been very near the truth, though that would have been to underrate the great contributions to nineteenth-century Socialist thinking of such Anglicans as Charles Kingsley and Charles Gore.[5]

Wilson did not bother to spell out the contribution he thought either Nonconformity or nineteenth-century Christian Socialists had made to the movement he then led. Presumably, at the time, the relationship was sufficiently commonplace, as Bullock had implied four years earlier, for Wilson not to feel the need to do so. The circumstances in which Morgan Phillips made his famous alliterative remarks are, however, rather more revealing.

Phillips, a Methodist who served as general secretary of the Labour Party from 1944 to 1961, made this claim on a number of occasions in the 1940s and 1950s, not least in his capacity as chairman of Socialist International from 1948 to 1957. He was thus speaking to other European parties that were mostly of a Marxist heritage, which had inherited or developed a distinctly anticlerical flavour in opposition to the entrenched power of both the Catholic Church and, in Northern Europe, Erastian Lutheran churches, all of which were perceived as bulwarks of the established order. In other words, Phillips was explaining to his European audience that the distinctiveness of British Socialism reflected an equally distinctive religious setting.[6]

Catholicism, for instance, though it had pockets of strength – especially in areas of heavy Irish settlement – was much weaker throughout Britain than in most Continental countries. This point can be illustrated by the reflections of the then Marxist J. T. Walton Newbold on why Marxism had such shallow roots in Britain. Writing in 1920 in the theoretical journal of that important forerunner of Labour, the Independent Labour Party (ILP), the man who two years later would become Britain's first elected Communist MP for the Scottish seat of Motherwell claimed: 'The ILP is a British institution … It has grown up in a historic environment peculiar to this country.' That he felt that this peculiarity lay in its religious history was made clear as Newbold went on to argue: 'In Scotland the dominant strain in the ILP has been that of the Covenanter. In England and Wales it has been that of the Nonconformist.'[7] Even though Britain had State churches established by law in England and Scotland (though not in Wales after the Church of England was disestablished there in 1920) these were very different from each other, as well as from their counterparts elsewhere in Europe. As Newbold indicated, the established church in Scotland had itself developed as a type of anticlericalism, in the form of seventeenth-century opposition to episcopacy. Presbyterian in order and Calvinist in doctrine, the Church of Scotland shaped a very different religious setting than that of England. This distinctive religious history of Scotland has thus meant that it has been largely excluded from the present study, except as the birthplace of many of those individuals, both clerical and political, who identified themselves as Nonconformists when they moved south of the border.

There the established Church of England was episcopal in character and more closely aligned with the political establishment than its Scottish counterpart. Into the mid-twentieth century its leaders, such as William Temple, archbishop of Canterbury from 1942 to 1944, could see it as the custodian of the English soul.[8] From the sixteenth century onwards, however, it faced a range of dissenters who were, by the nineteenth century, collectively referred to as Nonconformists. At the end of that century the more positive appellation of Free Churches was increasingly used for what was by then a large body of Protestant Christians who were not part of the established church. That around 50 per cent of Protestant church attendance was not at the parish church mitigated the establishment flavour of the Church of England.[9] It also ensured that the Labour movement emerged in the late nineteenth century in a much less anticlerical setting than elsewhere in Europe. Indeed, Nonconformity was itself a mild form of anticlericalism and the embodiment of radical traditions which, however tenuously could be traced back in England as well to seventeenth-century conflicts.

So distinctive was this Nonconformist witness for more democratic forms of church order and for liberty of conscience against State-sanctioned ideas that, in the midst of the Second World War, the leading Baptist, Ernest Payne, reflected: 'It is not fanciful to connect the failure of political democracy on the Continent with the absence there of a strongly religious tradition of the Free Church type'.[10] In contrast, in Britain, political radicalism did not necessarily lead to irreligion. This was apparent, for instance, at the international gatherings on Labour and religion hosted by F. H. Stead at the Browning Settlement in South London from 1910–15 and again in 1919 and 1922. Such distinctions also continued to be noted by Continental Socialists in the interwar years.[11]

Historiography

It is noteworthy that Newbold focused upon religious distinctiveness from Continental Europe. After all, there were a number of other distinctions as likely to influence a peculiar trajectory for the British Labour movement. There was, for instance, the differentially early emergence of trade unions in Britain and their subsequent financial dominance of the Labour Party they were instrumental in founding.[12] Particularly after 1918 there was a distinctive electoral system. There was also a much earlier move to industrialization and urbanization in Britain. Such factors, as David Redvaldsen has noted, shaped the sociological setting and electoral strategies pursued by Labour in comparison with sister parties elsewhere.[13] They also, of course, influenced the policies through which Labour sought to address the travails of the industrial heartlands of Britain suffering from international competition and long-term decline during the interwar years.

Redvaldsen concentrates on such factors rather than the religious distinctiveness that struck Newbold. In this, arguably, he follows a historiographical tradition that emerged from the 1970s onwards. The commonplace noted by Bullock had by then largely disappeared. Instead, claims that the historic roots of the Labour movement in the nineteenth century lay in Nonconformity were subjected to critical scrutiny.[14] Others, meanwhile, argued that Nonconformity's influence on the Labour movement in the late nineteenth century was limited and mainly at the level of personnel, moving from Nonconformity to a new religion of Socialism and the new organizational culture of Labour.[15]

It is, accordingly, not surprising that the commonplace Bullock wrote of has largely been explored by historians in terms of the origins of the modern British Labour movement between the emergence of Socialist organizations in the 1880s and the outbreak of the Great War.[16] Interestingly, in view of the distinction Newbold pointed to, one of the few exceptions which looks in detail at the relationship between

Nonconformity and Labour after 1918 is an interwar German doctoral thesis.[17] Differences in relations between religion and Labour in Britain and Germany, however, struck Stefan Berger much less when he returned to the comparative study of Socialist parties in the two countries sixty years later. As he rightly points out, there was a tendency to see Socialism as a new and competing religion in both countries, and a related inclination to adopt and adapt the familiar and morally powerful language of the Bible to the service of this new creed. He also argues it was easier to be a Christian within Labour's German sister party, the Sozialdemokratische partie Deutschland (SPD) after 1918.[18] Both he and Redvaldsen nonetheless concentrate largely on strategy and organizational issues.

This is a perfectly legitimate area of historical enquiry, though one with limited utility in capturing the ideas or aspirations of a political organization. Even at such a level, however, a relationship with religion may be traced. After all, the Labour Party was itself founded in the Congregationalists' Memorial Hall in Farringdon Street, London in February 1900, while the Methodist novelist Silas Hocking set up a fund to assist it after the 1909 Osborne judgement temporarily deprived Labour of the benefit of trade union levies.[19]

Accordingly, there is a need to explore Bullock's commonplace and its role in shaping a distinctive history for the British Labour Party between the wars on a number of levels. At the apex there is the social role played by religion, by providing framing devices that supply purpose and direction, moral values and the codes and mores which hold human society together.[20] I am here using religion in a Durkheimian sense rather than, as so often in existing histories of this period, more narrowly in terms of specific religious institutions. As such, it structures both the truths a society lives by and the nature of the moral economy, here understood as a framework for the pursuit of human well-being in spiritual, moral, social and economic terms. A particular moral economy thus involves a reading of human potential for good, both individually and collectively, a concept of what constitutes a good life and society, and views on the means to achieve these goals. How this thought-world structured ideas about social and political developments and possibilities is the first focus of this study. For Nonconformist thinkers, this was necessarily rooted in understandings of the relationship between humanity and God that were, in the second half of the nineteenth century, undergoing considerable change. Not least, there was a shift away from emphasis on individual salvation as the route to an improved humanity.[21] Understandings of social order were also changing, particularly in Nonconformist attitudes towards the State. In terms of the application of moral economy at the quotidian level of politics, this created space for a socialistic reading of its goals and methods. It meant that the language and values of Nonconformity could be adapted to serve the politics of Labour.[22]

The interaction between Labour and Nonconformity thus has to be traced at the level of ideas as well as institutions. To do this both local and national dimensions to the relationship need to be explored. After all, the Free Churches in the late nineteenth century were indelibly associated with support for the Liberal Party, and in 1922 the claim that the Free Churches were 'the regular chaplain to the Liberal Party' was still being repeated.[23] Indeed, such detailed historical work as has hitherto appeared on Nonconformity and politics in the interwar years has tended to focus on its relations with the declining Liberals.[24] Yet both at the level of the national Free Church leadership and of the local chapel, the picture was more complicated. Accordingly, the relationship also needs to be examined in terms of organizations, of personnel, and indeed of policies.

What are the Free Churches?

Any consideration of this relationship has to start by describing the nature of the Free Churches. The term 'Free Churches' embraces a disparate range of religious bodies varying greatly not only in size, but in church polity, theology, geographical distribution and the degree of political activism they supported or encouraged. The biggest were the Baptists, the Congregationalists and the three Methodist churches – the Wesleyan, the Primitive Methodist and the United Methodist – which came together in 1932 to form easily the largest Nonconformist Church, as can be seen from Table 1. Also substantial were the Presbyterian Church of England (sustained in part by immigration from their co-religionists in Scotland), the Presbyterian Church of Wales (also known as the Calvinistic Methodist Church) and the Salvation Army. The remaining Free Churches were strictly limited in size. None of the Unitarians, the Society of Friends (Quakers), the Moravians, the Wesleyan Reform Union, the Independent Methodists, the Countess of Huntingdon's Connection or the Churches of Christ could muster more than 50,000 members, and most were a good deal smaller.

Church organization and structure differed greatly between these various bodies. The main Methodist churches were organized as connexions, their chapels grouped in mutually supporting circuits. The resulting relative coherence of their church structures gave them more administrative and financial flexibility than some other Free Churches when faced with the new demands upon their resources posed by twentieth-century inflation. In contrast, the doctrine of the independence of each congregation, maintained most fully by the Baptists and Congregationalists, encouraged comparatively loose church structures. Independent and financially self-supporting congregations did not, however, prove well equipped to respond to twentieth-century difficulties. Always liable to become dependent upon middle-class support, they proved particularly vulnerable when situated in the inner city areas which, with the drift of the middle class to the suburbs, became increasingly working class in character in the late nineteenth century. By then, such developments were undermining independency, a process exacerbated by the growing concern felt at the inefficiency and hardship caused by the inadequacy of the ministerial stipends afforded by poorer independent congregations.[25] The inflation unleashed by the Great War added to the financial pressures on the Free Churches.[26] The Nonconformist press was hard hit by resulting hikes in printers' pay, falling advertising revenue, and paper shortages.[27] Moderators, in the Congregationalists, and general superintendents, in the Baptists, were introduced to superintend financial aid to the chapels and to assist in ministerial settlements and removals. Undoubtedly a sensible adjustment in straitened times, this process, however, led to consolidation and chapel closures.[28] Meanwhile, the

Table 1 Membership figures of the major Free Church denominations, 1918–1939

Year	Presbyterian Church of England	Presbyterian Church of Wales	Baptist	Congregationalist	United Methodist	Primitive Methodist	Wesleyan Methodist
1906	85,755	187,768	410,283	461,933	148,988	205,182	488,946
1918	85,551	187,834			140,230	200,539	459,399
1919	84,232	187,575	380,357		139,238	200,347	455,771
1920	83,710	187,220	379,976		138,921	200,175	452,957
1921	84,375	187,260	378,164		138,110	198,806	455,326
1922	84,462	187,746	379,674		138,947	198,471	458,628
1923	84,638	188,412	384,935		140,127	199,920	465,399
1924	85,054	188,970	387,699		140,940	200,986	473,742
1925	85,109	189,323	387,579		141,619	201,902	479,463
1926	84,729	189,727	389,625		142,151	202,533	484,364
1927	84,764	189,132	388,311	454,447	142,145	202,577	486,610
1928	84,598	187,892	384,360	453,814	141,949	202,591	488,289
1929	83,989	186,194	380,110	452,465	141,270	201,947	487,676
1930	84,146	185,827	379,318	449,497	140,957	201,491	487,853
1931	84,298	185.239	379,509	448,014	140,458	200,816	488,770
1932	83,413	184,257	378,733	444,369	139,019	199,549	488,990
1933	82,724	183,044	376,652	442,111		821,715	
1934	82,453	182,608	375,383	439,452		815,327	
1935	81,715	182,221	373,400	434,940		811,900	
1936	80,420	180,999	368,890	432,363		804,801	
1937	79,902	179,880	365,105	424,774		795,273	
1938	79,642	179,386	361,205	419,561		791,193	
1939	78,359	177,448	358,728	416,442		788,683	

Note: The peak year of 1906, following the Welsh revival of 1904–05, is included for comparison. The figure for the United Methodist Church is from 1907, the year it was formed from the amalgamation of three smaller bodies. The figures are all England and Wales, except those for the United and Primitive Methodists, which are England-only.

Source: Robert Currie, Alan Gilbert and Lee Horsley, *Churches and Churchgoers: Patterns of Church Growth in the British Isles since 1700* (Oxford: Clarendon, 1977), pp.133–50.

issue of ministerial exemption from military service during the Great War led the Independent Methodists to define more closely who their lay ministers were.[29]

With the exception of the Quakers and the Independent Methodists, the rest of the Free Churches had a ministry that had become increasingly professionalized during the nineteenth century. None, however, enjoyed as much spiritual and ecclesiastical authority as that of the Wesleyans. The laity nevertheless in general remained important, their authority exercised through varied forms of governance reflecting differing views of New Testament patterns.

There were also distinctive aspects to the geographical distribution of Nonconformist strength. Nonconformity was particularly strong in Wales, the South West, the North East, the Fenlands and in parts of Yorkshire, Lancashire and Leicestershire. To some extent this distribution reflected the local strength of particular denominations. For instance, Methodists were dominant in Devon and Cornwall, but less well represented in Wales, where Baptists, Congregationalists and Calvinistic Methodists were much more numerous. Meanwhile, Presbyterians had been strong in north-east England since the seventeenth century, where they were joined by significant concentrations of Methodists from the eighteenth century onwards. Regionalism was equally marked in the case of the smaller churches. The Wesleyan Reform Union and the Independent Methodists, for instance, were largely centred in geographically distinct and circumscribed areas either side of the Pennines.[30]

Theologically too, there were considerable differences. Most of the Free Churches shared an evangelical heritage in which distinctions of doctrine had largely diminished during the course of the nineteenth century.[31] Evangelicalism was, however, very much on the wane in the Society of Friends. Unitarians, meanwhile, did not even recognize the doctrine of the Trinity. This rejection of one of the central tenets of the Christian faith accounts for the hostility of the leading Wesleyan minister Hugh Price Hughes and others towards Unitarian attempts to affiliate to the National Council of the Evangelical Free Churches (NCEFC) in the 1890s.[32] However, Unitarians were readily admitted to several of the local Free Church councils that also emerged then in light of a perceived need to cooperate in mission, outreach and in response to social problems. Albeit on an informal basis, these councils gave a certain sense of unity to these disparate denominations, which otherwise only had in common their separation from the established Church of England. Their apparent unity thus reflected external constitutional factors whereby, historically, various civil and political disabilities had been imposed upon them by the State, rather than internal or religious ones.

This historically conditioned sense of common identity remained even though the factors that gave rise to it had, by the twentieth century, largely ceased to operate. As the Congregational theologian, Andrew Fairbairn, noted in 1897: 'It is harder perhaps to be a Nonconformist today than it has ever been in the history of England. The very decay of these disabilities from which our fathers suffered, has made it harder for us than for them to dissent.'[33] Instead, it encouraged his contemporaries to search for other sources of common ground, such as through local Free Church councils. Nonconformists had long made common cause in nineteenth-century pressure groups for temperance or disestablishment. Now, through the NCEFC founded in 1896, there was a body to claim to represent their place in the nation.

A willingness to speak politically to that nation varied from denomination to denomination. The Salvation Army generally sought to eschew party politics.[34] The Pentecostalist groupings that were starting to emerge in the aftermath of the 1904–5 Welsh revival were also generally politically quietist. Other more theologically conservative denominations, such as the Churches of Christ, were similarly characterized by lack of political engagement at official levels. Locally, however, it could prove a different story as is apparent from their radical chapels in Wigan, which in the 1920s provided the Labour leader of the council, Councillor Joseph Parkinson.[35]

The strength, vitality and prominence of the local chapel within the community seems to be the key variable here, rather than its theological profile. At the other end of the theological spectrum, it is possible to speculate that the wealth and local significance of their chapels was similarly a factor in the relative over-representation of Unitarians among politically active Free Churchmen. That their theological heterodoxy did not necessarily lead to radical politics is, however, reflected by their contributing proportionately more Conservative parliamentary candidates during the inter-war years than any of the other Free Churches.

This is apparent from the Appendix, which also makes clear that a high proportion of the inter-war parliamentary candidates for all except the Conservative Party came from Nonconformity. In turn, this reflects that Free Churchmen were disproportionately likely to be eminent in either local trade unions or businesses, the principal proving grounds for Labour or Liberal candidates. It also reflects that chapels remained important social institutions in their own right, bestowing prominence in the local community upon their leading adherents. Even small rural causes could prove disproportionately significant. The working-class autodidactism inculcated by the chapel made men like the Primitive Methodist local preacher George Edwards the obvious people to turn to by Norfolk farm labourers seeking to protect their livelihoods by forming a union.[36] In the interwar years similar factors ensured that Primitive Methodists remained over-represented in the ranks of the agricultural workers union and thus in the Labour Party in Norfolk.

The 'Free Church Notes' frequently carried by the local press in that period – particularly in the north of England – testify both to this status and to the chapel's position in the life of the community. The Labour press, particularly the local one, while not going to quite the same lengths, could hardly ignore such a major social phenomenon. Church events, pronouncements and sermons were reported in local party journals, such as the *Bolton Citizen*. In January 1929, for instance, the *Bradford Pioneer* was severely critical of some disparaging remarks about the No More War Movement (NMWM) made by A. E. Boyce, a local Wesleyan minister, in a recent sermon. It acidly commented that if Boyce found the NMWM too idealistic he must pray the Lord's Prayer with great insincerity.[37] Boyce's more radical colleague, C. J. Tribe, was however, reported much more favourably. This reflects the significance of chapels as community institutions, to be challenged or captured for Labour.

Examining Nonconformity and Labour

Such observations reinforce the point that the commonplace remarked by Bullock has to be scrutinized through a variety of means. This study has been constructed to explore the interaction between the Free Churches and the Labour Party successively through four different prisms. The first examines the Free Church leadership's response to the rise of the new party. The opening chapter starts by exploring the extent to which changing theological ideas reconfigured the moral economy of the Free Churches, producing a more receptive setting for Socialist politics, before tracing the extent to which Nonconformist leaders abandoned their traditional alliance with Liberalism during the interwar years.

This examination draws heavily upon a range of both local and national archives, as well as various contemporary publications, especially the Free Church periodical and weekly press. Apart from journals for each of the major denominations, the latter included two non-denominational newspapers, the *Christian World* and the *British Weekly*, which were eventually to merge in the post-war years. In his memoirs, Arthur Porritt, who joined the former in 1899 and became its long-serving editor in 1925, described religious journalism as a rewarding backwater. It was, however, a declining one. In its heyday in the 1880s the *Christian World* carried a wide range of news and had a circulation of 130,000 per week. By 1925 this had shrunk to 30,000, partly due to competition from more secular journals. The *British Weekly*, in contrast, was probably at the peak of its influence under its founder editor Sir William Robertson Nicoll during the Great War, not least because of Nicoll's close friendship with David Lloyd George and his barbed attacks on Lloyd George's predecessor as prime minister, H. H. Asquith.[38] During the interwar years, Porritt argued, the capacity of these journals to influence affairs remained 'in a degree far beyond the measure of its circulation, because so many of its readers are themselves people who influence public opinion'. Certainly, he and his counterparts at the *British Weekly* – as well as some of the other Free Church journals – commented extensively and regularly on political and public affairs, mixed with politicians of all parties, published their opinions, and reported on parliamentary proceedings. They saw themselves as representing the affairs of the nation to that great estate of the realm known as Nonconformity, and also acted as the means for reflecting Nonconformist attitudes, identities and concerns. The Nonconformist press was thus an arena in which the political and religious views of the Free Churches were debated, and the opening chapter examines how the representation of these in its pages changed during the interwar period.[39]

This is followed by a chapter detailing how political issues and policies changed the framework within which the Free Churches operated and which they sought to address. In the process, it reconsiders David Bebbington's conclusions about what was designated in the late nineteenth century 'the Nonconformist Conscience'. Both Bebbington and, more recently, Robert Pope have presented this phenomenon as essentially played out by 1914.[40] Here this view is reappraised by analysis of the responses of the Free Churches both to new issues, such as unemployment, foregrounded in part by the rise of Labour, and the continuance of traditional causes, such as temperance. In the process, the extent to which the latter remained politically significant, at least during the 1920s, is brought out. This makes clear the difficulty of treating the interwar years as an undifferentiated period given the pivotal shifts in economics, politics and culture that occurred at the end of that decade.[41]

The second prism is at the local level and follows a similar format. Chapter 3 starts by examining how social changes from the 1880s affected chapel society and the propensity of adherents to engage politically. Chapter 4 then looks at the consequences for electoral politics. In particular, the extent to which chapels aided or resisted the advance of Labour locally is explored.

Turning to the third prism, it should be noted that the core of Bullock's commonplace is the notion that the relationship between Nonconformity and Labour primarily operates at the level of personnel: that the Free Churches trained people like George Edwards who then brought the organizational and speaking skills they learnt in the chapel meeting or pulpit into the Labour movement. The extent to which this was the case is analysed in Chapter 5, both at the national level in the Parliamentary Labour Party (PLP), the party's National Executive Committee (NEC) and the general council of the Trades Union Congress (TUC), and through using various local examples. What Free Church ideals and attitudes they brought with them, and what effects these had on the wider party, is then discussed in Chapter 6.

The final prism is at the level of ideas and ideals. Chapter 7 examines how both the Free Churches and the Labour movement responded to the concept of class and the rise of working-class politics and of class consciousness between the wars. In the process, the dominance of narratives of class in explanations of the rise of Labour is questioned and religion added to the factors explaining the relative lack of Marxism in Britain.[42] Chapter 8 then examines the shift in Nonconformist attitudes towards the State, the ways in which the State's role in moral economy was reconfigured in the early twentieth century, and the impact this had upon both Labour policy and Socialist ideals.

It is useful to include a considerable local element in a study of this kind. For instance, the changes traced in Chapters 3 and 4 can only really be examined through local studies of the social and political changes affecting chapel society. An assessment of the numbers and effect of Free Churchmen on the Parliamentary Labour Party (PLP) has also been complemented by the examination of selected local Labour parties. Existing local studies have been supplemented by new ones in Bolton, Bradford, Liverpool and rural Norfolk, each with a reasonably successful Labour Party, yet differing greatly in their political, industrial and religious tradition.

Bolton and Bradford were both important textile centres on either side of the Pennines, one specializing in cotton, the other in wool. Bolton was a traditionally Tory, Bradford a traditionally Liberal stronghold. Nonconformity was well established in both places. By 1918, so was the Labour Party. In fact, Labour's rise in Bradford had by then pushed the local Liberals and Conservatives into a largely informal but nevertheless clearly observed and generally successful municipal alliance. Similar developments were occurring in other parts of urban England, but not in Bolton.[43] Bradford indeed has an important place in the annals of the new party, having hosted the inaugural conference of the ILP in 1893. In 1906, Bolton and Bradford became among the first places to elect Labour MPs. They were therefore selected to represent contrasting industrial areas of early Labour success.

Liverpool was the second port in the kingdom after London. It was therefore a shipping and insurance centre as well as the home of extensive docks and dock-related industries. Its political, social and religious history in the nineteenth and early twentieth century was very much defined by the groups of immigrants attracted by the port and by Merseyside's Victorian prosperity. Substantial communities of exiles from Ulster, Scotland and North Wales accounted for a large proportion of the city's Nonconformists. By far the largest and most important group of immigrants were, however, the Irish Catholics. Their presence divided the city into Protestant and Catholic; a division fully exploited by the Conservatives during their long domination of Liverpool politics until the second half of the twentieth century. Sectarian feelings, though diminishing, remained strong and sometimes violent throughout the interwar years.[44] This study explores whether Nonconformists still played a part in the local Labour Party in this charged atmosphere.

Agriculture was the predominant industry in rural Norfolk. The county contained great estates, tenant farmers and, especially in the wake of the legislation of the 1890s, a growing number of smallholdings. In the late nineteenth century it was one of the main centres of the agricultural trade unionism that flourished briefly in the 1870s only to disappear by 1896 in the face of the organized hostility of farmers, bad harvests and unemployment. Methodist leadership was notable in this first exercise in agricultural trade unionism, as it was when George Edwards played a leading part in reviving it in 1906.[45] In 1920, Edwards became Norfolk's first Labour MP. The Labour Party in fact, though unable to secure more than a dozen seats on the largely unpoliticized county council, enjoyed considerably more success in parliamentary contests in Norfolk than in any other rural area in that period. Norfolk was therefore selected, not so much as a representative rural area, but because it was one in which both the Labour Party and agricultural trade unionism were unusually strong.

Sources for this analysis are necessarily varied and partial. Good records generally exist for leading organizations such as Labour's NEC. Finding out personal details of all its many members during the interwar years, including what religion – if any – they espoused, is more challenging. The same is true in reverse for Nonconformist records. There are numerous chapel minute books, but these tend to be more informative on the need for new boiler systems than the political views of the congregation. Local trade union and Labour Party minute books are bound to be equally unrevealing, even where they still exist, though Hansard has been most useful in tracing the political behaviour of Labour MPs. Accordingly, reliance has been placed more on the national, Free Church, Labour and local press, including periodicals such as that of the hitherto strangely neglected Brotherhood movement, *Brotherhood Outlook*. In the case of the latter, this is the only way of circumnavigating the apparent lack of any archives, which may explain why this mass movement – so much larger and more significant than minor bodies like the Labour Church – has been comparatively overlooked by historians.[46] These press sources are invaluable in capturing the actions, intentions and attitudes of leading actors, but less useful in establishing mood, atmosphere and broad responses to change. They have therefore been supplemented where appropriate by oral testimonies.

Such a wide range of sources is necessary in an attempt to address the multilevel relationship between Labour and the Free Churches. If the result is only to flesh out and substantiate Bullock's commonplace, and revive it as a medium through which to see the early history of the Labour Party, then it is still an attempt worth undertaking. This study, however, seeks, more broadly, to examine how the irruption of Labour into the British political system altered views about moral economy, the place of religion in society, and the role of the State. As the quote from Keir Hardie at the head of this Introduction makes clear, Nonconformists in the party did not see its role or objectives purely in material terms. The values that maintained a moral economy were also needed. Otherwise, as the Wesleyan lay preacher and Labour MP C. G. Ammon warned in the 1940s: 'The danger lies in failure to see that the battle for improved economic and industrial conditions is almost won and that, by the pursuit of things material to the neglect or subordination of the spiritual … it may be lost.'[47]

1

Theological and Political Changes among the Free Church Leadership

Our political principles are properly conditioned and nourished by our philosophy and theology. For clearly there is such a close connection between politics and human nature that any political system presupposes, for example, a doctrine of man.

Gwilym O. Griffith[1]

To-day the Congregational Union scarcely succeeds in voicing Free Church opinion on great issues. Political questions are now mainly economic issues, and upon economic issues the Churches … are in alliance with capitalism and economic orthodoxy – or, at all events, the leaders are, and the younger and more ardent spirits are mute, if not gagged, at the denominational assembly.

Arthur Porritt[2]

The background: Developments c.1867–1914

'It is commonplace to say that we are passing through a time of theological unrest', wrote the Wesleyan W. T. Davison in 1926.[3] Changes in thought had indeed been marked in the second half of the nineteenth century and continued to reverberate in the interwar years. The old evangelical citadels of faith: the doctrines of eternal punishment in Hell, of substitutionary atonement, or of the literal inspiration of the Bible were first increasingly questioned and then subjected to frontal assault during the New Theology controversy launched by R. J. Campbell, minister of the Congregationalists' City Temple, in 1907. By the late nineteenth century the great Birmingham Congregationalist R. W. Dale could speak of them being 'silently relegated, with or without very serious consideration, to that province of intellect which is the home of beliefs which have not been rejected, but which we are willing to forget'.[4] As R. W. Thompson told the Congregational Union assembly in his 1938 Chairman's Address, their denomination had

> abandoned doctrines once thought essential: physical hell, total depravity, endless punishment for sins committed in this moment of life; Christ *punished* by God for

> others' sins; the predestination of some to eternal woe. Not all these dogmas were, I fancy, abandoned under pressure of abstract theological studies, but because the working minister found they simply could not be told as Good News to the people. *A true Gospel must be preachable.*[5]

The preaching of these long-held views had been sapped in part by developments within theology. Nonconformity may have initially reacted with hostility to the Bible criticism emerging from Germany in the early nineteenth century. Following a celebrated controversy in the 1850s, Lancashire Independent College, for instance, kept it off the curriculum until the 1890s.[6] However, by then, exposure to analysis of how and when the Old and New Testaments were composed was increasingly common within the ministerial training colleges. Another development – a shift towards emphasizing God's Fatherhood – was meanwhile also becoming palpable in their teaching.[7] This emphasis again drew upon German influences, in this case Albrecht Ritschl's stress on the idea of the Kingdom of God on Earth and Adolf Harnack's on man's brotherhood under God's Fatherhood. Not least, Harnack felt that this would impel a new higher morality that came to underpin the preaching of a Social Gospel.[8] Such influences were greatest among those, such as the Congregationalists and Presbyterians, with a tradition of reading German theology or of attending German universities. Receptivity to such ideas, however, was also encouraged by the growing tendency of figures like Dale to chide their forebears for overemphasis upon individual salvation. Instead, the increasing role of the ministerial colleges in professionalizing the Nonconformist ministry in the second half of the nineteenth century both stimulated and reflected a sense of the Church as a fellowship rather than simply as gatherings of converts,[9] and of Nonconformity's place within that wider Church. At the same time, Bible criticism undermined traditional claims that one or other forms of church order was closer to that of the New Testament. To such developments was added, from the 1880s onwards,[10] the impact of reflections on comparative religion in light of other faiths encountered in the mission field. The stress became less upon distinctive traits and more upon points in common across faiths. It is probably not coincidental that one of the most advanced theological modernists of the interwar years was Frank Lenwood, Secretary of the (Congregationalist) London Missionary Society from 1912 to 1925, who shifted towards seeing the distinctiveness of Christianity in terms of Jesus's example rather than his salvation.[11]

However, John Williamson suggested that these changes were themselves primarily the result of wider influences: 'The last fifty or sixty years have been a period of tremendous upheaval in every department of human life and activity. While change has been so busy in the scientific, the political, and the social world, it is not to be supposed that the theological world could remain unaffected.'[12] For example, the advent of Darwinism and humanism from the 1850s onwards and psychology at the end of the century both challenged evangelical assumptions and provided alternative ways of considering the human condition and the nature of sin.

Wesleyan Methodists proved particularly resistant to Darwinism: it was possible to pass through their colleges without encountering Darwin, Marx or higher criticism.[13] For those who did respond to the former, his work seemed part of a two-pronged assault on Genesis also stemming from Bible criticism. The Wesleyan theologian W. B.

Pope in 1880 therefore sought to defend the traditional view that the first book of the Bible presented an original Fall from grace.[14] Accepting the challenges to Genesis could otherwise invalidate both this conception of humanity and the concomitant idea of mankind's inherent evil. Furthermore, if people were not inherently evil, and therefore in need of Christ's salvation, how could the doctrine of eternal damnation be defended?

Nevertheless, by the 1890s even among Wesleyans there was a growing acquiescence to the theory of evolution.[15] Meanwhile, the leading Congregationalist J. D. Jones later observed that he accepted it from the first, for 'evolution by itself explained nothing, that evolution itself required to be accounted for' and therefore it could be explained 'as being the *method* of God's working'.[16] He, however, went on to note that this doctrine contributed to a growing optimistic and humanistic faith in improvement:

> Man, and the world he lived in, were on the way to perfection. There did not seem much room or need for the Saving Grace of Almighty God. The humanistic note became dominant in much of the preaching. The Social Gospel became the popular Gospel. Preachers concerned themselves with social conditions more than with the salvation of individual souls.[17]

Accordingly it was not necessarily that Darwin raised new theological challenges, or needed to be absolutely opposed. Indeed, the Nonconformist press was generally scornful of what a *Christian World* editorial described as the 'preposterous travesty' of the Dayton trial over the teaching of Darwinism in the United States in 1925.[18] The German-trained Congregational theologian Andrew Fairbairn instead reflected that Darwin merely added to the criticisms of Genesis and natural theology already supplied by Kant – that they argued at best for God as an architect, not as a creator.[19] He followed Kantian-influenced theologians such as Albrecht Ritschl in seeking a new Christian apologetics. This was encapsulated thus by his fellow Congregational college principal Sydney Cave in 1925:

> In an age and country where idealistic philosophy, destructive criticism and scientific materialism were imperilling the very existence of Christianity, Ritschl called men back to the central Christian certainty of the personal perfection of Christ in His vocation, which was at the same time the perfect revelation of God to men.[20]

When applied to soteriology this new apologetics led to a shift from emphasis on conversion to one stressing Christ's incarnation within the world and the development therein of the Kingdom of Heaven, a shift from righteous judgement to fatherly love.[21] Under the influence of post-Kantian philosophical idealism there was a similar shift as well from God as Lord to God as Father, immanent within the world. Christian teaching thus became more focused upon ethics, upon how humans should live rather than how they can approach God for forgiveness. This was, of course, conducive to and coincident with a growing emphasis upon the social mission of the churches.[22]

Such shifts also reflected new awareness of the often limited agency of those whom Nonconformists sought to save. Assumptions about the all-sufficiency of the call to repentance were therefore undermined. For instance, the campaign against the Contagious Diseases Acts between 1866 and 1886 sensitized the successful Wesleyan evangelist Hugh Price Hughes to the causes and context of sexual immorality. Sin became a matter of circumstances rather than simply a matter of personal choice, and to address the sin it became necessary to address the circumstances too.[23] Even someone as committed to mission as William Booth, founder of the Salvation Army, realized 'I have been a soul-saver all my life, but I find that many souls cannot be reached unless you deal with their circumstances.'[24] This led him to a change of tactics in the late 1880s, including the founding of hostels for the homeless and support for prisoners' families.

Part of the context for Booth's tactical shift was a growing awareness of resistance from the impoverished communities he was trying to reach. The 1851 religious census had drawn attention to the apparently godless state of the urban poor. This sense of the growing social, cultural, economic and geographic gulf separating the churches from slum denizens came as Victorian cities made manifest for the first time the social and spiritual needs resulting from unprecedented concentrations of disease, vice, poverty, criminality and poor housing among sometimes transient populations. Hughes was not alone in thinking that the gulf had to be bridged 'not by individualistic, but by socialistic Christianity'.[25]

Similar concerns prompted the 1883 London Congregational Union pamphlet, *The Bitter Cry of Outcast London*. This highlighted that the intemperance and vice that men like Hughes railed against was bred in the housing conditions and poverty of the slums. Accordingly, new forms of mission were required both to breach the gulf between the churches and the local populations of the inner city, and to change lives materially as well as spiritually.[26] Various Nonconformist denominations established such missions and settlements in the closing decades of the nineteenth century.

The ground for the sexualized approach to housing taken by *The Bitter Cry* had already been prepared by the horrified fascination of the mid-Victorians with this growing gulf from the 1860s.[27] In this pamphlet squalid overcrowding was depicted as leading to illicit sexual relations and incest. The surprise for the author[28] was not that slum-dwellers took to drink and sin, but that they were not more depraved.[29] The solution to this was for the State to 'secure for the poorest the rights of citizenship'; this was indeed necessary 'before the Christian missionary can have much chance with them'.[30] Indeed, Dale had already pointed out, 'if the drainage is bad and the water, praying will never save … from typhoid'.[31] Realization that collective social action could help to address such problems encouraged Nonconformists of the late nineteenth century to reappraise their traditional suspicions of an Erastian State from which they had historically been excluded.

A changing attitude towards the State was probably aided by a gradual diminution of that exclusion. First, civil and legal disabilities in comparison with members of the established church were gradually disappearing, even though in Wales they remained sufficiently prominent to aid the launch of David Lloyd George's political career.[32] Secondly, the growing emphasis on the ministry already noted, together with the demographic weight of Nonconformity revealed in 1851, encouraged a sense both of the churchmanship of Nonconformity and of the place of the various denominations within Christian ecclesiology. To some extent this was reflected in liturgical developments: while not repudiating their traditional rejection of credal formulations, the Baptists, for instance, introduced their first set of services in 1884.[33] For Dale, a key part of this process was Bible criticism in drawing attention to the relationship of the church to society and the State.[34] For others, no less important was the exploration of their churchmanship with Anglican interlocutors at the nascent ecumenical conferences organized by the Wesleyan minister turned travel agent Henry Lunn at Grindelwald in the 1890s.[35]

Meanwhile, the Forward Movement promoted by Hughes in the 1880s and subsequently copied by Baptists, Congregationalists and Calvinistic Methodists in the 1890s was not just about mission but also deliberately articulated a view that the Free Churches were no longer sects but instead had a national role. This was reflected in the following decade by the founding of the NCEFC thanks to the enthusiasm and finance of the Quaker chocolate manufacturer, George Cadbury.[36] Finally, the creation of this body spoke to a sense of the political as well as the religious significance of Nonconformity.

Improving communications and denominational development had already enabled the Free Churches to present an increasingly corporate and, by the close of the century, national voice. The franchise reform of 1867, while producing for the first time a working-class majority among voters, also ensured that this voice now spoke – often consciously – for enhanced numbers of Nonconformist voters generally, and sometimes noisily, aligned with the Liberal Party.

In the mid-nineteenth century this political alignment was such a commonplace that the *British Quarterly Review* could comment 'It may almost be said that there would be no Liberal party at all without Dissent.'[37] For Congregationalists, Baptists and Independent Methodists, Liberalism reflected a taste for voluntarism rooted in their tradition of independent congregations.[38] This also led to a witness for religious liberty and equality, and thus frequently to a stress on such matters as civil liberties and free trade as well. It has been argued that an essential Nonconformist unity around liberal individualism was a major source of its political influence in mid-Victorian England.[39] As Hempton has pointed out, notwithstanding their establishment origins, even the Wesleyans generally shared this Liberal alignment in a political system that by the 1850s was very much coloured by the contest between church and chapel.[40]

To this was added a moral certitude in politics developed during the campaign against the slave trade early in the century and nurtured by a mid-century emphasis on the need for a Christian government both at home and in the empire.[41] This, together with the elevated sense of Nonconformity as churches with a national voice, would in the 1890s lead to the coining of the term 'Nonconformist Conscience' to describe what has been characterized as an aggressive assertiveness against those traits, such as intemperance or adultery, which undermine Christian governance both in the individual and in society.

The occasion for Hughes's outburst, which led to the origins of this phrase, was the Irish Home Rule question, and specifically the revelation of the adultery committed by the leader of the Home Rule party, Charles Stewart Parnell.[42] Irish Home Rule was by then starting to undermine the seemingly monolithic Liberalism of mid-nineteenth century Nonconformity. A shift towards Unionism from the 1880s was perhaps most marked among Wesleyans and Unitarians, though J. D. Jones also found this to be the political faith of most of his Congregational deacons in Lincoln and Bournemouth.[43] Noting similar divisions in the Clapham church of the leading Congregational minister J. Guinness Rogers, Harry Jeffs argued that after the Liberals split over Home Rule in 1885–6, the Free Churches never again spoke politically with a single voice.[44]

Opposition to Irish Home Rule was indeed a core element in the Nonconformist Unionist Association organized by the Wesleyan Sir George Hayter Chubb in 1888. The future Conservative Chancellor of the Exchequer Kingsley Wood claimed in 1912 that 90 per cent of Wesleyans opposed Home Rule.[45] Another factor may have been the rise of a fiscally and socially conservative 'villa Toryism' in the suburbs after the changes to the electoral system in 1883–5.[46] Many Nonconformists (including Chubb in solidly middle-class Chislehurst) shared in this trend towards suburbanization.[47] There was also a move towards protectionism among some Nonconformist elites: for instance, in Sheffield, faced with growing international competition, leading Unitarian steel masters were shifting towards Conservatism by the 1870s. The local coalescence of an anti-Labour alliance under the Tories – after Labour became the city's dominant political force by 1926 – also helped to move, for instance, the Wesleyan steel master family, the Osborns, into the Conservative Party.[48] Generally, however, a shift towards the Tories among Nonconformists before 1914 seems to have been limited.

At the same time, suburbanization reinforced a sense of the growing gulf that Nonconformity had to try to bridge if it were, as Price Hughes put it in 1884, 'bring back the alienated masses to the social brotherhood of Christ'.[49] This and *The Bitter Cry* formed part of the backdrop to the establishment by a small group of leading Nonconformists around the Baptists John Clifford and J. C. Carlile of the Christian Socialist League (CSL) in 1887. A number of these Nonconformists, like Clifford, were also early members of the Fabian Society founded in 1884. The social-democratic use of the mechanisms of the State envisaged by the Fabians as a means of promoting social welfare were for figures like Clifford a more advanced means of pursuing existing political goals, often without compromising a continuing Liberalism.[50]

The CSL proved to be a short-lived body, folding in the 1890s. Its emergence had marked a reaction to the same growing conflict between capital and labour that was also to lead to the founding of the Labour Party. Within Nonconformity, however, such bodies began to be replaced by expressions of social concern along denominational lines in the form of Social Service Unions. While well-intentioned, this development did not necessarily help Nonconformity to address social and political issues. In place of the nineteenth-century pulpit policy entrepreneurs – such as Dale or Price Hughes –these organizations bureaucratized Nonconformist political witness into broad statements on social questions designed in large measure to maintain consensus within more politically diverse denominations.[51]

There was, nonetheless, another short-lived Free Church Socialist League established at the annual meeting of the NCEFC in 1909. The Quaker Socialist Society, founded in 1898, was a rare example of a denominational Socialist organization that survived into the interwar years.[52] Meanwhile, some ministers went further: a number of them became leading lights of local branches of the ILP. In such circumstances, they could find themselves ejected from their pulpits by Liberal-supporting diaconates.[53] In Bradford, Rev. R. Roberts, a Congregational minister who played a leading role in the early ILP, was the most prominent to be removed from his pastorate.[54] Most of his colleagues, however, were conspicuous in their support instead for the Liberal mill owner and Baptist Alfred Illingworth in his successful election fight with the dockers' leader (and Congregational lay preacher) Ben Tillett in the 1892 general election.[55]

Such attempts at moral leadership, however, were undermined in the fierce labour disputes of the early 1890s, such as the Manningham Mills dispute in Bradford in 1892, which formed the backdrop to the founding of the ILP. Lockouts of this kind suggested employers attacking working-class living standards. In place of the reciprocity of interests between masters and men assumed by mid-nineteenth century classical political economy (and many Nonconformists)[56] and exemplified by sliding-scale agreements whereby wages moved in line with wholesale prices, there were instead, from the 1880s, growing demands for minimum wages and conditions and certainty of employment in textiles and other industries in response to a period of often high and fluctuating unemployment.[57] In response, a minority of Nonconformist businessmen, such as the Congregational textile manufacturer Theodore Cooke Taylor – concerned about the effect of minimum wages on the viability of businesses – responded by introducing profit-sharing arrangements as a means of retaining reciprocal workplace labour relations.[58]

These industrial tensions spilled over into religious and political life. As the erstwhile Ulster Quaker S. G. Hobson later recalled, 'I soon realised that the ILP had appeared at a moment in time when Yorkshire Nonconformity was in a process of disruption [and] ... accordingly set out to capture the soul of Nonconformity.'[59] As Pope's work on Wales shows, these social tensions in the chapels, and their exploitation by the ILP, were by no means confined to Yorkshire.[60] Nonconformity, after all, provided for the new Labour movement an example of moralistic political activism that could be both imitated and challenged and a language of witness against oppression that could now be turned against the employing classes rather than the Church of England.

Arguably the last major example of Nonconformist resistance to Anglican Erastianism was the Passive Resistance campaign against the Tories' 1902 Education Act. Introduced to address the decaying conditions of Anglican elementary schools, this legislation was seen as 'an injustice to Free Church people by placing Denominational Schools on the rates'.[61] Indignant Free Churchmen felt that only Anglicans should have to pay for Anglican schools. Led by Clifford, a considerable number of Nonconformists – particularly Congregationalists, Baptists and some Quakers – therefore refused to pay part of their rates (a local tax on property values), in some cases persisting for years despite repeated fines or imprisonment. Even the Wesleyan conference voted by three to one against the legislation.[62] J. D. Jones later came to see this campaign as a blunder which 'encouraged the lawlessness and violence of the Suffragette Movement'.[63] At the time he, along with a number of other leading Nonconformist ministers, threw himself into the struggle to repeal the 1902 Act.

This both renewed and took to a high-water mark Nonconformity's alignment with the Liberal Party. Prior to the 1906 general election, a somewhat reluctant Liberal Chief Whip, Herbert Gladstone, was supplied with numerous additional

Nonconformist candidates to stand in, and sometimes unexpectedly win, seats that Liberals had struggled to contest in recent years.[64] When the campaign began, the NCEFC sent various Free Church leaders on extensive motor tours across the country to speak for the Liberal cause. The effectiveness of this effort might be questioned: Jones notes that not one of the candidates he and C. Silvester Horne spoke for was elected.[65] The Liberal landslide owed more to opposition to Joseph Chamberlain's protectionist campaign, and though Nonconformists generally shared in the Liberal support for free trade it did not feature prominently in their distinctive contribution to the campaign. They were, nevertheless, delighted to celebrate this apparent triumph. The *Christian World* proudly listed 188 Nonconformist victors (163 of them in English or Welsh constituencies), noting the dinner held for them by the NCEFC.[66] Reflecting the partisanship of the occasion, this list did not include the handful of Nonconformists elected as Conservatives. It did, however, feature those returned as Labour MPs.

An anti-Conservative electoral pact in a number of constituencies had enabled the election of some thirty Labour MPs, of whom eighteen were claimed as Free Churchmen in the Nonconformist press.[67] Bolstered by this success, the Labour Representation Committee founded in February 1900 decided to change its name to the Labour Party. The party was nonetheless aware that these electoral victories owed much to Liberal votes in the tactical absence of Liberal candidates. Nevertheless, just eighteen years later Labour had experienced its first taste of office and replaced the Liberals as the main opposition to the Conservatives. For the *Christian World* this reflected a 'transfer of the centre of gravity in politics from the prolonged struggle for freedom from social and religious oppression to the struggle for economic freedom'. This process, it warned, 'had left the Liberal Party stranded high and dry, and had deprived Nonconformity of its historic channel of political influence'.[68]

By then, the Free Churches had been debating the theological and political challenges posed by various conceptions of Socialism since the 1880s. Now, however, the pre-1914 flirtation of some ministers with Socialism was replaced by a more general need to come to terms not with the rise of Labour but with its arrival as a party of government. At the same time, Nonconformity also had to come to terms with the conflagration of the Great War which engulfed Europe between 1914 and 1918.

Theological changes

By 1918 the idea of coming post-war changes was a running theme in the denominational journals. The editor of the *Christian World* proclaimed, 'We are approaching the end of a year that will be memorable for all time. An old era is passing away and a new era is opening out before us.'[69] This tone was matched in presidential addresses to denominational assemblies in the last years of the war. Stress was increasingly placed on the lessons the churches could draw from the conflict for the future. For B. J. Snell at the 1917 Congregational Union's autumn assembly it reinforced the idea of fellowship that had been developing in the liberal theological trends of the previous decades. He went on to declare, 'The first Labour government can be trusted to see to the laws that impede fellowship'.[70] The following year his successor as chairman, Ebenezer Griffith-Jones, urged his audience 'to call upon all classes – welded in the fires of this war into a true social organism – to continue to make this world a fit place for the true brotherhood of mankind, and so prepare for the federation of the world'.[71] He was optimistic that Congregationalists could move on from the effort to secure political and civil freedom to the coming struggle for economic emancipation, for 'redemption is a social as well as an individual fact', and 'personal salvation is a lopsided and incomplete thing till it includes the salvation of society as well'.[72]

The war thus challenged the churches to speak to social ethics. Theology must always necessarily endeavour to reflect the context in which it is formulated and the concerns of a particular period for it is an attempt to explain the nature of God and the nature of humanity within a specific setting. As John Hutton noted, 'Every age has its own conscience and standard of goodness. Every age indeed has its own idea of the function of Christianity'.[73] The task now was to make that Christianity speak to a world that had passed through the trauma of the Great War.

Too often, it seemed, the churches spoke primarily instead to personal ethics, and in a negative tone. The spirit, courage and comradeship noted in the army could be seen as expressions of practical Christianity: perhaps mused B. J. Snell these rough soldiers were in fact nearer to God.[74] In contrast, the soldier's understanding of Christianity, as conveyed by the churches, all too often consisted of a litany of taboos. One YMCA worker reported that the soldier's 'idea is that Christian men must not drink, must not swear, must not (according to some authorities) smoke, must not grumble, and must not amuse himself, as to positive duties, he *must* go to church … We have got to connect the programme of the Church with their social ideals and programmes'.[75] In his presidential address in 1918, J. E. Roberts lamented to a Baptist Union assembly which included William Adamson, a Scottish MP and the then Labour Party leader:

> The Christian life should be a great adventure … Yet the Church has given the impression that it means eschewing tobacco … being afraid to say 'damn', drinking ginger-beer instead of whisky, looking askance at theatres or actors, whilst all the time the Christian may be as selfish, as proud, as bad-tempered, as cowardly, as harsh in business, as greedy of money, as the wickedest worldling from whom he turns away in such righteous scorn … Our ethical code seems to the outsider peddling, pettifogging, puerile: it strains out many gnats which other people don't dislike, but swallows enough camels to give the whole Army the hump![76]

Unsurprisingly, the Great War posed particular issues for the Quakers with their Pacifist traditions. In 1915 they replaced the Friends Social Union, which had been officially constituted in 1907, with a new War and the Social Order Committee (WSOC). This body took the traditional Quaker critique of war a step further by identifying social and economic forces at the root of international conflict. It concluded:

> We have come to see that the very existence of such conditions is a grave condemnation of our Christianity and our Quakerism. It is our paramount duty, not only

> to make sure that our manner of living places no burden on the lives of others, but also to seek that we may take our full share in the social reconstruction which, rightly conceived and executed, will remove the causes of both poverty and war.[77]

In 1918, this body produced *The Foundations of a True Social Order*, which remained an important reference point for Quaker social witness throughout the interwar years. It also led to a revision of the key Quaker text, *The Book of Christian Discipline*, which was also published the same year. This revision was partly prompted because 'Concern for the fullest opportunities of self-development, which is implicit in the Quaker belief', was 'leading Friends increasingly to explore the social conditions involved in the present economic system'.[78] Yet, it also reflected doctrinal change. Quakers had participated in the general trend towards an evangelical emphasis on personal conversion, together with the importation of traditions such as addresses and hymn singing, in the course of the nineteenth century.[79] Now such accretions were to be removed, with Quakers ceasing to record those they had previously termed 'ministers' from 1924.[80]

With their doctrine of the Inner Light of God in everyone, Quakers were particularly susceptible to the rise of Liberal theology. The augmentation of their numbers during and after the Great War by those attracted by their spirituality and Pacifist witness was to further undermine the maintenance of doctrinal positions within Quakerism. By the 1930s some commentators were observing a diminution of distinctive Christian elements and the rise instead of a vague ethical agnosticism or even a 'religious atheism' in Quaker worship.[81]

If less marked, a shift was also occurring in other denominations. Griffith-Jones, for instance, reminded the 1919 Congregational Union assembly of the immense distance that lay between his intellectual world and the pre-critical evangelicalism that he had encountered during the Welsh revival of the 1860s in his youth.[82] Even compared to the 1880s and 1890s, views which had then been heterodox were by the interwar years considered mainstream. J. D. Jones reflected, 'It is curious, with my present-day reputation for evangelical orthodoxy, to remember that once I was considered a rather dangerous modernist.'[83] His more radical colleague T. Rhondda Williams, after a crisis of faith and a move to modernist theology prompted by reading the scriptural criticism in R. F. Horton's *Inspiration and the Bible* (1888), was treated as a heretic by the powers that be in the Congregational Union and not invited to speak at the denominational assembly between 1891 and 1908.[84] In 1929, however, he became chairman of the Congregational Union for the coming year. Although there was some opposition from figures like J. D. Jones, J. H. Edwards noted that the warmth of his reception 'very conclusively demonstrated that the centre of gravity, as regards the doctrinal tenets of no small section of the assembly has undergone a striking change'.[85] This change was already becoming apparent in the theological colleges before 1914. Certainly, the dominant figures in Welsh Congregational and Baptist colleges by then were the theological Modernists.[86]

These shifts can be exemplified by changes to the doctrine of the atonement. Historically, this had been a point of division between Old Dissent's emphasis on a Calvinistic view of salvation that often focused upon a narrow elect and the Arminian approach of Methodists that salvation for all was possible through Christ.[87]

Amalgamation of Arminian concepts and Calvinistic rhetoric was essentially peculiar to the Welsh Presbyterians, also known as Calvinistic Methodists.[88] However, all agreed on the need for Christ's atonement for human sin. Views that the crucifixion was a substitutionary sacrifice, nonetheless, by the late nineteenth century were increasingly regarded as untenable. This was not least because of the awareness of the difficulty of reconciling this doctrine to the growing rhetoric of the Fatherhood of God. As early as 1859 the leading Congregationalist James Baldwin Brown had depicted the crucifixion not so much as the appeasement of God's wrath as emblematic of God's all-conquering and all-embracing love.[89] This idea of Christ's identification with humanity on the Cross was also taken up by the Primitive Methodist biblical scholar A. S. Peake echoing the earlier work of the German theologian F. D. E. Schleiermacher, whose influence was slowly spreading in Britain.[90]

So alarming did the slide from substitutionary atonement towards what he regarded as Socinianism appear in his own Baptist denomination that in April 1887 the eminent evangelical preacher Charles Haddon Spurgeon launched what became known as the 'Down-Grade' controversy through an article anonymously contributed to his journal, *The Sword and the Trowel*, by his colleague Robert Shindler. For Spurgeon this downgrade was also associated with the neglect of the Gospel and prayer meetings for entertainment and attendance at the theatre.[91] Railing, among other matters, against the downgrade of the doctrine of everlasting punishment, Spurgeon resigned from the Baptist Union in October 1887.

A carefully worded resolution reaffirming the 'fallen and sinful nature of man' at an 1888 meeting under the chairmanship of the then Baptist Union president, John Clifford, papered over the cracks.[92] Meanwhile, Spurgeon's resignation and death five years later may have magnified the apparent triumph of modernism among British Baptists. Arguably, in the 1880s, what was in fact occurring was the break-up of an evangelical consensus within Nonconformity and the emergence of a range of approaches which tended to produce theological divisions within rather than between denominations.[93] It is debatable how far a theologically liberal consensus replaced it. There were certainly still fears that T. R. Glover's stress in his 1924 presidential address to the Baptist Union on Christ reconciling man to God, rather than on his dying in order to appease the divine wrath, could provoke the vocal minority of Spurgeonite Baptists and reawaken the controversy that had split the denomination in the 1880s.[94]

Defence of the doctrine of eternal punishment had been, if anything, even more entrenched in Wesleyanism. Joseph Agar Beet's painstaking agnosticism on this subject in his *The Last Things* (1897) led to a prolonged controversy within the denomination. Leslie Weatherhead's denial of eternal torment in his first book, *After Death*, similarly led to him being interrogated for heresy by the Wesleyan conference in 1923.[95] Nevertheless, ideas of reconciliation, incarnation and of Christ suffering alongside rather than simply saving humanity from eternal punishment were gaining ground, promoted by figures such as the leading Wesleyan, J. Scott Lidgett.[96] Even among Primitive Methodists, the hellfire imagery of past revivalist hymnody was disappearing.[97]

Those within Wesleyanism who wished to 'make more vital the traditional faith of Methodism' increasingly had to found their own organizations, such as the

Southport Convention established in 1885. One of its leaders, Samuel Chadwick, wrote in 1919 of drift and disaster, not least through pursuing whist drives rather than prayer meetings, in tones reminiscent of Spurgeon thirty years earlier. The evangelistic fervour of Southport, however, could be treated with disdain within the denomination.[98] Furthermore, after Chadwick's death in 1932, Cliff College for the training of evangelists, of which he had long been principal, came under attack in Methodist circles, and was only finally exonerated of charges of obscurantism and antiquated teaching in 1945.[99]

Liberal theological perspectives were clearly increasingly in the ascendance. In 1929, W. F. Lofthouse declared in his presidential address to the Wesleyan conference that higher criticism was now universally accepted and the old attitudes to Hell universally shunned.[100] Acknowledging an intellectual debt to Lidgett, he went further in stressing Christ's mediation, representation and forgiveness as an alternative encapsulation of the atonement. For Lofthouse 'this was not to destroy the majesty of the moral law, but to place it on its true basis'.[101]

Not all, however, would have agreed that doctrine had indeed thus been re-established on a true basis. In 1926, its president W. R. Maltby lamented at the Wesleyan conference: 'we lost Hell forty years ago and Heaven ten years later, and have not put anything in their place'.[102] Indeed, as the Modernist Congregationalist A. D. Belden pointed out, there was not even a theory of the atonement, 'which may be described as entirely satisfactory to the modern mind'.[103]

The Presbyterian W. E. Orchard, who preached at King's Weigh House, one of the citadels of London Congregationalism, and F. W. Norwood, who preached at another, the City Temple, were among the few to seriously reconsider the doctrine of Hell in the interwar years. Both made use of the rise of psychology, with Orchard referring to hellfire as a metaphor for mental torture. Hell, he therefore concluded in an echo of the views that had led the Anglican theologian F. D. Maurice to lose his chair in 1853, 'may mean simply an intense sense of what the deprivation of God means, combined with an equally intense determination to deprive oneself of Him'.[104]

Maltby's solution instead was that 'we must lead the people to see God's meaning in everything … we must seek to make life sacramental'.[105] This understanding of sacramentalism probably reflected his involvement with the Swanwick Convention founded in 1920, a setting for attempts to revive Methodism's Holiness tradition within a more liberal setting than Southport amid intense spirituality, which also attracted a number of key Methodist Socialists such as S. E. Keeble and Donald Soper.[106] The risk, however, was that without following Maltby's anchoring of such views within a distinctive Christology, these doctrines could become merely pantheistic.

Some Modernists were indeed moving in such a direction, regarding Christ's divinity and/or the concept of the Trinity as at best ambiguous and at worst indefensible.[107] This process reached its apogee with the Blackheath Statement published by a group of Congregational ministers in 1933, in which they sought to replace Christ with a Jesus who was, 'but the highest expression of the law of our evolution, an example of the true order of divine humanity'.[108] Encouraged by Bible criticism to see St Paul as responsible for the attachment of divine accretions to an otherwise human Christ they rejected Pauline concepts and emphasized instead the teaching and humanity of Jesus.[109]

Modernism thus occupied a spectrum: from those like R. F. Horton, the Congregational founder of a Modern Free Churchmen's conference in 1926, who modified the atonement but abhorred Unitarianism,[110] to those who, like Lenwood, saw Jesus more as an exemplary leader. While defenders of traditional evangelical fundamentals were diminishing outside the Spurgeonite wing of the Baptists by the interwar years, positions such as Lenwood's could still be regarded with suspicion in the major denominations. In 1938 the secretary of the Union of Modern Free Churchmen complained of the bad treatment received by some of his members.[111] The most celebrated case was ten years earlier, the expulsion of Tom Nefyn Williams. The Calvinistic Methodists of Wales for whom he ministered had not been immune to liberal tendencies to emphasize the Kingdom of God. Nefyn Williams, however, went much further in presenting God as an impersonal, immanent force, a position he implicitly repudiated on readmission to the church in 1932.[112]

The centre of gravity in Free Church theology had nevertheless certainly shifted. Even the carnage of the First World War could do little to alter the optimistic humanistic idealism of those Modernists who could simultaneously believe it was a war to end wars.[113] The Congregational theologian, P. T. Forsyth, who had reacted against the New Theology before 1914 by re-emphasizing the centrality of the Cross, may have warned:

> The crisis has revealed anew the power and meaning of wickedness to a generation that was more credulous of good nature than sensible of moral death ... We have given up believing in original sin ... Liberal theology ended in the falsity of believing in a limited God while publicly praying to an Almighty ... Our religion was but the top storey of human nature, it was not based on the conversion of elemental passions and the regeneration of their power.[114]

Such fulminations, however, did not really begin to take effect until the theology of crisis of the Swiss theologian Karl Barth, which had first appeared in 1919, began to spread in British Nonconformity in the 1930s. In March 1939, J. D. Jones was among those Congregationalists influenced by this who signed a 'Call to Reformation' urging a restatement of the Gospel, the transcendence of God and man's need of grace.[115]

Meanwhile, A. S Peake argued that the war had raised no *new* theological difficulties, though it had given a new thrust to old problems such as suffering and the role of conscience.[116] Many Free Church leaders indeed do not seem to have given a great deal of thought to the theological problems and pastoral difficulties posed by the conflict.[117] This was despite the new pastoral demands the war brought both at home and at the front. Hitherto among Nonconformists only Wesleyans and Presbyterians had appointed army chaplains. With a mass army for the first time, initially composed largely of volunteers, most other denominations now followed suit. By November 1918 there were 302 Presbyterian (including Scottish churches), 256 Wesleyan, 251 United Board (Baptist, Congregationalist, Primitive Methodist and United Methodist), 10 Calvinistic Methodist, and 5 Salvation Army padres.[118] Some, like the Wesleyan R. J. Barker, whose idea of sin was transformed in the crucible of war from being a personal separation from God to being additionally a way of expressing the unchristian nature of Capitalist society, were pushed towards Socialism by their wartime experiences.[119]

In general, however, beyond a shift towards Pacifism, the war does not seem to have provoked the sort of theological agony for Free Church chaplains that their Anglican counterparts experienced.[120] One brother minister replied without any trace of irony to Barker's objections to air raids: 'This is no time for Christian sentiments'.[121] This was indeed what the Baptist Socialist Tom Phillips found: 'Try preaching forgiveness on the morrow of an air raid, with dozens of children lying stark and cold. War kills preaching'.[122]

The war did, nevertheless, encourage the flourishing of ecumenical concerns and initiatives in all the churches during the interwar period. Some of the principal obstacles in the way of this had already begun to disappear before 1914. Denominational differences became less sharp as Bible criticism undermined Protestant illusions that any particular church order or practice was uniquely sanctioned by the New Testament.[123] The exigencies of the mission field had also led to inter-denominational discussions at the 1910 Edinburgh conference.[124] Not least, the gradual disappearance of Nonconformist disabilities cleared the way for greater inter-denominational co-operation. This facilitated developments like the 1888 Lambeth Quadrilateral and the growth of the Student Christian Movement. Meanwhile, a desire for increased church efficiency and influence also prompted a growing interest in ecumenism of Free Church leaders.[125] These were among the considerations that led to the amalgamation of three smaller Methodist bodies into the United Methodist Church in 1907.[126]

Inter-denominational co-operation was both facilitated and required in the trenches of the Great War. The gulf between the churches and the soldiers presented in the evidence collected by the Scottish minister David S. Cairns in 1917 also conveyed a sense of urgency.[127] The Great War certainly had a major effect upon the timing and nature of the two great appeals that helped create the ecumenical ferment of the interwar years: J. H. Shakespeare's *The Churches at the Cross-Roads* (1918), and the Lambeth Appeal issued by global Anglicanism in 1920.

The urgency of these appeals ensured the pervasiveness of ecumenical concern in their aftermath. Furthermore, the need for denominations to respond corporately to the Lambeth Appeal, and to the ever-present pragmatic consideration of decline, revival or church provision in new housing areas,[128] tended to institutionalize ecumenism. This further stimulated an increased appreciation of the concept of the Church and the idea of church order among Nonconformists, as did the series of international and inter-denominational Faith and Order conferences held in the interwar years.[129] A paradoxical strengthening of faith in denominational principles was, however, sometimes the result.[130]

Another significant development was the way a growing sense of churchmanship led to liturgical development within late nineteenth-century Nonconformity, a process further encouraged by these interwar influences. For instance, Thomas Tiplady melded cinema and liturgy at the Wesleyan Lambeth Mission to give relatively untutored congregations a format and formulations through which to express their faith.[131] Some, such as Donald Soper, came to emphasize this greater sacramentalism as a 'sharing of God's bounty and love'.[132]

In the interwar years many proponents of this – still far from widespread – trend echoed Soper's view that this was part of a Free Church shift towards social concern and Socialism. As one writer put it:

> [I]t is not strange that following hard upon the quickening of the social conscience in the Protestant Churches there should come the emphasis on the sacramental concept of life. It could not be otherwise unless the social services of the Churches should run into a barren humanitarianism. Ethical values to persist must be grounded in eternal certainties'.[133]

It was this last point that transformed a New Theologian like W. E. Orchard into a sacramentalist.[134]

Sacramentalism acquired its radical tinge not only from an emphasis on sharing in the common meal and the common life but also from the ideals of mutual service and primitive Christianity expressed in, for instance, the liturgical comradeship of the Common Table and Community House R. J. Barker created in 1928 alongside Tonypandy Central Mission.[135] Orchard regularly emphasized the radical flavour of liturgical texts like the Magnificat in the sermons he published weekly in *The Crusader* in the early 1920s. Sacramentalist bodies like the Society of Free Catholics that appeared after the war, in which Orchard was a leading light, or the Methodist Sacramental Fellowship (MSF) (founded in 1935) therefore tended to be Socialist-tinged if not Socialist-dominated. They were, however, also small and subject to considerable suspicion, particularly after Orchard and the founder of the MSF, T. S. Gregory, converted to Roman Catholicism.[136]

Sacramentalism has often been completely overlooked as a factor in growing Free Church sympathies with Socialism. Both contemporary and subsequent commentators have tended instead to emphasize the role of liberal theology.[137] The relevant entry in *The Encyclopaedia of the Labour Movement* (1928) for instance stressed:

> Within the Free Churches the growing realisation of the common brotherhood of man, and the Christian communism which it implies, has of recent years been definitely deduced from the common Fatherhood of God.[138]

Both sacramentalism and liberal theology encouraged emphasis upon the concepts of the Fatherhood of God and the building-up of his Kingdom. It was realized that if the New Testament did not justify a particular church order it did say a lot about the Kingdom. For those drawn to the Left, this encouraged a growing emphasis on the law, truth and justice that were felt to be attributes of the Kingdom. It inspired criticism of the existing social order in the light of Christ's teaching and led to a new concentration, not only on personal morality, but on efforts to bring the social order into closer conformity with the Kingdom of God. As Rhondda Williams put it, men 'cannot be saved from their sin until they are saved from their systems'.[139]

This Social Gospel did not preclude Rhondda Williams from continuing to try and save men from their sin. He was described in 1928 as an 'evangelical modernist' who packed his church.[140] Evangelicalism was of course by then very different from that preached in the mid-nineteenth century. Free Church Socialists, such as the Wesleyans S. E. Keeble and Henry Carter or the Congregationalist Percy Carden nevertheless remained keenly interested in the call to conversion. Their Socialism was not necessarily merely a reflection of a humanistic or sacramental theology. The Baptist

Socialist W. Ingli James insisted that 'Only those who have been personally saved – saved from selfishness, from smugness, from snobbery – can retain their zeal for social righteousness.'[141] Free Church Socialists could retain the conviction that humans needed to be saved from themselves as well as the social system, and that the problem of sin remained a matter of alienation from God, as well as of the unchristian nature of Capitalism. After all, conversion implied a wholly changed attitude to life, as Henry Carter made clear when setting up Methodism's Youth and Christian Citizenship Movement in the 1930s. Conversion involved a commitment to change one's attitude to one's own life, and to the whole of society: 'If all who profess themselves Christian acted in this way, the difference in the world's life would be revolutionary.'[142]

After the chaos of the Great War, 'In the Christian Gospel we have the one secret of a new and better world', proclaimed his fellow Wesleyan Socialist, W. H. Armstrong.[143] Despite theological changes in response to new scientific, historical or psychological perspectives, this secret remained the Christian insight into the problem of human nature and sinfulness. Lovell Cocks therefore insisted, 'However uncongenial to the modern mind the consciousness of sin is inextricably bound up with the Christian revelation – which is either a word of deliverance from sin or nothing.'[144] Quite how to apply that revelation to the political problems that were facing Nonconformity nevertheless remained a challenge.

In many ways the New Theology of the Edwardian period had been an essentially political attempt to respond to those challenges, and in particular to find a Christian language through which to engage with Socialism. Reg Sorensen, who went on to be a Unitarian minister and Labour MP, was among those shaped by it. New Theology, however, proved too divisive to engage the churches, too indistinct to offer more than rhetoric to Socialists who increasingly needed policies as well, and too theologically deficient to maintain even the support of its main protagonists. Despite these inadequacies, it nevertheless remained significant as an attempt to bridge the political gulf Campbell had sought to address. In its aftermath, finding the language and ideas to turn Christianity into a means of delivering the new world of which Armstrong had spoken was elusive. At the end of the interwar period, the Unitarian Marxist John Lewis therefore feared that 'the Church has … given many the impression that, while it may wish to develop a social conscience, it is only a substitute for a social programme'.[145]

Some, however, solved this problem by finding their social programme outside the churches. On the 'road to fulfilment of the Christian message of Goodwill' Soper for instance realized, 'that politics must be party politics if it is to become the machinery of Goodwill on Earth'. He joined the Labour Party.[146]

Political changes

Nonconformity's traditional political alliance was being disrupted. J. D. Jones's autobiography contains a telling vignette of a conference between the Liberal Party and Free Church leaders to discuss Liberal policy and leadership in the wake of the 1902 Education Act.[147] There followed the campaign of conscientious objection to this legislation known as Passive Resistance. This campaign, however, came to seem paltry in comparison to the sufferings of those who on grounds of conscience refused conscription after 1916.[148] The atrophy of Free Church civil disabilities meanwhile worked to lessen the ties of interest and sentiment that historically had bound Nonconformity to the Liberals. The Congregational Socialist, Vivian T. Pomeroy, now argued it could no longer be said, as in the nineteenth century, that 'the issues for Free Churchmen were so clear cut their duty was obvious ... The one truth to be driven home is that the identification of Free Church politics with the Liberal Party must cease to be an understood thing'.[149]

Many, however, continued to mourn 'the passing of the "great days" of 1906'.[150] Nostalgia for the virtues of a vanished political era oozed through the eulogies and obituaries lavished on the great men of the past in the denominational press. The soft light of pre-1914 England came to bathe all the noble gladiators of that less intense and intolerant political culture in a roseate glow. This perhaps reflected the fact that, with the exception of some wishful thinking during the 1923 and 1935 elections,[151] few now discerned the possibility of another Free Church triumph like that of 1906.

It was not just the political world of 1906 that had disappeared, so too had the Free Church world that went with it. The number of effective local Free Church councils was diminishing, while unflattering comparisons were made between the apparent vitality of the NCEFC before 1914 and the timid leadership between the wars.[152] In 1912, the Baptist minister and future Labour MP Herbert Dunnico was already denouncing it as 'a party caucus controlled and subsidised by wealthy capitalists'.[153] 'It is run today by a little oligarchy in Farringdon Street', complained the *Methodist Times* in 1919, and

> to all intents and purposes elects its own officials and poses as representatives of the Free Churches, without gaining the authorisation either of their Conferences or their people. In recent years it has been marked by a paralysing timidity of action and fails to carry with it any serious weight of opinion.[154]

It however changed little, either in character or personnel, during the period. By 1936, the leadership of bodies like the disestablishmentarian Liberation Society or the NCEFC could be regarded as a sort of self-perpetuating gerontocracy.[155] This hardly made for flexibility and flair in the face of changing political circumstances.

The issues upon which political Nonconformity throve were meanwhile of declining significance in the interwar years. This was particularly true in Wales. Disestablishment of the Church in Wales weakened the close association between the Free Churches and the Liberals and helped to facilitate the growing support for the Labour Party apparent among the ministers and in the chapels of Wales by 1922.[156] By 1926, there was concern that: 'Modern Welsh Nonconformity ... having lost the rallying cry of the Disestablishment of the Church in Wales, seems also to have lost much of the unity, fervour and enthusiasm which were its most striking characteristics'.[157] The Welsh Free Church council indeed became defunct. Significantly in 1926 – the year David Lloyd George finally became leader of the Liberal Party – it was his brother William who led efforts to revive it.[158] These, however, met with limited success.

'Passive Resistance after a useless life' meanwhile 'died an unregretted death'.[159] The political partisanship it had encouraged was already being disparaged before 1914.[160]

The setting up of the Federal Council of the Evangelical Free Churches in 1917 was in part a reaction against this high political profile.[161] Its claim to be more representative was a check upon the partisanship which had characterized the NCEFC. Instead, it reflected two trends accelerated by the Great War: ecumenism and a concern to represent their role in national life. The Primitive Methodist H. B. Kendall could have been speaking of all the Free Churches in declaring:

> The War has helped to make our Church more National than, a few years ago, she could ever have dreamed of becoming. For four years we have been in the full tide of the nation's life, and never again, it is to be hoped, shall we subside into its shallows.[162]

This transformation was particularly symbolized by the attendance of the king and queen at the Free Churches' post-war service of thanksgiving at the Royal Albert Hall on 16 November 1918.[163]

Such trends enhanced national unity, but were not good for the cause of political dissent, as Griffith-Jones reflected during the renewed controversies over funding church education on the rates between 1930 and 1931:

> We are suffering from the secondary effects of the long years during which many of our prominent men have been absorbed in the Lambeth 'conversations' as to the conditions of corporate reunion with the Church of England … [W]e are now beginning to realise not only that they have failed, but that we Free Churchmen have come out of them much weaker ecclesiastically and politically, than when we entered upon these negotiations in 1918.[164]

In 1925, the Congregational journalist W. Haslam Mills told the Liberal Summer School, 'Politically, Nonconformity is dead and we shall have to do without it'.[165] The NCEFC was certainly both weaker and less closely associated with the Liberal Party. As early as the 1923 election, the *British Weekly* expressed a concern that Nonconformity had been too tied to one party.[166] By 1926, the NCEFC secretary, Thomas Nightingale, recognized that 'the Free Churches are now largely represented in each of the three parties', but held that this development would help 'to keep the leaders of each of the parties alive to the moral issues and the principles of religious equality and fair play that we stand for'.[167]

This did not mean either Free Church leaders or the denominational press abandoned political connections. Scott Lidgett, for instance, became the aged leader of the Progressives (Liberals) on the London County Council in 1918, a post he held for ten years.[168] Such connections, however, were no longer so automatic. Nightingale's observations were thus a pragmatic response to the rise of three-party politics.

The declining salience of traditional Free Church political issues was not the only significant change apparent after 1918. There was also the transformed potential of Labour politics aided by the more intrusive nature of the State, the wartime split in the Liberals and, in consequence, the greater willingness shown by the trade unions to fund Labour parliamentary candidates.[169] For some, this could seem a threat, not least in light of the impact of the Russian revolutions of 1917. During what proved to be the worst year of the war for industrial militancy, the Russian example prompted a conference that took place in Leeds in June 1917 to call for the setting-up of Soviets in Britain.[170] This development reflected Pacifistic concerns about the government's search for outright victory, rather than revolutionary pressures.[171] It was, however, followed by the Bolshevik revolution, raising the spectre of atheism as well as of Communism. Charles Ammon, an ILP activist, post office trade unionist and Wesleyan local preacher who had enthusiastically helped to organize the Leeds meeting, was not the only one to now have a change of heart, concluding 'not by force is freedom won'.[172]

With their Pacifist traditions the Quakers, whose numbers had been swollen by left-wing opponents of the war, were particularly challenged by the idea of class conflict promoted at Leeds. The Quaker Socialist society's journal, *The Ploughshare*, later complained: 'Marxian Socialism … puts such emphasis on the means, that the end to be attained is lost sight of'.[173] The founding of the Communist Party of Great Britain (CPGB) in 1920 accordingly proved to be a parting of ways with more ardent spirits: Quaker reluctance to countenance class conflict was later cited by Walton Newbold as his reason for resigning from the Society of Friends that year as part of his shift towards Communism.[174]

Free Church leaders, the Free Church press and Labour

The Free Church leadership and press thus had to respond to a more effective Labour movement that, after 1920, also had a Russian-flavoured challenger to its left. Rising interest among the denominational press in the Labour Party's importance was first marked in what turned out to be the final year of the Great War. This was stimulated by its disentanglement from the wartime Coalition and the high profile it subsequently attained through its definition of war aims, its new constitution and the promotion of *Labour and the New Social Order*.[175] Arthur Henderson, a Wesleyan local preacher and as secretary of the Labour Party, one of the principal architects of these developments, wrote two lengthy articles about these changes at the request of the *Christian World*.[176] His similar piece for the *Contemporary Review* was commended by Scott Lidgett in his presidential Address to the Wesleyan conference.[177] These articles appealed to Free Church leaders both by emphasizing the idealism and by minimizing the class nature of the Labour Party. There was also receptivity to the social programme Henderson outlined resulting from the searchlight the war had shone on the inadequacies and inequalities of existing social and industrial conditions: the retiring NCEFC president, the Congregationalist W. B. Selbie, confessed: 'There is a penitence that for so long Churchmen had been indifferent to Labour's legitimate demands'.[178]

Nonconformists became more likely to sympathize with Labour following the wartime Liberal splits after the formation of the Lloyd George Coalition in December 1916. The followers of the former prime minister, H. H. Asquith, now in opposition, proved reluctant to oppose their fellows still in government until mid-1918. Labour, in contrast, was transformed by its reorganization and the new programme from the small party that had helped to keep the minority Liberal government in office from 1910 to 1915. Its growing effectiveness as a party, not least through fielding far more candidates than in the last pre-war general elections in 1910, made it a viable alternative to the Liberals. Its war aims, meanwhile, appealed to those Nonconformists who favoured a negotiated peace and were impatient with the Coalition's continuing emphasis on the knockout blow against Germany.[179]

There were still, however, limits to the rapprochement of the Free Church leadership with Labour. The Baptist and future NCEFC president F. B. Meyer claimed in April 1918, 'We are moving on parallel lines towards the same objective'.[180] The Wesleyan-raised leading ILPer Philip Snowden noted optimistically that the 1918 NCEFC assembly had finally begun to criticize both Lloyd George and the war.[181] By August, Meyer's refusal to participate in a proposed international church conference at which Germans might be present had, however, again convinced Snowden that the NCEFC was 'neither Christian nor moral'.[182]

It was certainly not Socialist. Even among those who appeared on the platform of a Nonconformist and Labour rally at the Wesleyans' Kingsway Hall in London during the 1918 election campaign, few were by any stretch of the imagination Socialists. As they made clear in saying, 'Not all of us commit ourselves to the full Labour programme but in a case where it is Labour opposing the Coalition ticket we unhesitatingly urge all progressives to vote Labour',[183] this event was prompted as much by opposition to the Coalition and by the continuing strength of the Edwardian idea of a Progressive Alliance of Liberals and Labour as by a growth of Socialist sentiment. Leading Free Churchmen who remained Liberals all their lives thus voted Labour in 1918 in protest against the 'deep moral disgrace' of the coupon election.[184] Only those who actually campaigned on Labour's behalf, like Lloyd George's own minister, Herbert Morgan – an active ILPer who supported the Baptist minister who stood for Labour in Neath – can be seen as actual converts.[185] Most of the Nonconformist leadership supported Asquith in 1918. Only the *Baptist Times* under the editorship of J. H. Shakespeare, the prime minister's close friend and confidant, came out unequivocally for the Coalition.[186]

Others could praise Lloyd George as a new Elijah and yet regret the cleavage and defeat inflicted upon the Liberals. It was this effect on the Liberals, as well as their concern that important issues had been buried under the jingoistic rhetoric of the government's campaign, that fed the distaste of the denominational press for the Coalition and the coupon election.[187] The massed ranks of couponed Conservatives swept into Parliament with the aid of Lloyd George's endorsement amply confirmed the worst fears of John Clifford. Clifford's colleagues in the Baptist Union were however assiduous in their support of their co-religionist's administration. So was the leading Primitive Methodist, A. T. Guttery, notwithstanding the Pacifistic traditions of his denomination right down to 1914 and his own past as a pro-Boer during the South African War of 1899–1902. The elevation of this ardent proponent of the war and scourge of conscientious objectors to the presidency of the NCEFC in 1919 thoroughly disgusted Philip Snowden.[188]

It was not until the 1921 NCEFC assembly – when the Congregational Pacifist Leyton Richards succeeded in referring back to the executive a rather timid resolution on the government's Irish policy – that more critical attitudes towards the Coalition began to be expressed.[189] The policy of reprisals carried out by the Black and Tans prompted R. F. Horton to refer 'to our versatile and intermittently Christian premier' amid unkind laughter. There were indeed some who contended that the appointment of J. H. Shakespeare's son Geoffrey to the Downing Street staff was an attempt to stem this crumbling of Free Church support.[190]

Meanwhile, the penitence towards Labour expressed in 1918 bore fruit in a series of conferences between Nonconformists, Anglicans and local trades councils, often centred on a joint celebration of 'Industrial Sunday'. Some were even incorporated into denominational assemblies.[191] This growing receptivity to a Labour or Socialist message was marked at the Wesleyan conference, which in 1921 finally gave the veteran Socialist Samuel Keeble – one of the first Britons to read Marx in the original German – the honour of addressing them on 'Christian Responsibility for the Social Order'. That this scholarly review of the subject from apostolic Communism through patristic writings up to the present was published as the Fernley Lecture reflected official acceptance of Keeble's views, though it nevertheless still generated some hostility in the denomination.[192]

No less significant were the ecumenical demonstrations for Social Christianity in Hyde Park in 1921 and 1922 in which Free Church ministers and Labour figures featured prominently.[193] A rediscovered enthusiasm for peace also saw erstwhile jingo divines sharing predominantly left-wing platforms, particularly during the series of demonstrations around the country organized by the NMWM in 1922.[194]

One of the founders of the NMWM in 1921 was Wilfrid Wellock, an Independent Methodist lay minister and conscientious objector who had created what became *The Crusader* in 1916 as an organ of Christian Socialism/Pacifism.[195] The Great War otherwise did not prove a propitious time for left-wing Nonconformist-flavoured journals. The *Christian Commonwealth*, which had been the journalistic expression of the New Theology, ceased publication in 1919. So did *The Ploughshare*, partly because of the internal conflicts noted above. Meanwhile, the moment when it looked as if the *Methodist Times* might be captured for the Left with the retirement of Scott Lidgett as editor in 1918 did not, in the event, come to pass.[196] *The Crusader* thus remained in 1918 the only Free Church newspaper to maintain a distinctively Socialist tone. It was not however without troubles. Wellock and most of its founders left in 1921, dismayed at the increasingly Free Catholic direction it was taking under Orchard's influence.[197] By 1923, with the now dominant Free Catholics seemingly drifting away from Socialism, the last of its founders departed.[198]

The rest of the religious press was meanwhile forced to react to three elections in quick succession. In 1922 the battle lines were very similar to those of 1918, though Quakers and ministers in South Wales seemed to have discernibly shifted leftwards.[199] Relieved at the pre-election fall of Lloyd George's Coalition, Clifford and the *Christian World* looked for a reunion of the Liberals and a revival of the Progressive Alliance in the face of the succeeding Conservative government that narrowly won at that year's polls.[200] The Conservative prime minister Stanley Baldwin's decision in late 1923 to seek a mandate to introduce protective tariffs seemed to provide the basis for just such a revival.

In the ensuing general election Nonconformists rallied to the defence of the 'Christian ideal of Free Trade'.[201] Few were prepared to admit the force of Conservative arguments that protection was necessary in view of the rise of high-tariff industrial competitors, who were able to take advantage of British free trade without reciprocating the opportunity.[202] Although the protectionist stance of certain trade unions – particularly the Iron and Steel Trades Confederation – was later noted,[203] the denominational press could instead welcome the unequivocal support for free trade in the Labour manifesto:

> Tariffs are not a remedy for unemployment. They are an impediment to the free interchange of goods and services upon which civilised society rests. They foster a spirit of profiteering, materialism and selfishness, poison the life of nations, lead to corruption in politics, promote trusts and monopolies and impoverish the people.[204]

The imposition of duty was seen by all free traders as an unjust tax upon the consumer. The threat of protection both reunited the Liberals and restored the Liberal complexion of the Free Church press. The Liberals were, however, short of good candidates when the 1923 election was sprung on them. Sir Henry Lunn, prompted by the Liberals' Chief Whip, Sir Donald Maclean (a Presbyterian), therefore made considerable efforts to trawl up suitable Nonconformist candidates.[205] Together with the resurgence of Liberal support in Nonconformity, this may have helped the Liberals – as in 1906 – to many unheralded gains in what proved to be their best performance of the interwar years. In a year in which Labour left them with a straight fight against the Tories in many rural English seats affected by farming discontents, this enabled Liberal victories in seats not taken since 1906, if then. The Liberals also made gains in socially mixed urban constituencies.[206] The 159 seats attained on a similar vote share to Labour, however, only allowed them to flirt with power. When Parliament met in the new year it was Labour, with 191 MPs, that took office as a minority government.

Some Liberals – such as the Presbyterian MP W. M. R. Pringle – blithely assumed that in a hung parliament his party's numbers were such that, whether the Conservatives or Labour took office, it was the Liberals who nevertheless would be in power.[207] The Wesleyan Liberal MP Isaac Foot complained that the ensuing months proved to be a deeply disillusioning experience with Labour seemingly determined to scotch all such hopes.[208]

This policy did not endear the new government to the Free Church press, even if only the *British Weekly* had the gall to inquire whether it would fall under Russian atheistic influence; a suggestion swiftly denied by the Labour leadership.[209] The rest were less hostile, but wary of Socialism. Enthusiasm for Prime Minister MacDonald, especially after his speech to the NCEFC assembly, and general admiration for Snowden's free trade budget, nevertheless ensured a degree of cautious support. This was even extended to the government's efforts to establish diplomatic and commercial links with atheistic Soviet Russia, which in the end largely brought about its fall. Even the *Baptist Times*, habitually very sensitive to the plight of its co-religionists in Russia, supported these efforts.[210]

There was, however, concern that the Government was weak on temperance and too keen on class war.[211] Henry Carter had chaired Labour's internal Advisory Committee on Temperance Policy set up during the war, yet he shared the general view that the Liberals were sounder on this issue.[212] The animosity Labour had shown the Liberals, destroying in the process fond Nonconformist illusions about prospects for reviving the Progressive Alliance, also helped to ensure that the denominational press lined up against Labour in the 1924 election.[213] The release of the Zinoviev letter in the course of the campaign, helpfully complementing as it did the Tories' anti-Bolshevik propaganda, further confirmed their determination 'to register an emphatic protest against Socialism'. With the cash-strapped Liberals bound to an ungrateful Labour government and unable to field more than 340 candidates, Free Churchmen fearfully turned to the Conservatives.[214] The peculiar psychology of the moment was well illustrated by R. F. Horton, who voted Labour yet rejoiced at the Conservatives' landslide triumph.[215] The moderate nature of the Labour government did not quell fears of Red Clydeside,[216] following the return of erstwhile wartime union militants for Glasgow constituencies in 1922. Meanwhile, the need to respond to Labour's arrival as a party of government, and the dropping of protection, brought forth a new and winning moderation from the Conservatives, with the *British Weekly* later praising Baldwin as 'the best Liberal who ever sat on a Conservative bench'.[217] Kingsley Wood meanwhile established a Nonconformist Unionist League with the intention of wooing Free Churchmen alarmed by the rise of Labour. In contrast with Chubb's efforts in the past, this won an unusual amount of coverage in the denominational press, not least when Baldwin told this gathering that Free Churchmen would have to adjust to the new post-1918 political landmarks.[218]

By the time of the next election in 1929, Baldwin had worked hard to build on the opportunities to consolidate Nonconformist support for his cause. Unlike his rival party leaders, Ramsay MacDonald and Lloyd George, he could not claim to be a Free Churchman. However, he was transparently a sincere and devout Christian. Furthermore, although he was a good Anglican, Baldwin nonetheless had an eminent Wesleyan minister for a grandfather. His courteous disposition, and the character and faith that shone through his speeches, won the friendship even of arch-Nonconformists like J. D. Jones.[219] So did his readiness, unique in a leader of his party, to address Free Church gatherings. In 1925 he gave his first speech at a church conference to the NCEFC assembly.[220] This would have been, as the *Christian World* commented after his speech to a special Baptist Union dinner in January 1929, unthinkable in Clifford's day.[221] Two years later he addressed the Congregational Union assembly. The flatteringly intimate insight into the world of the Free Churches that these speeches featured undoubtedly owed something to the speech-drafting abilities and Calvinist Methodist background of Thomas Jones, the deputy cabinet secretary.[222] This was accompanied by a religious tone which struck Free Churchmen – who could bestow no higher accolade – as almost Gladstonian.[223] Randall Davidson, the archbishop of Canterbury, who had known W. E. Gladstone well, confided similar admiration for the generality of Baldwin's 1924 administration.[224] In contrast, among Free Church leaders, the only other Conservative to elicit much enthusiasm was another devout Anglican, Lord Robert Cecil, largely for his part in promoting the League of Nations Union (LNU).[225] Cecil, ironically, was increasingly estranged from his own party for much the same reasons. Baldwin's importance in making Conservatism respectable among Free Churchmen is therefore unquestionable.

However, not even Baldwin could rally any of the Free Church press to the Tory standard in 1929. Their ties with the Liberals were not killed by the Liberals' crushing defeat in 1924, as an immediate spate of articles in the *Contemporary Review* and the *Congregational Quarterly* made clear. Even in areas like Fulham, where Nonconformists were thin on the ground, Free Church councils apparently could still pick Liberal parliamentary candidates.[226] Except for the relatively unpartisan Quaker and Unitarian journals, the Free Church press continued to support them. There was, however, also increasing recognition that all three parties had claims to Free Church support. Both the *Christian World* and the *Baptist Times* therefore ran appeals by representatives of each party during the campaign.[227] This was partly because old Nonconformist battle cries were no longer at issue and the Prayer Book debates in 1927–28 had failed, despite J. D. Jones' optimism,[228] to revive the traditional alliance with Liberalism. It was also because, although the new Liberal programmes introduced since Lloyd George became party leader in 1926 had generated considerable enthusiasm, there was a growing reluctance in the Free Church press unequivocally to pass judgement on the economic issues that featured so strongly in the campaign.

Socialism was meanwhile becoming more acceptable within Nonconformity. Rhondda Williams, Tom Phillips and W. F. Lofthouse – Socialists all – were respectively chairman of the Congregational Union, president of the NCEFC and president of the Wesleyan conference in either 1928 or 1929.[229] Indeed, Table 2 shows the propensity of politically active Nonconformist ministers to stand for Parliament in the Labour interest.

At the same time, the coming together of various small societies gave a greater coherence to the Christian Left. The representatives of the Catholic Crusade, the Church Socialist League (both Anglican bodies), the League of Young Socialists, the Socialist Quaker Society, and *The Crusader* all participated in the setting up of the Society of Socialist Christians (SSC) in 1924.[230] This seemed to give the SSC a predominantly Anglican flavour, despite John Lewis's denials.[231] In fact, just under 50 per cent of its central committee and just over 50 per cent of those members of the new body who stood for Parliament in the Labour interest were Nonconformists. In 1925 it affiliated to the Labour Party.[232] By 1928 it had taken over *The Crusader*, which was then renamed the *Socialist Christian*. For the 1929 general election it issued *A Call to Christians* which was extensively used by the Labour Party during its successful campaign.

The SSC was not, however, the only example of Free Church radicalism during the 1924–29 Parliament. The answers to the question posed by the *Liverpool Daily Post* in 1926, 'Are the Churches Going Labour?' may have been generally in the negative.[233] By 1929, nonetheless, there were signs of increasing pro-Labour sentiment among students in theological colleges.[234] There were certainly signs of radicalism among some of the younger ministers. Pressure groups on specific issues also began to appear. These developments, however, seem to have had little effect upon the Free Church leadership. As S. Maurice Watts said of the Congregational Ministers' Crusade Against War:

> We may next be asked to join the Congregational Ministers' Crusade against slums, and I know these signatories well enough to be confident that they would

Table 2 Free Church ministers and ex-ministers standing for Parliament, 1918–35

	Baptist				Congregational			Unitarian		Prim		Wesleyan				Other[b]		TOTAL
	Lab	Lib	NL[a]	Other	Lab	Lib	NL	Lab	NL	Lab	Lib	Lab	Lib	NL	Con	Lab	Lib	
Candidates	5				3	1	3	2	1	1			1		1c			18
1918																		61.11%
MPs	1						3								1			5
Candidates	1				2	4	2	1	1	1		1	1	1			1	16
1922																		37.50%
MPs	1																	1
Candidates	2				2	9		2		1			2			3d	1	22
1923																		45.45%
MPs	1					3							1			1	1	7
Candidates	1				2	5		2		1		1	1			3	1	17
1924																		58.82%
MPs	1					1										1		2
Candidates	1	1		1	4	4		3		1	1	1	1			2	3	23
1929																		52.17%
MPs	1				1								1			2		4
Candidates	1			1	2			2						1		4	1	12
1931																		75.00%
MPs																		0

Candidates			1	1	2			3					1			1		9
1935																		66.66%
MPs								2										2
Candidatures	11	1	1	3	17	22	5	15	2	5	1	3	7	2	1	13	7	117
Lab %																		54.70%
Candidates	6	1	1	2	8	10	3	5	1	1	1	2	2	2	1	5	3	54
Lab %							3											50.00%
MPs	2				1	3	3	2					1		1	3	1	17
Lab %																		47.06%

Notes: [a]This category includes National Liberal and National Democratic Party supporters of the 1916–22 Coalition government and Liberal National and National Labour supporters of the 1931–40 National government.

[b]I have included in this column Rennie Smith and Wilfred Wellock, who both served as Independent Methodist lay ministers.

[c]Elected as a Unionist in Northern Ireland.

[d]G. M. Lloyd Davies stood as a Christian Pacifist but sat with Labour while in Parliament.

The abbreviations along the top of the table represent respectively: Lab = Labour; Lib = Liberal; NL = National Liberal; Con = Conservative.

> be the first to join. But where is this process to end? ... I want to see the whole of my denomination taking a radical stand.[235]

There was little sign of such a shift in the Free Church press. Its attitude towards Labour when it formed its second minority administration in 1929 was certainly more measured than in 1924. Nevertheless, there were still few Free Church leaders who were prepared to join Donald Soper in advocating a Labour vote, 'as part of my service to the Master',[236] least of all during the crisis election of 1931. During the previous two years the Labour government had struggled ineffectively to tackle rising unemployment. This and the resulting fiscal problems, together with a dramatic drain of the reserves, produced the budget crisis of August 1931 that led to the Labour government's resignation.

In this emergency, the denominational press readily accepted the necessity for the National government that Ramsay MacDonald formed to succeed it. In the face of a severe and largely unexpected crisis, its patriotic rhetoric and non-partisan complexion were particularly comforting. The Nonconformist press looked to it to restore international confidence in Britain's economy.[237] The apparent inability of the late Labour government to deal with either the budget crisis or the cuts deemed necessary hardly made it seem a viable alternative. As the Unitarian and Labour MP, Morgan Phillips Price, noted in his diary at the time, 'The country is thoroughly frightened and our Party has not proved that it has an alternative policy or the courage to put one through if it had one'.[238]

Traditional Liberal rallying cries like 'free trade' meanwhile were dropped in the face of the National government's plea for a 'Doctor's Mandate' to deal with the situation. It was realized that the government's need for revenue and unfavourable shifts in the balance of trade were bringing this principle under threat. Even Henderson, and with him most of the Labour Party, was prepared to accept a 10 per cent revenue tariff in place of the 10 per cent cut in unemployment benefit the National government had implemented in an effort to balance the budget.[239] Labour's objection to the unemployment benefit reduction was in fact the main plank in its election campaign. It was not without Free Church sympathizers. With predominantly unemployed congregations, it is likely that most ministers in South Wales joined M. Watcyn-Williams in supporting Labour.[240] The Unitarians' newspaper, *The Inquirer*, made clear its objections to the cut.[241] So did some leading Congregational ministers. They however failed to persuade the Congregational Union assembly to join them in their protest.[242] For most of the Free Church leadership, the crisis was more important than the cuts.

It was also now more important than free trade. It was still felt that free trade 'should be our ideal as the only way to world-peace and federation'.[243] The Free Church press in the 1931 election nevertheless generally supported a government in which protectionist Conservatives predominated, 'trusting to Mr. Baldwin to see that their faith is not betrayed'.[244] Lloyd George was taken to task by the *Baptist Times* for criticizing this naïveté. His call to free traders to vote for Lloyd Georgian or Labour candidates in defence of their principles went unheeded. His co-religionists were more impressed by the need to support the second budget of 1931 than by the fact that it was probably the last traditional free trade budget they would experience.[245]

They were encouraged in this by the presence of Liberals in the government. This was not, however, as important a factor as in the past. The Liberals, in light of their equivocal attitude to the 1930–31 education bills, were no longer relied on to defend Nonconformist interests. Several leading Liberals even helped to carry a Catholic amendment, which completely countered the traditional Nonconformist position that denominational education should not be publicly funded. The normally placid M. E. Aubrey (the Baptist Union secretary) responded: 'Never were old friends worse treated by old allies than Nonconformists were by the Liberal party. It is quite clear the old alliance is wiped out now.'[246] Feelings were not mollified by Lloyd George's explanation. The chairman of the Lancashire Free Church Education Association Henry Townsend fulminated, 'Our loyalties to the Liberal Party are being strained to breaking point.'[247] With the Liberals no longer the special defenders of Nonconformity, Free Churchmen could more readily contemplate other political associations. Liberal disunity and ineffectiveness while maintaining in power another minority Labour government did little to retain their diminishing affection.

Instead, Free Church leaders could take comfort from the liberal-minded leadership MacDonald and Baldwin gave the National government.[248] This new political alignment endured, even after the Liberals – though not Sir John Simon's protectionist Liberal Nationals – left the government in 1932 over the introduction of imperial preference through the Ottawa tariffs. By 1937, a suggestion that the NCEFC assembly protest against the National government could be laughed out.[249]

In the 1935 election there was more nostalgia than support for the independent rump of the Liberal Party that was now clearly unable to field sufficient candidates to contend for power. The *Christian World* lamented:

> Political freedom has been won, Free Trade, alas, is no longer in the sphere of practical politics (it never even became an issue at this election) and economic freedom can now be more properly left to the Labour Party.[250]

Liberalism had become an ethos, not a political programme. Government supporters like Geoffrey Shakespeare (now a Liberal National MP) thus spoke of infusing its legislation with Liberalism.[251] Otherwise it seemed to have little to offer on the dominant issues of rearmament or unemployment. For Dunnico, now a National Labour MP, the centrality of such issues meant that there was no alternative to the National government.[252]

These issues were also central to a meeting convened in 1935 by S. W. Hughes, the secretary of the NCEFC, in the Congregational Memorial Hall in Farringdon where Lloyd George was invited to speak. The veteran statesman had already spoken on unemployment at the 1933 NCEFC assembly, developing his 'New Deal' programme – involving a National Development Board overseeing rehousing, infrastructure projects and land settlement – in a speech at Bangor on 17 January 1935. At the Memorial Hall meeting Lloyd George 'urged the Churches to stop passing resolutions on war, and to take some definite steps to meet the situation that Hitler and Mussolini were creating'. From this was born what was called the Council of Action for Peace and Reconstruction (CAPR). This, with backing from the NCEFC, sought to put forward a broad programme of positive policies and solicit support for them from candidates of all parties, not least in the coming general election.[253]

The National government had already been invited to examine Lloyd George's 'New Deal' ideas, and was subsequently to adopt aspects of his proposals such as scrap-and-build in shipbuilding and nationalization of mining royalties. The generality of the scheme, however, was rejected in an official statement of 18 July 1935 on the grounds that the principal problem was underemployment, and that this problem was better treated by the National prescription of tariffs and industrial reorganization than Lloyd George's medicine.[254]

Even before the government's rejection was issued, many erstwhile Nonconformist supporters of the CAPR were distancing themselves. The *Baptist Times*, having praised the Bangor speech, turned rapidly against the new body as soon as its editor, the erstwhile Christian Socialist J.C. Carlile began to suspect it of being tied to the Welsh wizard's chariot.[255] There was certainly little enthusiasm for the idea of running parliamentary candidates. This was the principal reason for prominent left-leaning Methodists like Henry Carter and Robert Bond withdrawing their endorsements. Support in local Free Church councils across the country was also patchy and in some areas non-existent.[256]

Lloyd George's hostility to the National government helped to alienate those Nonconformist leaders who would have preferred to see the CAPR as a pro-government ginger group.[257] Baptists Carlile and Aubrey were certainly strong National government supporters.[258] So was the majority of the NCEFC leadership, which in 1935 invited Baldwin to address their assembly and warmly praised his speech.[259] Lloyd George's lieutenant on the CAPR, Scott Lidgett, shared this enthusiasm. He was therefore appalled when it became clear that his position might imply endorsement of the many Labour candidates who replied favourably to the CAPR's questionnaire. He wrote to Lloyd George:

> I look upon the declaration of the Socialist leaders as highly dangerous and, in the strict sense of the term, revolutionary. I had not completely realised the extent of my commitment to support any and every Candidate who might accept the policy of the Council of Action. As you are aware, the basis on which you and I co-operated in formulating our policy was that there was no likelihood of the Socialist Party accepting it.[260]

Impelled by this fear of Socialism he urged the return of National government candidates.[261]

One Methodist minister caustically observed that the CAPR had over 300 favourable replies from Liberal and Labour candidates and only 19 from government candidates and yet Scott Lidgett backed those 19 candidates.[262] Only 67 of the 362 endorsed candidates (of whom 180 stood for Labour) were elected and the National government again won a massive, if reduced, majority. Henry Carter's post-mortem recognized good motives but drew attention to the divisions in Free Church opinion the CAPR had caused. Though, contrary to his advice, the CAPR survived the election debacle and retained, after lengthy debate, the support of the NCEFC, it soon faded even from their discussions.[263]

The solidity of NCEFC support for the National government, meanwhile, should not be exaggerated. In the face of the unemployment and international tension bedevilling the 1930s, five members of its executive in 1935 issued a manifesto urging all Free Churchmen to vote Labour. One, A. D. Belden, had, as vice president of the NCEFC in 1931, played a leading part in the founding meeting of the Christian Socialist Crusade held at Whitefield's Tabernacle in Tottenham Court Road, where he was the minister. This later amalgamated with the SSC to form the Socialist Christian League.[264]

Conclusion

The gradual increase in the 1930s in the numbers of Socialist Free Church ministers seems to reflect generational changes. Scott Lidgett's fears were not shared by younger Nonconformists. The veteran Congregationalist theologian A. E. Garvie 'noticed among the younger men in the ministry a tendency ... to identify the Christian solution of the Social Problem with Socialism or the Labour Party'.[265] His fellow Congregationalist Claud M. Coltman argued in 1935 that Labour was now Nonconformity's natural ally:

> The Free Churches of today will not pull their weight in politics until they grasp the new economic situation which has arisen in this age of power, until they have overcome their social prejudices and recognised in the Labour Party – which they have done so much to build up – the natural inheritor of their political tradition and the only available vehicle for its effective expression. The Free Churches have played a great part in winning political freedom for the people, and they must go on to win their economic freedom.[266]

J. D. Jones, in contrast, saw in Labour not the means for economic freedom but a bureaucratic Socialism and retreated from party politics.[267] Others continued to nurture hopes of the Liberals. In 1945 the *Congregational Quarterly* confidently, if improbably, predicted a Liberal victory at the polls.[268] By then, however, Liberalism had long ceased to monopolize the political views of the Free Church leadership.

Nonconformist Socialists were increasingly attaining positions of influence in the Free Church leadership. Men like Soper and Owen Rattenbury were following Belden onto the executive board of the NCEFC. But the National government, and especially Baldwin, helped to shift the dominant political tone to the Right rather than the Left. Though Soper, Belden and a number of other Socialists had regular entry to its column inches, many on the Left were still confined to writing indignant letters to the denominational press.

2

The Nonconformist Conscience after 1918

As soon as we in this country passed from the tutelage of the old Manchester school, of the doctrine of industry unfettered by any state control, and the practice of individual bargaining between master and man, we began to move in perplexity. So we tried to study the difficult questions, to avoid using harsh terms of one side or the other, to affirm general principles, to recommend what progress we could in the less thorny paths of temperance. And all the time Labour, and others besides Labour, were asking why the organised followers of the Prince of Peace allowed the struggle to go on … with scarcely a protest. It was natural, pardonable, almost inevitable. It was like the tragic dilemma that faced us all with such terrible suddenness in August 1914. We did not call for war; we did not desire it; we loathed it; but we had no word, no plan, no device, to drive it from our midst.

W. F. Lofthouse[1]

Many a man cries out against the present social system when his real enemy is the bookmaker in his pocket and the publican down his throat.

Reginald W. Thompson[2]

What was the Nonconformist Conscience?

'He discovered unrighteousness all along the line in national life, and he was the leader of an army to destroy the unwholesomeness', was how David Andrea described John Clifford in 1936.[3] In the hands of preachers like Clifford, the Nonconformist Conscience that emerged in the late nineteenth century was a self-confident and assertive crusade against both domestic and overseas evils. The then Congregational minister of the City Temple Joseph Parker was far from alone in thundering against the 'Hellish iniquity' of the Ottoman Sultan.[4] In sulphurous language, nineteenth-century pulpit princes lambasted injustice and immorality. Thus in 1909 Clifford spoke of having 'a hand to hand fight with all the tyrannies and despotisms at once'.[5] The Nonconformist Conscience he preached expressed a pugnacious righteousness, through organizations such as the Passive Resistance League, Clifford's instrument for combating the 1902 Education Act. In the years before 1914 it had three principal characteristics: its proponents denied a boundary between religion and politics;

insisted that politicians should be men of highest character; and believed that the State should promote the moral welfare of its citizens.[6] They campaigned for the removal of evils ranging from sweated labour to intemperance.[7] Their attitude to political authority can be exemplified by Stanley Mellor's recollections. This Unitarian minister of Ullet Road, Liverpool, recalled that his 'passionate-hearted Radical' father believed

> [I]n representative government and all its institutions … respected the House of Commons … credited the ballot-box with a mysterious sanctity and power … upheld the duties and responsibilities of citizenship … regarded politics as a serious business … had faith in politicians and … believed in progress, marvellous and inevitable.[8]

Accordingly, they helped to create the atmosphere of mystique that attached to the exercise of the franchise and the idea of parliamentary democracy in the early twentieth century, evidenced by the numbers of early Labour MPs who graduated from the parliamentary debating societies of their native cities. With the 1918 extension of the franchise, however, the reverence for parliamentary democracy which William Mellor invoked seemed to pass into the constitution. Devotion to the causes of political and religious liberty remained noble, but these were no longer domestic issues.

The condemnatory Nonconformist Conscience, meanwhile, was arguably already in decline by 1910, damaged by the frustration of the high hopes – not least of overturning the 1902 Education Act – encouraged by the 1906 Liberal landslide.[9] Sectarian grievances had been reactivated by this legislation, which abolished school boards and gave rate support to denominational schools without corresponding public control, thus perpetuating the situation whereby Nonconformist children in the estimated 8,000 mainly rural areas where the only schools available were Anglican, were subjected to invidious and often prejudiced clerical influence.[10] Nonconformist teachers, similarly, had limited employment prospects in these denominational schools. The campaign against the Act, however, proved the Indian summer of militant Nonconformity. It achieved so little that, by 1935, the president of the NCEFC F. W. Norwood confessed that in recent years the Nonconformist Conscience had 'become rather a joke'.[11] There indeed seemed to be less need for it. M. E. Aubrey told the Free Church Federal Council in 1936, 'The fact that we have achieved so much of what we sought accounts for the fact that we are now less militant in the political sphere than our fathers were'.[12] It was also, Scott Lidgett suggested to the NCEFC, because the lives of great men were more moral and the Church of England more alive to moral issues.[13]

S. G. Hobson felt that the magnificence of its goals, salvation through Christ and, 'strike down the oppressor in his arrogance and vainglory, for only in liberty can man know God and realise himself', were incomprehensible to post-1918 cynicism.[14] This elevated witness for liberty was not, however, rendered irrelevant by the First World War. 'Liberty', reminded the *Methodist Times*, 'is a primary Free Church principle'.[15] Stanley Mellor's 1929 book *Liberation* was a paean to the concept of freedom. However, it was no longer enough to seek freedom from the political establishment or an Erastian church. As the Labour MP, Congregationalist, and leading light of the Socialist Medical Association Somerville Hastings put it in 1934:

> We who are Free Churchmen must never forget the debt we owe to our forefathers for the measure of political and religious liberty that is ours ... But civil and religious liberty can never be complete without economic liberty as well.[16]

This was a lesson, as Charles Ammon emphasised to the NCEFC assembly in 1921, rooted in Nonconformist teaching, for 'If Labour is wrong then the Free Churches have misled us; for they have taught us that human life is sacred'.[17]

Economic and wartime changes

Economic changes since the mid-eighteenth century meanwhile had encouraged a growing belief that the conditions people lived in were susceptible of systematic improvement. There had consequently been an increasing emphasis on people's economic needs and aspirations. By 1959, the Methodist Labour MP George Thomas could argue, 'Modern industry makes economic freedom a realistic policy for workers everywhere for the first time in history.'[18] It also produced a heightened sensitivity to social conditions. The churches increasingly had to address social and economic as well as spiritual conditions.[19] This required rethinking the relationships between these conditions. 'It was honestly thought at one time that the universe was so ordered that the man who best pursued his own interest was best advancing the interests of all' noted the distinguished Wesleyan economist Sir Josiah Stamp in 1926. Indeed, this was almost a direct quotation from the eminent early nineteenth-century Baptist minister Robert Hall.[20] The context in which Hall's belief had flourished had, however, been replaced by one characterized by high unemployment and pockets of industrial decline and transformed by the enfranchisement, education and aspirations of the working classes. It became a source of embarrassment. As the active Liberal and businessman Angus Watson explained in his chairman's address to the Congregational Union assembly in 1936:

> Our fathers failed to see that what they described as the uncontrolled operation of economic law and the beneficence of laissez-faire, 'each man for himself and the devil take the hindmost', was finally the law of the jungle; and they had no sense of reproach in the exploitation of their less fortunate and capable fellows.[21]

These predecessors had been unaware of any such deficiency. Karl Marx was unfamiliar to them. Nor was the idea of unemployment readily grasped before the work of the Cambridge economist Alfred Marshall in the 1880s began to circulate more widely. By the time of the ineffective 1905 Unemployed Workmen Act, the idea that unemployment was a temporary phenomenon eradicable by market forces was a swiftly disabused pious hope. As the empirical basis of the old iron laws of economics faded, they also came under ethical attack from those drawn to the critique that late nineteenth-century Socialism offered. The Unitarian minister and ILP pioneer H. Bodell Smith, for instance, complained that they ignored justice, resulted in waste, produced unemployment and poverty, and caused discord, war and crime.[22] Indeed, the empirical and ethical assaults on the ideas of long-dead economists went together: as an editorial in the ILP's *Labour Leader* pointed out in 1919, 'The Independent Labour Party was born in an unemployment crisis.'[23]

The days when Nonconformist businessmen could claim 'that no worker had the right to more than his services would fetch in the open market, and on the other hand, that no business could be held successful that was paying less than a 20 per cent dividend' were passing.[24] Laissez-faire was becoming discredited as it became increasingly clear that poverty was caused more by social factors than by sin.[25] By 1917, B. J. Snell could claim in his chairman's address to the Congregational Union assembly 'The policy of laissez-faire is ended' for 'it cannot be Divine Will that so many should have no chance of worthy independent human life.'[26]

This tendency was reinforced by wartime experience. War profiteering called business morality into question, undermining lingering beliefs that 'the existing economic system' represented 'God's will for industry and commerce'.[27] Accordingly, 'Ethically this war will ring the death-knell of the old-fashioned individualism', the future Labour MP Ellis Lloyd proclaimed in a novel published in 1919.[28] Similar views emerged from a survey of attitudes in the army published that year which concluded that 'no social order can be really Christian that is based on self-interest. The problem today is to construct one based on devotion to the common good.'[29] Both the 'war to end war' propaganda of the government and the ferocity of the conflict aroused the hope that the war would be succeeded by something substantially better than what had gone before. Furthermore, as one army chaplain observed,

> The commingling of all classes in the ranks ... bred a common sense of the social ailments which clamour for remedy, and a profound dissatisfaction with present social conditions ... It is quite evident that a critical and dangerous time is ahead of the nation after the war.[30]

Young men who had not been socialized into allegiance to existing political structures or parties during the long hiatus since the general elections of 1910 could prove prey to a radicalism that was a challenge to the churches no less than to a government that from 1919 onwards seemed more absorbed in the pursuit of economy than of the homes and jobs for heroes promised during the war.[31] A number were drawn to the National Federation of Discharged and Demobilised Sailors and Soldiers formed in April 1917 which, generally but not invariably with Labour support, fought twenty-nine constituencies in the 1918 election. It also put up candidates for municipal elections in places like Norwich.[32] This body, however, merged with other bodies such as the Tory-sponsored Comrades of the Great War in 1920 to form the British Legion. This new organization continued to address questionnaires on ex-servicemen issues to election candidates until the end of the 1920s, but its patriotic flavour ensured – as the Tory politician A. Duff Cooper pointed out – that it increasingly resembled 'a collection of Conservative working men's clubs'. However, only 10 per cent of ex-servicemen were represented by the British Legion.[33] After demobilization, too many of their ex-servicemen comrades went from being cannon fodder to becoming unemployment demonstration fodder.

The intractable unemployment of the period reflected structural problems in the British economy particularly embedded in Northern England, central Scotland, Northern Ireland and South Wales. Formerly staple industries, such as coal, cotton, iron and steel, and shipbuilding were all in long-term decline. This blight was particularly severe in the coal-exporting regions. Their exports to former markets like Italy were replaced by the coal Germany was required to provide as war reparations. Import substitution and the rise of oil as the principal maritime fuel also hit the coalfields of South Wales and Durham with especial force.[34] In South Wales, 180 pits closed between 1918 and 1937 and the number of miners more than halved.[35] Many left the valleys in search of work, often settling among the new industries to the west of London. George Thomas recalled: 'there was not a family in South Wales untouched by such misery; it was like a terrible war taking our people from us'.[36] Other export industries suffered similar, if not equally devastating, decline. In 1920, the Bolton and District Cotton Spinners annual report declared, 'a prosperous India reflects itself in the staple trade of Lancashire'.[37] By the 1930s they noted that Indian tariff barriers combined with the Gandhi-inspired boycott of British goods had hit their trade: exports to India were in 1938 only 10 per cent of the pre-war level.[38] The export potential of an industry whose malstructured nature prompted the local newspaper to launch an attack on the insane price war and overcapacity of Bolton manufacturers, was further weakened by the return of sterling to the pre-war parity of $4.86 in 1925 – raising the cost of British goods overseas – and by the emergence of cheaper Japanese competition.[39] Furthermore, the overcapitalization of Lancashire's cotton industry during the post-war boom of 1919–21 left an overhang of debt and firms found it difficult to restructure financially until the mergers forced by the Bank of England at the end of the 1920s.[40] Problems of organization and obsolete plant rendered much of Britain's older industry ill-prepared for the competition and crises of the inter-war years. Subsequent defensive mergers and concomitant reductions in employment in the industry still could not strip out enough overcapacity to avoid chronic short-time working in the 1930s.[41]

Such problems shaped the nature of class conflict in this period. Faced with declining competitiveness and profitability, all too often the only solution that captains of industry could see was the reduction of labour costs through cutting wages and increasing hours or duties.[42] The result was the erosion of the grounds for economic consensus.[43] One of the objects of the Bolton Card Room Operatives listed in their 1906 rulebook was 'to promote that reciprocity of good feeling which conduces so much both to the interests of employer and employed'.[44] In 1929 its general secretary commented sourly on the pressure for wage cuts exerted by employers: 'Those operatives, who have felt secure because they worked for firms who have a reputation for paying good wages, and working under reasonable conditions have had their eyes opened.'[45] Historic ideas of the commonality of interest of masters and men were being undermined by declining competitiveness.

These ideas were also undermined by the process of amalgamation and recapitalization either side of the First World War that transformed the ownership patterns, if not the efficiency, of British industry. Over half the spinning mills in Bolton changed hands in 1919.[46] Family firms were replaced by financiers; the latter described by Angus Watson as soulless asset-strippers who cared for the dividend-holder, and not the workforce.[47] When he and Ammon discussed 'The Reconciliation of Capital and Labour' at the NCEFC assembly in 1923, Watson pointed out that the consequent growth of joint-stock companies made it increasingly difficult to be a paternalistic employer identifying with his men. Ammon contended that this growth created both a useless body of dividend-holders, and class conflict.[48] As the *Rhondda Leader* put it in 1921: 'There was a day when the master took a paternal interest in "his men" … but today we have soulless companies and combines; the men have become machines for producing dividends for masters.'[49]

By 1919, 80 per cent of Britain's leading industries were allegedly controlled by these soulless combines.[50] In W. J. Edwards's father's time, coal owners and colliers had worshipped in the same South Wales chapels, equal before God. He, however, 'was a child of that malign revolution that placed a sinister wall around the masters and their minions, so that they became segregated and dwelt like stars in their own galaxies and free from personal relationships'.[51]

Social segregation compounded a geographical segregation already apparent in the second half of the nineteenth century as the middle classes moved out from the districts where they had once worked and worshipped.[52] This increased the difficulties of urban mission: as Ammon observed in 1933, for a minister of a central London chapel 'The heart of a lion and the spirit of a saint must be essentials'.[53] It also increased the risks of class conflict, as Thomas Tiplady found in surveying London's East End in 1924. He commented on the impoverished, predominantly working-class communities that remained: 'It is not the Communists who have made them class-conscious. It is the rich by forsaking them, and thus ostracising them.'[54]

Such developments were noted in a political landscape seemingly reshaped during the Great War. Trade union membership doubled between 1913 and 1920, with nearly half the male and a quarter of the female workforce unionized.[55] The exigencies of total war also led to similar increases in recognition of women's citizenship, culminating in the grant of the parliamentary vote for women ratepayers over thirty years of age in the 1918 Representation of the People Act. The following year the Sex Disqualification Removal Act opened civil and legal posts to women, who were then granted the franchise on an equal basis with men in 1928. There were calls for the churches as well to recognize female advancement. Garvie told the Congregational Union:

> [T]he new place women have won for themselves in society generally, and the new sense which is spreading amongst them of their wider function in society, is a summons to the church not to quench this new spirit among them, but to give them fullest opportunity for the realisation of their aspirations in the service of the Kingdom of God.[56]

Indeed, the NCEFC's 1918 manifesto called for the 'complete emancipation and equipment of Womanhood for service to the State'.[57] A year earlier, the first female Congregational minister, Constance Todd (later Coltman), had been ordained.[58] This service was presided over by W. E. Orchard, who even preached on the motherhood of God. In this, however, as in so many other ways, Orchard was unrepresentative of the Free Churches. His ordinand went off to serve in London's East End, but it was not until 1956 that the first woman chairman of the Congregational Union was appointed.[59] Progress among Methodists was even slower: despite John Wesley's appointment of female travelling preachers in the eighteenth century, and the view of the post-Union conference in 1933 that 'there is no function of the ordained ministry … for which a woman is disqualified by reason of her sex', in 1939 the denomination was just starting to consider women's ordination, a breakthrough that was finally achieved in 1974.[60]

For both trade unions and women, wartime gains thus proved more apparent than sustained. The former wrested from the Treasury the guarantees given in March 1915 that skills dilution through the introduction of unskilled labour to various industrial processes would only be for the duration of the conflict, followed by the restoration of pre-war labour practices.[61] This, however, did not secure pay levels that would compensate for wartime inflation. Ensuing high unemployment furthermore ensured that union membership fell back during the 1920s, before staging something of a recovery in the 1930s.[62] Meanwhile, the reassertion of gender stereotypes and marriage bars on employment in many industries meant that women's wartime advances in the labour market, and indeed within the trade union movement itself, were frequently not maintained.[63]

The Nonconformist response

There was, nevertheless, a widespread view within the Free Churches that the social circumstances they had to address were much changed by the conflagration. As a recipe for religious revival, the Congregational Modernist Frank Ballard pointed out, 'The well-meant suggestion in some Christian circles to dismiss all thoughtful estimate of the modern situation and simply continue in "prayer and praise" is worse than childish.'[64] A. R. Henderson devoted his chairman's address to the 1923 Congregational Union assembly to the idea that the Living God must be made meaningful by bringing God's judgement to bear on business, war, housing and all social relations as a lamp to guide post-war aspirations.[65] Mirroring wartime government propaganda about post-war reconstruction, several denominations had Reconstruction Committees by 1918 as offshoots of the Social Service Unions established in most of the churches around the turn of the century. Such developments did not, however, mean that all in the churches were wholly convinced of the need for the social application of the Gospel. Garvie found much hostility to his warning, as chairman of the Congregational Union in 1921, that

> [M]uch of the teaching and training in our churches bears still the impress of that excessive individualism which … has narrowed the range and lowered the quality of Christian testimony and influence in our Churches; and what we need is a pulpit competent to exhibit the application of all Christian principles in all spheres, domestic, industrial, commercial, social, national and international.[66]

This hostility resulted in the lack of finance and support for the Congregational and Unitarian Social Service Unions in the 1920s.[67] This seems to have reflected an antipathy towards Socialism. The Primitive Methodist Social Service Union complained in 1924, 'We are constantly encountering the charge or the fear that our Union is a branch of the Labour Party, or stands for the spread of Socialist doctrine. Most emphatically that is not so.'[68] Socialism was nevertheless well represented in some of the Social Service Unions. Only the first of the three secretaries of the Congregational body during the period, Will Reason, seems to have made the transition from Liberalism to Labour. The Wesleyan Methodist Union of Social Service was however led for most of the interwar years by Henry Carter, a minister with close associations with the inner workings of the Labour Party.

During this period the voluntary Social Service Unions were replaced by formally constituted denominational bodies. Some nevertheless remained distinctly radical in character, not least the Friends' Social Committee, whose moral earnestness reminded the erstwhile Congregationalist, Socialist journalist and Labour MP Fenner Brockway of the early ILP.[69] The Methodist Social Welfare Department meanwhile succeeded in giving social concern a much higher profile through initiatives such as the Youth and Christian Citizenship campaign of 1935. Furthermore, their *Declaration on Peace and War*, influenced by Carter's Pacifism, provoked considerable hostility from denominational leaders, including the editor of the *Methodist Times*.[70]

Nevertheless, it is noticeable that the handbook on which the Youth and Christian Citizenship campaign was based continued primarily to emphasize personal morality. Issues such as gambling and temperance were very much to the fore. It was, however, as Carter stressed, at least an attempt to explore what being a Christian meant in the contemporary social setting.[71] Instead, during the interwar years, Free Church bodies too often gave the impression that pious resolutions were being made to serve duty for the Nonconformist Conscience. In 1921, Thomas Nightingale, its secretary, claimed great things of the NCEFC's Manchester programme, while also admitting that they had not pressed their friend, Lloyd George, to make his government's policies more Christian.[72] The NCEFC certainly registered no protests against the Amritsar massacre or the Versailles Treaty. Even when critical resolutions were passed by church assemblies they were sometimes more for show than effect. Tiplady satirized them thus:

> It draws up a resolution calling upon some other body to intervene… .Up in a balloon, floating somewhere between heaven and earth, it sees or hears some evil on the earth. Someone eloquently proposes a resolution, someone eloquently seconds it. The resolution is carried unanimously. The Secretary writes it out on official notepaper and drops it over the side… . No one knows what becomes of it, but it is presumed that the resolution will cure the evil, and the balloon goes serenely on its way.[73]

With the application of Christian principles to the complex issues of the interwar years not always obvious and the churches divided in counsels, Garvie felt 'The Church corporately is not justified in making any authoritative declaration.'[74] Arthur Henderson however warned that if the Church failed to exercise moral leadership then that authority would pass out of its sphere to other secular bodies.[75]

War and conscience

The expression of this moral leadership had proved particularly challenging during the Great War. Nonconformist attitudes towards conflict had already been shifting in the late nineteenth century from an emphasis on peace towards the use of a forward foreign policy, and, in the hands of men like Hugh Price Hughes, a crusading imperialism, to tackle evils internationally as well as at home.[76] However, those like R. F. Horton and Clifford, who had not joined Hughes in supporting the 1899–1902 Boer War, nevertheless after initial doubts rallied to the cause after the German violation of Belgium.[77] This breach of international law brought a dramatic volte-face from the preaching of peace, which, like the international Church Conference in Constance convened by the recently formed World Alliance for the Promotion of International Friendship through the Churches, was interrupted and suddenly ended by the conflict.[78] The idea of Germany's moral bankruptcy encouraged Free Church leaders to strike a Cromwellian note in their denunciation of the militaristic tyranny of the Kaiser, while Guttery and others exalted the soldiers' Christian self-sacrifice in this righteous cause.[79] In the absence of conscription in the first eighteen months of the war, such rhetoric was particularly important to the recruitment campaign. The government even suggested appropriate texts for bellicose sermons.[80] It would not, however, countenance the use of the New Testament in criticism of the war. The publication of the Sermon on the Mount as a pamphlet without any commentary whatsoever was banned under the 1914 Defence of the Realm Act (DORA) as anti-patriotic propaganda. A Leeds Methodist was indeed gaoled for this offence.[81]

Some in the ILP, which largely opposed the war, denounced the churches as opponents of the Sermon on the Mount.[82] The Scottish miners' leader Bob Smillie at Easter 1918 told the ILP conference, 'The Churches keep his Crucifixion as a holiday, but they have forgotten his teaching.'[83] There were attempts to deal with this problem: the Wesleyan theologian J. H. Moulton, for instance, in 1915 explained in detail why he had concluded that his duty lay in resisting rather than acquiescing to German aggression.[84] Not all Nonconformists agreed however: there were lay-people and ministers in every denomination who opposed the conflict. Those who were male and of military age were faced with wrestling with their conscience over the dilemma Moulton highlighted after conscription was introduced in January 1916. Nationally, some 16,000 men refused to serve on either religious or political grounds, of whom 5,000–6,000 were imprisoned.[85] In 1919 the Congregational minister and Socialist Claud M. Coltman argued that their continuing incarceration after the war's end was for Nonconformity

> [A] fatal confession of spent strength and exhausted vitality. If freedom is the pride and glory of Britain, it is the very life-blood of Nonconformity. There can be no freed Church without free men, and no free men without free consciences. The safeguarding of the rights of conscience is the supreme charge of Nonconformity. Should Free Churchmen, for whatever reason, suffer these rights to lapse, they have lost their heritage, and with their heritage, their life.[86]

The moment of triumph for some, as the war enabled the Free Churches to win their place in the body politic, represented for him a pawning of the Nonconformist Conscience from which it did not recover.[87]

Coltman's reading of the Nonconformist Conscience drew on a tradition of exclusion from an Erastian State. In contrast, that State had now reached out in its need to embrace Nonconformity, in the process elevating one of its own to the high political office of prime minister. This gave those who supported an alternative reading of the Nonconformist Conscience – as the promotion of national righteousness – a chance to seize the initiative. Accordingly Robertson Nicoll, confidant of Lloyd George and the editor of the *British Weekly*, argued that Nonconformity would lose its place in national life – and thus its ability to shape the moral climate – if it did not fully support the war.[88] Most Nonconformist leaders joined him in the fight for Christianity against tyranny. This led some also to express impatience with conscientious objectors who would not support this struggle for righteousness. For instance, Arthur Pringle's lashing of conscientious objectors during his 1916 chairman's address to the Congregational Union on 'Conscience and Community' was greeted with a great crash of approving cheers.[89] The Wesleyans blacklisted their Pacifist ministers.[90] One minister even allegedly turned his own son from his door because he refused to fight.[91]

What the Liverpool Free Church council described as a 'notable victory for Righteousness' for most Nonconformist leaders overshadowed that fact that, as Garvie pointed out: 'We have during this war had to submit to a regulation of our concerns which at one time would have seemed intolerable and even inconceivable.' By and large, as he recognized, the Free Churches acquiesced.[92] Even the coercion involved in conscription was largely if somewhat reluctantly accepted by them.[93]

The moral right to dissent against this coercion nevertheless had some notable Free Church defenders, not least Horton who in 1915 also pressed the government to arrange neutral mediation as a means of ending the war.[94] Principally at the insistence of Garvie, Clifford and its secretary, F. B. Meyer, the NCEFC affirmed 'the sacred rights of liberty of conscience' from December 1915 onwards.[95] These three even had some success in pleading the cause of the conscientious objector with the war secretary, Lord Kitchener, in June 1916.[96] At the time the Congregational Union would not so much as discuss the issue. Congregational Pacifists like Leyton Richards were fined under DORA.[97] Quakers were meanwhile predictably conspicuous in the No-Conscription Fellowship (NCF) founded and led by ILPers like Brockway in 1915. The NCF was indeed largely funded by the Rowntree family of chocolate manufacturing Quakers.[98] The resulting propinquity to the ILP led J. W. Graham, Quaker and ILPer, to argue in the *Labour Leader*, 'Let us pull together', because of the common interest in the protection of liberty of conscience.[99] It was the anti-militarist ILP, not Nonconformity, which had led its defence.

The war thus revealed the limitations of a Nonconformist Conscience which concentrated on a struggle against tyranny. In its aftermath, the tendency to reduce issues into simple moral crusades became less marked. Not least, a growing appreciation of the witness of the conscientious objectors led to an increasing awareness of the complexity of the moral issues faced in the interwar years.

Issues and elections

The range of issues addressed by the Free Churches between the wars is reflected in the various societies and pressure groups on which the NCEFC had representation. These included the LNU, the Howard League for Penal Reform, the Temperance Council of the Christian Churches (TCCC), the Liberation Society, the Churches Committee of the NMWM, the (prohibitionist) United Kingdom Alliance (UKA), various Coalfields Distress Funds, and the National Council for the Abolition of the Death Penalty.[100] Changing emphases upon these various concerns are reflected in the statements released at the time of each general election by Free Church bodies outlining the principal issues as they saw them.

In 1918, despite the social aspirations released by the war, traditional issues remained strong. W. R. Wilkinson urged that since the new Parliament was supposed to be for post-war reconstruction, temperance might have been expected to take pride of place. Temperance was indeed the only issue mentioned in two Free Church journals.[101] The NCEFC's election statement also included support for the League of Nations and calls for adequate provision for ex-servicemen and their dependants, the prevention of unemployment during demobilization and afterwards, the establishment of partnerships between employers and employees, and the promotion of public morality, health, housing and education. There was a similar range of concerns, with a more socialistic emphasis, in the statement issued by the Wesleyan Union of Social Service.[102]

By 1922 the rise of the League of Nations as a good cause was marked by the fact that the Primitive Methodist general committee mentioned it in their letter on the election alongside the temperance programme that had been all-sufficient in 1918.[103] It was the first item on the NCEFC's manifesto.[104] It was not, however, greatly emphasized in that of the Wesleyan Union of Social Service. Instead, drawing from some of the more socialistic passages of scripture, they contended 'That the natural resources of the earth, such as land, minerals, etc., should be held as the gifts of God to the commonwealth.' They also stressed that this commonwealth must be based upon reciprocal responsibilities. Not only has the citizen an obligation to render service for the common good, but 'the nation has a corresponding obligation for the proper maintenance of its members, whether working or temporarily unemployed through no fault of their own; as also for their superannuation'.[105]

The problem of unemployment was receiving increasing attention by the 1923 election. The NCEFC pressed for industrial training, public assistance for industrial development and the full implementation of the 1918 Education Act as means of tackling this issue.[106] In February 1924, they dispatched a deputation to the Labour government to express concern about the demoralization of unemployed school-leavers, before urging increases in unemployment benefit at that autumn's election.[107] By 1929 their remedies for unemployment bore signs of the influence of the Liberal Yellow Book, as the NCEFC called for industrial training, relocation of industry close to redundant coalfields, public works, and those doomed dreams of the 1918 Education Act, continuation schools and the further raising of the school-leaving age to fifteen. In the wake of the 1926 General Strike, they called for industrial peace. They did not, however, neglect their traditional witness on temperance, which was for the

Baptist Times the main issue in the election. To these was added renewed concern about gambling prompted by the growth of gambling facilities in the 1920s.[108] These traditional concerns, however, were conspicuously absent from the joint Anglican/Free Church manifesto issued for the 1929 election.[109]

In the last two elections of the period there were no distinctive Free Church manifestoes. In 1931 the sense of national crisis precluded them. As noted in Chapter 1, in 1935 their place was taken by that of Lloyd George's CAPR, whose programme reflected the New Deal schemes he had tried to promote to the National government. Its solutions for unemployment featured – like Angus Watson's chairman's address to that year's Congregational Union autumn assembly – a mixture of nineteenth-century remedies, such as emigration to the colonies, land clearance and agricultural reform, with 1930s prescriptions like planning, public works and prosperity loans.[110]

Ministry, society and social order

The Free Church ministry was not necessarily very well equipped to address the problems of the interwar years. Ministers often came from sheltered backgrounds with little experience of secular work in the increasingly urban and industrial society they served.[111] Having generally been brought up in the church – and often in the manse – they spoke 'the language of Zion – a language the outsider did not understand'.[112] The college training, which by the end of the nineteenth century was becoming the normal route into the ministry, hardly made up the deficiency. Late nineteenth-century Methodist college principals were particularly distinguished by their lack of interest in or knowledge of public matters, while pastoral training was also neglected until the early twentieth century.[113] Men trained in this environment were ill-equipped to follow Christ's task of preaching the Gospel to the poor. They seemed to Keir Hardie, the founder of the ILP, to have learnt theology at the expense of Christianity.[114] Certainly, there was greater emphasis in their training on preaching and academic pursuits rather than pastoral work, a matter of increasing concern by the 1890s. One Baptist college did offer a course in economics.[115] Nevertheless, the Congregationalists' college in Nottingham, by the 1920s, was still unique in having a chair of Christian Sociology.[116]

Keeble, whose pleas for similar facilities in Methodist colleges had been rejected in the 1890s, continued to emphasize that,

> All Christian ministers should be at least as well versed in economics, industrial harmony, sociology and social facts, theories and remedies as the average intelligent trade unionist, Labour leader, employer and federation secretary or party politician.[117]

Nevertheless, a few years later Donald Soper left theological college almost totally ignorant of Marx, a deficiency which proved particularly embarrassing on his first attempt at open-air preaching.[118] Such deficiencies led the Congregationalist and future Labour MP, George Banton, in 1922 to suggest that a time of unemployment and suffering would be a better training for the ministry than a period at college.[119]

College training did at least become less regimented during the interwar years and there were signs of increasing appreciation that ministers needed to be aware of social conditions. Every newly ordained minister, F. W. Newland told the Congregational Union assembly in 1926, should be sent to the poorest parts of the country, 'for at least the first two years of his full service'.[120] One reason for the criticism of the evangelist training provided by Samuel Chadwick's Cliff College in the period is that it gave no grounding in Methodist thinking on social questions.[121]

Another sign of this increased concern about social conditions was the contrast between the largest Free Church benefaction of the nineteenth century, the Hibbert Trust, established essentially for theological purposes, and the 1924 founding of the Halley Stewart Trust, 'for Research towards the Christian Ideal in all Social Life'.[122] Two years later, the Wesleyans established the Beckly Social Service lectureship.[123] The most important of these developments was however the interdenominational conference on a Christian Order in Politics, Economics and Citizenship (COPEC) convened at Birmingham in 1924.

This ecumenical demonstration of the churches' concern for the social order was greeted with enthusiasm. Writing in the local ILP weekly, the *Bradford Pioneer*, Edward Siddle proclaimed, 'The Labour Movement has not been in vain.' He saw COPEC as the result of Labour's success, 'in focusing attention to the fact of the immoral nature of capitalism and the social implication of Christianity which were being largely forgotten by the churches'.[124] Such neglect was certainly admitted in the COPEC Basis. Much of the enthusiasm it generated seems to have been the result of this recognition. The plaudits won from Siddle or Keeble were for the mere fact that it occurred. At COPEC the churches were seen to be addressing a whole series of issues: from 1922, twelve commissions worked on preparing reports on topics such as education, the home, the relation of the sexes, leisure, crime, Christianity and war, and industry and property.[125] The originality of its conclusions was however less apparent. In some instances the very conclusion itself seemed unclear.[126] The Quaker Socialist, J. Theodore Harris, saw COPEC as a series of timid reports representing an advance in witness, but not in Christian social thought. He commented: 'The lack of clear thinking … seems to be due to the fact that the writers or groups of writers have had no clear or settled convictions by which to guide their thinking', a criticism local Labour parties were apt to share.[127] There was certainly a lack of intellectual cohesion at some of the regional conferences that followed. The Liverpool Conference in January 1925 seems to have become a forum for the promotion of pet ideas and projects.[128] In this it reflected one of the characteristics of COPEC and the Christian Social Council that succeeded it. These were meetings not of minds but of concerned individuals, serving more for the interchange than the development of ideas.

The development of ideas was not always the end in view. In the 1920s, the NCEFC habitually invited a businessman and a Labour MP to address its assembly, seeing its role more as the reconciler of the two positions. Nightingale considered, 'What we want to do is to get both Labour and Capital to see that each are necessary to the other. They must learn to live together.'[129] Many Free Churchmen were inclined to see industrial problems not in terms of how the means of production were organized, but as contests between capital and labour. Few questioned the validity of the view expressed by the Congregationalist-associated soap manufacturer, Lord Leverhulme, that capitalist wealth creation, far from being the cause of poverty, was the means to relieve it, or his vision of the future benefits it would bring.[130] The economic changes of the period were seen as necessitating not Socialism, but a new modus vivendi between employers and employees. There was accordingly considerable hostility among Free Church leaders towards what was seen as a class-based Labour Party. The Socialism it professed was opposed as a bureaucratic and demoralizing threat to freedom.[131] Free Church prejudices against both Socialism and nationalization were confirmed by the experience of wartime government controls, which were felt to have distorted markets and undermined profitability.[132]

Not all, however, agreed. Far from seeing private enterprise as a necessary form of wealth creation, E. B. Storr saw it as 'a euphemism for social exploitation'. He argued that Socialism would increase, not curtail liberty.[133] It would apply resources in order to eradicate social problems and to secure the fullest life for all: 'Socialism claims to be a way of organising economic forces – of harnessing them to human needs – so that the whole community shall use its energies to the best advantage, and shall pick the full fruitage of its work.'[134]

It was thus a means to achieve the Free Church ideal of the full and free development of human personality. As the Wesleyan minister Atkinson Lee put it:

> Through corporate ownership of the ultimate natural sources of wealth, through social ownership of accumulated capital, and by individual ownership of the lesser instruments of Labour, we may effect a distribution of property more calculated than the present to promote personality in the individual and justice in the whole of society.[135]

Not all Free Church bodies saw themselves merely as agents of reconciliation between capital and labour. Quakers were particularly assiduous in attempts to analyse the requirements of a Christian social order. Their WSOC and its successors produced a series of minutes and programmes on this subject. Having found in 1918 that 'Fellowship is the very essence of our Christian profession, and its practical expression in Industry involves the fullest measure of democratic control', the committee expressed its sympathies with Guild Socialism.[136]

This concept of worker control of production as a means of equitably distributing employment and resources had been developed in the Edwardian period. During the economic dislocation at the end of the war it had a wide appeal as a non-statist way to Socialism involving direct, economic democracy, rather than the parliamentary or municipal varieties.[137] Accordingly, Malcolm Sparkes, the Quaker prime mover behind the London Building Guild, one of the few practical efforts to realize this idea, saw it as the 'democratic control of a public service'.[138] Such a mode of industrial organization seemed in keeping with Quaker Pacifism. J. E. Hodgkin enthused, 'Industry for service, developed throughout the world, will ultimately destroy the roots of war, and render armaments absolutely meaningless in the face of the rising spirit of human comradeship.'[139] As the short existence of the London Building Guild demonstrated, however, it was not easy to maintain.

The WSOC was not the only denominational body that sought to explore how to apply a Christian social order in the interwar years. The *Bradford Pioneer* quoted with approval from the 1921 Basis of the Congregational Social Service Committee calls for equality of opportunity for the working classes to enjoy the fruits of their labour: 'for workers of all kinds remuneration adequate to provide the primary necessities and comforts of life; and for a cordial cooperation of brain and hand in the service of the community'.[140] No other Free Church body however came out with a statement which either in length or authority matched the Methodist conference's 1934 *Declaration concerning a Christian View of Industry in relation to the Social Order*.

This saw a Christian order in society rooted in the principles that humanity is one family in God, that each is of infinite worth in the sight of God's love and that men's actions should therefore be governed by the redeeming purpose of God. A Christian view of industry therefore stressed service for the common good. The spiritual consequences – in hopeless unemployment, in the placing of competition over conscience, and of material possessions over spiritual values – of a system in which there was poverty in the midst of plenty underlined the need for a Christian social order, which would abolish poverty, produce and distribute the fruits of industry according to ability and need, enforce the idea of moral obligations (especially in the matter of public health and slums) and foster the spirit of vocation.[141]

There was not, however, anything distinctively Socialist about any of these Free Church declarations. Those Quakers who felt that the Society of Friends should definitely repudiate Capitalism and give general support to the Labour Party and the principle of nationalization achieved little more than various Socialist-tinged epistles.[142] The Methodist declaration went no further.[143] Nor was it likely to, having to be balanced politically, even to the extent of being proposed by Henry Carter and seconded by Luke Thompson, the Tory MP for Sunderland.[144] It called for greater workers' responsibility in the direction of industry through works councils and conciliation machinery. It did not, however, resolve the problem of the ownership of the means of production, merely stating that if its transfer into public hands was shown to further substantiate the stated goals, 'then a convincing claim would thereby be made on the Christian mind'.[145]

The Nonconformist response to new economic challenges: Unemployment

Unemployment presented a particular challenge to the conscience of Nonconformists in this period. In 1923 the NCEFC urged 'Churches to throw open Halls and Schoolrooms for shelter and by music and in other ways to brighten this time of monotonous anxiety'.[146] Faced with widespread distress in the coalfields after the 1926 lockout, and then with the long-term unemployment which struck whole communities and industries in the 1930s, the Free Churches moved beyond such palliative measures. Most denominations set up distress relief funds, initially to provide for their co-religionists. These were supplemented by the Lord Mayor's Fund launched in 1927 by the then Lord Mayor of London, the Anglican Conservative MP, Sir Rowland Blades. Although this fund had reached £1.5 million by the time the Treasury offered an additional £600,000 in March 1929, it was still inadequate to tackle the poverty and malnutrition suffered in the coalfields, as the Primitive Methodist Labour MP Joseph Batey repeatedly pointed out in Parliament.[147] It nevertheless underwrote much of the palliative activities being provided and supported the efforts of bodies such as the Friends Allotments Committee to aid the 'development of the injured personality of the unemployed man'.[148]

In most cases this involved Nonconformity in establishing those social, educational and occupation centres for the unemployed vilified by the Communist-dominated National Unemployed Workers Movement (NUWM) as the 'dirty scab dope of organised Christianity to prevent the workers from organising to demand their rights'.[149] Yet there was little else churches could do to tackle the demoralizing effects of the dole and long-term unemployment except through the vocational training and recreational facilities provided by occupational centres. The congregation that could afford to spend £30,000 on plant to set up new industry for the unemployed was rare indeed, as was the shirt-making facility established by an interdenominational group in Wealdstone.[150] The Friends Allotments Committee admitted that though

> [O]ur experiences should furnish material towards finding the solution of what is a fundamental question for a religious society, namely the way in which the spirit and moral nature of man can best be developed ... We can only function in limited ways and in making small experiments.[151]

Their efforts in South Wales had been prompted by Emma Noble, a Quaker and a Labour councillor from Swindon moved by the suffering of the region in 1926. She and her husband William in April 1927 became the first wardens of the new Quaker adult education settlement at Maes-yr-haf in the Rhondda, the first of nine such institutions. By 1929 Maes-yr-haf had added the provision of both allotments and district nursing.[152]

Such endeavours attracted young middle-class Quaker Socialists from England, such as Margaret Pitt. Their arrival could, she recalled, prompt some hostility, not least from the local Labour Party and Miners' Federation of Great Britain (MFGB) branches, especially because of their attempts to encourage voluntary labour.[153] Nevertheless, by 1932 they had added minor relocation schemes and mild forms of public works provision, such as a new swimming pool in Brynmawr. Industrial retraining centres with an arts and crafts bias had appeared in South Wales, their main centre of operations. Small cooperative ventures, in boot- and furniture-making and metalwork were started, providing an outlet for creative craftsmanship, and some 100,000 allotments were in use.[154] They had few illusions that allotments – reminiscent of nineteenth-century schemes to solve unemployment by land colonization – were really a solution. These schemes were instead seen as practical ways of ministering to man's spirit, in the hope that their work might stimulate the 'more fundamental efforts' required 'if unemployment is ever to be a memory of the past instead of a bitter experience of the present'.[155] In autumn 1930, an impressed Labour government began to support the Quaker schemes which, because of general distress, could no longer be confined to the coalfields.[156] Given that unemployment stood at over two million for much of the 1930s, their effects were strictly limited. Nevertheless, with a degree of government funding, at their peak over 120,000 men were being assisted by Quaker programmes.[157]

Housing

Nonconformist concern about housing conditions was already well established by 1914, having been one of the principal themes of *The Bitter Cry*. The Congregational minister, C. Fleming Williams, was prominently involved in the campaign by the London County Council (LCC) against slum housing and the disease, squalor and immorality that it bred.[158] By 1918 the 'homes for heroes' wartime propaganda had greatly increased appreciation of the need for housing reform. The parlous condition of much accommodation was illustrated by the poor physical state of many conscripts. The industrial disputes that followed also drew attention to the insanitary conditions in which many industrial workers lived. The government, Tiplady commented, should seek to solve mining disputes by sending garden city builders, not soldiers, to the colliery districts.[159] Overcrowding into inadequate dwellings, though declining, was still considerable. Lloyd George's land enquiry in 1914 had calculated that some 120,000 additional cottages were required in rural areas alone. With production subsequently diverted by the war, by 1918 Labour estimated that an additional million homes were needed.[160]

To Rhondda Williams this shortage demanded government intervention. In 1920 he complained:

> The very lack of houses is an indictment of the private profit system. The criterion on which the nation operates is not does the nation want houses; but will it pay certain individuals to build houses? And because private individuals who ordinarily build houses do not see how they can make a profit, the nation goes without homes.[161]

Permissive legislation such as the 1890 Housing of the Working Classes Act did not offer a solution. George Haw – who six years later edited a book on religion and the Labour movement – used a series of articles in the Liberal-supporting *Daily News* in 1900 to draw attention to the poor quality of much housing in both urban and rural areas.[162] With building material costs subsequently soaring as a result of wartime inflation, encouraging profiteering in the building trade, the houses to replace them were not being built. The solution, argued the Labour MP George Hicks, was subsidized construction.[163]

A series of housing acts from 1919 to 1924 provided subsidies which facilitated significant building by local authorities. To F. W. Newland, warden of the Congregationalists' Claremont Settlement in Pentonville, progress in slum clearance was, however, too slow.[164] W. T. Spivey urged the Primitive Methodist conference in

1929 'To press the claim for the erection of houses of reasonable size ... which may be let at a reasonable rental to the families now living under conditions unworthy of Christian civilization'. Slum clearance would thus eradicate the conditions in which 'Bad health, vice, physical and moral deterioration' all flourished.[165] This also meant decent building standards, as specified in the report produced by the committee chaired by the Congregational Liberal MP J. Tudor Walters in 1918.[166] These minimum housing standards stressed not only the importance of an adequate water supply and sanitary and bathing facilities, but also of separate bedrooms for the parents and for the children of either sex.[167]

Some local church groups attempted to apply such principles in rehousing, slum clearance and beautifying schemes. COPEC sponsored a housing trust which did much work of this kind in Birmingham, one of a number of such local schemes.[168] In the 1930s, an equally ecumenical church group was responsible for transforming a St Pancras slum into a tiny garden city.[169] These were small-scale versions of the model factory villages built by Nonconformist philanthropists ranging from Leverhulme to the Primitive Methodist jam manufacturer, Sir William Hartley in the preceding century.[170] In 1898, Ebenezer Howard, who attended C. Fleming Williams's congregation, suggested replacing this paternalism with planning in his *Garden Cities of Tomorrow*.[171] Like the farm colonies developed in the 1890s by the founder of the Salvation Army, William Booth, these were small scale, intended to reconnect an increasingly urbanized population with the countryside. Nonconformists, especially Quakers, were heavily involved in the garden cities subsequently founded at Letchworth (1904) and Welwyn (1920).[172]

Among Howard's interwar disciples was Alfred Salter, a Quaker and the local doctor as well as the Labour MP for Bermondsey. Salter had been a medical social worker at Scott Lidgett's Bermondsey settlement. He also had suffered from the tuberculosis prevalent in this area of South London at the turn of the century. Slum clearance under his guidance focused on the replacement of slums with individual cottages (usually vernacular-style), space, light and gardens.[173] As a result of the efforts of Salter and his wife Ada, Bermondsey had by 1933 done 'more slum-clearance than the whole of the rest of London put together'.[174]

Despite the construction of nearly two million houses, slum clearance efforts in the country as a whole were, however, something of a failure. The rental on the houses built under the 1919–24 housing acts proved prohibitive to all but 'the aristocracy of the working classes'.[175] Extensive slum clearance only came when the National government in 1933 dropped these subsidies in favour of that provided under Labour's 1930 Housing Act, promoted by the Baptist Minister of Health, Arthur Greenwood. This linked subsidies both to clearance of insanitary districts and to the numbers rehoused, taking advantage of the fall in building costs in the 1930s. J. H. Shakespeare's son Geoffrey – junior minister at the Ministry of Health under the National government – later helped to promote Slum Clearance Sundays as part of a carefully orchestrated public opinion campaign accompanying this programme.[176]

Rents were still often high, causing hardship in some areas.[177] However, by 1939 the Quaker social investigator and chocolate manufacturer, Seebohm Rowntree, was able to point out that there had been a dramatic improvement in the condition of working-class housing in York since his 1901 survey.[178] Industrial conflict proved a much more challenging problem for interwar Free Churchmen.

Industrial disputes

The 1926 General Strike in particular seemed to seal the fate of the Nonconformist Conscience. Afterwards, the secretary of the Congregational Union, S. M. Berry, lamented: 'What part have we to play in the controversies and struggles which have shifted from the political on to the economic plane?'[179] This problem was exacerbated by the distaste with which Free Churchmen habitually viewed industrial conflict. G. Herbert East welcomed the 1927 Wesleyan conference to Bradford with the proud boast: 'There has been no serious and prolonged trade dispute in the City for many years. It is no idle boast that Methodism has played a decisive part in the production of this wiser mind.'[180] Peace-loving Quakers, steeped in their own consensual and highly democratic methods of settling disputes, shared this distaste. William Noble, for instance, before his move to Maes-yr-haf, played his part as a trade union leader in Oxford in preventing violence during the General Strike.[181] Nonconformist unwillingness to countenance industrial disputes was compounded by the way in which these conflicts reduced organizations like chapels, spanning social divisions, to impotent onlookers suffering collaterally from their effects. The revolutionary overtones which industrial unrest acquired around the end of the war only magnified this attitude.[182] Sympathy with the plight of strikers therefore did not necessarily extend to their motives.[183] Arthur Henderson's view was that the industrial unrest of 1919 was 'a moral struggle to attain to the complete development and fullness of human life which is the right of all but the actual attainment of few'.[184] In contrast, the *Christian World* responded to the coal dispute of that year by observing that in 'a fight between the miners and the State … the State must win'.[185] For Garvie, reacting to the 1921coal strike, it was 'that an industry on which the welfare of the whole nation depends should be so organised that the conflicts of capital and labour shall not be suffered to inflict untold injury on the whole community'.[186]

The idea of a need for conciliation between capital and labour proved particularly important in the industrial convulsions of 1926. Without it there seemed little room for distinctive Christian witness. This was not just because several leading coal owners and thousands of miners were Free Churchmen, but also because denominations were neither sufficiently expert to pontificate on the situation, nor in a position, by intervening, to transform it. In the face of these problems the only answer that some Free Church bodies could give to Berry's question was that they had nothing to offer. The Merseyside Free Church Federation for instance declared that 'it was not easy to determine upon a course of action, for the Free Churches are representative of all classes of the community, and while feeling was strong it could not justify the Federation in pronouncing upon the merits of this dispute'.[187] Not all, however, were content to take this attitude. What was needed was a role they could play in this confrontation. In declaring 'God has committed to us the word of reconciliation' (2 Corinthians 5.19),

Henry Carter was not just quoting scripture; he was proclaiming the nature of that role.[188]

The difficulties in exercising this witness were compounded by the deep-rooted nature of the conflict. In July 1926, the *Christian World* recognized that 'the present crisis is, in fact, only the final phase of a concealed crisis that has been retarded by the artificial and short-lived boom of 1919–20 and the equally artificial stimulant of the Ruhr occupation' by France and Belgium in 1923–24.[189] Even before the Dawes plan brought the occupation to an end, the coal industry's problems were made clear in a series of articles in the *British Weekly*. On the one hand, in many coalfields, miners' real wages were 50 per cent below 1914 levels. A Durham minister told of undernourished and indebted mining communities.[190] On the other hand, the colliery companies were far from financially buoyant. The loss of foreign demand was compounded by falling net output and output per person between 1913 and 1923 when unit costs all but doubled.[191] Accordingly, cash-strapped firms could only afford to improve miners' conditions, argued the Baptist coal owner and Liberal MP Sir Beddoe Rees by further increasing their labour costs, with the resulting increase in the selling price of coal hitting not only their own industry but also the profitability and export potential of other coal-dependent British industries.[192]

This situation was exacerbated by Winston Churchill's decision as Chancellor of the Exchequer in April 1925 to return to the gold standard. Although the *Christian World* initially agreed with Churchill that this move 'may do much to facilitate international trade', by July 1925 its editorial was claiming that:

> there is a growing consensus of opinion that the Government has made a capital blunder by their premature and precipitate (as Mr Lloyd George has called it) restoration of the Gold Standard before our credit was ripe for the step, making sterling dearer and forcing up the price of British coal.

Unemployment in the coal industry had already surged to 300,000, and two-thirds of the rest were on short-time employment.[193] Meanwhile, about a third of the pits were closed and 75 per cent were unprofitable.[194] The WSOC urged nationalization.[195] Instead, in June 1925, faced with falling exports and prices and widespread losses, the owners responded by posting wage cuts – to come into force at the end of July – for miners who were already, according to the *Christian World*, 'working for wages that would be despised by a Poplar scavenger'. Despite disliking government interference and subsidies, the newspaper therefore felt both were justified in these exceptional circumstances.[196] The prime minister, Stanley Baldwin, eventually came to the same conclusions, offering for nine months a subsidy eventually worth £23 million.[197] Meanwhile, the latest in a series of government inquiries into the industry was set up under the former Liberal cabinet minister Sir Herbert Samuel to advise on its future. This appeared on 10 March 1926, recommending reorganization short of nationalization, an end to the subsidy and – in light in the fall of living costs since the present wage agreement of 1924 – a temporary reduction in wages. Without such a reduction in costs, Quaker coal owners lamented, 'What is the Christian employer who does not want to go bankrupt to do?'[198] The MFGB, however, were implacably opposed to conceding either reduced wages or increased hours. The need instead for negotiation was urged by the *Baptist Times* in the aftermath of the Samuel Report both on the erstwhile Baptist lay preacher and MFGB secretary A. J. Cook and the coal owners.[199] However, when the government subsidy ran out at the end of April 1926, the vast majority of miners were locked out until they accepted substantial wage reductions which had merely been postponed.

In an attempt to negotiate a short-term continuation of the coal subsidy while a compromise was sought, the General Council of the Trades Union Congress (TUC) took up negotiations with the government and, when these broke down on 2 May, found itself managing a general strike. This was, as one correspondent in *The Inquirer* put it, an attempt to support the miners by withholding the only thing the working class control, their labour.[200] Accordingly, rather than a general strike reflecting revolutionary theory, the waves of workers called out by the TUC from one minute to midnight on 3 May were instead engaged in a national sympathetic action. Despite his Quakerly reservations Alfred Salter accordingly hailed it as 'The most Christlike action on a grand scale since Calvary'.[201] The Congregationally formed Yorkshire trade unionist, Ben Turner, similarly praised the Christian self-sacrifice of the strikers.[202]

However, the consensus of opinion in the correspondence columns of *The Friend* was that it was not a splendid example of passive resistance, as pioneered by Nonconformist protesters against the 1902 Education Act, but an unacceptable form of coercion. The *Methodist Times* similarly attacked undemocratic and dictatorial trade union tactics, instead praising Baldwin and those who attempted to run voluntary services during the nine days of the conflict.[203] This did not mean that the Free Churches helped to run these voluntary services. Despite being approached, the NCEFC did not, as the BBC claimed, place its organization at the government's disposal.[204]

In fact, the annual crop of church assemblies meeting in May at the time of the General Strike proved a good time for radical spirits to carry or reaffirm resolutions in favour of the concept of the living wage as the first charge on industry. Some conferences called for the maintenance of miners' living standards.[205] They were, however, less prepared to stipulate what sort of industrial organization would ensure this or lead in seeking resolution. It was the archbishop of Canterbury, Randall Davidson, who expended most efforts on conciliation. He was clandestinely encouraged in this by various leaders of the Labour Party, as well as Henry Carter and Scott Lidgett.[206] The archbishop's efforts culminated on 8 May when, with ecumenical support, he appealed for the resumption of negotiations on the basis of the cancellation of the strike, further short-term subsidies and withdrawal of the wage reductions. For Horton, this represented positive Christian cooperation.[207] The Tory Minister of Mines G. R. Lane-Fox however told Davidson that the appeal could only be harmful in raising unrealistic expectations of renewed subsidies.[208]

The appeal had no effect. Instead it was the TUC which called the end of the General Strike on 12 May. Alarmed at the prospects of a lengthy war of attrition they seized the prospect of resumed negotiation as a way of extricating themselves from the unpleasant predicament of responsibility for managing the dispute without authority to resolve it from an uncooperative MFGB.[209]

The miners' lockout nevertheless continued, accompanied by Christian efforts at conciliation. Quakers had responded to the General Strike in which, 'Each side claimed to be fighting for a moral end, the one for solidarity, law and order, the other for justice for the oppressed,' with the view that, 'the glaring signal of two such claims, each with its truth, should always be a signal to seek for some larger unity big enough to contain both'.[210] The only larger unity readily available to the eleven Free Church leaders and nine Anglicans who constituted themselves as the Standing Conference of the Christian Churches on the Coal Dispute (SCCCCD) was the Samuel Report. Its recommendations had, however, largely been rejected by both sides in the dispute. On 28 June 1926 the SCCCCD nevertheless began negotiations with the MFGB on the basis of a memorandum recommending a return to the pre-lockout conditions for four months covered by government assistance and the implementation of the reorganization recommended by the Samuel Report as soon as possible, with a joint board under an independent chairman to arbitrate at the end of the stipulated period.[211] These suggestions, however, offered the coal owners nothing. In August, the miners also rejected them in a ballot.[212] Even Baldwin eventually became exasperated, telling an interdenominational delegation that their efforts were as impertinent as the government attempting to negotiate a reunion between the Strict Baptists and the Anglo-Catholics.[213] In contrast with the way individual Nonconformists like Fleming Williams had intervened successfully in late nineteenth-century industrial disputes,[214] the attempts by the churches to do so in 1926 ended in inglorious rejection.

The principal significance of their intervention probably lies in the support that was generated in the denominational press. Though some Free Churchmen wrote critical letters to *The Times*, the point that this was a legitimate sphere of Christian concern was conceded by the much more enthusiastic line that prevailed in most Nonconformist journals. The atmosphere of 1926 worked in favour of those who held that the Free Churches must respond conscientiously to economic matters as well as to more traditional concerns like temperance, education or Sabbatarianism. Quite how, nevertheless, remained the problem. For instance, during the renewed coal disputes of 1936, the Methodist conference responded to a resolution calling for the nationalization of coal mining merely with a pledge of further investigation by the Social Welfare Department.[215] Such matters did not readily resolve themselves into the simple moral equations that had fuelled the nineteenth-century Nonconformist Conscience.

Traditional Nonconformist concerns: Temperance

The *Methodist Times* later congratulated itself that its Clean Film Campaign of 1931 was not only a success but was 'in complete accord with the Hugh Price Hughes tradition and demonstrated the fact that while the paper had passed through many and serious vicissitudes it had retained the full aggressive spirit of the founder'.[216] Questions of private morality remained those most emphasized by the Free Churches. Thus, in 1936, Scott Lidgett defined social questions largely as 'Sunday Cinemas, Temperance and the

Betting Pools', though he added the League of Nations and education in 1937.[217] These, together with disestablishment and immorality, may be taken as the archetypal fields of Free Church social and political concern. Socialist Free Churchmen were by no means unaffected by these traditional concerns. H. Bodell Smith and Henry Carter were both very active in the temperance organizations of their respective denominations. The Socialist and Congregational minister William Dick listed his four main foes in the impoverished East London borough of Poplar as strong drink, gambling, impurity and poverty.[218]

Of these traditional concerns the dominant one during the interwar years continued to be the cause of temperance. In the eighteenth century there had been much concern about the drinking of spirits, notably gin. The drunkenness unleashed by the 1830 Beerhouse Act demonstrated that beer, as well as spirits, could have an evil effect. At the time, a number of temperance societies were being formed around Britain. It was the 1830 Act, however, which two years later prompted the seven men of Preston, three of them Primitive Methodists, to set up the country's first total abstinence society.[219] From the mid-nineteenth century, teetotalism gained ground in all denominations, as well as ardent advocates like Price Hughes. By 1914, the ministry was predominantly teetotal in some denominations.[220]

Grounds for temperance included social, moral, economic and medical reasons. In 1931 the Friends Temperance Union (FTU) claimed that recent medical research had completely justified the total abstinence position.[221] 'As alcohol harms the body which is the instrument of personality and the dwelling place of the spirit of God immanent in man', a Congregational minister argued in the late 1930s, 'I regard drinking as … an act of irresponsibility unworthy of a man who seeks the highest moral life.'[222] Drink affected responsibility, critical faculties, and self-control. This could lead to brawling, domestic strife or the overlaying of children by drunken parents living in overcrowded conditions.[223] Drink indeed came to be seen by many Nonconformists during the closing decades of the nineteenth century as a prime cause of a host of social evils with those who became addicted to it descending into impoverishment and the slums.[224]

Slum housing, abject poverty and ready access to alcohol (in the centre of Liverpool in 1930 there was still one on-licence for every fifty-seven street yards) certainly tended to encourage drinking, and not just in urban areas.[225] The agricultural trade unionist and Labour MP, George Edwards, despite his credentials as a Primitive Methodist lay preacher and ardent teetotaller, recognized that the exhausted agricultural worker often found more warmth and comfort at the alehouse than in his own home.[226] As the *Labour Leader* pointed out, however, once there he succumbed to an opiate of the people far more potent than Christianity.[227] The resulting damage was invariably greatest where there was greatest need. Salter in his 1925 survey of Bermondsey claimed that the average family spent more per week on beer than on rent, rate, bread and milk put together, though his figures might have been distorted by the transient population locally.[228] In so doing he reiterated Seebohm Rowntree's earlier findings about alcohol driving people on marginal incomes into penury.[229] Drink might temporarily anaesthetize the pain of poverty, but it also compounded it.

The brewers were therefore condemned as exploitative businessmen impoverishing the community. The Trade, as it was referred to by both its advocates and detractors, was indicted for its effect on physical and industrial efficiency, disease and mortality, crime and poverty, and for the resulting cost to the community of institutions like gaols, hospitals or workhouses.[230] George Edwards considered drink a causal factor in nine-tenths of the crime he encountered as a magistrate.[231] The prohibitionist umbrella body for temperance organizations founded in 1853, the UKA, furthermore used painstaking statistical research in order to demonstrate that the costs of the Trade were not merely social. Annually, they estimated national expenditure on drink (Table 3). Even in 1926, a year in which beer consumption was hit by poor weather and the General Strike, they calculated that 800,000 working-class dwellings could have instead been built with the proceeds.[232] The Royal Commission set up by the second Labour government in 1929 meanwhile agreed that drink impaired industrial efficiency.[233] They were not, however, prepared to contemplate the drastic solution of prohibition that various temperance campaigners had advocated, particularly during the Great War.

Table 3 Annual drink bill, brewer's profit and government duty, 1918–39

Year	Annual drink bill (£m)	Estimated per capita expenditure[a]	Brewers' profits (£m)	Beer duty (£m)	Total duty (£m)
1913	166.7	3/12/5	10.0	13.2	41.5
1918	259.3	5/13/0	30.2	19.1	32.9
1919	386.6	8/8/0	32.4	25.4	52.3
1920	469.7	10/0/0	29.0	71.3	133.8
1921	403.0	8/10/0	19.7	123.4	201.3
1922	354.0	7/9/0	22.2	121.9	192.0
1923	307.5	7/2/0	23.2	100.0	161.0
1924	316.0	7/5/0	25.0	81.7	143.4
1925	315.0	7/4/0	26.5	82.0	141.5
1926	301.3	6/17/0	24.5	82.4	140.6
1927	298.2	6/15/3	24.0	84.2	136.6
1928	288.8	6/9/10	24.5	83.3	139.6
1929	288.2	6/9/9	25.0	75.8	130.5
1930	277.5	6/4/0	26.0	77.2	129.4
1931	259.8	5/15/0	23.0	75.7	125.2
1932	232.5	5/3/0	16.0	75.2	118.8
1933	224.8	4/19/4	18.0	73.7	166.8
1934	229.0	5/1/0	23.0	58.9	101.1
1935	237.7	5/1/0	26.0	58.7	100.2
1936	246.3	5/7/6	28.5	60.8	105.1
1937	259.4	5/12/9	31.5	62.7	109.1
1938	285.0	-	31.5	65.7	111.9
1939	310.0	-	34.0	65.6	111.4

Note: United Kingdom figures.

[a] Reliable population figures for 1938–39 were not available because of the war.

Source: *AYB* (1913–40).

The United States had introduced prohibition in 1917, prompting Leverhulme three years later to warn of greater American efficiency, productivity and competitiveness.[234] Alcohol-related problems had indeed led the Shipbuilding Employers' Federation in 1915 to press for similar prohibition for the duration of the war. Prohibition was again discussed in 1917 as a means of conserving food supplies during a time of shortage. Lloyd George however considered it impractical. Instead he suggested nationalization of the Trade.[235] Scandinavian experience in the late nineteenth century had promoted the idea of State purchase as a means of producing what was termed 'disinterested management', who had no interest in promoting consumption because their remuneration was not related to sales. Such schemes appealed both to various Nonconformists and to Labour figures like Snowden.[236] The UKA however considered State involvement in the iniquities of the Trade anathema. Such objections – and the government's concern about the cost of the scheme – led to its rejection in 1915.[237] Direct State ownership was only introduced on 4 January 1916 around the Royal Small Arms factory in Enfield and later extended to other areas like Carlisle and Gretna Green, where massive expansion of the munitions industry coincided with a similar growth of drunkenness and disorder.[238]

Indirect control meanwhile developed under the regulations of the Central Liquor Control Board (CLCB) set up by Lloyd George as minister of munitions in 1915. In addition to leading brewers, its members also included ardent teetotallers like Henry Carter and Snowden. Its regulations greatly reduced the strength of alcoholic drinks and cut licensing hours by two-thirds, while treating and buying drinks on credit were banned. Unlicensed clubs were placed under similar controls which, by 1916, extended over virtually the whole country. Licenses were suppressed and pubs replaced with billiard halls and industrial canteens. By 1920, annual average consumption had fallen from 214 to 80 pints of beer per person and the number of breweries halved to 3,000.[239]

The 1921 Licensing Act both wound up the CLCB and entrenched achievements such as restriction on hours of sale and abolition of grocers' licences. This was followed by the 1923 Intoxicating Liquor (Sale to Persons Under Eighteen) Act. In consequence, the nine-point manifesto of the TCCC in the 1918 election had, by 1923, been reduced to three. This ecumenical body had been set up during the war and was led for much of the interwar years by Henry Carter. After 1921, it made little headway with its remaining demands: local option to abolish or restrict licences, English Sunday closing, and the control of clubs. Nevertheless, the downward trends of consumption and drunkenness remained encouraging in the 1920s (Table 4). The spreading use of cars and thus the increasing menace of drunken driving added force to the temperance argument. This led F. W. Newland in 1932 to proclaim that total prohibition must eventually come everywhere.[240]

The centenary of the temperance movement proved however to be not the harbinger of further success, but a turning point. Tighter licensing controls and counter-attractions to the public house such as the cinema or the wireless undoubtedly reduced drinking. Drunks were no longer a common sight. The Mondays taken off work to recover from weekend sprees were a disappearing phenomenon. By the mid-1920s there were even signs that the reduced strength and menace of drink was leading to a drift away from total abstinence among Nonconformists.[241] The gradual decline in the

Table 4 Proceedings and convictions for drunkenness in England and Wales and alcohol consumption in the United Kingdom

	Drunkenness		Consumption[a]		
Year	**Proceedings**	**Convictions**	**Spirits**	**Wine**	**Beer**
1913	213,188	188,877	0.67	0.25	27.0
1918	32,703	29,075	0.33	0.25	10.0
1919	64,495	57,948	0.49	0.43	17.5
1920	103,632	95,763	0.47	0.32	20.8
1921	85,166	77,789	0.39	0.24	18.6
1922	84,257	76,347	0.36	0.27	15.9
1923	85,082	77,094	0.32	0.30	16.5
1924	87,511	79,082	0.31	0.34	17.6
1925	84,578	75,077	0.31	0.36	17.6
1926	75,787	67,126	0.28	0.37	16.9
1927	74,303	65,166	0.28	0.37	16.6
1928	64,331	55,642	0.27	0.30	16.2
1929	60,728	51,966	0.27	0.32	16.1
1930	61,455	53,080	0.24	0.30	15.7
1931	49,029	42,343	0.22	0.30	13.6
1932	35,407	30,146	0.20	0.27	11.0
1933	42,492	36,285	0.21	0.28	11.8
1934	46,293	39,748	0.19	0.30	12.7
1935	50,092	42,159	0.19	0.31	13.3
1936	52,988	44,525	0.21	0.33	13.5
1937	55,304	46,757	0.22	0.34	14.2
1938	55,688	46,603	0.21	0.32	14.2
1939	54,301	52,929	N/A	N/A	N/A

Note: [a] Figures are gallons per capita per annum.

Sources: *AYB* and *Alliance News*, 1913–40.

number of licensed premises (Table 5) meanwhile tempered long-standing demands for a local option.

There were six attempts by Labour MPs to pass local option legislation between 1922 and 1928. None of these, however, got beyond the first reading.[242] The Prohibitionist Bills put forward in 1923 and 1931 by the Wesleyan Scottish Prohibition MP for Dundee, Edwin Scrymgeour, meanwhile garnered only negligible support, even among teetotaller MPs. Instead, the idea of the improved public house as a place of hospitality as well as drinking, took increasing hold. These had begun to appear in the late nineteenth century. The claims in 1923 in the licensed victuallers' newspaper, the *Morning Advertiser*, that 'The notion that the public house is a place where the only refreshment to be obtained is alcoholic liquor is rapidly becoming a teetotal fiction' were certainly overstated.[243] The attractive inn as the best answer to the disreputable tavern was nevertheless an effective piece of propaganda for brewers' pressure groups like the True Temperance Association. This softening of the evils of the Trade contributed

Table 5 Licensed premises in England and Wales, 1918–1939

Year	On-Licences	Proportion	Off-Licences	Proportion
1913	88,739	24.04	23,632	6.40
1918	84,644	22.69	22,473	6.03
1919	84,038	23.29	22,288	6.19
1920	83,432	22.18	22,198	5.90
1921	82,739	21.84	22,155	5.85
1922	82,054	21.50	22,108	5.79
1923	81,480	21.22	22,097	5.75
1924	80,987	20.90	22,135	5.71
1925	80,420	20.68	22,131	5.69
1926	79,860	20.44	22,149	5.67
1927	79,330	20.19	22,174	5.64
1928	78,803	19.96	22,189	5.62
1929	78,307	19.77	22,171	5.60
1930	77,821	19.65	22,166	5.59
1931	77,335	19.36	22,125	5.54
1932	76,886	19.13	22,105	5.50
1933	76,418	18.94	22,055	5.47
1934	75,955	18.77	22,056	5.45
1935	75,528	18.58	22,102	5.44
1936	75,062	18.38	22,115	5.42
1937	74,681	18.29	22,094	5.41
1938	74,326	18.11	22,109	5.39
1939	73,920	17.94	22,052	5.35

Note: The proportion refers to per 10,000 of the estimated population.
Source: *AYB* (1913–40).

to increasing Nonconformist unwillingness to stress their temperance principles and thus to seem intolerant or puritanical. This explains why there was not a greater Free Church response to the campaign launched by the Brewers' Society in 1933 'to get the beer-drinking habit instilled into thousands, almost millions of young men who do not at present know the taste of beer'.[244]

Even in 1927, Salter was lamenting that it was increasingly difficult to get a temperance audience.[245] By 1939, he noted that the TCCC was underfunded and that the Free Churches were dropping the annual Temperance Sunday from their calendar.[246] Though the Quakers reaffirmed their commitment to temperance, the FTU complained of lack of support. Their Congregational equivalent faced similar difficulties.[247] Total abstinence was certainly becoming less characteristic among younger ministers.[248] Defensiveness in the face of this loss of concern showed in the strictures of the president of the UKA, the Baptist businessman Robert Wilson Black, against both church apathy and the improved public house.[249] Despite the mild upward trend in consumption from 1932 onwards, more because the low point of the depression had passed than because of the brewers' campaign, temperance reform was no longer considered urgent.

Gambling

The *Times*' obituary of S. W. Hughes argued that the Nonconformist Conscience was finding gambling a more intractable problem.[250] This was despite the tightening of the law by the Street Betting Act of 1906 passed by the Nonconformist-flavoured Parliament elected that year.[251] Though the national drink bill dwindled, there was an estimated three-fold expansion in net expenditure on gambling between 1920 and 1938.[252] Premium bonds were staved off in 1919.[253] Several other new ways of organizing mass gambling, aimed broadly at the working class, however spread rapidly. Greyhound racing, the Pools, the Irish sweepstake, the Totalisator, and in the 1930s, gambling machines arguably all made small-stake gambling easier. Illegal gambling was widespread.[254] Resulting problems, according to the Royal Commission of 1932–33, included the impoverishment of homes, deterioration of character, inducements to crime, the prevalence of fraudulent practices, the loss of industrial efficiency and public disorder.[255] This social cost was for the benefit of a trade which was subject to economic objections relating to its effects on employment or its absorption of national resources (gambling turnover was variously estimated at £300–500 million per annum), very similar to those used against the brewers. It was also subject to similar ethical objections.

'At no point is the spirit of love or service expressed in gambling', the Wesleyan E. Benson Perkins wrote in 1935.[256] Instead, it encouraged cupidity. Lotteries for gain, such as the Irish sweepstake, were therefore seen as self-contradictory, raising money for hospitals while appealing to sentiments that were anything but charitable.[257] They thrived on inculcating avarice and an unchristian belief in luck as opposed to Divine Providence.[258] Gambling, as the leading Presbyterian A. Herbert Gray pointed out, broke scriptural precept by seeking to gain the wherewithal to eat without doing any work for it. This criticism was, he argued, equally valid when applied to speculation in stocks and shares, 'even though certain respectable church-goers may indulge in the latter'.[259]

He was not alone in extending the argument in this way. Benson Perkins, the leading contemporary exponent of the Free Church position on gambling, proved equally prepared to condemn such speculation.[260] This concern was not however generally emphasized in Free Church resolutions on gambling. Their attack was rather on the gambling industry itself and the way it exploited the working classes. H. J. Taylor Lax won warm applause from the 1934 NCEFC assembly for his statement:

> I wonder when the working men and women of Britain will feel that not only are they to receive a reasonable means of subsistence, but that they are responsible for how they use it, and if they are going to squander it in building up the wealth of a few bookmakers and others, then they have no right to claim even a reasonable wage.

The enthusiasm such extreme views generated, significantly expressed just one day after the assembly had loudly called for the restoration of the 1931 Unemployment Benefit cuts, showed how much gambling continued to be seen as a cause of poverty.[261]

The Pools, argued R. J. Russell, Wesleyan, Liberal National MP, and a member of the NCEFC executive committee, were a particularly insidious way of encouraging people to gamble.[262] By the late 1930s, some ten million people were filling out their football coupons every week, spending some £40 million annually.[263] However, argued Russell, as they absorbed rather than created wealth, gambling on the Pools was clearly qualitatively, if not morally different from that indulged in on the stock exchange. Both Herbert Gray and Benson Perkins recognized that capital investment was necessary and beneficial, even if sometimes the motives were avaricious. There was therefore less emphasis on the evils of speculation. Resolutions enjoining the churches to avoid the taint of raffles and whist drives were frequently passed while resolutions condemning gambling in stocks and shares were less common. The Christian Social Council's committee on gambling was certainly concerned about stock market speculation.[264] Free Church attention was however more generally focussed on the evils of the dog-track or the Pools.

Nevertheless, the 1934 Betting and Lotteries Act, which they generally welcomed, was more a measure of regulation than abolition. It certainly did not entail the abolition of bookmaking, the racecourse Totalisator or the publication of betting news, as desired by the NCEFC.[265] Furthermore, the Pools were specifically excluded from its provisions, while Russell's 1936 private bill to rectify this and suppress the Pools was heavily defeated. Nonconformist attempts to protect the weaker brethren who succumbed to the gambling problem met with little success.

Sabbatarianism

The Free Churches were not conspicuously more successful in their attempts to defend Sunday from secular encroachment. For them, traditionally, it was a day set apart in commemoration of the resurrection of Christ, for the enjoyment of rest, and the worship of God in fellowship. A reverent attitude to Sunday was thus a way of life as well as an expression of faith. There was, therefore, more to the Free Church opposition to the incursions on the peace of the Sabbath of cinema, games or music in the parks, the secularizing components of the so-called 'Continental Sunday', than the view that 'it would be fatal to our Sunday school work if cinemas were allowed to open on Sunday afternoons'.[266] Quite apart from the dangers inherent in undermining this source of moral backbone with Hollywood fripperies – notwithstanding Charlie Chaplin's early if somewhat unhappy days at Christ Church, Westminster Bridge Road,[267] Benson Perkins felt his popularity was a particularly damning indictment of modern civilization – the secularization of the Lord's Day struck a blow at chapel culture and, in Wales, at national culture as well.[268] The mostly Nonconformist Liberal and Labour Welsh MPs therefore diligently endeavoured to exclude Wales and Monmouthshire from the provisions of the 1932 Sunday Entertainments Bill. 'It is not that we think going to church or chapel is indispensable to salvation', argued R. T. Evans, a Congregationalist and Liberal MP for Carmarthen, 'but somehow or other the observance of the Sunday . . . embodies the national conscience.'[269]

This conscience and the culture it gave rise to were, however, endangered by the proliferating leisure-related activities of the twentieth century. In the 1930s, the views they gave rise to even invaded the columns of the *Christian World*. The resulting denigration of the Victorian Sabbath by its youth correspondent 'Ariel' did not go unanswered.[270] The superintendent of Poplar's Methodist Mission W. H. Lax meanwhile recalled the four-service Sunday of his childhood as

> [A] gloriously happy day. When I compare those Sundays with the Sundays of today, spent in open disregard of divine sanctions and in frantic seeking after pleasure, without finding it; in futile pretence of happiness, I declare that for thrills and for satisfaction the old days far surpassed the present.[271]

His words evoked a stern, high-principled world before radio and motor car. With the arrival of Sunday activities such as Labour Party meetings or charabanc rides this world was under threat.

Free Church condemnation of these threats was an attempt to defend a culture centred upon Sunday observance. This was particularly true of the physical hostility displayed against Sunday golfers at Aberdyfi in 1927.[272] It was also reflected in reactions to Labour's Sunday political meetings. Devout Labour activists like George Edwards saw speaking at such meetings as expressions of their faith. Henry Carter, Labour supporter that he was, nevertheless continued to condemn these. Howard Williams's father, a Baptist minister in Mountain Ash, crossed a very real cultural divide in taking his son after the evening service to hear Nye Bevan address political meetings at the local working men's' club.[273]

In 1922, the Free Church advocate of Sunday games could be so savaged by his brother ministers that he was left feeling 'like a man who has been found doing something naughty'.[274] There was a major campaign in the same year against the decision of the Conservative-run LCC to permit Sunday games in the parks. Such campaigns, however, could suggest questionable priorities. The future Labour MP and Quaker George Gillett found 'nothing had disgusted him more on the London County Council than to find that whilst they were inundated with letters from religious organisations on the subject of Sunday games, not one was received from them on the subject of housing or unemployment'.[275] Quakers who held 'no Sabbath more holy than other days', were less prone to Sabbatarianism than Baptists, whose assembly in 1923 unanimously condemned the LCC's actions.[276] In contrast, the *Congregational Quarterly* hosted a debate about Sunday games following this unsuccessful campaign. In this, Frank Hall warned of the danger of appearing killjoys through stubborn opposition to what will come anyway because 'it is what the people want'. In summing up, Halley Stewart pointed out that they could not seek to impose their will upon the majority. Local councils were not there to coerce Sunday observance by denial of alternatives.[277]

In the early 1930s, some leading Free Churchmen adopted a similar attitude to the question of Sunday cinema. It was at least possible to argue that Sunday cinema reduced drunkenness and brought some pleasure into the drab lives of the slum dwellers and the unemployed. The Methodist evangelist Harold Murray also argued that Sunday cinema was at least better than the 'disgraceful monkey parades' of young men and women in urban high streets that was a feature of interwar courtship.[278] For these reasons, by the time of the 1932 Sunday Entertainments Act, Henry Carter and others had come to accept it.[279] Two years later, a quarter of the cinemas in England were open on Sundays.[280] Increasingly, such considerations tempered the Sabbatarian resolutions that Nonconformist assemblies continued to debate throughout the interwar years.

Peace and Pacifism

A number of Nonconformist ministers had been prominent members of the Christian Pacifist organization the Fellowship of Reconciliation founded in Cambridge in December 1914. Although some significant Nonconformist laymen like Henderson and Ammon were active in the Union of Democratic Control (UDC) founded in the same year, their ministerial brethren were much less evident. By the end of the war, however, the UDC prescriptions for ending secret diplomacy and promoting international understanding to prevent future wars were widely influential. Indeed, the Primitive Methodist and Labour MP Ben Spoor unsuccessfully nominated the UDC for the Nobel Peace Prize in 1920.[281] The inclusion of such ideas, especially an end to secret diplomacy, in the proposals of US President Woodrow Wilson led Clifford to praise him as the 'apostle of brotherhood'. The first of many Free Church resolutions welcoming the most significant outcome of these proposals, the League of Nations, was passed by the NCEFC in March 1919. By then Liberal Nonconformists like the Welsh coal owner and Calvinistic Methodist David Davies had played a prominent part in founding the LNU established in November 1918. The NCEFC was a very active cheerleader for the new organization, encouraging both congregations and the general public to signal their support, while Scott Lidgett and Henry Carter served on its Council.[282] Typical of Nonconformist enthusiasm was the Congregational Union resolution in 1923 about the Franco-Belgian occupation of the Ruhr: 'All the questions involved should be referred to the League of Nations as being the only body competent to express an impartial judgement which can be honourably accepted by all the Nations concerned.'[283] As archbishop Davidson recognized, this optimistic view of the League was almost universal in Nonconformity.[284]

Nonconformity thus shared in a general, if ill-defined, consensus for peace. The recent war had not prompted Nonconformists to thoroughly re-examine what they meant by peace, or how they hoped to achieve it. Some ministers were chary about associating with the left-wing successor of the NCF, the NMWM. For instance, one minister said of the Anglican Christian Pacifist, stalwart of the NMWM and future leader of the Labour Party, George Lansbury, 'He is such an extremist. He can never get away from the Sermon on the Mount.'[285] During the 1920s, however, the distinction between the Pacifism of the NMWM and the emphasis on international reconciliation and collective security of the LNU was not as apparent as it was to become in the succeeding decade. Free Church involvement with the NMWM was thus extensive, if nowhere like as near universal as with the LNU.

This general enthusiasm for peace meant that the 1924 Labour government's decision to build five of the new cruisers that had been planned by its Conservative predecessor was widely criticized. Two years earlier there was also a discernible lack of enthusiasm for the bellicose line Lloyd George took during the Chanak crisis that led to the downfall of his government.[286] This did not mean that the Turks, the bête noire of late Victorian Nonconformists because of their perceived tendency to slaughter subject Christian populations, had ceased to agitate the pulpit.[287] After the recent war, however, there was no real appetite to share Lloyd George's willingness to confront them.

Attempts to construct a more definitive Christian response to war not surprisingly commenced among Quakers before the Great War ended.[288] This was not least because, despite their traditionally anti-war stance, 1,200 members of the Society nevertheless joined the colours, including the future Labour MP Glenvil Hall.[289] Subsequently, the Congregationalists set up a commission in 1923–25, followed by an assembly devoted to the subject of war and peace in 1929. The results of such enquiries, however, were inconclusive.[290]

Pacifist resolutions were passed by bodies such as the Primitive Methodist conference and the Lancashire Baptist Union in 1928,[291] reflecting the contemporary enthusiasm for the Kellogg–Briand Pact. There was considerable Pacifism in the Old Paths Churches of Christ.[292] However, only the Quakers were fully committed to Pacifism, having reaffirmed in 1919 that 'in no form is war … in harmony with the life and teaching of Jesus Christ, and … that goodwill towards men, based on the love of God is a power that can be relied on as the true reconciler'. They, however, also recognized that others felt that justice, right and liberty needed to be upheld. Thus early Quakers saw, probably with greater clarity than LNU supporters (with the exception of those who followed David Davies in advocating an international police force), that the League of Nations might need to resort to economic or even military sanctions in order to uphold its authority.[293]

The ethical problems involved in such eventualities became acute in the 1930s. Accordingly the opportunities for acrimonious exchanges between Pacifists and non-Pacifists, already apparent at COPEC, grew more frequent.[294] These confrontations illustrated the fragmenting of the ill-defined consensus for peace of the 1920s under the shock of the failure of the League of Nations to tackle the Manchurian crisis and the rise of Hitler. Optimism generated by the World Disarmament Conference of 1932–34 under the chairmanship of Arthur Henderson, however, initially created opportunity for all shades of opinion to unite around the issue of armaments. For instance, Garvie's resolution passed unanimously by the Congregational Union assembly in 1933 spoke of abolishing all weapons forbidden to Germany under the Versailles Treaty, the reduction of all arms to the point where no nation could claim a need to rearm to regain parity or safety, and the international supervision of arms and arms manufacture.[295] A number of Free Church assemblies the following year felt that the latter required control of such manufacturers for, as the Methodist conference resolution put it: 'Arms for private profit constitute a serious menace to international peace.'[296] These calls for nationalization helped to prompt the establishment of an inconclusive Royal Commission on the subject in 1935. They did nothing, however, to halt the shift of the government towards rearmament from 1934 onwards.

British rearmament and the failure of the World Disarmament Conference brought to the fore differences between Pacifists and non-Pacifists. It became increasingly apparent that anything other than Pacifism could, in the end, mean support for war. Henry Carter accordingly publicly announced his Pacifism in 1933, just two months after Hitler's accession to power. Shortly afterwards, he and Soper established the Methodist Peace Fellowship for Pacifists within the denomination. This development was criticized by brother ministers concerned to defend the principles of collective security.[297] Conferences and assemblies became scenes of confrontation between these groups. In 1929, at the Congregational Union assembly, Leyton Richards was already urging the abolition of Officer Training Corps in Nonconformist public schools and a refusal to continue with the service chaplaincies which had been so hard won during the war.[298] Achieving the latter aim became a regular feature of Pacifist resolutions and the subject of a Congregational Union commission in 1931–32. However, in view of the fact that there were still Congregationalists in the forces who needed ministering to, no action was taken.[299] The attempts of Methodist Pacifists to abolish their Officer Training Corps and service chaplaincies proved equally unsuccessful.

Tom Bevan, in moving his Pacifist resolution to the Methodist conference in 1934 stressed that 'it is a case of saying we believe in spiritual power rather than material force'. Scott Lidgett's reply showed that he recognized that support for material force was now necessary if belief in the policing role of the League were to be maintained.[300] The Baptist Union in 1937 continued to call for disarmament and, in the face of widespread fear of the bomber's capacity for destruction, the abolition of aerial warfare.[301] Nevertheless, events like the 1935 Abyssinian crisis led to increasing emphasis upon the need to resist the use of force.[302] There was therefore no criticism of rearmament from the platform at the 1936 NCEFC assembly, horrifying Tom Bevan, who then complained that they were thus condoning 'a policy that can only stimulate a race in armaments and end in war'.[303] Quaker caveats about the League had at last dawned upon its supporters as they realized that collective security might need to be enforced. Those who took this line generally predominated, while Pacifists rarely secured more than a third of the votes at the Free Church assemblies and conferences of the 1930s. Even when the position was reversed, as at the Unitarian general assembly in 1936, *The Inquirer* remained committed to collective security.[304]

The fundamentalism of Pacifists, holding fast to the view passed by so many interwar conferences that 'war is contrary to the mind of Christ', was answered by the question, 'Is evil to go entirely unrestrained because we have perfected no way of restraint?' The questioner, Methodist Leslie Weatherhead, a former army chaplain who ministered at the City Temple from 1936 to 1960, had as a Pacifist suggested averting the Abyssinian crisis by offering Italy whatever territory might redress its legitimate grievances. Attitudes were, however, to harden during the Spanish Civil War, during which the Free Church press were solidly hostile to the Francoist cause.[305] By 1939 Weatherhead no longer believed that the dictators were amenable either to moral suasion or to pacificatory offers of territory. Few retained, like the Quaker Corder Catchpool, right up to the last the hope that such an offer would avert war.[306]

The Quaker Peace Committee had meanwhile by 1937 recognised that their perplexity in the face of the Spanish Civil War 'suggests that we have failed to think out the practical methods by which a pacifist can aid the advance of right as he sees it'.[307] Thereafter, Pacifists increasingly abandoned efforts to find practical methods and instead relied on faith. This, however, did not prevent increasing numbers of Nonconformists turning to Pacifism as war approached.[308] Appeasement also gained considerable support from the Free Churches in the later 1930s. In October 1938 in an address at the City Temple, Lloyd George emotionally lashed out at Nonconformity's failure to denounce the Munich agreement. Henry Carter was shocked by his 'ferocious and irresponsible speech'.[309] The Unitarian and Labour MP J. Chuter Ede, however, seemed to feel that the Nonconformist Conscience had at last spoken. 'One has been asking one's self for weeks what would Joseph Parker or John Clifford have said … If totalitarianism is tolerable, nonconformity is indefensible. Our leaders do not seem to have realised that.'[310] Indeed, by September 1939, in the face of Hitler's continued aggression, most Nonconformists had decided that the choice lay between the evil of war and the greater evil of passivity. Tyrants greater than any Turkish sultan needed to be denounced and resisted.

Education

Education was traditionally a key theme of the Nonconformist Conscience. From the eighteenth century, Nonconformists had been active in setting up Sunday Schools and adult schools. They also played a prominent part in founding mechanics institutes in the early nineteenth century, while the British and Foreign School Society was founded in 1808 to provide non-denominational elementary teaching.[311] Nonconformists also took an elevated view of the value of education. As Angus Watson reminded his fellow Congregationalists in 1935, the purpose of education was not just to learn facts, but to inculcate moral qualities.[312] Clifford's Westbourne Park Chapel took this to extraordinary lengths, featuring an educational institute with seventy classes per week and over a thousand members.[313] The Passive Resistance campaign he led after 1902 against the public funding of denominational schools was by no means the limit of his interest in education.

It did, however, bear witness to one enduring Free Church shibboleth: that education should be non-sectarian. 'What we desire', one passive resister stated, 'is that the education of the children in the people's schools should be free from all sectarian tests and teaching and under the control of the representatives of the public.'[314] The disestablishmentarian Liberation Society even felt that it was 'unjust for the State either to impart or pay for any form of religious instruction, and that the responsibility for such instruction rests upon parents and Churches'.[315] Their taste for secular education was not, however, shared by the majority of Free Churchmen. The views associated with Passive Resistance were more common. The civil disobedience associated with it, nonetheless, became increasingly rare. There were few like the Quaker Socialist Joseph Southall, who continued his protest by withholding a portion of his rates right up to his death in 1944. Passive Resistance as a protest movement did not survive the First World War.[316]

There was no redress for passive resisters in the 1918 Education Act. A Nonconformist memorial was sent to the Liberal president of the Board of

Education complaining that it did nothing to remedy clerical control in schools supported by public rates, the sectarian tests and environment in these schools, and the continuing ecclesiastical influence in State-supported teacher training colleges.[317] It did however, as Congregationalists recognized, promise 'a substantial advance in the provision of popular education'.[318] Many of its reforms were permissive rather than compulsory. Nursery schools, the prospect of the further raising of the leaving age to fifteen, and continuation schools up to the age of eighteen (a form of part-time further education pioneered by progressive firms like Rowntree's) nevertheless all proved most welcome.[319] There was therefore much Free Church hostility when many of the Act's provisions fell victim in 1921–22 to the post-war economy drive known as the Geddes Axe. Garvie protested: 'Education is the key to progress, and he who seeks to arrest the progress of education is one of the worst enemies of the commonwealth.'[320]

The main arresting agent on the progress of education was, as Geddes bore witness, lack of finance. Implementing the improvement envisaged in the 1918 Act and the 1926 Hadow Report recommending the universal provision of primary and secondary education with a break at age eleven proved a costly business.[321] Indeed, the problem of finance was such that many schools condemned as unfit in 1914 remained in use throughout the interwar years.[322] This problem was particularly acute for denominational schools. In York by 1936,

> [w]ith one exception all the voluntary school buildings which were in use … were erected between 1832 and 1899. Even in 1899 they were described by H.M. Inspector as 'old and in most cases poor'. Lack of funds has prevented the managers from re-building them or bringing them up to modern standards.[323]

Moreover, a large proportion of Anglican schools were in rural districts and were, with the advent of motorized public transport and rural depopulation, increasingly seen as too small and inefficient to be viable.[324] Many gave up the struggle and, encouraged by ecumenical sentiment, took the option of a locally agreed religious syllabus which most Free Churchmen favoured.[325] The number of Anglican schools accordingly declined steadily during the period (Table 6). Similar processes also affected the day schools of the Wesleyans, who did not share the general Nonconformist antipathy to denomination education. Their school numbers began to show a decline from the 1870s. Factors such as Price Hughes's association of denominational schooling with Romanism started this process, and it was compounded in the twentieth century by financial constraints.[326]

Reducing their numbers of denominational schools was not something Roman Catholics were prepared to do. Nor would they accept the agreed syllabus during the interwar years, on the grounds that inadequate teaching is halfway to being false teaching and that Christian education is a matter of the ethos of an institution, not of a syllabus.[327] They therefore responded to the financial difficulties presented by new legislation and the need to provide schools on burgeoning housing estates by demanding further support from public funds.[328] The ecumenical Anglican/Catholic Malines conversations, the 1927–28 Prayer Book controversy and the Catholics' apparently superior ability to cope with the chilly blast of the twentieth century were

Table 6 Schools in England and Wales, 1926 and 1938

	1926–27		1938	
	Schools	**Average attendance**	**Schools**	**Average attendance**
Total council and voluntary schools	20,723	4,973,656	20,916	4,526,701
(Wales)	1,906	405,753	1,909	322,478
Council	9,170	3,231,494	10,363	3,151,893
(Wales)	1,308	340,916	1,344	268,896
Voluntary	11,553	1,742,162	10,553	1,374,808
(Wales)	598	64,837	565	53,582
Church of England	9,927	1,349,403	8,979	1,004,117
(Wales)	530	50,018	501	38,597
Wesleyan	135	23,509	119	15,268
Roman Catholic	1,143	318,353	1,266	331,086
(Wales)	53	13,914	57	14,168
Jewish	12	5,291	13	3,973
Other voluntary	336	45,606	176	20,364
(Wales)	15	905	7	517

These figures were not fully tabulated before 1926–27. For comparison, however, the figures available for 1903 and 1919 are:

	1903		1919	
	Schools	**Accommodation**	**Schools**	**Accommodation**
Council	5,975	3,065,169	8,621	4,329,252
Voluntary	14,238	3,722,317	12,302	2,736,913
Total	20,213	6,787,486	20,923	7,066,165

Sources: Parliamentary Papers (1920) XV 45, *Report of the Board of Education for the Year 1918–1919* Cmd 722; *Parliamentary Papers* (1928) IX 39, Board of Education, *Education in England and Wales 1926–27* Cmd 3091; *Parliamentary Papers* (1938) X 661, Board of Education, *Education in 1938* Cmd 6031.

already fuelling Free Church fears for the safety of Protestant England. Especially in a place with a large Catholic minority, like Liverpool, the secretary of the Free Church Council found, 'Some of my brethren nearly go off their heads with fear of Rome'.[329] Catholic educational demands added to such fears and encouraged Congregationalists to reaffirm their position 'that public endowment of denominational interest is repugnant'.[330]

These demands complicated the necessary changes to school provision required to implement the Hadow Report. Having canvassed the various churches. Labour, therefore, conscious of their many Catholic voters, decided to avoid any specific pledges on the issue in the 1929 election.[331] This avoidance of the issue continued even after the new government committed itself to raising the school-leaving age to fifteen. The resulting lack of clarity seems to have encouraged Nonconformists to imagine that the president of the Board of Education, Sir Charles Trevelyan, was making concessions to the Catholics.[332] Catholics had no such illusions. In 1930, two bills had to be withdrawn because Trevelyan was unable to obtain agreement between the churches.[333] His third bill was mutilated by an amendment introduced by Catholic Labour MPs in January 1931 designed to ensure that the leaving age could not rise without commensurate financial assistance to church schools. The day after this passed, the *Christian World* rang with J. D. Jones's headline 'Free Churchmen Awake!'[334] The NCEFC's response to the emergency grants Trevelyan then proposed was hedged with formidable caveats which showed that they maintained their traditional position.[335]

Opposition to such grants being made to schools under denominational control remained so great that the Congregationalists' Education Committee recognized in 1935: 'The fear lest this demand should be conceded makes some of our people reluctant to support the raising of the school age.'[336] It was, however, clear that this could not come without concessions to the additional burdens placed on denominational schools. In 1934–35, the NCEFC therefore accepted an exceptional grant of 50 per cent, though this was to be for three years only, without precedent, and entailing no new building.[337] The regret Angus Watson felt about his role in the 1902 controversy and his increasing willingness, in the face of the declining influence of the Sunday School, to accept even sectarian education was not a general Free Church phenomenon.[338]

Although the National government's 1936 Education Act provided some encouragement for the adoption of the agreed syllabus, it therefore provoked concern in going beyond the provisos agreed in 1934–35 in featuring building grants and in failing to secure local government control over teachers.[339] Fears that the Free Churches' prime negotiator Scott Lidgett had conceded too much for the sake of raising the school-leaving age were clearly expressed at the following year's NCEFC assembly.[340] Disturbed by the 50 to 75 per cent grants, the Baptist Union Council suggested that the State should instead pay the lot and banish the evil of the dual system.[341] Protests against these grants, and against the new denominational schools appearing as a result, continued to be regular features of Free Church deputations to the president of the Board of Education and of local Free Church agitation down to the 1939 outbreak of war.[342] Ecumenism – a preoccupation of Scott Lidgett – and related desires to bury old denominational differences, had but limited effects on Nonconformist attitudes towards education in the interwar years.[343]

Immorality

In 1908, a survey of Liverpool's Free Churches noted: 'One of the recent reports on Rescue Work in Liverpool makes passing mention of poverty as one of the causes of immorality. This phase needs more attention than it has yet received.'[344] The linkage was not as novel as this suggested: mid-nineteenth-century initiatives had seen Nonconformists moving towards intervening with the young poor to try to prevent them from falling victim to social evils. The same period saw a steady growth in asylums for fallen women where they received food and shelter and were encouraged to consider repentance. Such an approach treated prostitutes as agents of their own downfall.

Attitudes, however, increasingly shifted following the Contagious Diseases Acts of 1864 and 1866. These were prompted by medical concerns about the difficulty of recognizing prostitutes and policing the health threat they posed to wider society. The campaign against the State sanctioning of prostitution, invasion of women's liberty and privacy, and sexual double standards embodied in this legislation drew attention to the extent to which women lacked agency.[345] Price Hughes, who was among the Nonconformists most involved in this campaign, realized, 'It is an awful fact that at this moment the only way by which a woman can secure bread is by the sale of her body.'[346] Fallen women thus came to be seen more as the victims of predatory male sexuality: as Tiplady pointed out forty years later, all too often their circumstance resulted from some sexual indiscretion, which led their shocked parents to drive them from their homes onto the streets where they, out of necessity, turned to prostitution.[347] Growing awareness that these women were as much sinned against as sinning led former asylums to become maternity hospitals or homes for unmarried mothers by 1914.[348]

State sanctioning of vice, for instance in the licensed brothels on the Western Front during the Great War, was nevertheless still condemned.[349] So were increasingly draconic attempts to tackle outbreaks of venereal disease in the army under DORA. Regulation 40D, introduced in March 1918, forbade women with venereal disease from soliciting or having sexual relations with soldiers. In practice, this involved arrests on suspicion, medical inspections and fines or imprisonment. This was, like the CD Acts, clearly discriminatory, placing the responsibility for sexual purity and the penalties for sexual indiscretion entirely on women.[350] The NCEFC claimed that their strong opposition had helped render 40D a dead letter, and Nonconformists must have been responsible for many of the over 200 resolutions against it received by June 1918. It nevertheless remained in force until 25 November 1918.[351] In his survey on *The Army and Religion* in 1919, Cairns argued that such regulations were not the answer to venereal disease and immorality. He emphasized the need for housing reform, for adequate female wages which did not need to be supplemented by prostitution, for better moral education and for a greater stress, not upon the evils of vice, but upon the inculcation of responsible attitudes to sex and marriage in both men and women. In the light of the changed position of women in society, it was also most important that legislation should not discriminate against them.[352]

This change in the position of women also encouraged emphasis on the positive virtues of a Christian view of sexual relations. The publication of Marie Stopes's *Married Love* in 1918 prompted a wave of marital literature explaining the joys of companionate marriage for a generation disrupted by war. Among the most notable examples, focusing more on men's need to express the 'iron strength and infinite tenderness' of Christ-like masculinity, was the 1923 publication of *Men, Women and God* by the former army chaplain A. Herbert Gray.[353] More controversially, Stopes encouraged the establishment of birth control clinics, thus separating the act and pleasure of sexual intercourse from processes of procreation. For her, birth control was also a means of reducing the financial pressures on couples.[354] For

Frank Lenwood, birth control could accordingly serve as a Malthusian means of tackling social problems.[355]

While individual Free Church ministers and laypeople thus commented on or promoted birth control, there was seemingly little appetite for official pronouncements on the issue. Garvie's reservations about the COPEC report on the relationship between the sexes indeed seem to have been prompted by the support it gave to the idea of official church guidance on birth control. In contrast to reactions among Catholics and Anglicans, these developments were little noted in the Nonconformist assemblies or press and birth control was generally tacitly accepted as a personal matter.[356]

There was more inter-church consensus at COPEC with regard to the importance of sharing, self-surrender and mutuality within Christian marriage.[357] Somewhat controversially Leslie Weatherhead, flushed with enthusiasm for Freud, felt that this Christian understanding of sexual relations could only be achieved by overcoming the taboo, guilt and ignorance he found often surrounded the subject. In *The Mastery of Sex through Psychology and Religion* (1931), he sought to provide a framework for understanding sex and psychology while remaining true to the traditional morality of self-control, abstinence before marriage, chastity and monogamy.

There was concern that this framework was undermined in the sugary world of the cinema. In this escapist environment, Benson Perkins complained, too many films stressed, 'sex, drunkenness, murder or some other form of unhealthy excitement'.[358] To W. H. Lax it was 'no wonder congregations are suffering, for people who are fed upon such pabulum are not likely to listen to anything that demands even the minimum of thought'.[359] Film contrasted strongly with the cultural treasures venerated by Alan Wilkinson's father, a Primitive Methodist minister. John T. Wilkinson instead always

> [S]trenuously endeavoured to enable his congregation to enter into the great literary, artistic and theological riches of the pre-1914 world in which he was reared. He had almost no interest in the characteristic novels, poetry, films, art or plays of the post-war period.[360]

Alan Bullock's Unitarian minister father, Frank, is another example of an eminent minister of the period with a similar cultural hinterland in which there was little or no place for the contemporary.[361] Some Nonconformists rejected it vehemently: R. J. Russell disliked the cinema as much as the Pools, arguing that it caused crime.[362] In January 1935, the Free Churches participated in a deputation to Prime Minister Ramsay MacDonald which unsuccessfully asked for an inquiry into the 'undesirable and disquieting character of films'.[363] There were further calls for drastic film censorship at the Methodist conference the following year.[364]

A minority, however, took a much more positive line. Soper described it as 'the biggest single creative force in the world … the most remarkable recreational and educational factor that we have, and … we must make use of it'.[365] Cinema services were pioneered at the Methodist East End Mission by F. W. Chudleigh and the Bolton Methodist Mission by Francis Woodmass. In 1917, the success of the entertainment provided by the latter provoked a letter from the Bolton Cinematographic Exhibitors' Association complaining of unfair competition.[366] In 1928, Tiplady went further and incorporated films into his services at the Lambeth Mission. He encountered far less criticism than expected and the film services were soon packed and being imitated by other inner city ministers.[367]

The films shown were not necessarily religious in theme. Tiplady believed any decent film would do Lambeth people good, if only by drawing them in from the surrounding dismal streets and slums and away from the temptations of the public houses. There was also recognition that many films were moral fables in which justice emerged triumphant. For both these reasons Tiplady attributed 'a great deal of the moral and social improvements of the last twenty-five years to the influence of the cinema'.[368]

Thomas Marks, a Methodist barrister from Ealing, West London, who felt mainstream cinema was instead too dominated by sex and gangster movies, responded by founding the Guilds of Light. His search for more wholesome fare led, with Tiplady's help, to the founding of the Religious Film Society (RFS) in 1933.[369] Backing was won from J. Arthur Rank, a wealthy Methodist flour miller, who saw films as a means of promoting Christian values. W. H. Lax was deliberately used as the star of their first film *Mastership* to help win over churchgoers. In the 1930s, Rank used his wealth to buy an increasing stake in the British cinema. As a result, by 1942, a member of the NCEFC executive committee dominated the British film industry.[370]

Disestablishment

Free Churchmen saw themselves as having been, from their very inception, the torchbearers of religious liberty and freedom to worship God according to conscience, untrammelled by the imposition of Prayer Book, tithe or State. The establishment of the Church of England, which involved all three impositions, risked the placing of social position before the spiritual Lordship of Christ, and of the comfort of endowment before the work of salvation. As Nonconformists moved towards numerical parity with the Church of England in the nineteenth century they increasingly resented the position and privileges establishment conveyed. The Anti-State Church Association was founded in 1844. Changing its name to the Liberation Society in 1853, it aggressively sought disestablishment legislation in the late nineteenth century.

Conflict was particularly acute in Wales over issues like education. The 1905 survey in response to Welsh demands for their own education board – successfully achieved in 1907 – demonstrated the Nonconformist preponderance in the principality and helped pave the way for the disestablishment and disendowment of the Church of England in Wales passed by the Liberals in 1914, though not actually enforced until 1920. Welsh Nonconformity thereby lost one of its cohering rallying cries.

The context of establishment, meanwhile, was changing in England, partly because a less Anglican-dominated Parliament also had less time for church affairs. Just before the outbreak of war the Church of England therefore set up a commission under Lord Selborne. By the time this reported in 1916, William Temple was leading his Life and Liberty Movement for greater spiritual independence. The confluence of these developments resulted in the proposals to establish a Church Assembly, diocesan synods and parochial church councils as means of managing the Church's affairs without requiring constant recourse to Parliament. These changes were enacted when Parliament in 1919 rapidly passed the Enabling Act.[371]

These changes, in turn, brought about a softening of Nonconformist attitudes. In moving a disestablishment and disendowment amendment to the Enabling Bill, the Congregational minister and Coalition Liberal MP T. T. Broad recognized that trying to force disestablishment now was a blunder; it could only come through its acceptance by the Church of England.[372] Despite some sympathies with the Bill's aspirations, it was nevertheless criticized by the NCEFC for expressly excluding sections of the community from having a say in what claimed to be a national church, for making it easier to undermine Protestantism, and for maintaining the compromising power of the State in a purportedly spiritual sphere.[373] Enthusiasm for reunion was clearly not yet tempering disestablishmentarianism. The objections of the arch-ecumenist J. H. Shakespeare to their hostility to the legislation were swept aside.[374]

Despite wealthy supporters like Sir Halley Stewart and Robert Wilson Black, the Liberation Society nevertheless increasingly struggled against encroaching impoverishment. Periodic disestablishment resolutions could not prevent it from becoming an old man's cause.[375] Remaining optimism was increasingly related to whether the justice of disestablishment appeared to be dawning on the Church of England, fuelled by the archbishop of Wales's satisfaction with the settlement there, or by the disestablishmentarian noises emitted by Bishop Hensley Henson of Durham.[376] Militant Nonconformity went into abeyance, waiting on the Church of England and only briefly surfacing when – as in the new Prayer Book of 1927–28 – that Church appeared to be moving in the wrong, not to say Romeward, direction.[377] The rejection of disestablishment in the Anglican Church and State report in 1936 also fostered a brief renaissance in the Liberation Society. For them, there was at least progress in the same year through the Tithe Act.

This and the new preparedness by Anglican spokesmen to recognize the limits of their claim to be the national church took the sting out of old ecclesiastical controversies. Nonconformists were anyway increasingly aware that inter-church strife would be of more benefit to Christianity's opponents.[378] It would, as the Quaker Carl Heath suggested in a 1938 memorandum to the Liberation Society, compound the impression of the churches' unpreparedness for the twentieth century. This memorandum pointed out that most of the younger people were not concerned merely about freeing the Church from the State. 'They wanted the Church to have its true place in the Community. If the Liberation Society is merely to keep hammering away at a Radical proposition of the Nineteenth Century it cannot be very useful.'[379] In 1959, the Society was disbanded.

Conclusion

Clearly something of the old Nonconformist Conscience died with it. But then Dissent could not remain what it had been. This was not necessarily, as Lloyd George cruelly suggested in 1938 (though not without some justification), because Nonconformist witness had been 'corroded very largely by the patronage of the ecclesiastical and official hierarchy'.[380] The style and rhetoric of their campaigning had certainly changed. If the Nonconformist Conscience betokens an aggressive, confrontational form of moral righteousness, then the many obituaries in the period and since were not premature. However, in the twentieth century, the Free Churches were faced with new issues or old issues in new guises. They had to learn how to conciliate, not criticize, to recommend, not admonish. The obstacles to human happiness were not tyrannies or vested interests so much as the failure to realize Christian ideals. Samuel Keeble nevertheless remained confident of their role: 'The Church cannot compel. It can only enlighten and persuade. In a rational and moral world that should suffice. Finally it will suffice.'[381]

3

Changes in Chapel Society

In many instances parents have allowed their children to go their own way both in religion and politics, to an extent that would have amazed and alarmed the generation before them. Finding protest unavailing the Church began to capitulate to youth's demands by organising entertainments, arranging social gatherings, giving facilities for recreation to a wider extent than ever before, in the hope of making religion attractive; though it must be confessed with very limited success.

A. Gordon James[1]

In most large towns the churches near the centre are the sanctuaries where once influential congregations worshipped but which are now left almost high and dry by the ceaseless movement of population outwards.

A. E. Wass[2]

England and Wales had a large stock of Nonconformist chapels and meeting houses at the close of the Great War. They varied greatly in size, from vast urban temples seating thousands to tiny rural causes with a handful of devoted members. All tended to be gathered in churches, serving their membership and a varying penumbra of adherents. Many had been built, extended or beautified in recent decades, and were often therefore encumbered with debt. During the ensuing twenty years, moreover, finance was to be only one of the challenges they faced, alongside population movement and social change. This posed the challenge of how to minister to their flocks in new ways.

New institutional models

A key response of late Victorian Nonconformity to this challenge in the inner cities was to reinvent the nature of the chapel, a process which continued into the following century. For instance, dramatic changes followed the arrival of the Socialist Sam Rowley as superintendent minister at an impoverished city centre Primitive Methodist chapel in Bradford during the Great War. Financial expediency as much as Rowley's social sympathies dictated the alterations he set in train. The chapel had for many years been accumulating debt.[3] He therefore followed the example of the Wesleyans who had in 1900–4 replaced the nearby Eastbrook chapel with a capacious and adaptable hall, not merely 'for the sake of the masses of non-worshippers for whose salvation the Methodist Church must be held largely responsible', but also because the money to maintain the previous cause had not been forthcoming from the 100,000 persons who dwelt within fifteen minutes' walk of its doors.[4] Like the chapels replaced by Central Halls during Price Hughes's Forward Movement in the 1890s, the former glory had departed with the drift of the middle classes from the city centre to the suburbs.[5] They left behind impoverished slum dwellers paying high rents for poor accommodation.[6] One sister at the Wesleyans' South London Mission was told, 'We poor people have no room for anything, not even to pray in.'[7] In such circumstances, the Wesleyan George Jackson complained; 'Religion has no more chance to flourish … than wheat in a coal-mine.'[8]

Nineteenth-century Nonconformity was by no means as middle-class in character, or as financially dependent upon the middle classes as both contemporaries and posterity have sometimes depicted it. There was, nevertheless, an uncomfortable awareness that the urban poor remained largely untouched by the message of the chapels. To bridge this gap the focus in the early nineteenth century had been on visitation and charitable support, supplemented by various social services such as those offered the Unitarian Domestic Missions that, inspired by American examples, began to appear in the 1820s.[9] From the 1880s, the Central Halls and settlements were a new attempt to address the same problem. Nevertheless, although some Central Halls succeeded in attracting working-class support, there was certainly truth in Charles Masterman's accusation that they also decanted existing support into the great preaching centres then created.[10]

Despite these efforts, chapel society became steadily more middle class during the nineteenth century. Even in poor areas, such as Bethnal Green, their principal constituency comprised clerks and skilled workers.[11] This made their causes financially vulnerable: the onset of poverty and unemployment in an area could cause the closure of local chapels for, as Tiplady pointed out, 'The lack of endowments tends to make Nonconformist churches the churches of the middle class and of the regularly employed working class.'[12]

Such churches were sustained instead by congregational offerings, even in the case of the Methodists with their more developed connexional arrangements. They thus required a commitment to the cause rarely encountered in impoverished areas. Appropriate financial and social adjustments were needed to maintain their work. Even chapels that drew substantial, if largely unemployed, congregations could ultimately prove doomed. The social concern and political and theological radicalism practised by inner city chapels like the Baptist Pembroke Chapel, Liverpool or Greenfield Congregationalists, Bradford, did not save them. A report by the Bradford Congregational Association just two years before Greenfield – which had once been blessed by the ministries of Rhondda Williams and Vivian T. Pomeroy – closed in 1938 recognized the inevitability of inner city closures in the face of the removal of members, indebtedness, the impossibility of paying a minister and the resultant loss of heart.[13]

The Methodists of Stourbridge Road, Bradford in 1934 urged, 'that a policy of severely restricting service to fit finance is not in the best interests of Bradford

Methodism'.[14] Finance, however, had to come from somewhere. Traditionally regular income for chapels had been supplied by pew rents. To appeal to the urban poor, the Central Halls eschewed these. Congregational giving, however, was never enough to fund their activities. Central Halls accordingly had to tap the generosity of the Nonconformist wealthy. The manufacturer W. J. Crossley found that when having tea with S. F. Collier, the first superintendent of the Manchester and Salford Wesleyan Mission: 'each cup cost him about £500'.[15] Notwithstanding his Socialism, Rowley was so far from wishing to alienate potential patrons that in his appeal for the assistance of shopkeepers, manufacturers and mill owners he urged:

> Surely the Mill and Factory girls are better and more regular workers for being associated with a Christian Mission? ... We have had Special Donations more than once during our Ministry from Masters and Mistresses because of the Christian integrity and worth of the servant associated with the Church.[16]

This did not necessarily make the Central Halls, as Snowden put it, 'the slave of rich men, who look upon the Church, aye, and its ministers too, as a valuable commercial asset'.[17] Tooting Wesleyan Central Hall may have been founded at the behest of the wealthy miller Joseph Rank after an encounter with a local Communist deriding Christianity, yet Rank made it clear to its minister that – Tory though he was – he would not interfere with what was preached.[18] Rowley's hall was freely lent to Bradford Trades Council during the General Strike.[19] Its connections with the Labour movement were more conspicuous than with those whose money sustained its work.

Rowley's Wesleyan contemporary G. Gilbert Muir of Eastbrook Hall nevertheless banned Labour speakers at its Brotherhood and generally adopted an attitude of unremitting hostility towards the party.[20] Increasingly, however, ministers attracted to this kind of work were generally sympathetic to Labour views. This was the case even with Roderick Kedward, the superintendent of the Bermondsey Wesleyan Mission in the 1920s, who was also briefly the local Liberal MP. Many labouring in this mission field were, like Kedward's assistant Donald Soper, in fact Socialists.[21] Wealthy benefactors – such as the famous contralto Clara Butt at the Baptists' West Ham Central Mission – enabled them to carry out their work but do not seem, in general, to have manipulated them.[22] The Central Halls instead tapped this wealth and applied it.

Central Halls emerged, primarily within Methodism, in the 1880s as a response to inner city decline. At Price Hughes's West London Mission founded in 1887, there was a carefully tailored mixture of evangelism, social work and entertainment: W. H. Lax even claimed that the Proms originated in the popular concerts the mission ran at St James's Hall.[23] There continued to be new foundations in provincial cities down to the 1940s, while the London Mission Committee, throughout the interwar years under the guidance of the Socialist C. Ensor Walters, spent £2 million – much of it provided by Joseph Rank – on developing Central Halls in the capital.[24]

In the 1870s, Clifford at Westbourne Park Baptists and later Silvester Horne at the Congregationalists' Whitfields Tabernacle were also developing the model of the institutional church in their respective denominations. The former was opened in 1877, furnished with fifteen meeting rooms. This architectural change facilitated a greater range of activities, in this case, principally featuring adult education classes until their transfer to Paddington Technical Institute in 1903. The campaign against the Contagious Diseases Acts, and that by the Congregationalist journalist W. T. Stead in 1885 against child prostitution, also led to the founding of a girls' home in 1886.[25]

A third means of church re-engagement with the urban poor was the settlement. The model was Toynbee Hall, founded by the Anglican Canon Samuel Barnett in Whitechapel in 1885. These brought middle-class, well-educated young men and women to serve among the urban poor. Nonconformist examples included the Congregationalists' Mansfield House Settlement and the university extension work central to Lidgett's Bermondsey Settlement. A variation on this theme was Kingsley Hall, established in London's East End in 1915 by the Baptist, Socialist and Pacifist Muriel Lester. By 1934, there were twenty-nine residential settlements in London and fifteen elsewhere.[26] Their aims usually were to promote social harmony and aesthetic improvement. Thus Mansfield saw itself as 'a centre for all classes', including as a meeting place with leaders of the Labour movement and as an oasis within a defiled environment where the local entertainment was a fight while for 'their architecture and their music they have strings of houses or returning drunks'.[27] Lester was unusual in focusing additionally upon an ascetic lifestyle, using her inherited wealth to pay for welfare services for the local population such as health clinics. This was really an idealistic community more than a settlement, though the Spartan food offered by Lester's Brethren of the Common Table does not seem to have helped its appeal to the local poor.[28]

Chapel culture

To be successful, chapels had to be not only situated among but also closely reflective of local society and its various strata. For instance, in the Yorkshire village of Idle in the 1920s, the perception was that the six chapels each had its place in the social pecking order.[29] Each formed its own tight-knit community.

Ministers also often remained figures of local eminence. Growing up in the late Victorian period W. H. Lax regarded the preachers at whose feet he sat as demigods.[30] Oral testimony indicates that ministers remained considerable figures in their local communities into the interwar years.[31] The extent to which both the local and national press were willing to report their activities and preaching indicates that they were still regarded as moral leaders and guardians.

Chapels accordingly fulfilled various social as well as spiritual functions. They also served instrumental needs as 'at that time there was no means of meeting people of the opposite sex except at chapel or work'.[32] Indeed, for the expatriate Welsh of Liverpool and Manchester their chapels not only acted as highly efficient dating agencies but also served as unofficial labour exchanges, helping new immigrants to find jobs. They were centres of Welsh community life in an alien and English environment.[33]

The chapel was also a major agent of socialization through debating societies and improving lectures. There were operettas, pantomimes, plays and choirs; the chapel was a house of culture as well as a house of God. These various activities reinforced the principles and values inculcated by the ordinary services, which were in turn focused outwards on the world as well as inwards on the chapel society. In the Durham mining village where the Methodist and future Labour Chief Whip Ernest Armstrong grew up between the wars, 'the Chapel was the powerhouse in the village and good chapel folk were expected to express their faith by active involvement in public life.'[34] This continuing close-fit between encouraging Christian leadership and an almost automatic Labour politics was also apparent in the Primitive Methodist chapel where Harold Miller grew up in the Derbyshire coalfield.[35] The Labour politics might not have been so readily apparent outside the coalfield. Nevertheless, particularly in rural areas, the chapel was still a major social institution. Into the 1960s in the Outwell–Manea circuit on the Norfolk/Cambridgeshire border, the Methodist chapel remained very much the centre of village life, so much so that in some hamlets the public house closed on Sundays owing to a lack of customers.[36]

By then, however, the chapel's place in village life in most parts of rural Norfolk was generally less assured. In 1933, J. W. Ewing lamented the passing of the days when, in his native East Anglia, 'The place of worship was the chief source of interest.'[37] The rural chapel proved no less vulnerable to social change and financial difficulty than its inner city counterpart. Weakened by the pecuniary impact of the 1923 farm labourers' strike and the agricultural depression of the 1930s, the Norfolk chapel's position in the community was eroded, Ewing alleged, by the coming of bus services, cars, Sunday sports and the cinema. This difficulty was compounded by the effects of steady rural depopulation from the 1860s.[38] A large proportion of Norfolk villages had by 1900 lost some 50 per cent of their numbers in this drift to the towns, which continued unabated in the early twentieth century.[39] In the interwar period the problems of rural chapels therefore provoked almost as much concern as those of the inner city.

Areas like rural Northumberland and Lincolnshire were already well provisioned with chapels before this rural exodus began. This had not, however, discouraged additional chapel construction. The chapel extensions in the rural Welsh fastness of Glan-Llyn ensured that seating was provided by 1901 for more or less twice the local population. Due to depopulation congregations accordingly looked increasingly thin. They also found themselves engaged in daunting struggles with building debt.[40] By the late 1920s, expedient amalgamations and consolidation of effort were being recommended.[41] Such a rationalization of resources was a key objective of the 1932 union of the Wesleyan, United and Primitive Methodist churches. This move did not, however, bring the revival that had been predicted. Indeed, unlike other contemporary ecumenical experiments such as the 1925 United Church of Canada, it did not even seem to arrest decline.[42]

Rationalizations they may have been, but these developments also brought in train the loss of a world of chapel anniversaries, Whit walks and Sunday School events which, across most of the country and across the denominations, were the characteristics of chapel life. Developments like the Methodist union were therefore not without pain. One Durham Methodist told Robert Moore, 'Closing a chapel is like taking someone's home away.'[43] Such closures and the forced amalgamation of circuits often ran counter to the identity and sense of community the chapel built up in its constituent congregation and among the associated adherents and social attendees. A Primitive Methodist suspicion that Wesleyans were weak on temperance also marred

Methodist union in several parts of the country. The fact that the resulting united church bore a rather Wesleyan stamp only exacerbated such problems.[44] The Labour MP C. J. Simmons gave up lay preaching as a result. True to his Primitive Methodism he declared, 'The straitjacket of orthodoxy was not for me.'[45] The *Methodist Recorder* in 1951, reviewing progress since Methodist union in 1932, declared that these changes and the chapel closures that had accompanied them were a necessary rationalization of resources, while admitting that they had led to the widespread destruction of long-established associations and traditions.[46]

The rough and the respectable

At the same time, the way in which the chapel was defined in relationship to the surrounding society was being eroded. Before 1914, there was often a stark contrast, in both village and town, between respectable chapel folk and the rest. 'In them days your parents were either interested in chapel and Sunday School or they were club and pub people', was a conventional, if sweeping view of the resulting cultural divide.[47] The drink-sodden districts around a chapel emphasized this divide. To County Road Methodists in North Liverpool, these furnished a readily available enemy, to be fought with relish.[48] The resulting process of definition also worked the other way round. Non-Methodists told Moore, 'Anybody who was anybody was a Methodist.' 'People who went to chapel were thought to be "somebody", looked up to and respected.'[49] This respectability was reflected in various activities encouraging thrift, individual responsibility and providence as well as sobriety. In the late nineteenth century, this contrasted starkly with surrounding improvidence: in East Bristol it was noted, 'It was very common among the neighbours to pawn things, except for the ones who went to the mission.'[50] Such virtues could still be a potent factor in conversion.

Another was drink. The Bradford Town Mission worked predominantly with 'the very poor of Bradford, men and women who live ever on the absolute border-line of abject need ... many of them have drifted into the condition in which they think "no man careth for my soul", and neither do they care for themselves'. An important part of their recovery of self-respect was the freeing from the tyranny of drink. This tyranny was itself a potent source of conviction of sin. Redemption from it brought not only new life in Christ but salvation from a life made wretched by drink, both spiritually and materially. Conversion and the signing of the pledge therefore often went hand in hand.[51]

The number of pledges secured by the Bradford Town missioners, however, declined year by year. The lodging houses and slums where they had traditionally ministered were gradually disappearing. Because of the restrictions on drinking hours, and the popularity of the cinema and the wireless, there were fewer drunkards on the streets. The treasurer of the Congregational Union Sir R. Murray Hyslop commented in 1932 that:

> Fifty years ago the number of drunken persons seen on the streets, the number of drunken cases in the police courts, and cases of crime directly due to drunkenness were horrible object-lessons to warn even moderate drinkers of what their drinking-habits might lead them to. Now drunkenness is so largely hidden away

> that it is rare indeed to see a drunken person in the streets, and many jump to the conclusion that there is no longer need for a Total Abstinence Movement.[52]

With the recently formed British Institute of Public Opinion claiming in 1939 that 37 per cent of the British population were teetotal, particularly among poorer households, the distinction between the rough and respectable was becoming blurred.[53]

This distinction was also blurred by their geographical separation. From the mid-nineteenth century onwards, the middle classes were moving out of the city centres. In the suburbs, the virtues inculcated by the chapels were less clearly relevant. A Baptist minister complained in the later nineteenth century that while in working-class areas, 'people almost made the chapel their home', in suburbia, 'the homes are comfortable and there is not the same necessity'.[54] A 1911 LFCC survey found, 'The migration to the suburbs develops a less sturdy type of Christian worker, with a tendency to once-a-day worship and general decline of earnest Christian activity.'[55] Scott Lidgett in 1918 complained of the indistinct witness of suburban Methodism and the pretentiousness of its dissenting Gothic.[56] Respectability was in danger of ceasing to be a sturdy Nonconformist trait, and becoming an architectural expression.

The disciplines of the regenerate were no longer to be fervently practised. The rise of State welfare called their necessity into question. In 1931 the *Baptist Times* complained, 'People are beginning to regard the State as a universal provider … The whole system is a negation of thrift and of the need of personal responsibility and independence.'[57] At the same time, improving living standards, increased material expectations and the growing availability of hire purchase by the mid-1930s all seemed to undermine the need for thrift. As a result, respectability, as inculcated by the chapels, was of declining social value. This was compounded by the diminution of the problems of slums and poverty in the interwar period. Respect for chapel values and appreciation of the services it provided began to disappear. In 1921 the Liverpool North End Domestic Mission reported, 'The "church" is looked upon as the centre of all true charity by hundreds of people who never enter its doors.'[58] In contrast, by the 1950s the Manchester Methodist Mission stopped its lodging house work because they could no longer get the men to listen.[59]

The Sunday Schools

At the same time, rising standards of local authority-provided education made the educational facilities provided by the chapel seem less tangibly useful. Matured Christianity in any case did not necessarily result from the large Sunday School attendance of the pre-1914 era. Its inadequacy was revealed during the Great War. One army chaplain wrote,

> A course of catechumen classes … served to reveal the vague, confused and ineffective religious ideas of men who, without exception, had passed through the Free Church Sunday Schools and had been in more or less regular connexion with the churches, short of actual membership, up to the outbreak of war.[60]

But though the residue may not have been great, a chapel background had been an essential part in the upbringing of millions, even if only because of the delights of the Sunday School outing.[61] By 1939 two million cars and relatively cheap rail travel had devalued the outing. Before 1914 the children of the slums that surrounded Eastbrook Hall had been glad of a place to meet, the various treats, the outings and the Christmas parties. In the 1960s and 1970s, bringing in the inner city children of the area resulted in them trying to smash the place up.[62] When George Edwards was growing up in the middle of the nineteenth century, the Sunday School was his only source of schooling.[63] In contrast, a *Punch* cartoon of 1921 showed the proud working-class mother replying to the question 'And what is your religion?' with, 'Well, Miss, I'm Church and me 'usband's Chapel; but little Maudie's County Council.'[64]

The number of Sunday School scholars nevertheless remained substantial (Table 7). Surveys suggest that a majority of children continued to attend Sunday School during the interwar years, though some 12.5 per cent only for brief periods. Numbers seem to have begun to decline faster in the 1930s.[65] However, successful Sunday Schools could still be found, even in the most deprived areas. Cannock Chase Congregationalists had declining membership in the 1920s when it was repeatedly hit financially by the consequences of coal disputes, but its Sunday School was overcrowded. Similarly, in 1937 the Socialist William Dick of the Poplar Congregational Mission complained that his problem was not too few scholars but too few teachers for overcrowded classes.[66] Most, however, were not so thriving.

Arthur Hardman of Bank Street Unitarians, Bolton, writing of his own chapel around 1945 noted:

> At its peak the roll of scholars numbered about 350 and the average Sunday afternoon attendance was nearly 200. It was not a casualty of the first war. Its peak was after that, but like many others, it is a casualty of the last thirty years during which time prosperity and the affluent society have done so much of these things that were the very existence of Sunday Schools . . . Who would suggest today the need for Sick Societies or Chapel holiday saving funds. In the 1920s holidays with pay were not even a distant dream. The Bank Street peak payout before the Bolton holidays was over £1700, and that is a lot of money, even today. So the weekday life of the Sunday School, that beacon of the past, that filled so many needs is largely no longer required. Many of the things it did are now done better by the State or municipal authorities.[67]

Innovations like the graded Sunday School, which was designed to lead children gradually to full church membership, were less of an answer to this problem than an attempt to grapple with the long-established fact that 80 per cent of the scholars did not retain their church connections.[68] Most scholars left around the age of fourteen. The future Labour deputy leader Herbert Morrison was a typical example: 'Like most children I went to Sunday School until I got my first job and became a "man"'.[69] In the 1930s youth clubs began to appear in an attempt to retain the interest of older children. Neither these nor uniformed youth organizations like the Boys Brigade and the Scouts were complete solutions. Arthur Black found in his survey of church attendance in

Table 7 Sunday School scholars of the major Free Church denominations, 1918–39

	P	PW	B	C	UM	PM	WM
1906[a]	88,609	193,599	586,601	732,466	315,723[b]	477,114	1,013,391
1918	66,526	166,624			268,182	427,013	863,538
1919	67,139	166,876	498,460		262,593	416,937	869,334
1920	64,064	165,656	508,759		264,113	424,452	849,861
1921	65,050	163,512	514,411		262,595	419,245	850,871
1922	64,466	161,836	519,933		267,583	419,927	854,746
1923	63,993	162,049	526,233		263,482	419,632	859,317
1924	63,423	160,721	526,306		259,499	414,678	854,312
1925	62,588	159,782	521,219		253,242	407,571	840,205
1926	61,630	155,941	520,822		246,832	398,923	830,318
1927	59,341	155,759	504,419	522,350	242,886	394,050	825,604
1928	57,484	152,070	494,587	541,210	237,269	386,412	813,839
1929	56,671	146,724	483,710	522,051	231,420	378,581	800,292
1930	55,283	145,294	477,929	512,592	224,767	368,782	763,075
1931	55,158	142,970	473,887	506,184	222,430	361,307	759,968
1932	53,066	139,932	471,380	498,356	218,050	355,169	752,855
1933	50,845	136,841	460,079	486,356		1,297,953	
1934	48,953	133,399	448,577	470,213		1,249,669	
1935	46,474	128,970	431,592	450,771		1,187,056	
1936	43,345	122,422	413,168	436,608		1,138,795	
1937	41,923	116,612	396,577	411,448		1,056,175	
1938	40,730	113,961	381,794	395,239		1,006,800	
1939	35,753	108,771	371,837	382,326		980,005	

Notes: Great Britain figures.
[a] This year, a peak in the wake of the Welsh revival, is included for comparison.
[b] This is the figure for 1907, the year the United Methodist Church was constituted.
The abbreviations along the top of the table represent respectively: P= Presbyterian Church of England; PW= Presbyterian Church of Wales; B= Baptist Union; C= Congregationalist; UM= United Methodist; PM= Primitive Methodist; WM= Wesleyan Methodist.

Source: Robert Currie, Alan Gilbert and Lee Horsley (eds), *Churches and Church-Goers*, pp. 175–91.

Roehampton and Putney in 1927–28 that the latter tended to bear fruit in improved character rather than chapel membership.[70]

Some have accused the interwar Sunday School of a lack of innovation, imagination and enthusiasm.[71] There is certainly evidence of class antagonisms marring their work.[72] One suburban minister was even reported as saying of the nearby working-class district: 'Of course we're not particularly anxious to have those children. If they were to come in any numbers our own children would stay away.'[73]

Nevertheless, other Sunday Schools, and the steadily spreading Christian Endeavour classes, continued during the interwar years to have inspirational lessons extolling service for the community as well as teachers whose example and ability to relate the scriptures to the lives of their charges proved of lasting influence.[74] In an earlier generation, the Baptist and former conscientious objector Morgan Jones recalled that the Sunday School was not only where he first experienced public speaking and debating, but also the only place he could learn his native language.[75] His fellow Labour MP the Calvinistic Methodist R. T. Jones indeed declared in 1923, 'The Sunday School has done more for Wales than any other institution.'[76]

Y Capel

Even in Wales, where the chapel's nurturing of so much of the national culture, from the eisteddfod to the language itself, had traditionally given it a pre-eminence unrivalled even in the most Nonconformist parts of England, there was no guarantee of invulnerability to the financial or social pressures of the period. The Welsh revival of 1904–5 may, paradoxically, have been one of the factors undermining the position of the chapel. After all, it was in part itself a reaction against the formality of Nonconformity and a call for practical religion.[77] Therein lay the problem. Converts filled with idealism and enthusiasm found, 'All we got was nebulous phrases. Hence we looked far more closely to the emerging Labour Party and we recognised that therein lay salvation.'[78] The chapels failed to garner the harvest. Nor did they emerge with credit during the ensuing controversy provoked by the 'New Theology' preached by R. J. Campbell, Rhondda Williams or, in South Wales, by T. E. Nicholas. Attempts to minister to the demand for social reform which had developed during and been partly inspired by the revival, at a time of increasing industrial tension in the South Wales valleys, were broadly rejected by the chapels. Even those who tried to present a Social Gospel continued to emphasize the need for individual conversion. This left many converted mineworkers and ironworkers instead to seek and find their socially relevant theology in the doctrines of Karl Marx. In the travails of a region devastated by industrial closures and resulting unemployment and industrial conflict, Marxism often seemed a more illuminating commentary on the plight of the worker than the nostrums of the pulpit.[79] South Wales was traditionally praised for the erudition of its congregations. To W. J. Edwards these were however increasingly being offered not bread but stones.[80]

This did not mean that the chapels ceased to be either the source of moral standards or of community life, or that the values and qualities they had formerly inculcated were no longer valued. When a group of Llanelli non-chapelgoing trade unionists were asked in the 1950s to give local examples of persons embodying their ideal leadership qualities, 'the five persons named were all leading members of chapels, were all middle class, and in all but one case were Liberals'.[81] In the Durham coalfield, similarly, Methodists often became checkweighmen because of their reputation for honesty. This resulted in their also holding a disproportionate and misleading preponderance of posts in the local mining trade union. The bulk of the local miners, like their counterparts in Llanelli, respected but did not attend chapels, which they recalled as declining in community significance by the 1930s.[82]

Arguably, this decline was more noticeable among the male population. As institutions that encouraged female participation, in contrast to the trade unions and working men's clubs in which the menfolk were increasingly absorbed, the chapels continued to be important to the lives of the women of the mining districts.[83] There were some exceptions among, for instance, the Churches of Christ, which certainly included male-dominated chapels.[84] The Quakers were fairly evenly balanced between the sexes until the twentieth century. However, in general, a female preponderance – most noticeably among Congregationalists and Baptists – was already well established and widespread in the nineteenth century. These women also increasingly played leadership roles in the chapels.[85]

These processes were exacerbated by industrial conflicts and impoverishment. It is significant that, in the western half of the South Wales coalfield, the turning point in church membership statistics seems to coincide with the 1926 lockout.[86] Then, in the 1930s, about 250,000 mostly young people left the valleys in search of work, depriving the chapels of a generation of potential leaders (a problem also experienced in the equally hard-hit Durham coalfield). Of the population that remained an estimated 65 per cent, in 1937, were affected by unemployment. With impecunious congregations, total chapel debts in the area rose to an estimated £125,000. Many chapels could not afford pastors.[87] The English as opposed to Welsh-speaking chapels were particularly affected. In 1929 David Walters pleaded urgently on their behalf, predicting many closures if no help was forthcoming.[88]

Financial and social pressures

Financial acumen was already a much-needed attribute in a minister in the light of the debts incurred in the late nineteenth century wave of chapel building. Such matters, however, were conspicuously absent from the training college curriculum. Accordingly, the skills of someone like Robert Rowntree Clifford, who could in three years turn around a failing chapel with £1,000 debts and develop a thriving Baptist Central Mission in West Ham, remained uncommon.[89]

Financial skills became even more valuable in the face of the inflation during and immediately after the Great War. Thereafter, inflationary pressures were replaced by deflation. However, the high interest rates introduced to combat deflation in turn also hit the finances of heavily indebted chapels. Meanwhile, pew rents were increasingly abandoned from the 1890s, regarded as financially inefficient as well as socially divisive. They provided a fixed, predictable but inflexible income. Their replacement with a weekly envelope scheme – already widespread by 1920 and near universal by 1939 – was seen as a more buoyant and equitable form of fundraising, even if it did not prove any more lucrative in practice.[90]

The demands made upon chapel finance were increased by the population movements which continued unabated during the interwar years. Nearly four million houses were built between the wars, almost half on new estates. Meanwhile, in the old inner city areas the population was either vanishing or changing dramatically in character. The resulting 'vast areas of unoccupied pews each week' provided 'a short-cut to depression'.[91] In London's East End the difficulties accruing from the fact 'that as soon as men and women rise spiritually and socially they leave us for pleasanter surroundings' were compounded by their replacement with immigrants who proved more impervious to the appeal of Nonconformity.[92] Protestant church attendance declined dramatically in the older working-class areas of London in the first thirty years of the century.[93] The Congregationalists' Church Building and Extensions Committee therefore in 1929 recommended:

> Congregationalism has its work to do in down-town areas, but there are districts which have become largely industrial and commercial areas, and the Committee recommends that such problems should be boldly faced and that the remaining workers in the Churches in such areas should consider moving out to continue their work in new areas where the opportunities are larger.[94]

Such areas were plentiful: two years earlier the committee had declared: 'all over the country, but especially in the larger towns, there is a crying need for new churches'.[95] The urgency of this, in terms both of spiritual provision and of establishing a community, was realized by Anglicans and Free Churchmen alike. The Vicar of Heaton, Bradford, wrote in 1928:

> One of the chief problems of the Church to-day is presented by the sudden growth of large new housing areas, which have come into being in such abundance since the war ... The houses spring up with almost lightning rapidity; a large population appears within a very short time ... most of them with no close connection with any Church or Chapel.[96]

Without the advantage of a parish church or the greater financial resources of the Anglicans, the Nonconformist response to new estates was sluggish. Attempts to set up Free Church parishes in order to avoid overlapping efforts had lapsed since 1914. Faced with 'many churches ... in hopeless positions', and the need to group village chapels and population movements to new suburbs, the *Christian World* renewed the call for the setting up of Free Church parishes in 1925.[97] Arthur Black also concluded from his 1927–28 survey that this development was still desirable. Although a United Church Extension conference had met on the subject, Black felt that the necessary local cooperation had, however, become less evident in the face of 'the elaborate development and steady pressure of denominational machines upon ministers and churches'.[98] Church extension was meanwhile also hampered by the continuing burden of debt in the old residential areas. By 1938, it was clear that 'in Liverpool the Anglican and Roman Catholic churches are rising to the occasion in a wonderful way. The Free Churches are moving more slowly, though the Methodists show enterprise'.[99]

'Too often a large estate is built upon and the houses occupied before we have a church ready for the new residents', W. H. Lax lamented in 1934.[100] By 1937 twelve million people lived on estates built since 1918, which were devoid of much except housing. Community associations therefore arose in the 1930s to fill the void left by the builders. The community centres these provided often featured many of the aspects of the chapel community, including activities of a religious nature, but all within a secular context.[101] This complicated the chapel's task of establishing itself in what Lax recognized could prove unpropitiously soulless territory.

There were other financial challenges as well. Death deprived chapels of dominant patrons. In 1938 Victoria Road Methodists, Bradford, were still mourning the death of

David Yewdall in 1874, for, 'from that time until the present the Church has struggled alone without any dominant financial personality'.[102] Such patrons were of great importance in the nineteenth century, not least in the planting of new causes. In West Yorkshire the paternalism associated with great Nonconformist businessmen like Sir Titus Salt was so frequently extended to the chapel as well as the mill that several Congregational churches of the Riding were colloquially known by their benefactor's name.[103] When in the 1930s the local Methodist minister Fred Pratt Green opened a new chapel in Girlington, Bradford, largely financed by the mill-owning company Isaac Holden & Sons, he was amused to find that the letters IHS on the pulpit fall were associated by some in the congregation not with Christ's monogram, but instead with the initials of this local firm.[104] In South Wales these patronage connections had direct implications for employment. A Quaker report in 1926 noted:

> In the past it was impossible (it is still extremely difficult) for a man to get any post if his name was not on the membership roll of a Chapel. I have heard it stated that if a mine manager transferred his membership from one Chapel to another, it was the practice for the men in his employ to follow him for fear of losing their jobs.[105]

Certainly, colliery managers could be the financial mainstays of chapels in Durham into the twentieth century.[106]

Powerful patrons, such as Dame Sarah Lees of Hope Congregationalists, Oldham – a Liberal stalwart and the first female mayor of the town in 1910 – were, however, disappearing.[107] In 1926 in Liverpool it was noted, 'The problem of Finance has become acute. The death of large subscribers and the considerable increase of costs, have coincided with a period of trade depression that has affected all religious and charitable work adversely.'[108] Benefactors of the scale of Sir William Hartley or the first Lord Leverhulme were not replaced. The family of the Congregational businessman Sir Albert Spicer did not inherit his attitude to the text, 'honour the Lord with your substance and with the first fruits of all your increase' (Proverbs 3.9), and increasing taxation discouraged them from imitating his munificence.[109] West Yorkshire mills were taken over by firms that lacked both a local base and a relationship with the local chapel, which sometimes failed to survive the subsequent removal of support.[110] The generosity of J. Arthur Rank, his father Joseph, or Robert Wilson Black was increasingly exceptional. Thrifty self-made businessmen who gave thanks to God for their success by patronizing chapels were not a prominent feature of the interwar years.

Faith and culture

It has been suggested that these financial pressures help to explain shifts in the emphases of chapels. Simon Green has noted that in the late nineteenth century experiential religion was in decline in Nonconformity. For instance, class meetings were less common in Methodism, and even where they persisted, they 'ceased to be a means of grace'.[111] An emphasis on evangelism was instead replaced by associational culture, an emphasis on fellowship. In turning to a variety of activities, starting with bazaars and gradually encompassing a range of social pursuits, as means both of tapping additional finances and reaching out to the unchurched beyond their doors, the nature of chapel society subtly altered.

This trend was also encouraged by the theological changes of the period. There was less emphasis on the need to maintain the disciplines of the spirit. The value of recreation was at the same time increasingly appreciated. Chapel sports clubs and facilities, providing healthy recreation untainted by gambling, began to appear in the later nineteenth century.[112] Hitherto, one chapel history reflected 'Entertainments as we know them in present day church circles were then "taboo" and prayer meetings and classes served as a relaxation from daily toil.'[113] Unconsciously, worship was thus conflated into a range of relaxation activities, rather than as the regimen of the regenerate.

Some Nonconformists however continued to fulminate against the 'Devil's Amusements'.[114] In 1920 the eminent Baptist evangelical F. B. Meyer threatened to resign from his distinguished pastorate at Christ Church, Westminster Bridge Road, should dancing be permitted. The Free Churches, he complained, 'could not go in for amusement for the unregenerate without lowering the standards of the regenerate'.[115] The regenerate, however, were frequently no longer willing to accept such standards. Attendance at Attercliffe Congregationalists in Sheffield largely collapsed after W. W. Clayton arrived from rural Norfolk in 1925 and banned dancing just when it was becoming increasingly popular.[116] Indeed, the rapid spread and commercialization of dance halls in this era seems in general to have elicited little anxiety from the Free Church press.[117]

Concern remained much more about the public houses and music halls. With increasing leisure time, the provision of wholesome entertainment – far from being the work of the devil – was seen as a way of combating such unhealthy influences. One Wigan chapel of the Churches of Christ saw the departure of thirty members in 1939 over the unbiblical introduction of an organ.[118] Such rigour was, however, by then increasingly uncommon. In the Edwardian period chapels like Wigan Road United Methodists, Leigh, were incorporating billiards rooms in their design, while nearby Hope Congregationalists, Wigan, even had a nine-hole golf course.[119] Such facilities and the concerts, plays and even dances that had begun to appear were part of the chapels' service to the community. They could also assist evangelism. Berkeley Street Congregationalists, Liverpool, was revived as a result of a social club started on the premises in 1919.[120] Through the beneficence of Dame Sarah Lees, Hope Congregationalists, Oldham (and other local churches), enjoyed thriving youth organizations, including football and cricket pitches, tennis courts and a bowling green.[121] Local church-based football or cricket leagues were not uncommon, and by the end of the 1930s, neither were drama clubs.

Entertainment and recreation could be portrayed as part of, rather than distractions from, the church's mission. They were, Eastbrook Hall noted, 'a means of grace through which the Master of all life is able to approach the boy or girl who is afraid of sentiment but revels in ardent exercise and adventure'.[122] The entertainment they provided was justified by evocations of muscular Christianity. Necessarily developing their own membership and subscription systems, however, these sports clubs and leagues steadily become more autonomous from their chapels of origin.

It is striking that Nonconformist churchgoing started to decline just at the moment, around the 1880s, when this associational culture began to proliferate. Robin Gill's meticulous statistical work is used to argue that overbuilding helped to create this crisis.[123] The churches drew the wrong lesson from the single datum point of the religious census of 1851: that there needed to be more provision for worshippers. For instance, the Methodists were prompted to set up their Metropolitan Chapel Building Fund in 1861 in the belief that '10% of those resident in London should find a spiritual home within the Methodist family', and built accordingly.[124] Combined with shifting populations, the result too often was over provision in the wrong places: the chapels accordingly both appeared empty and were burdened with debt.[125] For Simon Green, the associational culture used to tackle this debt was a cure worse than the disease. It undermined the distinctiveness of the chapels and their doctrines. Their congregations' relationship to them also became more instrumental and shallow, just when increasing numbers of secular organizations and activities were appearing that could challenge them. Turning the chapels into leisure organizations made them vulnerable to this competition.[126] All the main threats listed by Black in his analysis of church decline in 1927–28 were social distractions: the gramophone, wireless, cinema, the growth of weekend charabanc rides and the Sunday press. In addition, old church connections were broken and not renewed in the population movements of the period. With the State increasingly taking responsibility for social conditions, the working classes increasingly looked to the State for justice, not to the churches for charity.[127] The churches in consequence became more peripheral to the community.

Arguably, however, associational culture was a subsidiary rather than the prime cause of this marginalization. The churches, in providing associational activities, were responding to a rising demand for leisure and recreation affecting the whole of society, churched and unchurched. It was this demand, and the associated tendency to see church attendance as a lifestyle choice, that the churches were reflecting and unconsciously furthering through the provision of associational culture. As a result, although doubt played a part in Black's explanation for falling attendances, it was relevance rather than plausibility that was the problem. Associational culture could maintain the social relevance of chapels, but undermine their spiritual relevance. Men might go to them to play snooker, but not to be saved.

This need for salvation was less apparent in the interwar years. In 1932 the leading Methodist (and Socialist) J. Ernest Rattenbury complained, 'There is little consciousness of sin … Men feel no need of a Saviour.'[128] In the same year J. W. James introduced his senior deacon to a discussion group of working-class non-churchgoers he had set up. The deacon's reaction was:

> When I was a young man, and was asked to join the Church, I felt myself too unworthy, too sinful to do so. But those young fellows last night, without exception, spoke as if they were too good to join the Church. They think the Church isn't good enough for them. I can't get over it.[129]

Neither could the churches. They were faced with an intangible, but progressive loss of a sense of sin and personal responsibility. As one YMCA worker explained of the soldiers on the Western Front: 'They have a great admiration for Jesus Christ and look upon him as a great example for men, but since they have no real conviction of sin, they naturally do not look upon Him as their Saviour.'[130] A large proportion of these men would have been to Sunday School, but the religion they there acquired seems to have been exemplary – consisting of precepts and maxims – rather than soteriological. At the front the widespread use of talismans suggests that it was also infused with quasi-magical properties. Such practices, however, reflected folk religion that already had wide currency in the nineteenth century.[131] It is too simplistic to suggest that it was encouraged by the associational culture of the late nineteenth-century churches. It is also too simplistic to suggest that shifts in belief and relations with the churches were dramatically disrupted by the First World War.

After all, although unbelief was rare in pre-war Britain, 80 per cent of the army had no vital church connection, a tendency which increased as the war went on.[132] Chaplains like Gray commented on their existing alienation from the churches, their pettifogging rules and effete clergy.[133] This seems to have been particularly marked among those more subject to the pettifogging rules of the army itself in the base camps of the ever growing number of non-combatants.[134] For those in the Line, soldiers' experience of facing death seems neither to have brought about drastic loss of an already often vague faith, or the revival that many in the churches hoped and energetically worked for. It is true that some were driven from the chapels as a result of the frequently unsympathetic response to conscientious objectors, but to be driven out they had to be there in the first place.

Meanwhile, for the minority who attended before 1914, the realization that the chapels had changed far less than they had did not necessarily discomfort the returning soldiers. Initially at least they offered a comfortingly familiar world after harrowing experiences.[135] There were many widely scattered chapels that grew serenely in the 1920s. Efforts were made to welcome the returning servicemen, even as efforts had been made to keep in touch with them through the dispatch of news and parcels throughout the war. By the 1930s, however, the re-establishment of familiarity may have seemed less reassuring in the face of the Slump. Benson Perkins found that the Men's Own meeting for the unemployed that he inherited on coming to the Sheffield Methodist Mission in 1935 was full of bitter, Communist-flavoured invective against the churches.[136]

This process seems also to have been encouraged by an increasing popular emphasis on being modern and up-to-date, attributes which were not readily associated with the church, as a result of the considerable social and economic changes of the period. A Merseyside survey in 1934 suggested a missing generation in Protestant churches, the results of the depredations of death, deprivation, distractions or doubt.[137] By 1951, Seebohm Rowntree and George Lavers found that apathy and ignorance characterized the attitude to religion of large sections of society.[138]

This does not mean that conversions became entirely things of the past, though there is evidence that the adherents from whom they were frequently drawn were in overall decline, especially in the 1930s.[139] In the 1920s T. Wilkinson Riddle habitually succeeded in drawing an extra congregation of two thousand to the Palace Theatre, Plymouth, in addition to his regular thousand-strong Sunday evening throng.[140] In 1935

F. W. Chudleigh, the Socialist who ran the Methodist East End Mission, proclaimed, 'The days of dramatic conversions are with us and are not passed.'[141] Revivals certainly did not cease after the great Welsh eruption of 1904–5. The most successful of the interwar years seems to have been that on coastal Norfolk in the early 1920s.[142] Inland, however, 'the apparent inability to get men and women to a definite decision' for Christ complained of in Attleborough Wesleyan circuit in 1922, seems to have been the more common state of affairs.[143]

Before 1914, week-long missions to win conversions had been a common feature of chapel life. These, however, became less conspicuous in the interwar years. Though professional evangelists like Gipsy Smith continued to draw crowds on preaching tours, doubts about the value of such efforts were increasingly expressed. There was a distinct lack of enthusiasm in some chapels. Gipsy Smith's biographer complained: 'I could name churches where when there has been a mission nearly all the leading members have deliberately absented themselves.' Ministers were often similarly lukewarm.[144] Some were perhaps dubious about the theology of the evangelists. Seaward Beddow, the Socialist and Pacifist minister at Wycliffe Congregational Church in Leicester, considered that their preaching ignored social Christianity. Soper was similarly dubious about evangelism.[145] There was also concern that the souls won by such efforts were either rapidly lost once again or proved to be existing church members reaffirming their faith. The fact that many chapels were unprepared to provide a spiritual home when converts were referred to them did not help matters: 'There have been well-authenticated cases in which a conventional Church had no means of attracting and keeping and employing the poorer converts who signed, so advised them to go straight off to the Salvation Army.'[146]

Traditional evangelical methods made little headway in depressed or inner city areas. Before turning successfully to films Tiplady tried a fortnight mission, including house-to-house visitation, open air and weeknight meetings: 'In a provincial town such an effort would have filled any church, but in Lambeth it brought nobody in.'[147] In 1936 a Baptist evangelical team active in South Wales for four years questioned whether traditional forms of evangelism were really appropriate, especially given the hostility they had encountered in the valleys.[148] In contrast, the industrial missions of S. E. Keeble and others to South Wales in the 1920s had some success. In Tonypandy, Keeble was told by a group including the Baptist Labour MP Will John that his influence had helped them to a concept of Socialism harmonious with and derived from Christianity.[149]

Social witness

The chapels had to respond to the social conditions and unemployment endemic in South Wales and elsewhere during the interwar years. The *Methodist Times* suggested that they should be as available for demonstrations against the moral evil of unemployment as those of drink or gambling.[150] Even the NUWM cooperated with London chapels and the Brotherhood in organizing such demonstrations in

1924.[151] In Liverpool, Hope Street Unitarians supplied free food and medical attention to the unemployed.[152] J. Vint Laughland of Pembroke Chapel was meanwhile busily organizing them.[153] His depth of involvement with left-wing unemployed agitation was, however, somewhat unusual for a minister. Chapels as institutions generally concentrated on relief work. Those in mining areas were particularly active in this field in 1926 and after.

The Congregationalists' Social Service Committee recommended that chapels provide reading rooms and material; alleviation of special distress; help with claim forms and finding re-employment; facilities for craft work, boot repair and similar activities; and the arrangement of concerts, games and amusements.[154] Complying with these was of course beyond the resources of many chapels. In Liverpool such efforts were therefore essentially confined to the larger chapels.[155] In many cases it was the local Free Church Council, not individual chapels, which made these provisions. The most ambitious efforts to create work and a sense of community were undertaken by the Quakers, primarily in South Wales. The various enterprises they established, most notably at Brynmawr, were echoed by those set up by R. J. Barker at Community House in Tonypandy.[156]

In South Wales the chapels also shared fully in the mobilization of the community against the impositions of the household means test introduced in 1931 as a condition for long-term unemployment benefit. Leon Atkin used his Central Hall in Bargoed to house the unemployed and circumvent its provisions.[157] As the Quakers pointed out, by taking any household earnings into account in benefit calculations, the means test penalized those Nonconformist virtues of thrift and self-help.[158] The Gateshead Methodist minister Maldwyn Edwards also noted the effect on families: 'It was particularly galling when a son or daughter's wages were virtually supporting the family – it was hard for the young people but most humiliating for the parents.'[159] The *Baptist Times*, influenced perhaps by the fact that the Liberal National Minister of Labour, Ernest Brown, was a Baptist, nevertheless seems not to have understood why Baptist ministers and chapels in South Wales were so opposed to the indignities this involved.[160] In areas where the unemployed were less noticeable within the congregations, the chapels were less active in criticizing the manner of their relief. It was only after William Dick organized the Workers' Christian Fellowship in 1936 with the assistance of several Labour MPs that the role of pressing for better treatment for the unemployed (through a Christian alternative to the NUWM) was added to that of ministering to them.

Meanwhile more well-established facets of chapel social witness were in unspectacular decline. The diminishing vigour of the chapels' commitment to temperance, and dismay at the way in which social convention was intruding drink into the Nonconformist lifestyle was a constant refrain of the UKA by the 1930s. 'In far too many cases the old Band of Hope has been allowed to cease and the juvenile organisations which have taken its place either neglect the temperance question altogether or do not place sufficient emphasis on it in their programme', Robert Wilson Black lamented.[161] Young Quakers were already abandoning temperance in the 1920s.[162] Though denominational leaders urged that there should be no congregation where children, 'are without efficient instruction on this subject which so vitally affects their temporal and spiritual welfare', the numbers of Bands of Hope declined steadily.[163] In 1914–15 the Band of Hope Union had 34,502 constituent societies and was still expanding.[164] By 1939–40 only 8,674 were reported.[165] The rate at which the chapel was ceasing to define the social attitudes of its congregation must not, however, be overestimated. Mass Observation's anthropological investigations in Bolton in 1938–39 found anti-drink sentiment still entrenched in the local chapels.[166] The advent of the improved public house and the increased sobriety of the interwar years were gradually modifying Nonconformist attitudes to drink. Drinkers were, however, still far from numerous in the congregations.

This did not mean that there were not Nonconformists who drank or bet, nor chapels which resorted to the dubious device of raffles in their search for funds. The chapel ethos produced by anti-drink and anti-gambling propaganda was neither universally promoted nor respected. Breaches of the ethos were, however, rarely public and there was little debate about its validity. Anti-drink and anti-gambling attitudes continued to characterize chapel society.

So too did an enthusiasm for peace. A large minority of Nonconformist congregations affiliated to the LNU, though this figure peaked at 2,090 in 1932 and then almost halved during the rest of the decade.[167] In 1929, 246 Congregational, 171 Unitarian, 114 Wesleyan, 93 Primitive Methodist, 81 Presbyterian, 57 Baptist, and 25 other Nonconformist congregations were also affiliated to the World Alliance for Promoting International Friendship through the Churches.[168]

Few, however, were committed to Pacifism. A handful of Pacifist chapels set up by conscientious objectors ejected from their own churches appeared in the aftermath of the Great War.[169] Thereafter their visibility declined before re-emerging amid the increasing international tensions of the 1930s. Pacifist resolutions were then passed by assemblies of Welsh Baptists and Independents.[170] In Pratt Green's North London circuit at the end of the 1930s, he and a colleague were the only non-Pacifists out of seven Methodist ministers.[171] With such ministerial enthusiasm, Pacifists could even come to dominate a particular congregation, as with Soper's Islington Mission.[172] The same happened at Queen's Road Baptists, Coventry, where Ingli James's dissatisfaction with Labour's position on the subject led him in 1937 to attempt to found a Christian Pacifist party.[173]

However, by 1939 there were at most 15,000 enrolled with Christian Pacifist societies.[174] Most Nonconformists accepted war against Hitler as they had a generation earlier accepted war in defence of Belgium, yet they approached it in a more tolerant and regretful spirit. This both reflected the effect of interwar peace propaganda and that conscription meant that there was no need for the chapels to take part in justifying the war, with the accompanying rhetoric and tensions. There was therefore none of the bellicose pulpit language of 1914–18. The hostility Pacifists had faced in many chapels was nevertheless still far from absent.[175]

In contrast, church/chapel relations were improved from the mutually exclusive communities frequently found in the nineteenth century. Passive Resistance in 1902 certainly revived old animosities, but was largely a middle-class phenomenon. Nevertheless, it was not without influence on working-class Primitive Methodists, especially in rural districts, where the denomination was strongest and where the abundance of single school areas and the dictatorial insensitivity of some incumbents encouraged strongly disestablishmentarian sentiments.[176]

There were denominational, regional and class-related variations in the chapel's attitude to education and the related issues of disestablishmentarian and anti-Catholic sentiment. The impact of the Irish on the local labour market encouraged the anti-Catholicism expressed in the Free Churches of Merseyside, not least during the controversies over building grants for Catholic schools that ensued from the 1936 Education Act. However, even in Lancashire, the most Catholic county in England, there was no unanimity about the evils of denominational education. The Wesleyans, Baptists and Unitarians all had elementary schools in the county.

Disestablishmentarian sentiment was meanwhile undermined by growing cooperation with the Church of England, even in rural areas. The disappearance of the arrogant hostility that formerly characterized many clergymen's attitudes to Nonconformity was an important factor in such developments. It was this process which had, by 1959, according to the *Christian World*, made the Liberation Society's existence increasingly unnecessary.[177]

Sabbatarianism also gradually declined. Whereas in the nineteenth century the formal membership, if not the adherents, could be expected to attend several times on a Sunday, this discipline was relaxing. The world in which all secular activities – even in some cases shaving or cooking the Sunday joint – had been suspended for a day, was hard to recapture after a war which was no respecter of the Sabbath. The fact that Alan Wilkinson's father in 1922 published a pamphlet in defence of the English Sunday showed that it increasingly needed defending.[178] In the interwar years, secular entertainments increasingly encroached on the Sunday. The Congregational minister and Labour MP Gordon Lang lamented in 1931, 'There are those who regard the Sunday – and some of my hon. Friends, no doubt, will be putting this case shortly – as a day of Christian festival, and consider that, after their celebration, they are entitled to enjoy themselves and spend the rest of the day in pleasure.' The Unitarian and Conservative MP Neville Chamberlain observed during the same debate:

> One has only to go into the country to-day and look at the golf courses, the tennis courts and the main roads on which people drive from London and other big towns to take their pleasure in the country, to realise how much the idea of what is proper and decent to do on Sunday has changed since the days of our forefathers.[179]

Conclusion

The rituals and disciplines of chapel life were disappearing. Already by 1914, many nineteenth-century characteristics of Nonconformist worship were moribund.[180] The prayer meetings and class meetings had encouraged worshippers to define their relationship with, and experience of, God. They supplied a means whereby ordinary members of the congregation could live and describe their faith, thus mitigating the traditional dominance of the pulpit in Free Church worship. Nor were they necessarily testamentary. They could become 'forums for industrial dispute', where the Lord was urged to intervene on behalf of the workers against certain stiff-necked employers.[181] An inspirational vein of idealism ran through the prayer meetings at John Taylor's Primitive Methodist chapel in Durham in the 1920s.[182] By then, however, few Nonconformists shared this experience. Despite periodic lamentations throughout the period that the demise of camp meetings, prayer meetings and class meetings had severely affected both experiential religion and conversion, it seemed few wanted to. The testimonies and prayers of the converted had little appeal for a generation less enthusiastic about the public examination of their souls. Changing social sensibilities, which also contributed to the disappearance of the hallelujahs and amens that formerly punctuated services, clearly had a role in this development.[183]

The increasing reluctance to speak of religious experience also bore witness to declining ability to define its nature. Its clarity was undermined by the theological developments of the later nineteenth century. The ensuing rise of liberal theology removed both the note of urgency from preaching and the fervour from conversion experience. The Social Gospel emphasized everyday social experience more than it did spiritual experience. The exhortation to personal religion and scriptural holiness became less pronounced, and so did its practice. The prayer meetings therefore ceased to concentrate upon experience of God. Like liberal theology itself, they came to reflect an interest in fellowship, not redemption. E. Middleton Weaver found in his survey of Huddersfield Methodism that those class meetings that survived had metamorphosed into Fraternals, Fellowships or Home Circles.[184]

The sermon had always been a particular glory of Nonconformity.[185] Its centrality to Free Church worship was enhanced by these developments. This situation placed the chapel's fortunes in a position of vulnerability to the capabilities of the preacher unparalleled among Anglicans and Catholics, and a tendency to blame inadequate sermons for declining attendance was a natural if not entirely justifiable reflection of this. Nowhere was this more marked than in Liverpool. William Paxton, whose considerable talents restored the declining Congregational Chapel in Great George Street to its former glory, was moved publicly to deplore the fickle attention Liverpool paid to a preacher, and not a church.[186] The departure of a popular preacher almost invariably affected the congregation adversely, though the retention of class meetings helped County Road Methodists to maintain congregational loyalty and tide themselves over times of poor preaching.[187]

The dominance of the preacher could overshadow the spiritual life of the chapel. Nevertheless, the declining tolerance of extempore worship as evidenced by the demise of prayer meetings and the gradual disappearance of family prayers, also affected the sermon. An increasing reliance on preaching did not necessarily lead to its exaltation, but to the diminishing of the whole art of worship.[188] One church, Pratt Green noticed, had even resorted to the inducement, 'We guarantee that our service will be over within an hour.'[189] Furthermore, oligarchic cliques did not always pass on leadership to the younger generation until it was too late.[190] This did little to preserve the vigour of an increasingly ageing Nonconformity.[191]

Its principles were no longer emphasized. A 1908 survey of Liverpool Nonconformity found large numbers of chapels had no classes on church membership or Free Church convictions.[192] Affected by the ecumenism of the interwar period, those symptoms became more general. 'We don't stress the points on which we differ from the Established Church', J. D. Jones complained in 1938. 'Our people are no longer instructed in their principles. They don't know why they are Free Churchmen. They are Presbyterians, Congregationalists, Baptists, Methodists – not by conviction but simply by tradition … Consequently their Free Churchism is a rather feeble and ineffective thing.'[193] The shift to supply the recreation and entertainment demanded by congregations increasingly familiar with the wireless and cinema did little to preserve either the vigour or the values of chapel society. The BCA found that it led to 'the almost complete absence of literary and debating societies which in former days did so much towards the training of thinkers, workers and speakers for our various organisations' – or indeed for outside bodies such as the Labour Party.[194]

This was not the universal experience, but it was the trend of the interwar years. While the chapel remained central to the lives of many, its influence became more diffuse. The expulsions that had enforced the chapel ethos upon the congregation dwindled rapidly from the 1880s onwards.[195] Newer disciplines did not take their place. The world of the chapel became less distinctive, less definite. By the 1930s the chapel, not least because of the atrophy of some of its characteristic organizations and principles, was no longer so central an influence on the attitudes of its congregation.

4

The Politics of Pewmanship

Free Churchmen no longer instinctively and as a whole turn to the Liberal Party to secure their aims; they have become so divided in their allegiances that leaders of political parties no longer find it necessary to take the views of Nonconformists into serious consideration.

Albert Peel[1]

Most preachers … are acquainted with the prosperous layman who lays a condescending hand on one's shoulder after a pulpit reference to a glaring industrial evil. His eyes are wistful, and there is pathos in his voice as he explains that what he wants when he comes to church is not economics, but the 'simple Gospel'. He usually means that if his parson dares to suggest that the Gospel is going to interfere with the profits of respectable business there will be trouble.

W. G. Peck[2]

Chapels and the interwar electoral setting

Nonconformists as a percentage of the electorate peaked between the 1867 and 1884 Reform Acts. This was also the period in which their alignment with Liberalism was consolidated, before the Irish Home Rule issue drew off the Liberal Unionists led by the Unitarian Joseph Chamberlain, taking with them into the Conservative fold a considerable number of Free Churchmen. In 1892, it was estimated that a fifth of Unitarians were now Unionists, concentrated in the wealthier chapels of the denomination. If anything, the effect among Congregationalists was even greater in particular areas: a survey of London Congregationalists in 1894 revealed that 35 per cent of those replying were opposed to the recently defeated Home Rule Bill.[3]

The peculiar circumstances of the 1906 election, and the way in which the chapels acted as auxiliaries to sometimes reluctant Liberal associations in that contest, nevertheless gave the appearance of a solid Nonconformist voting bloc, not least to those Free Churchmen who campaigned hardest in the Liberal cause. By 1909, however, the notion of a particular Nonconformist contribution to politics was being disparaged, while in London it was by then recognized that 'Nonconformity is largely leavened with a Conservative element'.[4] The political cohesiveness of the chapels – as well as their cultural cohesiveness – was in decline. Furthermore, as Arthur Porritt pointed out, following the enfranchisement of 1918 Nonconformists were proportionately much less significant electorally.[5] His newspaper accordingly noted, following that year's election, that only eighty-eight Nonconformist MPs had been returned to Parliament, the lowest number since 1880 (see Appendix, which draws on wider sources and gives the higher figure of 119).[6]

If Nonconformists were over-represented in the pre-1918 electorate, the young were massively under-represented. Adult males between the ages of twenty-one and thirty were a third of the 1911 adult male population, but only one-seventh of the electorate. They were particularly under-represented in the boroughs, where the urban working classes were concentrated.[7] This changed when the 1918 legislation effectively provided for adult (over twenty-one) male suffrage for parliamentary elections. It also enfranchised women over thirty who qualified as local government voters either in their own right or through their husbands. For local elections the franchise remained linked to property: of the 4 million new male parliamentary electors three-quarters were young lodgers who – as tenants of furnished rooms – continued to be unable to vote locally. Young women who inhabited furnished rooms also continued to be excluded from both franchises until the parliamentary voting age for women was lowered to twenty-one in 1928. Thereafter younger women, more likely to be living in furnished rooms, remained less likely to have the municipal vote.[8] This situation only changed with the equalization of the franchise qualifications passed in 1948.

In 1948 the plural vote was also abolished. Hitherto a qualified elector could vote twice (unlimited times before 1911). This gave a certain advantage to the Conservatives: indeed, the Tories had deliberately widened the qualification for the business vote with this in mind during the passage of the 1918 Act.[9] This business vote dominated some local government wards such as St Peter's, Liverpool and probably also helped the Unitarian Peter Eckersley win Manchester Exchange as a Conservative in 1935 general election.

The 1918 changes thus only partially transformed the British electoral scene. Pre-war voters (and their wives) formed the bulk of the new electorate. Radical changes to the electoral system were contemplated, but abandoned during the passage of the legislation. The only constituencies which in the end adopted the Single Transferable Vote (STV) that had been mooted were the university seats retained, like plural voting, until 1948.

Since STV was designed in the mid-nineteenth century to protect the representation of minorities, it might be speculated that it could have been used by Free Churchmen to ensure a reasonable sprinkling of candidates in favour of schemes such as temperance in the multi-member constituencies. In practice, neither Nonconformists nor bodies like the UKA seem to have scented this opportunity. Moreover, although the Liberals belatedly converted to electoral reform in the early 1920s when it became apparent that they were now an electoral minority, changing the franchise did not feature prominently in Free Church discourse. The Quaker and Labour MP C. H. Wilson was a member of the executive committee of the Proportional Representation Society and secured an important amendment to introduce the alternative vote to the Electoral

Reform Bill introduced in January 1931. The minority Labour government which brought in that bill in order to retain Liberal support, however did not generally share Wilson's enthusiasm for the cause, and nor did the Free Church press.[10]

Other electoral changes were introduced which proved inimical to Nonconformist political mobilization. Elections from 1918 took place on a single day, rather than over several weeks. This placed a premium on the ability to get the vote out in a particular constituency, rather than the rolling bandwagons of pre-war elections. The electorates of these constituencies were also much larger and their boundaries were redrawn in 1918 to make them more socially homogenous. This process created more defined working-class and middle-class seats, particularly in urban areas.[11] It did nothing, however, to assist the electoral significance of local cross-class bodies such as the chapels. In that sense, the interwar electoral system was restructured against the interests both of the Liberals and the Nonconformists.

The increased social homogeneity, particularly of urban seats, helps to explain an apparent trend towards class-based voting which impressed historians in the 1970s.[12] Contemporary observers, however, lacked detailed information on such matters until the first, largely unremarked, opinion polls commenced in 1937. Electoral commentary accordingly tended towards the impressionistic. While inflected with languages of class in the period, it was not until the pioneering psephological studies of the 1950s and 1960s that it was to become the dominant narrative.[13]

In part, this was because a class-based model had clear limitations. The Liberals, for instance, retained a number of urban seats in places as far-flung as Bethnal Green, Middlesbrough or Birkenhead until the Second World War and in none of these did they benefit from a substantial Nonconformist presence. An identity of interest between Labour and working-class voters was not successfully inculcated everywhere, and arguably in Bethnal Green was thrown away by the conduct of the local party.[14] It therefore appears that electoral sociology in the form of class was only one of four factors (discussed more fully in Chapter 7) shaping voting patterns in the period: the others being the structuring of the electoral system; its effects on party strategy and behaviour; its geography; and issues and events.

The latter arguably bulked relatively large in a number of the elections in these years. The elections of 1924 and 1931 were fought against backdrops of either external or economic panic in which large swathes of voters were stampeded into the Tory fold to keep out the untrustworthy and inexperienced Labour Party. The desire for the stability that the Conservatives or the National government seemed to offer probably contributed to the phenomenon of crowds of Nonconformists cheering 'like mad at each Conservative success' that so distressed the *Yorkshire Observer*'s Free Church correspondent in 1924.[15] Certainly, there is evidence that, in the widespread absence of Liberal candidates, the Nonconformist vote went more to the Conservatives that year.[16]

The salience of issues (as well as the effects of the re-structuring of the electoral system) is also apparent in the extent to which all parties felt constrained to make national rather than sectional appeals. Indeed, for Labour this was particularly important given the way in which it was painted by its opponents as an unpatriotic party pursuing narrow class interests.

Issues could nonetheless still differ according to setting or region. Thus, while the 1923 election saw a Liberal resurgence in defence of free trade, in the last election in which this subject mattered, that revival was swollen in rural areas as the Conservatives reneged on promises to support corn prices when farmers were hit by post-war losses, and by Labour's lack of candidates and inexperience in contesting rural areas.[17] It was not until 1929 that Labour was really able to fight a national campaign, in an election in which the countryside was specifically targeted by the party.[18] Until then, a concentration on more promising areas led to potential rural breakthroughs not being followed up. For instance, in South West England wartime unionization saw Labour's vote share climb locally to 29.4 per cent in 1918, before falling back.[19]

The most westerly part of this region was Cornwall. This was the poorest English county. Its poverty, however, did not lead to class-based voting. Instead, it was an area of relative Liberal success between the wars. Given that it was also England's most Nonconformist county, this coincidence has often been seen as proof that a local concentration of Free Church voting strength in such regions could still deliver for their traditional political allies.[20] According to the maverick Oxford historian, sometime Labour candidate and professional Cornishman A. L. Rowse, chapels in the county in the 1920s acted as 'virtually Liberal recruiting stations'.[21]

However, a number of caveats need to be offered. First, Labour did not have a local concentration of heavily unionized industrial workers to draw on in the region in the way that commonly gave them a core vote elsewhere. Even where there was arguably such a concentration, in nearby Devonport for example, the overlay of defence and imperial interests in the naval dockyard meant that maverick Tories like Nancy Astor or maverick Liberals like Leslie Hore-Belisha tended to prove more successful than their Labour opponents. Secondly, this illustrates that such interests continued to overlay class identities. Arguably this was a facet of the entire South-West, given the success of Liberal appeals to the interests of small traders in a region characterized by small-scale industry rather than the agglomerations of workers in large factories and social housing estates which elsewhere proved more conducive to building a working-class identity and Labour voting habit.[22] Thirdly, there is the problem of disaggregating what are class interests. Clearly, the notion that voting is determined by either identity or instrumentality is a false dichotomy.[23] Class, after all, is often simply an unconscious rationalization of instrumental attitudes and interests. What is apparently either 'class-based' or 'religion-based' voting may in practice simply involve the application of labels to attitudes derived from more material considerations. Finally, there was a distinctive quality about these religious identities in Cornwall. Nonconformity in the county was dominated by Methodists. Liberal candidates such as Isaac Foot and Walter Runciman were also usually Methodists. The former in particular, in revivalist-style campaigns, would play on this identity of interest with many of his electors.[24]

This dominance of local Nonconformity by one particular denomination occurred in various regions of the country. In addition to Cornish Methodism, there was the strength of the Calvinistic Methodists in areas of North Wales, the Presbyterians in rural Northumberland and Congregationalism in parts of the West Riding. This needs to borne in mind when considering the apparent lessons of Table 8. This uses Michael Kinnear's calculation of the size of the Nonconformist vote in 1922, constituency by

Table 8 The relationship between the size of the Nonconformist vote (1922 figures) and seats won by each party in the general elections in England, 1918–35

% Nonconformist 1922	% Won by Liberals[a]	% Won by Labour	% Won by Conservative	No. of seats
Over 20	40.0	2.9	57.1	5
15.0–19.9	34.8	20.5	42.9	16
12.5–14.9	20.7	12.1	67.1	20
10.0–12.4	17.9	23.9	57.0	82
7.5–9.9	13.8	23.8	61.8	117
5.0–7.4	9.1	17.5	71.3	111
0.0–4.9	5.5	30.7	61.5	62

Note: Excludes London, Middlesex county divisions and the university seats.

[a] This figure includes the various Liberal groupings. These figures have been recalculated and differ slightly from Kinnear's.

Sources: Michael Kinnear, *The British Voter: An Atlas and Survey since 1885* (London: Batsford, 1981), pp. 125–9; F. W. S. Craig, *British Parliamentary Election Results 1918–1949* (Glasgow: Political Reference Publications, 1969).

constituency, to analyse its electoral effects. Ostensibly, this shows a positive correlation between the success rate of a contracting Liberal Party and the local size of the Nonconformist vote. This variable does not seem to have significance when applied to the electorally dominant Conservative Party. However, this table could be read to suggest that chapel voters had a clearly negative effect on Labour's electoral prospects. A number of caveats need to be expressed about such findings. The apparent correlation with lack of Labour success reflects the fact that the most Nonconformist seats tended to be rural, in areas where Labour generally was less effectively organized. Accordingly, party behaviour – as much as Nonconformity –was a factor in the results. These findings reflect that – notwithstanding the large numbers of Nonconformist candidates which Labour ran, often in constituencies where they had few co-religionists – the party's electoral core lay in urban working-class seats with a limited Free Church presence. They by no means prove that Nonconformists did not vote Labour, simply that chapel voters did not have a significant impact on Labour's propensity to win seats.

Similar considerations apply to the apparent correlation with Liberal success. This is partly because the sample of heavily Nonconformist constituencies was relatively small. Historically, these were areas of Liberal success, and many of them had the same, locally popular candidates standing in the Liberal interest regularly throughout the period. These candidates largely held these seats when, as in 1931, the Liberals fought few constituencies but were given clear runs by the Tories in most of these. Nonconformity thus may help to explain why these seats came to be seen as Liberal in the first place, but party behaviour also reinforced Liberal successes in them. It might also be noted that the Tories did even better than the Liberals in these very Nonconformist areas, which suggests that even if Nonconformity were an important factor it was by no means the only one.

Finally, many of these heavily Nonconformist areas of continued Liberal success were also dominated by one particular denomination. Insofar as Nonconformity was a factor, it is likely that it was shaped by this situation. In particular, it meant that social competition was not so much between the various Free Church denominations, but between a dominant denomination and either Anglicanism or Catholicism. In such settings, ostensibly religious voting can reflect other factors: for instance, Methodist farmers in Cornwall or Norfolk voting against Anglican landlords or because of tithe disputes. These differential strengths and concentrations in religious groups particularly shape voting behaviour when:

(a) They map onto other cleavages, such as in the local labour market, as in the Protestant/Catholic divide which was particularly marked in Liverpool but also found in a number of other Northern cities;
(b) There is a large religious identity to respond against, such as Catholicism in these locations;
(c) The dominant religious identity was able to mobilize its adherents politically, either directly through a defence of their interests, or structurally, by shaping value systems in ways which impinge also upon wider society.

The first two of these factors helped to structure the strident Protestant Toryism of Lancashire, particularly among those who felt more economically threatened by Irish immigrant labour. Thus, into the 1950s, Stephen Mayor found that whereas the middle-class members of his Congregational chapel in Merseyside voted Liberal the working-class members were correspondingly Conservative.[25] The third factor includes the idealistic internationalism that became a particular feature of interwar Liberalism, but only seems to have had significant electoral appeal in places like Cornwall.[26]

Outside such areas, religious adherence seems to have been less likely to significantly shape voting behaviour. Accordingly, in Andrew Thorpe's case study of Derby, although there were strong religious traditions, not least for Nonconformity, no particular denomination predominated and religion did not become a key identifier of politico-social cleavages and thus a mobilizer for one party or another. In Thorpe's view, this made it relatively easy for Nonconformists to switch to a new political identity of Labour – particularly given that this railway town furnished the core of regularly employed unionized labour around which the new party could gather support.[27]

Chapels and labour

A change in issues aided this process. Core messages widely shared by Liberals and Nonconformists before 1918 were either no longer salient, such as Welsh disestablishment, or no longer so distinctly Liberal, such as temperance reform. Newly enfranchised younger Nonconformists and those not socialized into Liberal voting during the long gap between the elections of 1910 and that of 1918, thus found their electoral choices less obvious than for their forebears.

Furthermore, many of the new voters, the generation brought up since the rise of Socialism in the 1880s, had never voted before. They rose to adulthood and political maturity after the consensus about a liberal political economy, which formed the voting habits of Philip Snowden's father's generation, had been replaced by the uncertainty about unemployment and the dilution of skilled wages ushered in by a more competitive global economy and volatile labour market at the end of the nineteenth century. The dilution of skills and resulting changes to pay differentials broke down historic horizontal boundaries within the working classes which had restricted class solidarity. Meanwhile, the creation of mass culture in the second half of the nineteenth century through the rise of entertainment forms such as the music hall or the popular newspaper helped to consolidate the working class. So did the advent of universal and free elementary education after 1891.[28] In the process, these developments also helped to diminish the social and educational advantages and distinctiveness that a chapel background could bring.

As Michael Childs has demonstrated, even before 1914, these young male working-class voters hitherto differentially excluded from the franchise were expected by Liberal analyses to take any opportunity presented to support the new left-wing party. The Liberals also seem to have been correct in assuming that they would be differentially affected by the enfranchisement of this group and of women.[29] In Nonconformity as well, there is evidence of an intergenerational shift by the 1930s, depending on class, away from the Liberals and towards their Labour and Tory opponents.[30] When George Thomas's mother joined the Labour Party in 1915 she was told by her father, 'The Liberals were the radicals when I was young. If I were your age, I'd probably be joining the Labour Party.'[31]

Many portrayed such decisions as natural outcomes of their faith. Thus the Bolton Labour councillor W. M. Farrington explained at a Labour meeting, 'I was converted to Socialism through being a Sunday School teacher.'[32] For many among the first generation of Labour politicians, both local and national, the chapel was the cradle of the idealism they took into the movement. For these men and women, growing up in the late nineteenth century when Nonconformity and its Sunday Schools were at their height, chapels provided opportunities of advancement and training not readily available elsewhere. To varying degrees chapels were democratic societies within which the humblest of laymen could, in theory at least, enjoy the experience of preaching or of administrative or financial office. In 1927 it was estimated that one in every five or six members held some sort of chapel office.[33]

Accordingly, the Primitive Methodist and Labour MP Jack Lawson recalled, 'Apart from the meagre elementary education, one great force held the field in the matter of personal development and that was the chapel.'[34] With most of the working classes continuing to receive no more than an elementary schooling, this largely held true into the interwar years. Thus, Lawson's fellow Prim and Labour MP Bertie Hazell – who grew up not in the mining districts of the North-East in the 1890s but in rural Norfolk in the 1920s – also learnt in Methodism the speaking and leadership skills that led him to head the agricultural workers' trade union, 'because formal education came to a dead halt and chapel provided an outlet'.[35] It was in this setting that organizational skills, the management of meetings, and means of communication and proselytization were inculcated.

In urban areas, there was a greater range of alternative forms of intellectual formation available. There were Radical Clubs in London and elsewhere that had long supported mock parliaments, which introduced young working-class speakers to the rules of debate, the democratic virtues of oppositional advocacy and engagement with the principles of policy. Many early Labour MPs, including Nonconformists, learnt their debating skills in such settings.[36]

R. J. Barker brought these traditions together in the 1930s by establishing a mock parliament at Tonypandy Central Hall.[37] By then, however, such bodies were less conspicuous in the chapels. In complaining that 'our task is to create a disinterested community of people willing to accept changes which may seem to strike at their own private interests because they have learned from Christ to love their neighbours more than property and privilege. A hard task! Harder than singing hymns and attending meetings and playing cricket', Pratt Green hinted that the rise of associational culture had undermined such activities.[38]

Baptist chapels were particularly inclined to eschew political discussion, to the frustration of some future Labour leaders such as Ernest Bevin of the Transport & General Workers Union.[39] Nevertheless, as one Baptist minister and Socialist who grew up in the interwar years later recalled, although 'party politics never entered Church meetings … there were in Bible Studies references to rich and poor and God's attitude to them and their responsibility to God'.[40]

The chapels thus did not simply afford many their first experience of public speaking and debate. The refining of thought that these processes involved took place within the context of the challenging ethics of 'an inspired Book that sets up standards that touch every phase of human life'.[41] The Bible was not just the source of political language which gained power through the beauty and familiarity of the King James Version, but it was also a series of statements of what should be and of how men should order their society under God. In calling for a return to the clear-cut revolutionary implications of texts like Psalm 24.1: 'The earth is the Lord's and the fullness thereof', Wilfred Wellock gave expression to its moral imperatives.[42] Labour also continued, at least during the 1920s, to publish works by people like Wellock which had a religiosity of tone redolent of Snowden's celebrated *The Christ That Is to Be* (1903).

Scripture gave a measure against which to view society. Margaret Bondfield – a Congregationalist who became the first female cabinet member in the 1929 Labour government – found from her study of the Old Testament, 'We could not think religion and not think of the needs of the poor'.[43] The Bible helped to focus attention upon the duty to respond to such needs. Accordingly, the Unitarian domestic missioner Henry Gow argued in 1919, 'Religion rightly preached is a revolutionary force; it awakens men to unselfish love and makes them realise the suffering of others.'[44]

This same Christian message of unselfish love and service could equally be taken up by Conservatives, and was indeed the theme of many of Stanley Baldwin's speeches.[45] Baldwin could also share the emphasis of his Labour opponent, Somerville Hastings, on 'the sacredness of human personality and the infinite value of every individual in the sight of God'.[46] The implication that Baldwin, and his Nonconformist followers such as Kingsley Wood, derived from this stress, however, was the need for personal responsibility without the sometimes coercive social utopianism they detected in their political opponents.[47]

H. G. Romeril, a Baptist and Labour MP, may have come into the Labour movement because Campbell Morgan's preaching at Westminster Chapel made him 'realise very keenly that I had a duty towards my neighbour'.[48] Campbell Morgan's popular evangelicalism was, however, far from politically radical. It could be interpreted as either to imply a social duty on the individual to aid others, or as a call to remake a fairer society. Even the latter did not necessarily imply a conversion to Labour. Such a political imperative could nevertheless be derived by some in the congregations. Lawson suggested that this was indeed a general lesson in telling the NCEFC assembly in 1921 'if Labour is wrong then the Free Churches have misled us', with their emphasis 'that human life is sacred' and 'that mankind is one'.[49] This was, of course, an appeal for political support. Not all, however, would agree that Labour voting was the logical outcome of those ideals. The Conservative MP and Methodist lay preacher R. J. Soper accordingly was clear that political economy should not be broached in the pulpit, not least because different implications could be drawn from Christian teaching.[50] His fellow lay preacher, Charlie Ammon, for instance, felt in 1932 that the lessons of the Slump were that

> much of the luxury and wasteful extravagance, which is so marked a feature of modern life, should be eliminated in a more equitable distribution of the profits of industries in salaries and wages, and so bring about a more uniform standard of living and a consequent consumption of primary commodities.[51]

There ensued a debate in the correspondence columns of *The Times* in which General George Cockerill responded: 'Socialism differs from Capitalism in that effort is non-competitive, and therefore less effective; it tends to become compulsory. The reward of effort … is fixed arbitrarily by an oligarchy, which becomes an autocracy and eventually a tyranny. To Christianise Socialism is not easy.'[52] Such views, and the concerns about the Soviet Union which helped to inform them, could certainly lead to Free Churchmen drawing wholly different political conclusions from Ammon. A conscientious objector and trade unionist who was very much radicalized by the First World War, including a close involvement with organizations such as the 1917 Club, Ammon was an early (if later repentant) admirer of the Soviet Union.[53] Doubts about the wisdom of such enthusiasms, if nothing else, help to explain the considerable numbers of Nonconformists who signed the nomination papers of his Tory opponent when he was first elected to Parliament in a by-election in Camberwell, South London in 1922.[54]

Free Churchmen may, like Ammon, have seen Labour support as an extension of their faith, but they were more likely to do so if there were, as in his case, other factors, such as trade unionism or unemployment, inclining them towards Labour as well. Accordingly, a Bangor minister wrote in 1926, 'It is notorious that in the quarry districts of Caernarvonshire there has been a great transference of allegiance from the Liberal to the Labour Party',[55] but this primarily reflected the decline of the quarry industry after the great industrial disputes over wages and conditions of 1896–1903. Nonconformist voters merely joined this trend. In the process, Nonconformity may have helped to provide a rationale for such developments, but their prime cause was material. Nor did it exclusively drive in that direction, even in places which, during the interwar years, became impregnable Labour strongholds. In the 1920s, for instance, the membership at Hope Congregationalists, Wigan included a Liberal MP, the Tory leader of the opposition on the local council and the first female member of that council, elected for Labour.[56]

The Brotherhood and Adult Schools

Nevertheless, there were certain factors which arguably did encourage growing Labour support on the pews. One was the Brotherhood movement, of which Ammon was national president in 1929 and 1945.[57] This was founded by the Congregationalist John Blackham in West Bromwich in 1875, stimulated by the recent mission of the American evangelists Dwight Moody and Ira Sankey, as an attempt to reach those who would not come to church. Within ten years, over 100,000 were attending what were originally known as Pleasant Sunday Afternoon Meetings.[58] Never an exclusively working-class movement, its combination of idealistic appeal under the motto, 'One is your Master, even Christ, and all ye are brethren' (Matthew 23.8), and 'brief, bright and brotherly', not to mention thoroughly unecclesiastical meetings, nevertheless succeeded in drawing large numbers of working-class non-churchgoers into its ranks.[59] 'Here at any rate', proclaimed William Ward, the ex-President of the National Brotherhood Council in 1911, 'has come into being a movement that is bridging the gulf that for so many years has existed between the churches and the working classes.' At the time attendance was estimated at between 500,000 and 750,000 and increasing. Ward was hopeful it would soon top the million mark.[60]

The message of Christian Brotherhood also had political resonances, which seem to have drawn Labour figures into the movement. Debates at Brotherhoods, like the one run by the radical Liberal MP C. Silvester Horne at Whitefield's Tabernacle in London before his untimely death in 1914 were 'challengingly political', a tradition sustained by his Socialist successors S. Maurice Watts and A.D. Belden.[61] During the Edwardian period the Brotherhood was seen as a means of reaching out to anticlerical and irreligious masses of the Continent and demonstrating the compatibility between religion and labour, with Keir Hardie leading a Brotherhood mission to Northern France and Belgium in 1910.[62] This association was enthusiastically embraced by some, such as F. H. Stead, W. T.'s brother and the superintendent of the Congregational Browning Settlement in Walworth, South London. As noted above, his church was the setting for a series of international conferences on religion and labour, featuring Socialist leaders from Britain and various European countries from either side of the Great War. This may explain why a number of chapels were unwilling to support the Brotherhood movement before 1914.[63]

In much of the country, however, as the ILP subsequently acknowledged, the Brotherhood then appeared almost as a religious counterpart of the Labour movement. It was certainly far more important, both numerically and in terms of influence, than other organizations such as the Labour Churches which have nevertheless received far more attention from historians. In 1918, Brotherhoods even helped to distribute Arthur Henderson's *Aims of Labour* in which the Labour general secretary and twice Brotherhood national president set out to woo the electorate to a party which had been revamped in wartime. Many Brotherhoods marked the end of the conflict by passing pro-nationalization resolutions. The fact that Tom Sykes, the movement's general secretary (himself a Labour supporter), still had to deny that it had any Socialist tendencies indicated the extent to which a certain political reputation had been established.[64] In 1922, there were even some who felt that it was exploited by Socialists for their own ends.[65] The *Labour Leader*, in contrast, felt that the recent international Brotherhood conference, at which Henderson was the only Labour statesman, indicated the decline of pre-war closeness.[66]

By then, however, the Brotherhood was much changed. Two-thirds of the membership enlisted in the Great War.[67] Significantly, the drop in membership from 1914, which Tom Sykes reported in 1919, was 65 per cent.[68] Membership in 1925 was apparently down to 100,000, though it seems subsequently to have by 1937 gradually climbed to around the 250,000 mark.[69] The motives of those attending, however, may have been mixed: addressing a meeting in South London's Old Kent Road in 1933 Ammon noted, 'A good attendance, the most pathetic part being the gallery half full of unemployed men attracted by the chance of a free tea'.[70]

By then, although the bulk of the membership seems to have remained working class, both the movement's Nonconformist and leftish identity was diluted. Anglicans played an increasingly prominent part in the Brotherhood in the interwar years. In 1935 Canon Dick Sheppard replaced the Baptist lay preacher and future Labour Cabinet minister A. V. Alexander as its president. His leadership of the Pacifist Peace Pledge Union (PPU), nevertheless, guaranteed his radical credentials. This was not true of fellow Anglicans like the Conservative MPs Sir Rowland Blades and Lord Henry Bentinck, who also became prominent in the movement in this period. It is clear from the columns of *Brotherhood Outlook* that many Liberal and Conservative MPs also regularly addressed Brotherhood meetings. In 1930, Stanley Baldwin was invited to deliver for the Brotherhood the tenth John Clifford Lecture.[71] No doubt that former stalwart of the movement turned in his grave at the thought of a Conservative party leader delivering a lecture named in his honour.

The Brotherhood as a means of linking religion and labour still impressed Continental observers. Franz Linden's 1932 Leipzig thesis explicitly explored the distinctive religiosity of the Labour Party and highlighted the conspicuous role played in shaping this by the Brotherhood. He argued that most of the speakers at Brotherhood meetings then were still members of the Labour Party.[72] Certainly, of the 390 Labour MPs elected for England and Wales between the wars at least 143 can be positively identified as having spoken at Brotherhood meetings. While this number included Nonconformist lay preachers like Ammon and Alexander, it also included a good number of Catholics, lapsed Anglicans like Clement Attlee, and even people like Frederick Montague, who was probably an atheist. Speaking at a Brotherhood might then have become more of a way of combining ethicalism with electioneering. However the Brotherhood's national president in 1931, W. H. Bolton, reported fewer 'labour' and radical addresses.[73] The experience of attending and speaking at Brotherhood meetings may have remained part of the development of post-war Labour politicians like the Methodists Peter Archer or George Thomas. The political identity was, however, gone.

Another rather different nineteenth-century movement linking Nonconformity to the working classes was the Adult School. Starting in Nottingham in 1798 it spread as Sunday morning Quaker-run schools instructing the urban working classes in reading, writing and Bible study. At the movement's peak in the Edwardian years, Adult Schools even offered labour exchanges and benefit societies.[74] As with the Brotherhood, there was a parallel female section. The Sisterhood seems to have become comparatively more significant numerically during the interwar years. This was certainly the case with the female membership of the Adult Schools: they went from being outnumbered two to one to completely reversing this ratio between 1911 and 1937.[75]

The movement remained closely associated with the Quakers, even after what became the National Adult School Union replaced loose control by the Society of Friends in 1899. Although most of the seventeen interwar Labour MPs who can be identified as having Adult School connections were Quakers, there was a wider impact on the movement, through the involvement of trade unionists such as Ernest Bevin. He recalled of his Adult School in Bristol,

> It taught you to think, to reason, to be tolerant of the other person's point of view, to examine the facts; and it helped you to develop the ability to exercise judgement; added to which of course, there was the good fellowship, the social outlook, the awakening of a social conscience.[76]

Such emphases were encouraged by the Great War. The movement's unofficial creed, formulated in around 1921, stressed cross-class comradeship, public spirit and morality, responsible citizenship and equal opportunities.[77]

By then, however, the movement was in decline. The Quakers were becoming increasingly involved instead in the setting up of educational settlements and colleges. Fircroft College, Birmingham for instance, was founded in 1909 as a residential college for adult workers offering courses such as industrial history and economics, industrial and trade union law, international relations, or the history of politics and sociology.[78] The extension of elementary education and the growth of other, more secular types of educational provision for the working classes, also adversely affected the Adult Schools. Membership by 1937–38 was down to 33,301, though this meant that it was still the largest adult education movement. Its character had, however, changed and its direct impact on the working classes, especially men, had declined. There was less of the visiting culture which had been so important a feature, prompting Seebohm Rowntree's interest in social analysis. Instead, there was if anything more of an emphasis upon the Adult Schools' religious nature.[79]

Political conflict in the pews

The Brotherhood and Adult Schools may have acted as training grounds for future Labour politicians and trade unionists. The political rise of Labour, however, produced tensions and resistance within chapel communities. When, in the 1890s, for instance, H. Bodell Smith made the egalitarian gesture of abolishing pew rents at Crewe

Unitarian Church and alienated wealthier members of the congregation by arranging Socialist lectures by men like Keir Hardie or Tom Mann, the resulting financial crisis forced his departure.[80] Although seemingly less common, such tensions persisted after 1918. For instance, Mount Gold Christian Socialist Church, Plymouth, was established in 1926 as a result of the virtual expulsion of members of the local Wesleyan chapel for supporting the miners in the lockout of that year.[81]

Splits and expulsions often focused upon the minister's political profile. Sometimes these crises were provoked by a particular minister changing the social composition of the chapel. Vint Laughland hinted that his resignation from Unity Church, Sheffield in 1919 was forced by prominent laymen desirous that the chapel should again 'degenerate into a limited company run by two or three families as a hobby'.[82] In Shrewsbury in 1929, in contrast, it was the minister's openly political stance and his liberal and too readily articulated views on sexual matters that split the Unitarian chapel. After a resolution calling for his resignation passed by the narrow majority of two, a number of his supporters followed him into the Shrewsbury Free Religious Movement which he then set up. Objections to politics in the pulpit could not then prevent him campaigning and standing in the November municipal elections as a Labour candidate.[83]

Actively campaigning on behalf of Labour candidates could still lead to trouble. Ingli James and Accrington Baptists parted company when his support for the Quaker Labour candidate Roden Buxton in the 1922 election proved unacceptable to many Liberals in his congregation.[84] Another minister in the North of England was made to resign for similar activities in 1926. His congregation declared that they would have no objections to a minister active in the Liberal cause.[85] Indeed, ministers in places like Norwich continued to display a marked Liberalism, while the Unitarian-cradled Labour MP John Parker found that the chairman of the local Liberal party, when he was first elected in 1935 in Romford, was a Methodist minister.[86] This did not mean even then that such ministers would always be free to use their pulpit in unashamed service of their party. On occasion, the intrusion of outspoken Liberalism into the sermons of D. Ewart James of Cliff Town Congregationalists, Southend, led one of his deacons to rise in protest.[87]

Ministers continued to appear on party hustings at election times in various parts of the country. In 1918 in Bradford, there were still twelve ministers on Liberal platforms to two on Labour hustings.[88] A London Labour candidate in 1929 complained that all the local Nonconformist ministers were Liberal, with the one whose Congregational chapel hosted the pre-election service for all three candidates having signed the Liberal's nomination papers.[89] Such partisanship was even more marked in 1931. The peculiar circumstances of that election led to a whole crop of pro-National government sermons in Bradford.[90] At the Labour Party conference of that year, E. A. Lucas was told by a Methodist lay preacher: 'We have all the powers of Hell against us in this election – both the Press and the Pulpit.'[91] This was certainly true of the religious press. A letter to the *Christian World* in September 1932 commented: 'Your customary analysis at the last general election revealed that approximately two-thirds of the Free Church candidates stood in the Labour-Socialist interest, although unfortunately the influence of your paper was ranged with the opposition with which they had to contend.'[92]

Such tensions could affect lay preachers as well as ministers. Preaching at one Accrington chapel in the 1930s, the Methodist and future Bolton Labour councillor Alan Brigg was afterwards told by one of the stewards, 'We didn't like your sermon much. You see we're all Tories here.'[93] Agricultural trade unionist and future Labour MP Edwin Gooch met with so much opposition and animosity to his trade union and political activities in Wymondham Primitive Methodist circuit led by H. G. Stone, the secretary of the local Free Church Council and a former vice-president of the Primitive Methodist conference, that in 1920 he resigned both his lay preaching and membership.[94] The 1923 Norfolk farmworkers' strike exacerbated such tensions. Incensed at his use of his preaching powers in the service of the union during the dispute, Jack Quantrill's employer, a farmer on the same preaching plan, told him when the strike was over, 'Jack, you and I part company … and what's more you won't get another job within a ten mile radius.'[95]

To some extent this reflected traditions of class hierarchies in the chapels, made more visible by the pew rent system. Even with the widespread disappearance of pew rents, in Rossendale in the 1930s, the relative wealth of the members nevertheless continued to be reflected in where they sat, with the richest nearest to the back of the church.[96] Hope Congregationalists, Oldham, treated their benefactress Dame Sarah Lees 'as if of royal blood. When she attended the Operatic Society's production, a throne-like seat was set on a dais for her, regardless of those sitting behind in the auditorium.'[97] Fenner Brockway claimed in 1929 that though 'the working class membership is largely Labour where before it was Liberal', the chapels as a whole were 'still dominated by rich Liberals' like Dame Sarah.[98]

Ellis Lloyd expressed this relationship in his 1919 novel, *Scarlet Nest*. His Socialist protagonist tells the Calvinistic Methodist minister, 'You ministers are to a large extent class agents and party hacks … It is the moneyed men in the chapels who are your real masters.'[99] A deferential attitude certainly was felt to be expected at some chapels.[100] These 'wealthy laymen count for too much in the Free Churches' complained Arthur Porritt in 1922.[101] In recognition of this danger Garvie warned the NCEFC, 'A tied pulpit is worse than a tied public house.'[102] Mindful of this, East Glamorgan Baptists in 1920 passed a resolution urging churches

> [C]arefully to scrutinise the social and economic attitudes of their members, and to discipline, and in extreme cases to exclude, such persons as may be proved to procure for themselves financial advantages for which they have tendered no service to the community.[103]

Sensitivity over such matters can be illustrated by the controversy in the correspondence columns of the *Methodist Times* following the criticisms levelled by the Wesleyan travel agent Sir Henry Lunn at the lack of charitable bequests from and size of the estate (worth over £1 million) left by Sir William Hartley after his death in 1922.[104] This was, however, somewhat unfair on Hartley, who built up his jam business from humble origins and always considered himself 'simply the steward of the Lord's money', giving a third of his income to church and charity, to hospitals or to unemployment funds, while fostering high wages, recreational facilities, free medical facilities and profit-sharing in his factories at Aintree where he built a model village for his employees.[105] As the Socialist W. H. Clouting pointed out, the real issue was not whether Christians can die rich but whether the poor can live.[106]

Nonconformist coal owners did not always seem as generous as Hartley. There were notably philanthropic colliery companies, like the Lancashire firm of Fletcher Burrows. Their philanthropy was reflected in the introduction of the first pithead baths in Britain in 1913, and through the strike pay, relief work, entertainments and generous early settlement that characterized the firm's conduct during the 1926 lockout. Robert Burrows's part in this and in the welfare activities of the company however contrasts sharply with the bitter hostility of his fellow Baptist coal owner W. Dale Shaw towards the miners.[107]

With changing patterns of ownership and control in the coal mining industry during the interwar years, figures like Dale Shaw were becoming rarer. The Bradford weaver and Primitive Methodist, Joseph Wilson had worked his way up from the shop floor to running his own paternalistic firm. As the companies that such men created passed with their decease into history, so too did the nineteenth-century vision of class collaboration evoked by Wilson's view, 'that employer and employees were all members of one big family, with the same interests, the same aspirations, the same needs, subject to the same trials and responsive to the same pleasures'.[108] Wartime inflation and trade union recognition, compounded by post-war expectations, tended to undermine this model of workplace industrial relations.[109] The Conservative MP Sir John Randles in 1921 indeed urged the Wesleyan conference to amend its rule preventing trade union meetings being held on Methodist trust property, although this was primarily so that trade union branches would not be constrained to meet in taverns.[110] More broadly, Seebohm Rowntree argued in 1922 that progressive firms must now seek to secure for the worker sufficient earnings, reasonable hours, both job security and provision for his old age, a share in deciding the conditions of his work and an interest in the prosperity of industry.[111]

Yet there was a continuing need for incentives, for both employers and employed. Theodore Cooke Taylor had recognized this when pioneering profit sharing in the late nineteenth century. In contrast, in 1922 he lampooned left-wing views:

> That capitalism is the enemy, that the man, therefore, who denies himself and saves capital becomes the enemy of others; that spendthrift ways are really more desirable, that the wage system is slavery and Socialism would be freedom; that the present industrial system is so bad that nothing could be worse; that men would work more assiduously for the State than they do for themselves or for each other; that collectivism would immediately develop an amazing burst of altruism; that under communal control a great outburst of general prosperity would occur; that it is the duty of the State, that is everyone else, to provide a man with all he wants; that if he happens to be out of work he has a moral right to Trade Union rates for doing nothing.[112]

In contrast, the concerns on the Left were frequently that men could work at all during years of economic depression and industrial rationalization. Even the Quaker firm of Cadbury's could not avoid minimal redundancies when faced with rationalization in 1929. They were then accused of giving up the attempt at Christianity in order to maintain profits by their fellow Quaker, the Socialist Will Chamberlain:

> I confess that as members of the Society of Friends I had hoped for great things from Quaker employers. I had hoped that they might have given a bold lead to other employers. But with the action of the Cadbury family my hopes have vanished, and I now know that we shall have to wait for a Socialist government to secure for the workers not 'benevolence' but justice.[113]

The Cadburys were nonetheless among those Quaker business families which switched to supporting Labour in the interwar years. The Quaker cotton mill owner J. Percival Davies indeed stood for Parliament several times as a Labour candidate and various members of the Rowntree family became active in Labour politics, though Seebohm remained a Liberal. Examples of Nonconformist businessmen in other denominations making a similar switch, however, are conspicuous by their absence.

Some Nonconformist business dynasties were instead already Conservative. For instance, Richard Pilkington, who was both a pillar of St Helens Congregationalist chapel and a member of the family whose glassworks dominated the town, sat as Conservative MP for nearby Newton in 1899–1906, while his daughter Margaret twice stood for the Tories in St Helens in the 1920s and her brother Richard sat as Conservative MP for Widnes between 1935 and 1945.[114] Local factors, such as the Pilkingtons' South West Lancashire setting in a traditionally Tory area, may have be the key determinant of such developments. Certainly, Barry Doyle found little evidence of such moves among Congregational families in Norwich like the Cozens-Hardys with whom the Pilkingtons intermarried. In a city with much stronger Liberal traditions Doyle argues that it was only with generational change and the loss of old rallying cries such as free trade after 1932 that local Nonconformist business elites moved in bulk to the right.[115]

In other areas, however, there was some evidence of movement towards the Conservatives by the 1920s. The rise of Labour even before the First World War prompted expedient municipal alliances between Liberals and Conservatives and these became more widespread thereafter.[116] In 1920, lecturing on goodwill in a Yorkshire chapel, Tom Phillips was told: 'We are practising it in this municipal election. Liberals show the greatest goodwill towards the Conservatives. I am afraid neither of us loves Labour.'[117] These local Liberal/Conservative alliances peaked in the 1931 municipal elections.[118] Although these have been widely seen as leading to the atrophy of local Liberalism, where it remained strongly entrenched in the middle classes, as in Norwich, such anti-Socialist alliances might actually have helped the party's survival. There were also continuing alliances, such as in Preston up until 1929, between Liberals and Labour at the local level.[119] In settings lacking a strongly unionized core, however, chapel folk seem to have been as likely to turn to the Tories.[120] Party behaviour and local conditions thus helped to structure Nonconformist voting.

Political affiliations in the pews

Nonconformity was an independent variable affecting social and political attitudes, but other factors may have been as or more important. Accordingly, addressing a men's meeting at a Congregational church in Lewisham, Ammon 'could not but feel the audience was typical of little suburban snobbery'.[121] These social and political distinctions according to geography and social status were noted by contemporaries even in the case of the Primitive Methodists, traditionally seen as the most working class of Nonconformist denominations. George Edwards, for instance, found that 'some of the members of my own Church in the Division were my bitterest opponents'.[122] Indeed, a *Methodist Times* inquiry in 1922 suggested that the Prims were becoming as politically divided as the Wesleyans notoriously were: 'In the mining areas the Primitives may be expected to vote for Labour; in the industrial areas for Labour and Liberalism; in suburban areas for Lloyd George Liberalism and Conservatism.' After the election of that year it added, 'There is growing up a steady volume of Tory opinion in the Denomination coincident with a rise in the social status of its adherents.'[123]

Some politically radical ministers clearly tried to reshape the politics of their chapels. They were most successful at this when they drew in outsiders. Thus the speeches about the virtues of Soviet Russia delivered by John Lewis in the 1930s on the steps at Ipswich Town Hall led to an influx into the local Unitarian chapel of people politicized, if not converted by its minister.[124] There is less evidence of ministers having a major political effect upon existing congregations. C. J. Tribe, who revived the inner city cause of Kirkgate Wesleyans, Bradford, by attracting a large and political evening congregation with his left-wing preaching, perhaps came close. In the process, he turned it into a 'People's Church' and initiated a magazine called *Comrade*. However, as at Pembroke and Greenfield, such moves were no guarantee of long-term success: Tribe faced some resistance from his congregation and, after he left, by 1935 the chapel was for sale.[125] Congregations in general were not so swayed. For instance, the left-wing stance of the Methodist minister in nearby but more rural Baildon in the late 1930s does not seem to have alienated his predominantly Liberal congregation, but nor does it seem to have led them to follow his politics.[126]

Certain chapels nevertheless had very clearly defined political positions in the period. The peculiar relationships in Liverpool that Ullet Road Unitarians and Sefton Park Presbyterians had respectively with the Liberal and Conservative Parties of the city were already noticeable in the nineteenth century. With the interwar contraction of the Liverpool Liberal Party its identification with Ullet Road became more marked: by the late 1930s practically all the city council's Liberal group were pew holders at the chapel. Sefton Park was equally remarkable for its stream of Conservative Lord Mayors and parliamentary candidates.[127] Such particular traditions on the part of various chapels, though related to an unusually high proportion of wealthy shipowners in the case of Ullet Road, perhaps reflected the sectarianism of Liverpool. This was certainly true of the Protestant Martyrs Memorial Church. This powerhouse of militant anti-Catholicism spawned the city's Protestant Party, led by its pastor Harry Longbottom. Though interwar housing development, the decline of church attendance and the bomb damage of the Second World War all tended to destroy the discrete communities of Catholic and Protestant and with them the intensity of sectarian feeling, this church still supplied some Protestant councillors into the 1960s.[128]

In contrast, a study of South West Wales in the 1950s noted that the more democratic the chapel polity the more working-class its composition and the more radical its politics.[129] However, as Peter Ackers's analysis of the relationship between religion and politics within the relatively democratic and millenarian Churches of Christ in the generally Labour-supporting area of Wigan has shown, church polity was not necessarily the key determinant of political views. Within the same denomination and area there was a difference between the radicalism of Platt Bridge chapel, dominated as it was by miners, and the more Liberal persuasions of Rodney Street, in which the clothing-manufacturing Coop family had a strong influence.[130]

Regardless of denomination, the vast majority of chapels did not have clearly defined political identities. While it is relatively easy to assess the politics of their more eminent members, identified as they are as councillors or parliamentary candidates, it is harder to estimate the political affiliations of the bulk of the congregations. Because Free Churchmen were always disproportionately over-represented in the candidates' lists (see Appendix) their presence in a particular constituency was not a good reflection of the size or the political character of the Nonconformity of that area.[131] The number of Free Church Labour MPs in Durham, for instance, did not indicate that the chapels of the county had, like the miners of the area, converted to Labour politics. For instance, the Liberal opponent of Ben Spoor in 1923 and 1924, the Labour MP for Bishop Auckland, preached on the same Primitive Methodist circuit plan.[132]

Oral evidence, which is often the only basis upon which the political complexion of the chapel community can be assessed, has in fact been used to argue that even among Primitive Methodists Labour supporters predominated in only one out of every three chapels during the interwar years. The proportion seems to have been even smaller in the other branches of Methodism.[133] The Independent Methodist Rennie Smith, soon to become Labour MP for Penistone, argued in 1924 that the village chapel was still the stronghold of Yorkshire Liberalism.[134] Liberalism was also far from routed in the mining districts of Lancashire. Tensions over his support for the Labour rather than the Liberal candidate led George Tomlinson to resign his membership of Farnworth Congregationalists after the 1924 election.[135]

Only in the comparatively well-documented case of the Society of Friends – itself not without a Conservative element – is there evidence of a considerable and early shift to Labour. 'Today many Friends are joining the Socialist bodies and finding a place in the great Labour Movement, for which the recent constitutional revision of the Labour Party has opened a wider door', reported *The Friend* in 1918.[136] It was the war rather than the Labour Party's constitutional reforms that most encouraged this process. In its aftermath the pre-war reluctance of Quaker editors to open their columns to the discussion of Socialism disappeared.[137] The anti-war stance the Society of Friends shared with the ILP encouraged Quakers to consider the economic as well as the moral objections to war. It also led to many Quakers joining the ILP, and to ILPers in turn becoming convinced Quakers. Though some older and more affluent Friends viewed the resulting influx of Socialists into the Society with deep misgivings, this process continued through the 1920s.[138] In declaring her continuing allegiance to the Liberal Party, Elizabeth Cadbury was forced to admit, 'It takes courage to make such a statement at the present time in any Friends circle! It is the fashion to join the Labour Party and those who do not do so are considered "back numbers."'[139] By 1926 it was estimated that half the Society were Labour supporters and that this preponderance was still increasing.[140]

Conclusion

The Society of Friends was a relatively small body. Another small body, the Old Paths Churches of Christ, also seems to have shifted substantially towards Labour, again not least because of a Pacifist tradition they shared with the Quakers.[141] With respect to the larger denominations, it cannot be argued with equal confidence that their sympathies were shifting in that direction. There is sufficient evidence of Nonconformists remaining differentially likely to vote Liberal throughout the later twentieth century to suggest that the Quakers offer the best instance of such a shift not only in terms of evidence for it, but also in terms of the degree to which it occurred.[142] Indeed, increased Conservative support and the degree of enthusiasm for the National government in the 1930s suggest that many chapelgoers were moving in the other direction politically. Those who did, nevertheless, move to Labour may have been informed by their faith in doing so, yet they were as likely to have been prompted to do so for economic reasons. Nonetheless, many came forward, with Labour having the largest number of Nonconformist parliamentary candidates in 1924, 1931 and 1935 (see Appendix). It was in producing such candidates, rather than through electoral support, that the chapels made their main contribution to the rise of the Labour Party.

5

Free Churchmen and Women in the Labour Party

The political Labour movement, which developed out of the Trade Union Movement, and drew the majority of its early Parliamentary leaders from it, received much of its driving force and inspiration from radical non-conformity. It is a demonstrable fact that the bulk of the members of the Parliamentary Labour Party in any given time during the last twenty five years had graduated into their wider sphere of activity via the Sunday School, the Bible Class, the temperance society or the pulpit. No British political party has ever had such a large proportion of lay-preachers and Sunday School teachers in its ranks as has the Labour Party in Parliament, and even today, despite the increased pressure of their public duties many of them continue still their religious activities in one form or another.

Arthur Henderson[1]

I am in the Labour Movement because I believe that it has the ways and means of bringing Jesus Christ's teaching and doctrines to our fellow men.

William Carter[2]

Methodism and Marx

As noted in the Introduction, in a series of speeches in the 1940s and 1950s Morgan Phillips coined the alliterative observation that Socialism in Britain owed more to Methodism than Marx. Phillips was sketching out what was distinctive about the development of British Labour in comparison with the growth of Socialism elsewhere. These distinctions were earlier explored by the series of international Labour conferences held by F. H. Stead at the Browning Settlement in Walworth. Following his 1919 conference Stead concluded:

> On the Continent religion has been too largely the bulwark of the upper and official classes, a convenient department of state for the buttressing of the established order. In this country, thanks to the variety and vitality of the Free Churches, the official grip has been much slackened.

He thus explained the absence of the anticlericalism of Continental Socialists – which had developed as a response to monolithic systems of truth bolstering the established order, generally in the form of the Catholic Church, with which they were often faced – with reference to Nonconformity. Ramsay MacDonald indeed claimed in 1930 that relations between Nonconformity and working-class movements were 'of the most intimate kind'.

Stead nevertheless continued, probably with more accuracy, that 'English religion has been painfully bourgeois. It has rarely or never been frankly proletarian.'[3] As noted in Chapters 3 and 4, it was not the generality of the working classes but the autodidacts among them who were differentially likely to have attended chapel. The skills they there acquired, not then readily available to working men through other routes, meant that they were accordingly more likely to be elected to trade union and thence to Labour Party offices.

Chapels provided them with the drive and ideals, speaking and organizational skills and reputation for honesty, which enabled them to climb the ranks of trade unions and other Labour organizations.[4] A succession of such figures were celebrated in the series of books charting the relationship between Methodism and working-class politics since the late eighteenth century that poured from the pen of R. F. Wearmouth between 1937 and 1959.[5] Wearmouth, who came from mining stock in North East England and served in the Great War as a Primitive Methodist chaplain, established this orthodoxy for a whole generation of Labour figures, including Morgan Phillips and Harold Wilson. Jack Lawson, who came from the same background as Wearmouth, reviewed the latter's *Some Working Class Movements of the Nineteenth Century* in 1949 thus: 'I always knew Methodist organisations had been the pattern for social and political movements. Did not the Independent Labour Party in the North in my own time have its plan of Speakers based on the Local Preachers' Plan?'[6]

Nonconformity and the PLP

Nonconformists in the Labour Party could prove very conscious of their heritage. In early 1931, C. H. Wilson convened a committee of Nonconformist Labour MPs to watch over Free Church concerns. The *Christian World* was soon able to report, 'Already about forty Labour MPs have sent in their names, apart from the Free Church members of the Government.'[7] There is an irony here, because it was the policies of the then Labour government that prompted this move. Sir Charles Trevelyan, the president of the Board of Education, may have been claimed as a Unitarian.[8] In exploring the attitudes of the various churches to the implications of raising the school-leaving age he, however, seems to have assumed that only Liberal MPs could represent Free Church interests. Trevelyan's invitation of Conservative Churchmen, Liberal Nonconformists and Labour Roman Catholics to present the case of their various churches is an interesting comment on the perceived denominational allegiances of the various parties. It is impossible to know how long Wilson's initiative in response would have survived had not the National government's landslide victory shortly afterwards robbed him and many others of their seats. Thus ended the only attempt to give Nonconformity an institutional voice within the PLP along the lines of the group led by Robert Perks and George White within the parliaments of the Edwardian era.

Nonconformity in Parliament was nevertheless now preponderantly represented in Labour rather than the Liberals. Though the Parliamentary Liberal Party's Nonconformist core of the Liberal Party in Parliament became, if anything, more pronounced in its decline, the bulk of Free Church MPs were from 1922 onwards (with the extraordinary exception of 1931–35) in the Labour Party (see Appendix).

Table 9 attempts to map the religiosity of interwar Labour MPs. This is, of course, not an exact science. On one level it is complicated by the tendency of a number to change denominations. Henderson and Tomlinson started as Congregationalists and switched to Wesleyanism, while the Sheffield precious metal-smelter C. H. Wilson continued to be a Congregational deacon after he also became a Quaker. It is also complicated by the issue of degrees of adherence. If, for instance, the stringent test that David Bebbington uses to define a Baptist as someone who has undergone believer's baptism and is in membership with a Baptist church is applied, then figures like S. P. Viant (who attended Clifford's church) or Arthur Greenwood (who clearly identified as Baptist) should be excluded.[9] In Table 9, both are recorded as Baptists. So indeed is Ness Edwards, despite his sparing attendance at chapel in adulthood.[10] This was a tendency shared by several other Labour figures brought up as Nonconformists. In most instances, however, they seem to have grown away from their chapels, rather than Christianity itself. Like the miners' leader A. J. Cook, an erstwhile lay preacher ousted from the Baptist pulpit for his Socialist views, they retained some faith and certainly chapel culture if not their chapel connections. Instead, it was those of a more middle-class background, who had been brought up at home and at university in a humanist milieu who, like Mary Agnes Hamilton, treated theistic religion with 'polite disregard'.[11] Those who had a faith to lose, nevertheless, frequently remained shaped by it. Where appropriate, those MPs who seem to have continued to attend chapel occasionally, to have been seen as Free Churchmen and to have been temperamentally Nonconformist themselves,[12] have therefore been treated as such in Table 9 and in the listing of parliamentary candidates in the Appendix.

Table 9 demonstrates that 44 per cent of interwar Labour MPs were Nonconformist. This figure is less than the 60 per cent of the first cohort of Labour MPs in 1906 that were apparently Nonconformist.[13] Many of this first cohort continued in Parliament after 1918. Although people like Henderson lost their seats, 66 per cent of Labour MPs elected in that year were Nonconformists. Their weight within the PLP, however, gradually diminished over the interwar years, not least because of generational change as those born in the 1860s and 1870s, when Nonconformity was at its numerical height, retired or died. Of the new intake in the 1935 election, only 20 per cent were Nonconformist. Nevertheless, because of the survival of Free Church members of earlier cohorts, Nonconformity continued to be a strong feature of the PLP throughout these years.

Defining Nonconformists in the way set out above is not necessarily less valid than an ecclesiastical definition when attempting to assess the religiosity of the Labour Party in the interwar years. An ecclesiastical definition is indeed perhaps somewhat inappropriate given the degree of animosity sometimes expressed within the movement

Table 9 Religious affiliations of Labour MPs in England and Wales, 1918–39

Joined PLP in	Total	W	PM	UM	B	C	P	Q	CM	U	ONC	TNC	LP	CO	Min	B/AS	RC	A	UD	J	Eth	CS	Theo	Par	II	NR
1918	54	7	8	5	4	8			3		1	36	20	17	1	21	3	8							5	2
1918–21	17	3	1	1	2	1			1			10	4	6		8			2		1				4	
1922	72	11	2	1	4	10	3	2	2	1	3	38	16	22	1	35	3	10	1		2			1	12	5
1923	58	9	2	1	3	2	1	4	1		1	27	14	15	1	29	6	3	1	1			1		13	6
1924	17	2	1							3	1	4	3	2		6	2	4							6	1
1925–28	8					1		1			1	3	1	2		3		2							3	
1929	100	10	5		3	9	2	4	1	3	1	38	21	17	2	34	7	14	6		2		2		19	12
1930	3	1										1						1							1	
1931	9				2						1	3	1	1		4		3							2	1
1932–34	7										1	1		1						1					3	2
1935	30		3				1			2	1	7	2	2	1	2	1	2	1	1		1			16	2
1935–39	15		1		1	2		1				5	1	2		1	1		1						8	
TOTAL	390		74		19	33	7	12	8	9	11	173	83	87	6	143	23	47	12	3	5	1	5	1	92	31

Note: The abbreviations along the top of the table represent respectively: W = Wesleyans, PM = Primitive Methodists, UM = United Methodists (after 1932, the Methodist figures are united); B = Baptists; C = Congregationalists; P = Presbyterians (including adherents of Scottish churches sitting for English and Welsh constituencies); Q = Quakers (Dorothea Jewson is recorded here as a Baptist rather than the Quaker she later became); CM = Calvinistic Methodists; U = Unitarians; ONC = Other Nonconformists (those who cannot be accurately placed by denomination); TNC = Total Nonconformists; LP = Lay Preachers; CO = Chapel Officers; Min = Ministers; B/AS = MPs active in the Brotherhood and Adult School movements; RC = Roman Catholics; A = Anglicans; UD = Undenominational (those recorded in various sources as Christians of varying degrees of orthodoxy, but unaffiliated to a particular church); J = Jewish; Eth = Ethical Society; CS = Christian Scientist; Theo = Theosophists; P = Parsee; II = Insufficient Information; NR = No Religion (those known to be atheist).

Source: Sources for this and subsequent tables in this chapter include the denominational and local press, Franz Linden's analysis, memoirs and biographies. Cross-checking like this is necessary: after all, the Primitive Methodist Charlie Simmons was habitually missed in the lists of Nonconformist election candidates in the *Christian World*.

towards the churches. Some, like Wilfrid Whiteley, frustrated at the churches' failure to interest themselves in the economic welfare and social life of the people, made Socialism their religion.[14] Impatience with the shortcomings and Liberalism of the chapels, and the related tendency to see the Labour Party itself in a quasi-religious light meant that the religiosity of Labour activists was not always expressed through the churches. A devotee of the New Testament and of the Brotherhood Movement, like Ben Turner, could refer to himself as 'not religious in the orthodox sense'.[15] His perceived heterodoxy was as much political as theological. Partly related to his infrequent church attendance, it largely reflected the view that he could do more to achieve practical Christianity through Labour than within the churches and chapels. This background and intellectual formation has been reflected in Table 9 and Turner has been recorded as a Congregationalist, despite the fact that he did not appear in the lists of Nonconformist parliamentary candidates compiled in the denominational press at each general election.

Those who retained church membership could express frustrations similar to those of Turner. In 1919, Walter Barber and T. W. Stamford (both chapel-raised) told the Spiritual Advance Committee of the local Wesleyan district on behalf of Bradford Trades Council (BTC) that their former church either opposed or did not know Labour's aims.[16] The Congregationalist and Labour MP Robert Young, who was later to be a member of the NCEFC executive, even separated himself entirely from his church for ten years. At the end of that time, however, he decided that, 'in spite of all our political and industrial movements, the teaching of the Scriptures was essential for the political, economic and industrial life of our people'.[17]

Others only retained tenuous links with organized religion. In his study of the PLP between 1929 and 1931, Linden came across 45 MPs who simply described themselves as 'Undenominational'. They, however, stressed that their 'Non-Churchianity' should not be confused with 'Non-Christianity'.[18] It might seem odd to be unable to ascribe to them a formal affiliation. Their position, however, seems entirely consistent with widespread working-class practice in the late nineteenth and early twentieth century.[19]

Conversion to Socialism did not invariably mean rejection of Christianity. The hostility of an E. P. Thompson, whose father was a Methodist missionary, was not ubiquitous. Another missionary's son Fenner Brockway could no longer think of himself as Christian, but retained a deep reverence for Christian values and ideals, continuing to pay tribute to his Congregational upbringing and to Christ.[20]

Relatively few came to reject all religion. 'I could complain about ministers not coming up to my ideal of a minister', declared the Prim and Labour MP Tom Cape, 'but my leaving the Church will not make them any better.'[21] Ben Turner's view of the religiosity of the Labour Party should be borne in mind by those wishing to assess it:

> Most men and women in it are very religious. They may not go to church or chapel – that does not make a man or woman religious – but even from that standpoint there is no other party in the land with as many local preachers within its ranks, or leaders of religious activity, as our party has.[22]

Nonconformity in the wider Labour movement

It is more difficult to assess Free Church numbers in other sections of the Labour movement, such as the trade unions. Trade union leaders were not subjected to the same biographical scrutiny as MPs. There are no lists of Free Church members of the General Council of the TUC (as the central body of the trade movement became known from 1922). Obituary notices are not necessarily any more enlightening. Furthermore, trade union records do not tend to reflect the religiosity of their members. It cannot, however, be assumed that failure to uncover church connections either in these or in the *Labour Who's Who* that appeared in 1924 and 1927 indicates their absence. Therefore, although Table 10, showing the religious affiliations of members of the general council of the TUC in the interwar period does not demonstrate a degree of Free Churchmanship comparable with that of the PLP, it cannot be presumed complete.

Even so, it appears that over a quarter of the members of the general council during these years were Free Churchmen, though their preponderance steadily declined. In some areas and industries the degree of correlation between trade union leadership and Nonconformity is striking. There were, for instance, many Congregationalists and Methodists among textile union leaders in the Bolton area. Primitive Methodists were prominent in the agricultural workers' union.[23] Few trade union documents, however, record the strength of the Free Church presence, and Wearmouth has been shown to have exaggerated its influence in the North East.[24]

Free Churchmen nevertheless retained prominent positions in the mining unions. Their dominance was less than in 1890, when the *Methodist Times* alleged that at least half the delegates at that year's MFGB conference were local preachers.[25] Nevertheless in 1925 the MFGB's former general secretary Frank Hodges – himself an ex-Prim local preacher – reported, 'It is true to say that in most of the English counties the old and many of the present leaders of the Miners' Federation were, and are still, influenced by the Methodist Church.'[26] Three out of five of the MFGB presidents in the interwar years were indeed Methodists.[27]

It can be even more difficult to pinpoint the churchmanship or otherwise of Labour's NEC members in the period. The governing institution of the party, and its policymaking core, had been remodelled through a hard-fought process at the 1917 and 1918 Labour conferences. Labour was then preparing for the post-war electoral situation, not least by drawing up the new constitution and approach that Henderson assiduously promoted in 1918–19. At the same time – in the changed circumstances brought about by the Great War – the unions indicated much greater willingness than hitherto to finance the party. The unions, however, in the reshaping of the NEC sought their reward through enhanced influence over this body. In an NEC increased from sixteen to twenty-three, they secured thirteen union representatives, in addition to five representatives of constituency parties, four women and the party treasurer. They also ensured that all twenty-three members would henceforth be elected by a conference dominated by their votes.[28]

The influence of the unions in shaping the membership of the NEC might explain the findings in Table 11. The role of Nonconformists at the apex of the PLP and in the upper echelons of the trade unions no doubt influenced their weight in the NEC. Thus,

Table 10 Religious affiliations of members of the Parliamentary Committee/General Council of the Trades Union Congress, 1918–39

Joined in	Total	W	PM	UM	B	C	P	CM	TNC	LP	CO	B/AS	RC	A	UD	II	NR
1918	18	2			1	3			6	2	4	1	1	1		9	1
1919–21	23					1	1	1	4	1	1	4	2	4	1	11	1
1922–24	7	1		1					3		1	1				3	1
1925–27	7	1			3	1	1		6	2	3	2				1	
1928–30	9													1		7	1
1931–33	6	1	1						2	1		1		1		2	1
1934–36	12		3				1		4	1	1	1				8	
1937–39	8															7	1
TOTAL	90		10		4	5	3	1	25	7	10	10	3	7	1	48	6

Note: The abbreviations along the top of the table represent respectively: W = Wesleyans, PM = Primitive Methodists, UM = United Methodists (after 1932, the Methodist figures are united); B = Baptists; C = Congregationalists; P = Presbyterians; CM = Calvinistic Methodists; TNC = Total Nonconformists (including two who cannot be placed by denomination); LP = Lay Preachers; CO = Chapel Officers; B/AS = those active in the Brotherhood or Adult Schools; RC = Roman Catholics; A = Anglicans; UD = Undenominational (those recorded in various sources as Christians of varying degrees of orthodoxy, but unaffiliated to a particular church); II = Insufficient Information; NR = No Religion (those known to be atheist).

Table 11 Religious affiliations of members and officers of the National Executive Committee of the Labour Party, 1918–39

Joined in	Total	W	PM	UM	B	C	P	Q	CM	U	TNC	LP	CO	B/AS	RC	A	Eth	II	NR
1918	30	1			1	5	3	2			13	4	4	8		5		9	3
1919–21	23	2	3	1	3	2		1			12	4	5	12	1	1	1	6	2
1922–25	18		1		3				1	1	7		2	4	3	1		7	
1926–29	14	2			1						3	1	2	3		2	1	5	3
1930–32	11						1				1			2	2	2		4	2
1934–36	9		1								1	1	1	1		2		6	
1937–39	12					1		1			2		1	1				9	1
TOTAL	117		11		8	8	4	4	1	1	39	10	15	31	6	13	2	46	11

Note: The abbreviations along the top of the table represent respectively: W = Wesleyans, PM = Primitive Methodists, UM = United Methodists (after 1932, the Methodist figures are united); B = Baptists; C = Congregationalists; P = Presbyterians; Q = Quakers; CM = Calvinistic Methodists; U = Unitarians; TNC = Total Nonconformists (including two who cannot be placed by denomination); LP = Lay Preachers; CO = Chapel Officers; B/AS = those active in the Brotherhood or Adult Schools; RC = Roman Catholics; A = Anglicans; Eth = Ethical Society; II = Insufficient Information; NR = No Religion (those known to be atheist).

although the considerable number of relatively obscure individuals makes tabulation of its religious affiliations more complex, it seems that over 30 per cent of the members and party officers recorded in the NEC minutes were Free Churchmen.

Nonconformists were equally apparent within the party at the local level, and seem to have been in the majority in places like Loughborough.[29] They were just as important in shaping the Labour movement in the Black Country. Wesley Perrins recalled:

> [T]he Labour movement in this part of the country was, in its origins, very largely a Christian crusade … Christianity in this area, of course, was pretty well synonymous with Methodism, and many of the early leaders of the Labour movement here were prominent Methodists.[30]

Nonconformity was indeed characteristic of the early leadership of many Labour groups on borough, city or district councils across the country. In places as varied as Accrington, Exeter, Birmingham, Derby, Huddersfield, Plymouth, St Pancras, Leigh and Wigan the first leaders of Labour groups and/or the first Labour mayors were Nonconformists.[31] Peter Lee, miners' leader and Prim lay preacher, meanwhile led the dominant Labour group on Durham County Council. Of this council, Labour-controlled since 1919 (except for a short break in 1922–25), J. T. Bell wrote in 1936, 'A very large percentage of its members are members or adherents of the Primitive Methodist church. Many of them are local preachers, Sunday School teachers or actively engaged in the work of our Church in other ways.'[32]

Durham was not unique in this respect. The earliest Labour councillors in Bolton were Methodists and local party leaders habitually stressed the numbers of local preachers and Sunday School teachers in their ranks, particularly to emphasize their respectability in the run-up to the annual round of municipal elections each November.[33] In a town with strong Methodist traditions this is unsurprising, as is the finding in Table 12 that a large proportion of Labour's Bolton councillors in the period were Nonconformists, as was every Labour mayor. Except for 1928–35, when George O'Neil, a Roman Catholic, was its chairman, the leadership of the Labour group was in the hands of Methodist local preachers. Two of the town's three Labour MPs in the period were also Methodist local preachers.

Free Churchmanship was also well represented at Bradford, especially in the early leadership of the local Labour group (Table 13). This is despite the traumatic effects that the rise of Socialism in Bradford apparently had on the city's chapels. It was alleged that the founding conference of the ILP, held in the city in 1893, cost Bradford's Baptist churches scores of members and adherents.[34] The extent of the rejection of Nonconformity should not, however, be exaggerated. Both the decline of its religious content and the growth of social concern within the Free Churches ensured that the Labour Churches that sprang up in the 1890s never became an alternative to Nonconformity. By 1914, in many areas, not least Bradford, the Labour Church movement was either extinct or moribund. Chapel connections for many were, nevertheless, subsequently attenuated. Their former loyalties and affinities, however, clearly continued to influence men like Alfred Pickles, Tom Blythe and Fred Jowett.[35]

Table 12 Religious affiliations of Labour councillors in Bolton, 1918–39

Joined in	Total	W	PM	B	C	Q	U	IM	SA	TNC	LP	CO	B/AS	RC	A	UD	Spr	II	NR
1918	4	3	1							4	3	3	2						
1919–21	13	3			1					6	1	5	2	2				5	
1922–24	8						1		1	4	1	4		1	3				
1925–27	13	1			1	1		1		6		2	1			1		6	
1928–29	10	1								1		1		2	1		1	4	1
1931–33	11		1		2					3	2	3	3	1	1			6	
1934–36	7	1		1						2						1		3	1
1938	3							1		2									1
TOTAL	69	10		1	4	1	1	2	1	28	10	18	8	6	5	2	1	24	3

Note: The abbreviations along the top of the table represent respectively: W = Wesleyans, PM = Primitive Methodists (after 1932, the Methodist figures are united); B = Baptists; C = Congregationalists; Q = Quakers; U = Unitarians; IM = Independent Methodists; SA = Salvation Army; TNC = Total Nonconformists (including eight who cannot be placed by denomination); LP = Lay Preachers; CO = Chapel Officers; B/AS = councillors active in the Brotherhood or Adult Schools; RC = Roman Catholics; A = Anglicans; UD = Undenominational; Spr = Spiritualist; II = Insufficient Information; NR = No Religion (those known to be atheist).

Table 13 Religious affiliations of Labour councillors in Bradford, 1918–39

Joined in	Total	W	PM	UM	B	C	Q	SA	WRU	Mor	TNC	LP	CO	B/AS	RC	A	J	II	NR
1918	20	3	2		1	4		1	1		14	2	7	2	1	2		3	
1919–21	14	1		1	1						3	1	3	1	4	1		4	2
1922–24	11					1	1			1	3		2	1	2			6	
1925–27	12	2				1					5	1	2	1	1	1		5	
1928–30	14	1		1		1			1		4	1	2		1	2		5	2
1933–34	7		1		1			1			3	2	1		1	1	1	1	
1936–38	6		1								1	1	1	1		2		2	1
TOTAL	84		13		3	7	1	2	2	1	33	8	18	6	10	9	1	26	5

Note: The abbreviations along the top of the table represent respectively: W = Wesleyans, PM = Primitive Methodists (after 1932, the Methodist figures are united); B = Baptists; C = Congregationalists; Q = Quakers; SA = Salvation Army; WRU = Wesley Reform Union; Mor = Moravian; TNC = Total Nonconformists (including four who cannot be placed by denomination); LP = Lay Preachers; CO = Chapel Officers; B/AS = councillors active in the Brotherhood or Adult Schools; RC = Roman Catholics; A = Anglicans; J = Jewish; II = Insufficient Information; NR = No Religion (those known to be atheist).

Free Churchmanship also remained very characteristic of the Liberal groups in both Bradford and Bolton. Indeed, in their decline, their characteristic Nonconformity seems to have become if anything, even more marked. Free Churchmen in the Labour groups of Bradford and Bolton, numerous though they were, achieved no comparable predominance. Even in these areas where Nonconformity was strongly represented in Labour, Free Churchmanship remained more typical of the Liberals.

It also remained more typical of the Liberals in areas where Nonconformity was much less apparent than in Bolton or Bradford, such as Liverpool, where it was the Catholicism of the large Irish community which set the tone of the Labour Party. This was especially true after the creation of the Irish Free State and the rejection by archbishop Downey in the late 1920s of the concept of a specifically Catholic party.[36] This helped Labour to absorb the former Irish Nationalist support of the heavily Catholic riverside wards of the city. The resulting Catholic pre-eminence was only partly represented by the number of individual Catholics who actually became Labour councillors in the period. Table 14 does not convey the much greater security of tenure enjoyed by Catholic councillors who, though now standing for Labour, continued to dominate most of the old Nationalist wards where Irish Catholic voters could account for as much as 85 per cent of the electorate.[37] Nor does it convey the important part Catholic support played in forming the electoral basis of the Liverpool Labour Party. Indeed, the wooing and winning of this support was perennially an important consideration for many local Labour parties. For instance, Catholic candidates were deliberately chosen alongside the Wesleyan local preacher Albert Law in the two-member seat of Bolton, while targeted Labour propaganda, it was alleged, was even distributed after Mass in Bradford.[38]

Nonconformists could be targeted in a similar way, particularly in the absence of a Liberal candidate. At the 1924 by-election in Burnley, for instance, Henderson successfully played upon his impeccable Free Church credentials to persuade voters that he was 'the next best thing to a regulation Liberal'.[39] Henderson remained wedded to this approach to campaigning throughout his career. He came close to resigning in 1927 as the party's general secretary over the drift away from temperance sentiment within the NEC because he felt, Hugh Dalton grumbled in his memoirs, that it was still an electoral asset for winning over former Liberals.[40]

In the aftermath of Labour's 1931 defeat, when there was a dramatic decline in the number of Liberal candidates, Henderson continued to focus on playing to erstwhile Liberal voters. While such tactics certainly paid dividends at Burnley in 1924, and arguably retained utility as Labour continued to build its constituency during the 1920s, they, however, had little appeal among comrades eager to take the fight to the National government in the early 1930s. Attacked in the NEC and at the 1932 party conference, Henderson resigned as Labour leader shortly after the latter and, although he retained the title of general secretary until 1934, became a marginal figure in the development of party tactics.[41]

Henderson's approach tended to assume the Liberal tendencies of the Free Church voter. From the point of view of his detractors, the result was a compromising of the party message in order to appeal to these electors, rather than a concerted drive to win them over. This association of Nonconformists with Liberalism meant that, apart from

Table 14 Religious affiliations of Labour councillors in Liverpool, 1918–39

Joined in	Total	PM	B	P	U	TNC	LP	CO	B/AS	RC	A	UD	J	II	NR
1918	9				1	1				4	2			2	
1919–21	14		1	1		2				3				8	1
1924–26	11			1		1				5		1	1	1	2
1927–28	22				1	2	1	1		14	2			3	1
1929	23				1	1				13	1	1		5	2
1930–33	8	1				1	1	1	1	1			1	3	2
1934–36	17									4	1			11	1
1937–39	7									4			1	1	1
TOTAL	111	1	1	2	3	8	2	2	1	48	6	2	3	34	10

Note: The abbreviations along the top of the table represent respectively: PM = Primitive Methodists; B = Baptists; P = Presbyterians; U = Unitarian; TNC = Total Nonconformists (including one who cannot be placed by denomination); LP = Lay Preachers; CO = Chapel Officers; B/AS = councillors active in the Brotherhood or Adult Schools; RC = Roman Catholics; A = Anglicans; UD = Undenominational; J = Jewish; II = Insufficient Information; NR = No Religion (those known to be atheist).

Table 15 Analysis of lobby voting in the House of Commons on John Scurr's amendment to the 1931 Education Bill, 21 January 1931

	For	Against
Free Church Labour MPs	99	10
All Labour MPs	188	35
Free Church Liberal MPs	23	3
All Liberal MPs	28	8
Free Church Conservative MPs	-	9
All Conservative MPs	-	211
Result of the division	249	282

Note: It is important to reflect that the amendment was carried primarily on the votes of the Conservative opposition. The 'For' column represents the votes for the government, while the 'Against' column reflects the votes in favour of the amendment.
It should be noted that all parliamentary statistics in this chapter exclude Scottish and Northern Irish MPs unless otherwise stated.

in certain areas, even when Liberal candidates were absent, they were not courted so assiduously by Labour as their Catholic counterparts. As electoral ballast, they were clearly less significant than the much more culturally distinct (in addition to church-enforced endogamy, the Irish tended to have their own Labour clubs), geographically concentrated and rather more thoroughly working-class Catholics.[42]

This can be illustrated by the lobby voting on the Catholic amendment to Trevelyan's 1931 Education Bill, moved by a group of Labour MPs led by the East End Catholic, John Scurr. Bradford was by no means as Catholic in complexion as Liverpool. Nevertheless, three of the city's four Labour MPs (two of them Nonconformists) voted for Scurr's amendment, while the non-churchgoing William Leach, who sat for Bradford Central, actually seconded it. Similarly, the only Nonconformist Labour MP in Liverpool, Joseph Gibbins, supported Scurr's amendment. Encouragement to do so was no doubt provided by the knowledge that his fellow Nonconformist, Joseph Cleary, had been deselected and replaced by a Catholic for the East Toxteth by-election in Liverpool of February 1931 because of his views on the education controversy.[43]

Labour Catholic voting on the amendment was solidly in favour, despite the fact that it involved opposing their own government. As Table 15 shows, they were joined by 10 per cent of the party's Nonconformist MPs. Interestingly, a higher proportion of Free Church Liberal MPs (13 per cent) also supported Scurr (for more tactical reasons, so did 100 per cent of Free Church Conservatives). Liberal voting for the amendment in general was also proportionately considerably higher than among Labour MPs, which perhaps explains the ire subsequently directed at the Liberals by the Nonconformist press. On this issue at least, Nonconformist attitudes were better represented by Free Church Labour MPs than their Liberal counterparts, despite the consideration a number of the former gave to the likely attitudes of their Catholic voters.[44]

Labour was not always beholden to these voters. For instance, conflicts between Catholic and non-Catholic factions on the Liverpool council's Labour group were common in the 1930s.[45] In particular, the extraordinary split in the party over the question of the siting of a new archdiocesan Catholic cathedral atop Brownlow Hill demonstrated willingness to face Catholic hostility.[46] This willingness, however, did not extend to the issue of Catholic education. When this issue became central to Liverpool politics in the late 1930s as the dominant Conservatives shored up their support among working-class Protestants by declining to make the grants to denominational schools stipulated under the 1936 Education Act, few in the Labour group failed to back the Catholic demand for the maximum grant permissible.[47] This reflected the importance of Catholics within the Liverpool Labour Party. The position of Free Churchmen in Liverpool was negligible by comparison.

Norfolk provides an interesting contrast to Liverpool. There the proportion of Nonconformists to the general population was a little higher than on Merseyside. It, however, did not have Liverpool's ranks of Catholic working class to provide an obvious alternative dominant group. Indeed, there were not any Catholics among Labour's county councillors in the period. In these circumstances, Nonconformity's contribution to the Labour Party in Norfolk was even more remarkable than in Bolton. The pre-eminence of Free Churchmen in the Norfolk Labour Party in the interwar years is suggested by an analysis of those elected as county councillors in the period (Table 16). These, like their borough counterparts in places like Bradford, were elected for three years. However, unlike the annual election of one of three councillors in three-person wards that characterized the other locations analysed here, the whole council was elected at once every three years. That made progress more difficult for a relatively cash-strapped party with limited organization. The size of wards was another challenge; one which local party organizers could find not readily appreciated by their counterparts in urban Britain.[48] The relative scarcity of railways meant that the county also lacked the railway trade unionists who provided Labour's representatives in other rural areas such as Brecon and Radnor.[49] Accordingly, the one labour organization the party could fall back on to help it slowly consolidate in areas of strength was the agricultural labourers union George Edwards had re-established in 1906. Prims like Edwards were very strongly represented in this body. There may not have been many Nonconformists in rural Norfolk, but a large percentage of them were Primitive Methodists. This denomination provided the autodidacts to lead otherwise unschooled labouring men. They also stood outside the alliance of the squire and clergy that could be seen as the common source of the 'rotten landed system that helped to enslave the labourer'.[50] In these circumstances, Labour seems to have been peculiarly reliant for personnel upon Primitive Methodists. In Itteringham in North Norfolk, for instance, the same people ran their chapels, the local Labour Party and the agricultural labourers' union branch.[51] The Prims supplied an astonishing 46 per cent of Labour county councillors, while their centrality in the local party organization continued after 1945.[52]

Having such support networks in the local chapels could prove important as otherwise Labour campaigning in such rural areas was apt to be fraught with difficulties. The party often did better than it expected in the countryside, despite split votes meaning that it won relatively few seats.[53] This was despite the way the tied-cottage housing system continued widely to give farmers considerable social and political leverage over employees who were also their tenants. Wilfrid Winterton claimed that in Leicestershire villages,

Table 16 Religious affiliations of Labour county councillors in Norfolk, 1918–39

Joined in	Total	PM	UM	C	Q	RM	TNC	LP	CO	B/AS	A	II	NR
1918	3	1		1			2	2	2	1			1
1919–21	6				1	2	3	1	1	2	1	2	
1922	5	3					3	2	2		1	1	
1925	2	1	1				2	2	1	1			
1928	2	1					1	1	1				1
1930–31	3	2					2		1			1	
1934	3	3					3	3	3				
1937	2						1						1
TOTAL	26	12		1	1	2	17	11	11	4	2	4	3

Note: The abbreviations along the top of the table represent respectively: PM = Primitive Methodists, UM = United Methodists (after 1932, the Methodist figures are united); C = Congregationalists; Q = Quakers; RM = Railway Mission (an undenominational evangelical organization); TNC = Total Nonconformists (including one who cannot be placed by denomination); LP = Lay Preachers; CO = Chapel Officers; B/AS = councillors active in the Brotherhood or Adult Schools; A = Anglicans; II = Insufficient Information; NR = No Religion (those known to be atheist).

NB: Party politics only slowly appeared on the county councils and Norfolk was no exception. Although Sam Peel, the Quaker elected in 1919 and two of the three Prims elected in 1922 were initially recorded as Labour, they seem to have subsequently joined the vast majority of the council in sitting as Independents. Peel, indeed, endured considerable Labour hostility as a result of his opposition to the 1923 farm workers' strike.

> Labour speakers had to pitch their voices towards the outside walls of houses where the voters within might possibly hear them through open windows or doors left ajar … too fearful to venture out-of-doors lest they were observed by those who had the means and the power to register their disapproval by economic pressure.[54]

Glenvil Hall, the defeated Labour candidate in the Isle of Ely constituency in 1922 alleged, 'The farmers threatened [to] reduce wages by 5/- a week if I were successful.'[55] The survival of the tied-cottage system until 1976 ensured that even in the 1960s farmers retained considerable influence. At that time in Norfolk, some still kept watch over the way their tenants voted. Nonconformity encouraged its adherents to stand up to these employers. Part of the appeal of Sydney Dye, the Methodist lay preacher who was Labour MP for South West Norfolk in the 1950s, was his ability to do just that.[56]

What has been termed 'deference' was in rural society often economically rational, reflecting complex and reciprocal social hierarchies and bonds.[57] Nonconformists, being already somewhat outside that social order because of their churchmanship, were more likely to take part in and lead rural agitation. Only the often agnostic trade unionists who came from Norwich to assist the Labour cause in the countryside and who, because they were not part of rural society, were unlikely to be overawed by those who held power within it, shared this advantage.

There was another factor which contributed to the pre-eminence of Methodists in particular both in the agricultural unions of the late nineteenth century and the Norfolk Labour Party of the twentieth. Lay preaching did not just train them in the art of public speaking, important though this clearly was, and not just in Norfolk.[58] It also took them far beyond their native villages, giving them a status and prominence across the wide boundaries of a country circuit in a way few other organizations or activities then could. This was significant elsewhere too. By the time he became the Labour MP for the Lancashire mining constituency of Farnworth in 1938, George Tomlinson was already well known throughout the constituency because of his lay preaching.[59] Lay preachers were also able to know what was going on beyond the confines of their parish. Arthur Amis found this aspect of his lay preaching of particular value in his work as a Labour Party agent for North Norfolk from 1958 to 1970. It was another way of keeping in touch with the constituency in an area in which Methodist votes were still seen as being of major importance, especially to the Labour Party.[60] The county was indeed one of the few areas where Labour pursued Nonconformist voters with the same commitment shown to Catholic voters in places like Liverpool. In 1970 Labour even distributed Donald Soper's *Why I Vote Labour* in South West Norfolk in a vain attempt to recapture the seat.[61]

They also seem to have deliberately selected Methodist candidates in South West Norfolk from 1945 to 1964. A similar policy was pursued in North Norfolk through to the 1970s, though, from the list of those put forward at the death of Edwin Gooch in 1964, it was virtually certain that a Methodist would be selected anyway.[62] The selection of Nonconformist candidates was also considered expedient in a number of other areas. Not being a Nonconformist was certainly regarded as a political disadvantage for a candidate in areas like Cornwall where Methodism was particularly strong.[63] The large numbers of Free Churchmen chosen as Labour parliamentary candidates during the interwar period cannot, however, be entirely explained on these grounds, especially as many were clearly selected in areas where the Nonconformist vote was negligible.

This demonstrates that the pre-eminence Nonconformists could acquire in the local Labour organizations which helped to secure them parliamentary selection was by no means confined to areas like Norfolk. The attributes acquired in the chapel certainly contributed to this pre-eminence. So did a concomitant commitment to public life: as the Baptist Labour MP Frederick Messer put it, 'The teacher or preacher sees how social life conflicts with all he has been teaching or preaching and he attempts to relate that to religion and has to show that there should be a connection between actual life and religion.'[64] A differential propensity for Nonconformists to participate in public life continued to be observed in surveys in the 1950s and 1960s.[65] Christian convictions proved a powerful political impulse for this. A. V. Alexander said in 1931: 'The basic reason as to why we are politicians is this – that we are going sincerely to labour for the improvement of the conditions of those for whom Christ died.'[66] It seems likely that this sense of commitment contributed significantly to the numbers of Nonconformists active in the Labour Party in the interwar years.

This presence was considerable in most sections of the Labour movement, not least in Alexander's Co-operative Party. Some 50 per cent of its English MPs, though not so high a proportion of its candidates, were Free Churchmen, while its two secretaries in the period, S. F. Perry and Jack Bailey, were both Wesleyan local preachers.

The case of the ILP

Initially at least, Nonconformists were similarly active in the ILP. Even if Ramsay MacDonald's view that 'at least 90 per cent of the ILP belong to church or chapel and a considerable percentage of them are lay preachers and actively absorbed in religious work' was probably exaggerated, the pre-1914 ILP of which he wrote clearly included considerable numbers of Nonconformists.[67] This is despite the view of subsequent historians that many of those joining the ILP lost their faith.[68] While evidence for this can certainly be produced, committed Christians like Salter and Ammon nevertheless played a key role in founding pre-1914 ILP branches in places like South London.[69]

After the First World War, the ILP changed in character. It grew rapidly in the immediate aftermath as its opposition to the war made it, in the eyes of Egon Wertheimer (the London correspondent for the SPD's journal, *Vorwärts*):

> [A] refuge for all those radical bourgeois malcontents whose war experience and disillusionment had brought them into contact with the Socialist movement, or those from the Universities who were seeking a way into the Labour movement and who sought a platform for the propagation of ideas of the most varied kinds.[70]

In the process, its centre of gravity shifted away from the Nonconformity of Lancashire and Yorkshire. In the 1920s, Nonconformists were, however, still of considerable importance within the party. In 1926, about half of the English members of the National Administrative Council – the party's governing body – were Nonconformists. As is clear from the frequent references in the ILP's newspaper, pre-1914 ethical Socialists with a strongly chapel-infused message, such as Katherine Bruce Glasier, the daughter of a Congregational manse, continued to serve as ILP missioners. So did the Prim lay preacher, Charlie Simmons. Reg Sorensen and his fellow MP, the Congregational minister Gordon Lang also led ILP missions in the 1920s.[71] Furthermore, throughout that decade, the *New Leader* regularly featured religious stories and poems or even, in a column entitled 'Between the Furrows', occasionally explored the nature of sin.[72] Its Quaker satirist, 'Yaffle', in 1928 wrote an appreciation of the revolutionary doctrine based almost exclusively on fraternity, which emphasized the forgiveness of sins, the loving of enemies and the discouragement of wealth.[73] Christianity was not, however, appreciated by all in the ILP.

The party chairman ousted by the Glaswegian MP James Maxton in 1926 was Clifford Allen. The year before he declared, 'To all intents and purposes religious creeds have gone.'[74] His view of the redundancy of religion gained ground in the ILP in the 1920s, though even before 1914 some ILP branches had been very active in pushing both the literature and the message of the atheistic Rationalist Press Association.[75]

Rationalistic scepticism informed a series of articles that appeared in the *New Leader* in 1928–29. Tutored by Freud to regard religion as a way of reconciling man with the burden of civilization and by Marx to identify it as 'at once the instrument of the rich and the bridle of the poor', its author, who used the pen-name '27', sought to demonstrate that the problems to which Christianity most overtly addresses itself, of sin and moral responsibility, were now being solved by psychoanalysis and Socialism.[76] 'For the first time in history', he enthused, 'we are in a position to begin the real conquest of our baser self.'[77] For Freudians, this baser self was seen as the product of repression, especially sexual repression. Resolving sexual problems could be seen both as a means of liberating the individual and of tackling wider social issues. One ILPer wrote in 1930: 'Poverty, ill-health, and mishandled sex life are the three main miseries of mankind; and it is strange to reflect that, if the last of the three were wisely handled, the first would in time largely disappear, and the second would to an unexpected degree diminish also.'[78] This Pelagian faith in human perfectibility through some form of self-realization also encouraged some of the less circumspect of Freud's disciples to eagerly associate this repression with religious faith.[79] It was necessary for the Primitive Methodist minister Eric Bilton to remind them in the *New Leader*: 'There is a well-known code of ethics which declares if everyone pleases himself, everyone will be happy. It isn't true of toothache, much less of sex relationships or religion'.[80]

Some Nonconformist Socialists were nevertheless drawn to psychology. Ammon established a psychological clinic for his constituents after he was elected to Parliament in 1922, where his advice was 'sought on the most intimate personal questions'.[81] Two years later, A. Herbert Gray founded an 'informal spiritual and moral clinic' at his Crouch Hill Presbyterian Church in North London. Gray, who later helped to found the Marriage Guidance Council in 1942, wrote extensively and influentially on sex and marriage. He felt counselling could help to improve existing marital relations, rather than liberate individuals from the need for them.[82] The 'avalanche of protest' that greeted C. E. M. Joad's 1929 article in the *New Leader* condoning a more casual approach to marital fidelity suggests that there were still plenty in the ILP who agreed with Gray. Katherine Bruce Glasier proclaimed, 'Self control in the individual, for the sake of a whole society as for the whole man, the control of all our appetites, whether in eating or drinking, or revenge or greed of any kind that would invade other people's rights … was the first essential of a Socialist Society.' Speaking of the early ILP she argued that 'The chief object of Socialist effort was to make human life sacred and not property rights. Socialists recognised that the monogamous family had long ago been proved by experience to be the best cradle of the human race. They sought, therefore, to found that family upon the firm foundations of a love marriage.'[83]

Despite her long connections with the party, Katherine Bruce Glasier, however, quit the ILP in 1932, the year it disaffiliated from the Labour Party.[84] Most Free Churchmen, indeed most of its members outside Scotland, left the ILP as it drifted away from the party that it had done so much to create. Thereafter, although the Methodist Kate Spurrell continued to sit on its National Administrative Council,[85] Free Churchmanship ceased to be a noticeable feature of the leadership, membership or character of the ILP.

One young Nonconformist addressing his local ILP branch in 1931 on 'The Need for a Religious Basis for Social Reform' found:

> I had a terrible time. The atmosphere was hostile from the first. In discussion time I had absolutely no support. The bitterness against religion of any type, against religious bodies and people professing it has to be heard to be credited … Simply the verdict was – religion is an utter failure – socialism is good enough … If that ILP is typical the taunt of Socialist-Atheist is true.[86]

A correspondent to the *Labour Leader* in 1922 (the year it changed its name to *New Leader*) certainly claimed that this was true of some 50 per cent of British Socialists.[87] His downright hostility to Christianity was undoubtedly shared by some in the Labour Party. But though his denunciation of it as charity instead of justice could be heard from some Labour platforms it was the implicit praise of Christianity, as a vision of the most equitable and just manner of ordering society which the churches, branded as hypocrites, were failing to achieve or aspire to, that was more typical. Complaint was not so often against Christianity as against the unchristian nature of the social order, and against the churches' failure to denounce this. Thus, the *Bolton Citizen* railed in 1937:

> The preacher from his pulpit proclaims that all men are brothers and that they should love one another. The same preacher fails to condemn an industrial system which forces men, even against their will, to struggle with each other in a jungle of trade and commerce for the mere material things of life.[88]

Though the churches were often portrayed as having fallen short of their own high calling this did not mean, however, that Labour was generally hostile to Christianity.

Language and Labour

In the same year Clement Attlee, by then party leader, argued that 'There are probably more texts from the Bible enunciated from Socialist platforms than those of all other parties.'[89] It cannot be assumed that this was simply because of the numbers of lay preachers, accustomed to building their arguments upon a scriptural passage, active in the Labour movement. Lapsed Christians like Attlee could prove as ready with apt Biblical quotes and allusions. Eagerness to shrug off the label of 'Atheist' or the notion that Socialism was an alien creed, with which their opponents tried to brand the Labour Party, might be one reason for this. More importantly, the Bible was very familiar and generally respected, not least among Labour's political opponents. It possessed, for supporters and adversaries alike, both powerful resonances and authority. Its universality as the word, not of some Socialist theorist but of God, made it an ideal stick with which to beat opponents. For instance, the emendation of the Decalogue, which in 1927 appeared in the Labour press as the 'New Trade Union Commandments', was a pointed satire on the Conservative government's recent trade union legislation.[90]

A year earlier, the police had raided the *New Leader* office during the General Strike. One officer noted that its editor, 'read extracts from the Bible while we went through his things'.[91] This was, as E. P. Thompson has noted of an earlier period, the use of the Bible to criticize authority, including that of organized religion.[92] The Bible did not, however, merely lend itself to such uses. It conjured up images of a providential order blighted by the self-seeking nature of Capitalism.[93] The spirit of the text, 'He who would be greatest among you let him be servant of all' (Matthew 23.11) was presented as virtually absent from the ethics of the existing economic order.[94]

The language and nature of the Bible furnished ready material for such condemnations. 'What modern Labour man', asked Keir Hardie in 1912, 'ever used the same strong language towards the rich as Christ did?'[95] It also provided a stock of familiar precepts such as 'Feed my lambs' that could serve Labour rhetoric, even for atheists like Jack and Bessie Braddock.[96] This was a favourite passage that Rhys Davies, the Congregationalist and Labour MP for Westhoughton, turned to when he wished to remind the Bolton guardians of their responsibilities to dependants of miners locked out in 1926.[97] So frequently did Bob Smillie resort to this sort of use of scripture during the Royal Commission on the coal industry in 1919 that one of his fellow commissioners, Lord Durham, was moved to ask, 'Is this an ecclesiastical examination?'[98]

This use of scripture, however, differed somewhat from that of nineteenth-century radicals. Labour speakers drew their texts more from the New than the Old Testament. This was partly because of the relative decline of issues like land or free trade, which had been addressed in the Victorian period with language suffused with Old Testament references.[99] Another factor was an understandable shift to stressing the issue of peace. Its importance in the interwar years encouraged an emphasis on the Sermon on the Mount. Texts such as this or Paul's first letter to the Corinthians were regularly used on Labour platforms or in Labour propaganda. Passages such as these or John 15.12: 'Love one another as I have loved you', were not, however, simply a basis for Pacifist testimony. These texts also provided the guiding principles of a Socialist order in which 'Service, Brotherhood, Love (or to call love by its economic equivalent, co-operation), must be the basis of our social system instead of self-interest, individualism and competition.'[100]

The extent to which the scriptures were used to express a vision of Socialism should not, however, be exaggerated. Many Nonconformists spoke on both sides of the parliamentary debate on the shortcomings of Capitalism initiated by Philip Snowden in 1923. Of these, the only one to quote the Bible was Walton Newbold when he described St Paul's dictum (2 Thessalonians 3.10) that 'If a man will not work neither shall he eat' as 'the principle of Communism'.[101] Within the confines of a parliamentary debate it perhaps was not easy to join Katherine Bruce Glasier in emphasizing the responsibilities of power in Biblical terms thus: 'With Socialists it is "first things first". We ask the rulers of our day, as Jesus asked those of His day: "Have you fed the hungry, clothed the naked, cared for the fatherless and widow?"'[102] It nevertheless seems clear that such language (including St Paul's dictum) was, in the interwar period, a fairly standard feature of Labour platforms, particularly in the more Nonconformist parts of Wales and the North. Simmons often found that meetings in these areas continued to show a strongly revivalist tinge.[103]

Conclusion

These gave the Labour Party a religiosity of tone that was generally Nonconformist in flavour. They confirm the impression of a considerable Free Church presence within the Labour Party suggested by an appraisal of the religious affiliations of its members. It is, however, possible that this impression is exaggerated. It cannot be claimed that any of the tables through which these religious affiliations have been examined are wholly accurate or complete. The most substantial sources for the national figures, the lists of Free Church candidates published at each general election in the denominational press, are not above reproach. Compiled as these were from information sent in by readers, they were neither devoid of exaggerations (as the editor of the *Christian World* hinted when, in asking for his 1935 list, he stressed, 'Such a list … should be confined to Free Church candidates who have definite denominational associations') nor inaccuracies.[104]

They also contain many omissions, as is revealed by cross-checking with local and other national sources. Members of smaller denominations, such as D. B. Lawley, a member of the Churches of Christ who stood for Labour in 1922,[105] were particularly likely to be overlooked. There is therefore a possibility that the number of Free Churchmen in the Labour Party at least in some localities has in fact been underestimated. Given the relatively large amount of biographical material this is least likely to be true of the Labour MPs of the period. In cases where good biographical material – such as the potted biographies of newly elected councillors that disappeared from the Bradford press after the First World War – is more scarce, this possibility is much greater. This is certainly the case where most levels of the Labour Party, outside of parliament, are concerned. Despite these deficiencies of detail it is nevertheless evident that the Free Church presence in the Labour Party, albeit diminishing slowly, remained substantial by the end of the interwar years. So did its influence upon the tone of the party.

6

Labour and the Nonconformist Conscience

[T]he Labour Party should hesitate to don the fatal shirt of the Liberal Party ... Who demands local veto? Not the great body of workmen who have always been and will be opposed to it. No-one but the Chapels. It appears from those other observations that the Labour Party is becoming the captive chained to the chariots of the Chapels.

B. T. Hall[1]

I would not cross the street to support a candidate of my own party who was not sound on the temperance question.

Philip Snowden[2]

Liberals, Labour and the Nonconformist Conscience

Under the Coalition government of 1918–22, as in the Edwardian heyday of Liberalism, the temperance committee of the House of Commons coalesced around Liberal MPs like the Congregationalist P. W. Raffan.[3] The voice of the Nonconformist Conscience in the first Parliament after the Great War, when it spoke at all, still tended to be expressed and orchestrated by Liberals. Outside Parliament, Liberal and former Liberal MPs remained conspicuous on the executive committees of Free Church bodies. Labour had no comparable place in the councils of Nonconformity.

Nor did Nonconformity hold a comparable place in the Labour Party. After the 1922 election there were more Labour than Liberal Free Church MPs. In the opinion of one failed Liberal candidate however,

> [I]t certainly cannot be said by anyone who knows the industrial North East (particularly as a parliamentary candidate) that the mantle of Liberal Nonconformity has fallen upon the Labour Party ... any attempt to identify the Labour Party with Nonconformity would be laughed to scorn by great numbers of its adherents. The fact is that the Labour Party is a coalition in itself.[4]

Though all political parties – not least the Liberals themselves – are, to a greater or lesser extent, somewhat of a coalition, this was true of the Labour Party in a particular way. For the Liberals, Nonconformity was a historically important external interest group: in Labour's case, the important interest groups were within a party which had been founded as a coalition of such groups and continued to have some of those characteristics even after individual membership was introduced in 1918. This did not mean that Labour was constrained to represent only the interests of the trade unions who contributed the bulk of its votes, members and money and whose position within the Labour alliance was formalized by the creation of the National Joint Council of Labour in 1921. It did mean that Labour was a less obvious conduit for Free Church opinion than the Liberal Party.

This was compounded by the insistence upon independent Labour politics which had led to the foundation of the Labour Party. When Joseph King – one of Horton's deacons at Lyndhurst Road Congregationalists in Hampstead and a former Liberal MP who joined Labour after the First World War – was asked by his fellows on the Liberation Society's management committee to ascertain his new party's attitude to disestablishment and questions of religious equality, he warned them, 'the Labour Party was jealous of any action from outside'.[5] Though the Liberation Society, through individuals like King, nevertheless managed to get its views expressed within the Labour Party, it was not able to exert institutional pressure upon it.

The Liberals were more susceptible to this kind of pressure. It may not always have affected the whole party's policy. However, the relatively loose-knit structure of the Liberal Party accommodated the formation of interest groups within it. Labour was more centralized and monolithic. It was, accordingly, less tolerant of interest groups, even when, as in the case of the ILP, they originated within the party, particularly when they threatened party unity, hence the expulsion of that body in 1932.[6] This was even more the case when the interest groups concerned were responsive to organizations outside the formal structure of the party. For instance, having endorsed 183 of the Labour candidates at the 1935 election, the Council of Action for Peace and Reconstruction sought to incorporate the 34 elected in an all-party group in the new Parliament.[7] Labour's NEC responded with the resolution

> That membership of, and joint action with, the Council of Action for Peace and Reconstruction are not consistent with the pledges given by Parliamentary candidates upon joining the Party, and that their association with this Group in the House of Commons should be terminated.[8]

Free Church Labour MPs were among those taking a dim view of this attempt, as they saw it, to undermine party loyalties.[9] Other efforts to influence the party from outside were no more successful. Initiatives such as the invitation of the National Emergency Committee of Christian Citizens (NECCC) to the NEC to be represented at a conference on greyhound racing and betting were apt to be met with polite refusal.[10] Individuals could and did become involved with such bodies: Ammon becoming treasurer of the NECCC and C. H. Wilson its secretary.[11] Corporate involvement, however, was resisted. This attitude was similarly common among local Labour parties.

Labour, rhetoric and righteousness

This resistance to external pressure made it impossible for Free Church bodies, as institutions, to attain the kind of influence in the Labour Party they had once exerted within Liberalism. It did not, however, prevent Free Churchmen in the party from expressing themselves in Nonconformist rhetoric. The moral crusades of the Nonconformist Conscience of the late nineteenth century found an echo in the sense of moral outrage at the social injustices perpetrated in an allegedly Christian country expressed from many a Labour platform. For instance, in 1925, Fred Jowett declared: 'I want the poor to be discontented. I want them to nourish a deep sense of the wrongs they suffer and to feel, with an intensity which cannot be deflected from its purpose, that the responsibility for their condition lies with the supporters of the present immoral and un-Christian social order.'[12] A cartoon in the *Washington Labour News* in 1923 spoke of whipping the usurers and whited sepulchres, 'out of their mansions – the stock exchange and Parliament – as the Saviour whipped them out of the Temple nineteen hundred years ago'.[13] Accordingly, 'What movement can be more sacred', George Edwards asked, 'than the one which has for its object the uplifting of man, the beautifying of human nature and the restoring of that likeness and image of God which man has so long lost?'[14]

Labour was thus in many ways the heir of a righteousness of tone redolent of the Nonconformist Conscience. Indeed, the formative years of its principal founders were when that movement was at its height. These men and women adapted and extended that rhetoric, applying it first to lambast those aspects of contemporary society they sought to condemn. Charlie Glyde, the Congregationalist-cradled Bradford anarcho-Socialist, is one such example. When not leading back-to-the-land attempts to recapture a simpler and more equitable society, he inveighed against 'the brutal, callous treatment of the poor … invented by Capitalism in a country that is crowded with churches and chapels, brotherhoods and sisterhoods'.[15]

Secondly, this rhetoric was used in a spirit of rivalry to claim Labour's moral superiority over churches which had failed to heed their own message. For instance, in March 1933 an article in Labour's local monthly, the *Bolton Citizen*, on 'Socialism in the Early Church' highlighting choice patristic writing, not only drew the lesson that 'the Church has neglected its own business, has disregarded its own teachers, is ignoring its own past and is now declining its original lesson among men', but also inferred that the discarded mantle had fallen on the Labour Party.

The high profile political role of Nonconformity in the late nineteenth century set it up to be judged and found wanting, particularly in terms of its (lack of) actions to tackle socio-economic problems.[16] So did its shift towards an emphasis on fellowship rather than salvation. In these circumstances, J. R. Clynes essentially dropped the outward forms of religion – those intended to promote the inward acquisition of grace and salvation – concluding that conduct alone was the central object of religion.[17] Clynes was nevertheless claimed as a Congregationalist by the denominational press, but from the chapels he appears to have derived an idealism and sense of righteousness which he attached to Labour: 'Many of us have found in political life not a splendid career but an expression of our religion. A position has not been viewed as a job but as a Cause.'[18]

Thirdly, then, this righteousness was also readily attached to the Labour programme. The idea that the party existed as a kind of secular church to project righteousness into national life was promoted on many a platform. Indeed, the use of figures with a preaching background, such as Charlie Simmons, encouraged such conflations of Labour with righteousness. He accordingly declared, 'My political ideals were a projection of my Christian faith … I believed in the application of Christian principles to social problems.'[19] Wilfrid Wellock in 1922 claimed, 'A Labour programme based on New Testament ethics would shake society to its foundations.'[20] Clynes as Lord Privy Seal in the first Labour government in 1924 indeed assured a deputation from the churches that government policy was based upon the Sermon on the Mount.[21] The *Methodist Times* may have been sceptical about this claim in light of the government's ambivalent position on issues like the building of battle cruisers or the Welsh Local Option Bill.[22] The fact that it was made, however, indicates how readily Labour politicians adopted the Nonconformist habit of identifying themselves as an outsider group working for righteousness in national affairs against the self-interested resistance of the established order.

Such attitudes remained current in the Labour Party after the Second World War. Of the legislation of the Attlee government George Thomas recalled:

> There was a feeling of crusade as we took into public ownership the essential industries of coal, gas and electricity. Each night as we trooped through the division lobbies someone would call out, 'Come on, George. Strike up!' and I would start to sing 'Guide me, O thou Great Jehovah'. Instantly there would be a mighty choir singing its way through the lobby.[23]

This tone of moral crusading and righteousness was adapted to the programme of the party. As King found, however, the party was unwilling to adopt as righteous the causes of others. Accordingly, Nonconformity was more likely to find a voice within Labour through the agency of willing individuals. In particular, by the 1920s, the Society of Friends was increasingly using Quaker Labour MPs as its parliamentary spokesmen. In 1923, Roden Buxton and Alfred Salter were called upon to present a memorandum on capital punishment to the House of Commons declaring:

> We reaffirm our belief in the sacredness of every human life, and the infinite possibilities of spiritual reclamation. We regard the Law of God as binding upon the community and we cannot rest satisfied whilst what is wrong for a single person is practised by the State. We base our opposition to legal killing on this belief.[24]

Two years later the Quakers helped to launch the National Council for the Abolition of the Death Penalty with another Quaker E. Roy Calvert as its secretary.[25] The NCEFC was soon represented on this organization's executive through its secretary Thomas Nightingale.[26] By then, the 1924 COPEC conference had called for the abolition of capital punishment.[27] Though large numbers of Labour MPs were in sympathy with this call, the first three Labour home secretaries, all of whom were Nonconformists,[28] did little to gratify it.

Henderson, in the first Labour government in 1924, appears to have given little consideration to the subject.[29] The issue, however, was raised much more directly in 1929. It was not a Quaker but a Wesleyan, W. J. Brown, a newly elected Labour MP, who took advantage of the advent of the second Labour government to put forward an abolitionist motion. Clynes, as home secretary, gave his approval. However, on an amendment moved by the (Jewish) Liberal and former home secretary Sir Herbert Samuel, a Commons select committee was appointed to investigate.[30] This eventually recommended, by a majority of one, a trial suspension for a period of five years.[31] However, though the *New Leader* furiously compared Clynes to Pontius Pilate, no action was taken or promised by the government.[32] Chuter Ede, as home secretary in the Attlee government of 1945–51, was still sending men to the gallows. It was only after he left office that he came to oppose capital punishment.[33]

This conversion was somewhat behind that of the bulk of Free Church opinion, and certainly behind that of Ede's own church, for the Unitarians had conducted a lively debate on this subject in *The Inquirer* throughout the interwar years. However, neither for Clynes nor Chuter Ede was this matter of public morality one readily reducible to the certainties they attached rhetorically to the righteousness of Socialism.

For many of their Nonconformist parliamentary colleagues, such certainties were more likely to arise in the context of the keenly attended and contested Prayer Book debates of 1927 and 1928. The proposed replacement of the Church of England's 1662 Prayer Book with an updated version seen by swathes of suspicious Protestant opinion to have been infected with Anglo-Catholicism galvanized many on all sides of the Commons to reveal unsuspected depths of theological and liturgical learning. These debates also, as Clement Attlee rightly observed, 'revealed a great deal of latent Protestantism in unexpected places'.[34] The view that the new Prayer Book posed a threat to the Protestant settlement in England led a number of Labour MPs vehemently to oppose the Measure. 'My puritan ancestors arose before me in solemn array', recounted the Unitarian Josiah Wedgwood. 'All the changes were in the direction of dogma and that authority which chills the spirit, which I had ever fought in the field of politics and thought.'[35] Deploring the subsequent defeat of the Prayer Book Measure the *Socialist Christian* complained

> [W]hile in the Churches, Socialism has hitherto seemed to appeal mainly to those at the superficially opposed poles of (a) Quakerism and (b) Sacramentalism, in the rank and file of the Labour Movement, and among Labour members of Parliament, 'Christianity' more commonly means some form of Evangelical Protestantism.[36]

This was, however, a misleading explanation of the conduct of the party as a whole in these debates. Labour certainly acquired something of a reputation as a Protestant party as a result. Around this time as well, MacDonald, who Porritt regarded as the most religious premier since Gladstone, confided to the editor of the *Christian World* his anxieties about the weakening of Nonconformity and fears of 'Catholic influences'. Nevertheless, fewer than half the Labour MPs who sat for English and

Welsh constituencies in fact voted against the Measure when it was first debated in December 1927 and only a slight majority of them joined those who rejected it when it returned to the House in June 1928. MacDonald was not among them. Some of the most vehemently Protestant of Labour MPs were nonetheless his fellow Scots, speaking and voting against a Measure which did not affect them. One of these, Edward Rosslyn Mitchell, by common consent made the most powerful speech in opposition to the Measure, supplementing his words by dramatically acting out transubstantiation.[37]

Not all those MPs from south of the border who joined him in defeating the Measure did so simply because they shared Wedgwood's righteous Nonconformist indignation. The Anglican Labour MP J. M. Kenworthy, in supporting the Measure, pointed out that its defeat would only work in favour of those who rejoiced in the Church of England's discomfiture. Several of the Labour MPs, such as Ernest Thurtle, who were most prominent in the opposition to the new Prayer Book fell into this category.[38] Not all those who opposed the Measure did so for the highest of Protestant motives.

The Prayer Book debates thus only reveal Labour as a Protestant party to a strictly limited extent. Nor do they reveal much about the Free Churchmanship of the party. In contrast to their Liberal counterparts, who were, it seems from George Thorne's citation of telegrams from various Nonconformist leaders, closer to the bulk of Free Church opinion as they united in rejection of the Prayer Book Measure,[39] the only Free Church Labour MPs to refer to their Churchmanship in the course of the debates were those who spoke *for* the new Prayer Book. Nonconformist Labour MPs nevertheless were divided by roughly three to one in favour of the rejection of the measure. Protestantism no doubt largely accounts for these votes. So did the hope that rejection might bring disestablishment closer. Ammon, in contrast, voted in favour on the same grounds. He also saw the debate as a distraction from the party's principal concerns: 'Would that half the enthusiasm, half the keenness and half the energy which has been devoted to this problem had been devoted to social, moral and economic problems.' He pleaded that the measure be passed so that the Church could turn its attention to such matters.[40]

Labour and drink

One moral problem that concerned Ammon throughout his life was temperance. He was one of a number of Labour figures who enthusiastically pursued this well-established Nonconformist cause. Nor were Free Churchmen the only temperance advocates in the party, although they may have constituted the bulk of the party's teetotallers. There were, however, among the Anglicans, Catholics and those of no religion in the party, men and women of equally firm temperance convictions. The Free Church press was nevertheless unconvinced that Labour had succeeded to the temperance witness of the Liberals. In the early 1920s, the Liberals continued to be seen as the leaders on the issue, with Isaac Foot chairing the parliamentary temperance group in 1924.[41] Meanwhile, in 1922, the *Primitive Methodist Leader* warned its readers that Labour was unreliable on the temperance issue.[42] A number of Nonconformist Labour MPs were certainly seen as such. Herbert Dunnico may have been a Baptist minister, but he nevertheless

Table 17 Analysis of lobby voting on the Wales (Temperance) Bill, 15 February 1924

	For	Against
Free Church Labour MPs	45	17
All Labour MPs	68	46
Free Church Liberal MPs	51	-
All Liberal MPs	83	3
Free Church Conservative MPs	-	4
All Conservative MPs	9	171
Result of the division	201	229

Note: The Bill was accordingly defeated on its second reading by a majority of 28.

disappointed the chapels of his constituency with his attitudes on temperance.[43] Bolton Free Church Council's 1924 interview with their (Wesleyan) Labour MP Albert Law similarly revealed that – probably for good electoral reasons – his views on the Welsh Local Option Bill and the registration of clubs were most unsatisfactory.[44]

Labour's conduct on the second reading of this bill, introduced by the Liberal Congregational Rhys Hopkin Morris in 1924, for the denominational press proved the party's unreliability on the temperance issue. This was a particular moment shortly after the advent of the first Labour government when it became apparent to Nonconformity that Labour was establishing its own identity and that a progressive alliance with the Liberals would not prove feasible. As Table 17 shows, Labour MPs – including Nonconformists – were much more divided than their Liberal counterparts on this legislation. This reflected growing ambivalence within the party about how to handle the temperance issue.[45] It also reflected that forces other than the chapels weighed upon the minds even of the most ardent Nonconformists within the party.

Under the terms of Hopkin Morris's Bill, the local electorate would regularly be given the option of voting for either no change in licensing policy, a reduction in licences, or no licences, as had been the case in Scotland since 1920. This was a measure predominantly Nonconformist Welsh Liberals had been pressing for since the 1890s.[46] It had also generally been Labour's adopted policy before 1914. During the Great War, Lloyd George's nationalization schemes, however, suggested an alternative. The Baptist party official, Arthur Greenwood, subsequently established a Labour Campaign for the Public Ownership and Control of the Liquor Trade. He also persuaded Labour's Advisory Committee on Temperance Policy, by then chaired by the Wesleyan minister Henry Carter, to support his ideas. Their resulting report was endorsed by the NEC in March 1920.[47]

That autumn, the party conference debated and decisively rejected Prohibition. The NEC recommendation of nationalization was much more narrowly defeated, probably as a result of a change of heart by Snowden. Before the war, he had campaigned vigorously for a variant of nationalization, the adoption of the Gothenburg system of municipal control.[48] Struck, however, by the levels of drunkenness in the nationalized pubs of Carlisle, his advocacy helped to ensure the reaffirmation in 1920 by a large majority instead of the policy of local option.[49]

This was not to remain the case for long. To manage the tensions in the party the 1922 conference instead remitted temperance policy to an inquiry under Sidney Webb. The resulting 1923 report indicted drink on both social and economic grounds. For ardent teetotallers like Henderson, drink also stood in the way of the achievement of Labour's goals. In 1921 he promised that given, 'an army entirely dissociated from strong drink … it would not be long before they would crush the very life out of Capitalism'.[50]

The more measured findings of the report were that not only would the social costs of drink in terms of bad health, poverty and criminality be lessened, but it would also soon be possible to achieve important objectives, such as the solution of the acute post-war housing shortage, could the amounts then expended upon drink be redirected to that end.[51] It ended by reaffirming the policy contained in *Labour and the New Social Order*, the 1918 manifesto, which advocated a combination of local option and the expropriation of those private interests which exacerbate the drink problem by 'promoting the utmost possible consumption'. However, Webb's report also concluded that no useful purpose could be served by pursuing temperance reform at that time.[52]

The grounds for this could be found in the party leader's preface to the report. Here MacDonald complained:

> What is known as 'the Drink Question' is one of the most troublesome and difficult that the honest politician has to face today. The 'Trade', the clubs, the prohibitionists, the local vetoists, one and all, are apt to come down upon him just at the critical moment of an election, and present an ultimatum that if he does not do exactly what they want they will throw their influence against him.[53]

He nevertheless took Labour into the 1923 election advocating nationalization of the Trade.[54]

Local option, however, clearly continued to have many supporters among Labour MPs. J. H. Thomas introduced a local option bill for England in 1922 and various Labour MPs were unavailingly to resubmit this five times by 1928.[55] It also was alleged that of the 288 Labour MPs returned in the 1929 election, a clear majority of 163 were supporters of local option.[56] Nevertheless, by 1923, only the Liberals continued to advocate this policy at elections.

Snowden may have defended local option in 1921 by claiming: 'Labour is unmoved by the argument of the Liquor trade that Local Veto is an unwarranted interference with personal freedom … Labour believes that the community has a right to restrain personal freedom where its exercise is manifestly injurious to the individual and the community'.[57] This was a formulation remarkably similar, of course, to the arguments in favour of the restraints on personal freedom of Socialism itself. However, it was a view widely rejected by local party branches in their responses to the Webb inquiry. The party files dealing with the inquiry are scattered with identical resolutions denouncing local option as 'antagonistic to Individual Freedom'.[58]

This resolution seems to have been promoted by the active hostility of the Club and Institute Union (CIU). The CIU was the largest of the working men's club organizations, with some 1.15 million members in its 2,400 clubs.[59] In 1924, it was particularly concerned about the attempt in Part III of Hopkin Morris's Bill to extend to the clubs the controls on Sunday opening which had been in place in Wales since 1881. This was the facet of the Bill the chapels most strongly supported, irritated by the defiance of Sunday closing by Welsh working men's clubs. In the debate many Labour Nonconformists, nonetheless, seem to have taken the side of the clubs rather than the chapels. Arthur Henderson Jr, for example, may have shared his father's faith and teetotalism and he also voted for the second reading of Hopkin Morris's Bill. However, he criticized the provisions covering Sunday closing of the clubs, and called for this section of the Bill to be withdrawn.[60] His attitude, and that of many Labour Nonconformists, may well have been influenced by the publicity the CIU general secretary B. T. Hall gave to his view that 75 per cent of his members voted Labour.[61] Upon the defeat of Hopkin Morris's Bill, the CIU's periodical, the *Club and Institute Journal*, rejoiced that the debate had seen Labour freeing itself from 'the domination of the little Bethel state of mind into which one or two of its leaders endeavoured to thrust it'.[62]

Nonconformist teetotallers like Gordon Lang may have argued, 'The ideals of Labour will never fructify amidst unchecked whisky palaces and its intellectual appeal will fall in vain upon a drink-sodden democracy.'[63] The CIU contention that 90 per cent of the male working-class population consumed beer and that the party which sought to be the representative of those working classes should pursue reductions in the price of this 'most common commodity in working class consumption' rather than control of its availability was a powerful counterargument.[64] No doubt such considerations animated the concerns about the wartime reductions in beer supply emphasized by the Primitive Methodist and Labour MP Alfred Waterson in his 1919 maiden speech.[65] This was particularly the case when many party workers were among those drinkers. In 1927, Salter complained that so attractive were the social and intoxicating pleasures to be had from beer that even party activists could find that their enthusiasm for the cause was flagging as closing time drew near.[66]

By the 1924 election, the party had dropped nationalization as a policy as well as local option. While James Nicholson, the leader of the National Union of Vehicle Builders, had told the Webb inquiry that temperance advocacy was an electoral liability, he also took the view that nationalization would cost too much in compensation. Instead, he argued that the party should encourage improved public houses.[67] The party did not seek even to do that. Both in 1924 and 1929, Labour simply suggested setting up a Royal Commission to advise on alcohol policy. The UKA's *Alliance News* on the latter occasion had no doubt that this offer merely reflected internal divisions on the issue.[68] Any more positive approach was indeed rejected by the NEC in 1927, with only Ramsay MacDonald and Arthur Henderson (who carried his dissent close to the point of resignation) offering serious opposition.[69]

These divisions were reflected in the PLP. By 1924, even former teetotallers like Ben Tillett were closely associated with brewing interests.[70] Although a good proportion of Labour MPs remained teetotal – including apparently 73 out of the 154 elected in 1935 – many others, some of them Nonconformists, including Greenwood and Spoor (who died of an alcohol-related illness in 1929) more than made up for this.[71] In 1929, George Strauss found 'the element of drunkenness in the Labour Party …

really shameful. Some were drunk every night, usually the same ones, and quite a lot of people … drank too much occasionally.'[72] Some seemed to treat the Commons as a social institution, rather than a workshop. The Anglican teetotaller George Lansbury as party leader in 1935 accordingly attempted to revive the pre-war pledge first introduced by Keir Hardie, whereby Labour MPs promised to abstain from alcohol while Parliament was in session.[73] Neither attempt, however, proved successful.

Temperance advocacy became the preserve of individuals, particularly after an attempt at the 1928 party conference to rally support behind Ammon's local option bill was heavily defeated.[74] At the following general election, some of these temperance advocates faced hostility from their own side or the clubs.[75] J. H. Hudson was reprimanded by the NEC for campaigning for temperance in another Labour MP's constituency.[76] By 1934, the local party in Portsmouth was even complaining to the NEC about the mere association of Henderson, who had but recently been party leader, with the Workers Temperance League (WTL).[77]

The WTL had been set up in 1931 in response to the Royal Commission on Licensing established by the Labour government in 1929. Its foundation reflected the increasingly marginal place temperance had within the movement. The improved public house and the failing of Prohibition in the United States made the drink issue appear both less urgent and less susceptible to legislative solution. As a pressure group within the party, it therefore had little success in persuading Labour to adapt, 'a LEGISLATIVE PROGRAMME which shall include the Temperance Recommendations in the Report of the Royal Commission on Licensing'.[78] For instance, Salter's 1933 efforts to get the clubs to conform to the same hours of sale as licensed premises simply provoked the rejoinder from his fellow Labour MP George Hicks that 'the club movement has been a very valuable agency on behalf of Labour'.[79] This was despite the fact that the clubs also worked through Tory MPs: the Conservative Methodist Gilbert Gledhill introduced a liberalization measure at their behest in 1936.[80]

By then the CIU claimed 4 million members.[81] As Table 18 shows, the number of clubs also steadily expanded during the interwar years. Faced with the difficulties of satisfying both their temperance and clubmen supporters, not least when in government, Labour first temporized, and then opted for the avoidance of an alcohol policy. This process was assisted by agreement between the three political parties in 1929 that the way to avoid the lobbying MacDonald had complained of earlier was to agree that their candidates should not respond to any questionnaires by organizations from outside their own constituencies.[82] An increasingly professionalized party was trying its best to avoid becoming the captive of either the chapels or the clubs.

With the decline of the Liberals, however, the Nonconformist-dominated WTL nevertheless became the principal parliamentary advocates of temperance.[83] Hudson, its secretary from 1934, also came to be a key figure in the National Temperance Federation.[84] Meanwhile, his fellow Nonconformist Labour MPs came to replace Liberals at denominational temperance rallies. The Labour Party may not itself have proved the successor to the temperance witness of the Liberals. It is, however, clear that by the end of the interwar period it was Labour MPs who were leading the temperance forces in Parliament.

Table 18 Registered clubs in England and Wales, 1918–39

Date	Number	No. per 10,000 estimated population
1913	8,457	2.29
1918	7,972	2.14
1919	8,049	2.15
1920	8,994	2.39
1921	9,924	2.62
1922	10,663	2.79
1923	11,126	2.90
1924	11,471	2.96
1925	11,780	3.03
1926	12,138	3.11
1927	12,481	3.18
1928	12,775	3.24
1929	13,132	3.32
1930	13,526	3.42
1931	13,947	3.49
1932	14,377	3.58
1933	15,010	3.72
1934	15,298	3.78
1935	15,657	3.85
1936	15,982	3.91
1937	16,297	3.99
1938	16,563	4.04
1939	16,951	4.11

Source: AYB (1940).

Labour and gambling

In the early 1920s, Labour did not give the same attention to gambling as to temperance. The Labour MP John Banfield (of no known religious affiliation) nonetheless shared the Free Church view that this problem was on the rise, declaring in 1934: 'I am satisfied that gambling is a bigger curse to this nation to-day than drinking has ever been.'[85] Two factors were instrumental in this development. First, the gambling industry was more diverse, more accessible, more respectable and cheaper than before. In place of the rough and illegal pursuit of street betting there was the brightly lit dog track, complete with crèche. In place of the difficulty and expense of taking a day off work to go to the racecourse, there was the charabanc picking up people from the factories for one of the vastly more frequent evening race meetings in the greyhound stadium. Even more convenient for the small gambler was the advent of the Pools coupon.[86]

Secondly, the idea that the state could usefully tap gambling revenues resurfaced when Winston Churchill, as Chancellor of the Exchequer in 1926, introduced a betting duty. This reflected both his search for means of balancing the nation's budget, and a view that luxuries and indulgences should be taxed.[87] Snowden, the Shadow Chancellor, opposed this state recognition of gambling. He was also immediately shown by J. H. Thomas – who, unlike Snowden, gambled – how the duty could be evaded.[88] It was, however, the bookmakers and their threats to campaign against the Conservatives in the 1929 election that eventually led Churchill to modify the measure.[89]

In a more successful attempt to tackle the illegal bookmaker and increase revenue, Churchill also supported the introduction of the Totalisator in 1928. This prompted Snowden to accuse him of making the State 'nothing less than a bookie's tout'.[90] Arthur Hayday, despite United Methodist antecedents, may have become associated with brewing interests, but not the gambling industry: he denounced the Totalisator as a machine which facilitated cheaper, easier and – worst of all – greatly increased betting.[91] Like other innovations of the gambling industry in the period, it seemed specifically designed to make gambling cheap and more accessible for those least able to afford it.

The opposition to both this and the betting duty won the full backing of the Free Churches. For them, there was no justification for State involvement in a trade which both exploited folly and bred cupidity. Their reaction was not quite matched by that of the Labour Party. While no Labour MP voted for the Racecourse Betting Bill, not all were perhaps as convinced as Rhys Davies that the Totalisator was 'an infernal instrument'.[92] Opposition was largely confined to the same small group of MPs and was even more muted in the Lords.[93] The left-wing Wesleyan MP Ellen Wilkinson drew a furious tirade from Davies when she admitted that though she agreed about the parasitic nature of bookmaking, she could not understand why some of her fellow Labour MPs were so agitated by 'Tote' bills.[94] 'Is it nothing to the Labour Party when the State becomes a partner in bookmaking?' he asked. 'Is it conceivable that within the Socialist State we would exploit the vices of the people for revenue purposes?'[95]

Notwithstanding the fervour of Rhys Davies, the answer to this second question has to be yes. Many local Labour parties and trade unions exploited the vices of their members for revenue purposes in just this way.[96] This method of raising money by appealing to a capitalistic desire for personal gain, rather than more altruistic motives was condemned both by NEC officers and by the National Union of Labour Organisers and Agents.[97] However, sweepstakes and lotteries were the financial mainstay of many Labour branches, a fact that could encourage the most impeccably Nonconformist of Labour agents to accept their existence.[98]

Gambling was similarly a mainstay of the Labour movement's newspaper, the *Daily Herald*, wholly owned by the trade unions until 1930. Although Lansbury, its founder, was fervently anti-gambling, the widespread pursuit of this pastime among its working-class readers meant that failure to carry racing reports would make poor business sense.[99] The newspaper indeed initially welcomed the advent of dog tracks in 1926–27, though by 1928 it was supporting the private bill introduced by the Scottish Conservative John Buchan to allow local option on their provision. About half the PLP supported Buchan's Bill and only four, including Wedgwood (who took a libertarian approach to gambling) opposed it. Among the most vehement Labour opponents of greyhound racing was J. H. Thomas.

Thomas's opposition was based less on moral grounds than a concern about working-class domestic economy. He claimed that dog racing was much more objectionable than horse racing because it took place most days, rather than just on Saturday afternoons.[100] Many of his parliamentary colleagues joined him in opposing some forms of gambling – particularly this one – rather than others. Other interwar gambling innovations, such as the Irish Hospitals Sweepstake, indeed won considerable sympathy among Labour MPs, possibly because it had more altruistic overtones than some of the alternatives. At a time when there was no immediate prospect of government control or finance of perennially under-funded hospitals, sweepstakes offered a potential solution to their problems argued the Conservative MP Sir William Davison in introducing his Hospital Lotteries Bill in 1931. The background to this was the wide and illegal circulation in Britain of Irish sweepstake tickets.[101] Even so, only sixteen Labour MPs supported Davison's Bill, which accordingly did not proceed beyond the first reading. Most of the 118 Labour MPs who rejected it probably agreed with Isaac Foot's argument that hospital sweepstakes did not encourage genuine philanthropy, they only, 'cover[ed] cupidity with a thin smear of charity'.[102]

Although C. H. Wilson became the chairman of the National Anti-Gambling League in the mid-1930s,[103] Foot was probably the leading parliamentary anti-gambling campaigner of the interwar period. However, the most significant piece of legislation on this issue during the period was neither the product of the Liberal benches on which he sat, nor of the Labour Party. These parties did not develop specific policies to address the gambling menace, though Snowden as Chancellor of the Exchequer in 1929–31 removed the last vestiges of Churchill's betting duty.[104] It was left to the succeeding Conservative-dominated National government to appoint the Royal Commission of 1932–33 in view of mounting concern at increasing numbers of sweepstakes, dog tracks, tote clubs, and other inducements to gamble. Unlike Labour's Licensing Commission, this bore fruit in the Betting and Lotteries Bill of 1934.

This, in addition to severely curtailing the operation of the Irish sweepstake in Britain, sought at last to attack other forms of gambling that did not possess even a thin smear of charity. Its principal objectives were the closing down of tote clubs, the introduction of various restrictions on track betting, and the prohibition of newspaper gambling competitions.[105] A few Labour MPs, because these were essentially working-class forms of gambling, saw in this evidence of class bias, though only two actually voted against the legislation. One of these, the Liverpool Catholic David Logan, also led the opposition to the government's decision to restrict dog racing to 104 days a year. His views, however, had negligible support among the PLP, most of whom had supported another greyhound racing local option bill in 1932.[106] On the other hand, on the third reading, three-quarters of the PLP abstained and only eleven Labour MPs voted for the Betting and Lotteries Bill. Most of these were Welsh Nonconformists or Scot Presbyterians.[107]

Even they used a different, less paternalistic, tone to justify their stance. In the wake of the allegations of a 'banker's ramp' bringing down the second Labour government in 1931, there was more focus upon the evils of gambling on stocks and shares and the association of gambling with the very nature of Capitalism.[108] Rhys Davies thus lambasted the capitalistic exploitation of an industry that sowed nothing but greed and misery:

> I am offended beyond measure that there are men and women in this country who have not sufficient honour to see that, when they combine together in a capitalist group to exploit the known weaknesses of their fellows for their own personal profit, they are doing an injury, not only to this nation, but ultimately to the human race as a whole.[109]

The dog tracks were at this time making large profits. Tom Williams (one of the undenominational Nonconformists recorded by Linden) opposed this form of gambling, commenting: 'I suppose that if I owned a greyhound track I should be almost as silly as those who own such tracks now, and want to destroy the nation so long as there was profit in it for me.'[110]

He saw the Pools and their promoters in much the same light and was most disappointed when the government decided not to include these in the terms of the Betting and Lotteries Bill, taking the view that 'Of all swindles the football pool is probably the biggest of any.'[111] In supporting the Betting (No.1) Bill of 1936 designed to suppress the highly profitable Pools companies Williams declared:

> We talk about abolishing Capitalism or the capitalists, and about industrial magnates who have no sympathy or care for their workpeople; here is a case in which the proprietors have only one interest in life, and that is in getting as much interest out of these 5,000,000 or 6,000,000 people as they possibly can.[112]

In this indictment he was at one with the Free Church press. Indeed, the 1936 Bill might almost be considered a Free Church bill, promoted as it was by R. J. Russell, a member of the NCEFC and Liberal National MP. The extensive support Russell's Bill won from the denominational press was not, however, matched among Nonconformist MPs.

Labour had supported suppression of the Pools in 1920. The Ready Money Betting Act 1920, however, proved a wholly ineffective measure and was easily evaded by the Pools promoters. The subsequent growth of this business led the National government to drop the Royal Commission's recommendation to ban Pools betting from the 1934 Act. After all, by the mid-1930s, 10 million people a week were filing coupons for what was then the most popular form of betting. This development also helped to change the minds of Labour MPs on the subject from 1934, when a large majority of the PLP had supported reinstatement of the Pools betting clauses into the Betting and Lotteries Bill.[113] In 1936, Tom Williams declared he had received more letters from constituents threatening never to vote for him again if he supported Russell's Bill than over any other issue since he entered Parliament.[114] Nevertheless, he was one of only thirteen Labour MPs to vote for it. Only six Free Church Labour MPs voted in its favour, while twenty-two others opposed the Bill. The Labour Party as a whole voted heavily against it.

This illustrates that by 1936 Pools betting had become as acceptable to most Labour MPs as to their constituents. Labour did not share the Free Churches' growing concern about gambling, and the nature of its attitude towards that vice also shifted. After 1931, there were rhetorical flourishes against capitalistic gambling on stocks and shares to be curtailed in future within the planned economy that had, by the 1935 election, become the main plank of Labour's proposals. Meanwhile, a new generation of MPs whose moral preconceptions were less formed through the framework of paternalist late Victorian assumptions of the need to protect people from themselves came to the fore.[115] As in the field of temperance, whatever the attitudes of those like Rhys Davies, the party as a whole had moved towards accepting gambling as part of working-class culture and away from presuming the efficacy of moral prohibition.

Labour and the Sabbath

In the late Victorian era the nascent Labour movement had acquired some characteristics of a moral crusade as an alternative to the churches. This had included the creation of new institutions which adapted religious form to serve Labour ends, particularly in the form of the Labour Church and the Socialist Sunday Schools (SSS). The first, however, was largely moribund by 1914, though in a few places like Stockport it transformed into a Labour Fellowship and survived into the 1930s holding lectures on personal development and entertainments of an essentially secular kind.[116] The second emerged at around the same time at the start of the 1890s, and sought to create a distinctive cultural milieu to nurture children into appreciation of the goals and morality of the just social order advocated by the new movement. The ideal that Socialism was a religion continued to appear in its teachers' manual in 1923, though the rising influence of more militant figures meant that revolutionary objectives were by the late 1920s emphasized more. This, the splitting off of the ILP which had helped to develop the SSS, and the institutionalization of the Labour Party as a vehicle for the political aspirations of the organized working classes, all undermined the distinctive role of these bodies by the 1930s, although a few lingered in the West of Scotland until the 1960s.[117]

Free Church concern was more focused upon the Labour tendency to hold political meetings on Sundays.[118] These meetings were expedient for a working-class party in the days before the development of mass media, when the working week was long and leisure time short and generally concentrated in Sundays. They, however, more than the SSS, gave the party the appearance of being irreverent and secularist. At the 1931 general election, the minister of Leeds Road Baptists, Bradford, allegedly suggested this as a major reason for voting for the National government.[119] Certainly, the secretary of the Baptist Union, M. E. Aubrey, in 1929 expressed his hope that no Baptist would support a candidate who thus disturbed the Sabbath.[120] Some Labour candidates, notably Arthur Henderson and Ramsay MacDonald, indeed promised not to hold Sunday political meetings.[121] However, as Labour candidates were nevertheless the main culprits, Aubrey's comments were tantamount to advice not to vote for their party. The *Methodist Times*, at the previous election in 1924, similarly concentrated fire on Labour's culpability in this respect.[122]

D. J. Vaughan's suspicions that this attitude was animated as much by party bias as by Sabbatarian feeling were, for him, confirmed by his experience as a candidate in the

Bristol South constituency in the 1920s. A Wesleyan local preacher, he held no Sunday meetings though, unlike Henderson, he had no moral objections to doing so. It was his Liberal opponent Sir Beddoe Rees, a Baptist coal owner and the then treasurer of the NCEFC, who held Sunday political meetings. Rees, however, received no protests from the chapels.[123] Nor had Nonconformists always proved averse to Sunday political meetings in the past. Clifford in the 1890s addressed rallies on Sundays.[124] The essentially Nonconformist Leicester Vigilance Committee certainly held their protest meetings on the Sabbath.[125]

Labour complained that their meetings were just as appropriate for the Sabbath. 'Politics are applied religion and best propagated on Sunday', argued the *Bradford Pioneer*.[126] Many Free Churchmen in the party, seeing their Socialism as the application of their Christianity, agreed. Indeed, George Edwards's Sunday meetings in Norfolk were often virtually indistinguishable from Primitive Methodist camp meetings.[127] He, however, had to be dissuaded from offering his resignation as a local preacher in 1924, so upset was he by complaints against Sunday Labour meetings from Primitive Methodist circuit meetings in the county, 'as being a needless competition with the Churches and a desecration of the Sabbath'.[128]

There was thus a divergence in attitude between the Nonconformist leadership and both the Labour Party and Free Church Labour MPs on the issue of Sunday political meetings. There were also tensions at the local level. In Bolton and Liverpool, the best allies of the local Free Church Councils in their defence of Sabbatarianism were the Conservative-dominated councils. It was Liverpool city council which regularly baulked Labour's demands for Sunday concerts in the municipal parks. Such concerts had begun to appear in London in the 1880s, and gradually spread in the provinces. Congregationalists like Edward Siddle joined with fellow Labour councillors in calling for Sunday music in the parks of Bradford.[129] The Bradford Labour group was, however, split on the issue of Sunday cinema performances.[130]

The Conservative-controlled LCC had largely turned a blind eye to the spread of Sunday cinema in the capital since before the First World War until a court decision ruled that these Sunday performances were illegal under the 1780 Sunday Observance Act. This presented the Labour government in 1931 with the dilemma of either enforcing the 1780 Act or bringing in new permissive legislation.[131] Choosing the latter, Clynes as home secretary accordingly introduced the 1931 Sunday Performances (Regulation) Bill, designed to allow local authorities to give or refuse licenses for Sunday cinema performances as they saw fit. Though Liberal Nonconformists like Goronwy Owen led the opposition to this Bill, appealing 'to the House not to let it be said that we in this generation made legal what our fathers regarded as wrong and as a sin against the Divine Law', the Free Churches showed surprisingly little hostility to this proposal.[132] Even Ammon – a former LCC councillor who had been severely criticized in the *Daily Herald* for his part in the Free Church agitation in 1922–23 against the LCC for permitting Sunday games in the London parks – supported its provisions.[133] As Table 19 shows, so did a small majority of his fellow Free Church Labour MPs, in contrast to their Liberal counterparts.

After Clynes's Bill failed with the fall of the Labour government in August 1931, to be taken over, slightly altered and expanded to cover Sunday concerts as well by

Table 19 Analysis of lobby voting on the Sunday Performances (Regulation) Bill, 20 April 1931

	For	Against
Free Church Labour MPs	63	38
All Labour MPs	145	55
Free Church Liberal MPs	3	26
All Liberal MPs	6	33
Free Church Conservative MPs	5	5
All Conservative MPs	97	85
Result of the division	258	210

Note: The Bill accordingly passed its second reading, but it fell with the Labour government and it was the National government the following year that passed new statutory provisions in the form of the Sunday Entertainments Act.

the incoming National government, Liberal Nonconformists continued to lead the opposition to these measures. A few Welsh Labour Nonconformists sounded a Sabbatarian note in support. Speaking to an amendment to exclude Wales from the terms of the 1932 Sunday Entertainments Bill, the Calvinistic Methodist Tom Griffiths declared, 'The most important thing that the people of Wales believe in is the Resurrection, and that Resurrection took place on a Sunday.'[134] Such sentiments could not, however, prevent the defeat of the amendment.

Sabbatarianism was not widespread within the Labour Party. There was, however, considerable concern about Sunday labour. Even those more inclined to stress strict observation of the Sabbath, like Rhys Davies, were as likely to focus on this question.[135] The PLP indeed introduced an unsuccessful amendment to the 1932 Sunday Entertainments Bill in an attempt to protect the interests of those workers affected by the measure. Winding up the discussion on this amendment, the Roman Catholic Joseph Tinker declared: 'As it is a special Bill, we are anxious to see special protection given to those who will be called upon under it to work on Sundays. On these benches there are differences of opinion as to the Bill, but on this point we are agreed.'[136] A similar concern marked the efforts of the Methodist John Leslie to restrict the relaxation of Sunday trading laws (under which about 26,000 prosecutions had hitherto annually taken place during the interwar years) introduced in the 1936 Shops (Sunday Trading Restrictions) Act.[137]

Given proper safeguards for those required to work on Sundays however, many Labour MPs saw positive advantages in the introduction of Sunday cinema. Ammon was vehemently against this but his fellow Methodist Ellen Wilkinson, speaking in the debate on the Sunday Performances (Regulation) Bill 1932 was clearly concerned that this day of rest should not involve the Sabbath gloom 'of very real dread' she had known as a child.[138] Sunday cinema not only lightened that gloom, but it was also seen by supporters of these bills as a service to the community, both because of the money it generated for charity and because, in many areas, it offered the only alternative to the streets and the taverns. George Lansbury accordingly declared that no social worker in the East End would vote for the closure of Sunday cinema.[139] Several Free Church Labour MPs indeed felt that the terms of the bills were too limiting: they looked for the Sunday opening of theatres as well. This is not indicative of support for the commercialization of Sundays. It was simply that many Labour MPs were more interested in providing wholesome entertainment for the working class on their day of rest than in inculcating strict Sunday observance.

Peace and Pacifism

There was greater consensus, particularly in the 1920s, between the Nonconformist leadership and the Labour Party on the issue of peace. In the aftermath of the Great War they were initially united in their desire to avoid a repetition. The LFCC and the Labour Party locally, for instance, cooperated in organizing No More War demonstrations.[140] Party policy was designed to ensure that these expressed more than pious hopes. It reflected the criticisms of the policies and the international system that had failed to prevent conflict in 1914 levelled by the UDC in which so many figures later influential in the formulation of Labour's foreign policy – not least Ramsay MacDonald – had been prominent during the war. Not least of their targets was what they saw as the dangerous and discredited policy of maintaining the balance of power in Europe.[141] By 1917, their solutions were reshaping Labour policy from the simplistic pre-war reliance on an international general strike to maintain peace, a hope which had clearly been overwhelmed by events. A special conference in December of that year overwhelmingly endorsed an NEC memorandum which called for the complete democratization of all countries, the limitation of armaments, the abolition of private arms manufacture, the establishment of an International Court and Legislature, self-determination and the holding of plebiscites to decide territorial disputes; virtually the whole programme of the UDC.[142]

Such recommendations reflected and informed the faith of the time in a restructured international system as a guarantor of peace. This system, as it emerged from the chaos of the war at the summit meetings of Versailles, was however a grave disappointment to the architects of these recommendations.[143] Labour nevertheless accepted the principal creation to emerge – the League of Nations – though with markedly less enthusiasm for that or Versailles as a whole than the Free Church press.[144] By 1928, renunciation of war, to be replaced by negotiation through the League of Nations, was part of a policy that continued to reflect UDC perspectives: stressing the jurisdiction of the Permanent Court of International Justice, international economic cooperation, the presentation of all international engagements to Parliament, and arms reduction by international agreement to the minimum necessary for police purposes.[145]

This did not prevent Free Church criticism of Labour's defence policy. The Labour government of 1924 sanctioned building five of the eight cruisers planned by the outgoing Conservative administration. In response, the *Methodist Times* complained, 'It has quoted the Sermon on the Mount and has voted for the building of more battle cruisers.'[146] This criticism was echoed in other Free Church journals, probably reflecting the Liberals' attitude to the issue. Liberals may have been no more inclined to treat the Sermon on the Mount as a sound policy guide (in the 1924 debate on the Army Estimates, the Presbyterian W. M. R. Pringle declared, 'it is simply an absurd futility to talk, in these days, of expecting the nations of the world to have their conduct governed by that Sermon').[147] They nevertheless moved an amendment calling for the scrapping of the cruiser building programme. The Labour government's rejection of this amendment demonstrated that – despite the opposition expressed by many of its members to the First World War, including both the prime minister and the parliamentary secretary to the admiralty Charles Ammon – it could hardly be described as Pacifist. Nor, however, did it entirely deserve the strictures of the denominational press.

After all, the government's defence strategy, including the decision on the cruiser building programme, hardly bore signs of belligerence. 'We have scrapped a dozen ships; we are proposing to put five in their place', Frank Hodges told the House of Commons. According to his defence of government policy, their objective was a small but effective navy.[148] This objective was supported by most Labour MPs and by the formerly vehemently antimilitarist *New Leader*.[149] Only fifteen Labour MPs (including three Scots) for Pacifist reasons joined the Liberals in supporting their amendment. Even former conscientious objectors like Morgan Jones voted in support of the government. Few joined Ben Turner in arguing:

> You have either got to scrap the preparations for war, or scrap the New Testament, and I am not going to scrap the New Testament … If the Ten Commandments are right, and the Sermon on the Mount is right, then building cruisers cannot be right, because it is contrary to the principles contained in the Ten Commandments and the Sermon on the Mount.[150]

While recognizing the validity of this view, Tom Stamford pointed out that not even the churches were prepared to recommend it. Both he and Jack Lawson took refuge in Labour conference decisions in favour of the service estimates and steady progress towards international disarmament. Some of their less Nonconformist colleagues responded far more scathingly. Fred Montague was most anxious to correct any impression that Labour was a Pacifist party. To him, Pacifism was a sort of political equivalent of Christian Science, vainly persuaded of the non-existence of evil. This implied that Pacifists were naive. Few on the Labour benches shared their colleague Dr Haden-Guest's view that they additionally suffered pathological tendencies.[151]

It was nevertheless a Labour MP, the Quaker W. H. Ayles, who moved a Pacifist amendment to the 1924 Army Estimates, to reduce the army by some 150,000 men to a force not exceeding 11,600.[152] He, however, won scant support. Even Quaker Liberals like T. E. Harvey opposed this amendment. Only fourteen Labour MPs (seven of them Scots) demonstrated their Pacifism by voting for it. Surprisingly enough, none of these supported their arguments with the sort of economic critique of militarism as wasteful and destructive employment of talent paid for by excessive taxation that the Society of Friends had, since the Great War, come to stress.[153] Nor did many of them share the scripturally based rhetoric of Ben Turner. Only three of the fourteen were Free Churchmen.

There were other strains of war-resistance in the Labour Party than that derived from Christianity. During the Great War, there was a tendency, especially in the ILP, to denounce the motives of all combatant nations as capitalistic and imperialistic, a view that the publication of wartime Allied secret treaties by the Bolsheviks upon their seizure of power in Russia, did little to dispel. This Socialist critique of war was however not exactly Pacifism. *Ploughshare*, the journal of the Socialist Quaker Society responded to the enthusiasm with which many of its protagonists greeted the Russian Revolution: 'We have no right to call ourselves pacifists, to challenge war at all times and in all places, and then set to organising committees the success of which is to depend upon the potential use of the Army or parts of it on the Russian model for the English Revolution.'[154]

This anti-capitalist critique of war tended to fall into abeyance when war was neither taking place nor threatened, as was the case in the 1920s. Better suited to the reactions from the horrors of the last war and the optimistic hopes of avoiding another so prevalent in this decade was the utilitarian, humanitarian Pacifism typified by the Peace Letter circulated by the agnostic Labour MP Arthur Ponsonby in 1925.[155] The central tenets of this view: that all war is too horrific to be justified and that all international conflict is susceptible to peaceful, rational solution, however, differed little from the assumptions that continued to underpin Labour's foreign policy when it returned to office in 1929. There accordingly remained broad consensus between Pacifists and non-Pacifists in the party on the conduct of foreign affairs and defence (Ponsonby indeed generally supported the service estimates introduced by Labour governments).[156]

Limited progress towards naval disarmament through the negotiations that culminated in the 1930 London naval treaty went some way towards justifying these assumptions. This, together with a certain amount of enthusiasm for Snowden's defence of British interests at the September 1929 reparations conference at The Hague, ensured more initial support for the foreign policy of the second Labour government than of the first from the Nonconformist press. The *Methodist Times* was less inclined to carp when one if its directors, Arthur Henderson, was foreign secretary. Henderson's announcement in 1930 that no new capital ships would be built before 1936 was greeted optimistically. In the same year, the withdrawal of the last Allied troops from the Rhineland marked a further stage in the return of Germany to the concert of nations.[157] Meanwhile, plans were laid for the resolution of international differences at the Geneva disarmament conference starting in 1932 under Henderson's chairmanship.

The conference, however, did not develop into a triumphal display of the virtues of UDC ideals. After Germany deserted it for the second and final time in October 1933, it could only limp purposelessly on into the next year, achieving nothing. This total failure, together with the simultaneous rise of the sinister and unscrupulous figure of Hitler, increasingly called into question the assumptions upon which Labour's defence and foreign policy had hitherto been based.

In 1929, disarmament had been seen both as a way of reducing international tension and supplying a moral lead. If Britain disarmed, J. Percival Davies, asserted, 'We should not be attacked, because no people would allow their government to engage in such wanton aggression as an attack on an unarmed nation.'[158] In the wake of the Japanese attack on Manchuria in 1931, such assumptions became increasingly difficult to sustain, recalled the Unitarian and Labour MP F. W. Pethick-Lawrence:

> Inside the Labour party these foreign events were beginning to create a division of opinion. Up to then, it had seemed possible to ride at once the two horses of pure pacifism and loyalty to the League. But now it had become apparent that the time might come when they would take us in opposite directions. Loyalty to the League meant support of collective security and a willingness, if need arose, to co-operate in the application of sanctions. If there was actual aggression, that might involve us in war. It was therefore necessary for the members of the Labour party, individually and collectively, to choose which horse, in that event, they would continue to ride.[159]

There was, however, reluctance to abandon long-held attitudes. The 1933 Labour Conference indeed responded to the worsening international situation by returning to the pre-1914 policy of calling a general strike in the event of war.[160] The international aggression of the decade, however, rendered such an approach futile. It was dropped in 1934, but an emphasis on negotiation and international arms control remained much in evidence. There was nevertheless growing awareness that if this failed, collective action might be necessary to curb an aggressor nation. In 1934, Labour therefore recommended a 'Yes' vote to all the questions to be raised in the 1935 LNU Peace Ballot, including support for military action against an aggressor state.[161]

The following year, the need to react to Mussolini's invasion of Abyssinia made the implications of this, for the TUC at least, extremely clear. The trade unions were already antipathetic to Fascism in the light of its crushing of independent trade unionism. Abyssinia reinforced this position. There was a feeling that such acts of aggression justified military sanctions, a feeling that was fully shared by some Labour MPs, such as Pethick-Lawrence.[162] The TUC secretary, the Presbyterian-raised Walter Citrine, told Congress, 'There is only one way of dealing with a bully and that is by the use of force. Moral resolutions are no good … There is no alternative now left to us but the applying of sanctions involving, in all possibility, war.' The TUC conference overwhelmingly agreed.

For Labour Pacifists, re-emphasizing their Pacifism was increasingly their only option as the party shifted towards policies which might ultimately involve support for war. Such dilemmas were highlighted when, during a debate at the 1935 Labour Conference on the same sanctions resolution that the TUC had so heavily endorsed, Ernest Bevin launched a furious attack on the compromises into which the Pacifist George Lansbury had been led through his position as party leader, prompting Lansbury's resignation shortly after the resolution was successfully carried.[163] The subsequent launching in 1936 of a Parliamentary Pacifist Group by three Labour Quakers – Salter, Hudson and Wilson – reflected recognition of the clear difference of principles that now existed.[164]

A number of Labour MPs became involved with Sheppard's PPU; though not all remained supporters as sympathies for the republican cause in the Spanish Civil War (which tested even Lansbury's Pacifism), rearmament and, finally, the outbreak of war itself, all took their toll.[165] Lansbury called for a Truce of God, featuring a conference at Jerusalem convened by the Pope; and devoted much of the few remaining years of his life to visiting the major statesmen of the world and trying to arrange such an event.[166] Even when war broke out, faith in such solutions to the various economic and territorial tensions they saw as leading to war remained strong among parliamentary Pacifists. In November 1939, a group of Labour MPs put their names to a memorandum calling for an immediate armistice and the convening of a conference of this type.[167]

Free Church Labour MPs predominated in this group. For most Labour Nonconformists, however, the evils of Hitler and Mussolini had become greater than the evils of war. Pacifists and those who denounced all war as a capitalistic or imperialistic exercise made increasingly little impact at Labour Conferences from 1936 onwards. There was, however, a continuing reluctance – which even the most hawkish Nonconformist Labour MPs shared – actively to prepare for war. The Air Raid Precautions introduced by the National government were still being criticized by local parties in places like Bradford in 1939 for producing a war atmosphere, despite a party circular of August 1935 declaring that they were necessary.[168] Nevertheless, by late 1936, the only important local authority still refusing to implement them was Labour-controlled Barnsley.[169] In the Commons, the PLP continued to oppose the service estimates until 1936. Thereafter, Labour abstained on the issue, though in 1937 the Congregational Hastings Lees-Smith moved the rejection of the Defence Loans Bill.[170]

At the same time, there was a growing sense of frustration with the inadequacy of the government's diplomacy and its civil defence preparations. This view was confirmed by the 1938 Munich crisis. The threat to Czechoslovakia that prompted it had been a casus belli for the Labour Party. While Pacifists like Wellock rejoiced, Ammon lamented that the 'lamp of freedom has been considerably dimmed – and at our hands'.[171] He, like his party in general, nevertheless went on to oppose the limited Military Training Bill Chamberlain hastily introduced after Hitler's invasion of Czechoslovakia in the spring of 1939.[172] In retrospect, it seemed to Morgan Phillips Price:

> We wanted to stand up to Hitler and Mussolini, but thought it should only be done through the League of Nations. Labour opinion was confused. We were afraid to re-arm in the ordinary way because we had argued ourselves into thinking that all armament meant war. We could not bring ourselves to believe that they might deter an aggressor.[173]

Ultimately, however, the aggressor had to be confronted. The views of the Methodist George Tomlinson, elected at the January 1938 Farnworth by-election as a Christian Pacifist committed to disarmament and the League of Nations, may be taken as representative of the process whereby the large majority of Nonconformist Labour MPs reconciled themselves to support for war:

> I held the view that if a nation was strong enough to disarm and set an example to the world the moral forces of the world would be sufficient to prevent its being overrun. The rise of Hitlerism demonstrated the impracticality of my theories.

> I came to the conclusion that there was nothing else to do but fight for the things in which I believed, even if fighting appeared contrary to my Christian principles. Until Hitlerism was destroyed, that in which I believed had no value.[174]

Confronting the Nazis had become more important than maintaining peace.[175] In justifying Labour's support for the war effort in early 1940, Attlee invoked the moral standards of Christianity abrogated by the conduct of the German government.[176] Such moral claims may not have been universally accepted when Labour's pro-war majority in the First World War defended their stance on the basis of a Christian duty to protect small nations. By 1940, and despite the party's Pacific intentions throughout the interwar period, they commanded much wider support.

Education

Fred Jowett had little sympathy with the Passive Resistance campaign against the 1902 Education Act, noting:

> The vast majority of working class parents are quite indifferent on the subject; and as for the children they cannot understand. The most important of all questions, that which concerns the bodily and mental development of child life (without which the capacity to feel and the desire to live in a truly religious sense is stunted if not destroyed) is lost in the faction fighting between rival sects. And they have the impudence to say that their fight is for education![177]

Accordingly, until 1914, Labour favoured the introduction of a wholly secular education system.[178] The party contained few passive resisters, except in rural areas like Norfolk, where Anglican domination of education was more noticeable than elsewhere. There were, nevertheless, considerable similarities in the attitudes of the Free Churches and the Labour Party to education.

They were certainly agreed on its intrinsic value. Some of Labour's first educational initiatives, such as the pioneering of school meals or the establishment of nursery schools, indeed reflected the concerns of Free Churchmen and women in the party. Reformers such as the Congregationalist pioneer of open-air nursery schooling, Margaret McMillan, saw education as an essential component in 'the creation of a new society – a society that will make the beautiful life possible for all'.[179] The moral qualities and intellectual capacities Socialism demanded indeed required a well-educated society. Education was important as a means of equipping trade unionists, 'to participate effectively in the management and control of industry'.[180] A Labour publication in 1948 continued to emphasize: 'divorced from authoritarian dogmatism, the ethical and moral values of Christian teaching combine these very virtues of love, brotherhood and toleration, without which no real civilisation is possible'.[181]

Ayles in his 1922 general election handbill declared, 'I am in favour of a sound free system of education, extending from the primary school to the university, and an adequate system of maintenance grants. The children of to-day are the citizens of tomorrow.'[182] Education, stressed the Brotherhood National Charter drawn up in 1922 by Arthur Greenwood, was fundamental in preparing these future citizens for responsible membership of society.[183]

The 1928 *Labour and the Nation* programme reflected this desire for quality and equality of opportunity in education. It recommended more nursery and special schools, the reduction of class sizes with the necessary improvements in facilities this entailed, the raising of the school-leaving age to fifteen (to be facilitated by maintenance grants), and much wider opportunity of access to both secondary and higher education.[184] Such improvements, however, could only further overstrain the already stretched budgets of denominational schools. Warned of the dangers of reopening old Edwardian religious controversies by Scott Lidgett and Nightingale, the party decided to refrain from any pledges on the education question during the 1929 election campaign.[185]

This reticence disguised the extent of Labour's willingness to share Free Church antipathies to denominational education. After all, Labour's incoming president of the Board of Education was Sir Charles Trevelyan, who as a Liberal MP had fully supported the Nonconformist opposition to the 1902 Education Act.[186] J. D. Jones's apprehension that Trevelyan had abandoned his former views appears to have been misplaced.[187] In a letter to Bertrand Russell in 1929 Trevelyan declared, 'I am absolutely determined that the Labour Party shall not get into the hands of any religion, least of all the Catholic. I represent a constituency swarming with Irish Catholics. I would rather lose the seat than give the priesthood a bigger power in the schools.'[188] Nor was he averse to expressing in the House of Commons the dislike with which he viewed the dual system of provided and non-provided (denominational) schools set up under the 1902 Act.[189]

Trevelyan made considerable progress in reducing average class sizes, increasing secondary school places, promoting school building and providing nurseries and playing fields.[190] In the course of a series of conferences with denominational leaders on the cardinal issue of the raising of the school-leaving age he managed, however, to antagonize both Nonconformists and Catholics. The upshot was Scurr's amendment reflecting Catholic fears that Trevelyan's Bill would impose on them additional burdens without commensurate financial assistance.

The Labour government's unsuccessful opposition to this amendment received the thanks of the NCEFC. Nevertheless, in the actual debate, the *Baptist Times* felt that only Ramsay MacDonald represented the views of the Free Churches. Allowing for Isaac Foot's speech, the sole contribution from the Liberal benches, this view was substantially correct. Nor did the NCEFC feel able to support the new proposals which Trevelyan submitted in February 1931. These were far from representing the full Nonconformist position of insistence on the agreed syllabus in religious education and local authority control of the teachers and of any building grants that might be made to existing denominational schools. There was Nonconformist relief when this Bill was rejected by the House of Lords.[191]

With two million children in denominational schools, however, Trevelyan recognized they could not be abolished, observing 'We must, in some way, enable the voluntary schools to be reconditioned in a good many cases, or in many parts of the country thousands of children will be left without a proper chance which we are trying to give to all.'[192] His successor, Lees-Smith, therefore reintroduced the Bill under the 1911 Parliament Act procedure for overruling the Lords.[193] Lees-Smith's readiness to take on this task illustrates the limited extent to which Nonconformist principles in education found expression even among Free Church Labour MPs. C. H. Wilson's subsequent establishment of a Nonconformist parliamentary group nevertheless demonstrated that the educational controversy did stir up feelings. Both this group and Lees-Smith's Bill, however, perished with the fall of the government and Labour's annihilation in the ensuing general election.

The issue did not arise again until the National government introduced a new attempt to raise the school-leaving age in 1936. By now it was clear that this could not occur without some concessions to the additional burdens that it would place upon denominational schools. Clearly, the implementation of the Hadow proposal of separate teaching of eleven- to fifteen-year-olds would also adversely affect such schools. Catholic interests in the Labour Party were not, however, represented on the subcommittee on denominational education set up by the NEC on 28 November 1934. This, accordingly, did not recommend generosity in the matter. Chaired by Lees-Smith, it proposed that building grants should be restricted to the improvements required under the Hadow Report or for the sake of raising the school-leaving age and should represent no more than 50 per cent of costs. It also advocated restrictions on the number of reserved teaching positions in denominational schools.[194] These recommendations were very similar to those already adopted by the NCEFC. Though the Labour Party in Liverpool, reflecting the Catholicism of the area, pressed for the full 75 per cent building grants permitted under the 1936 Act, for new as well as existing schools, this was not typical of the party as a whole. Indeed, Joseph Cleary, the deputy leader of the Labour group on Liverpool council, opposed his own party on this issue.[195] Accordingly, while not prepared to consider itself the representative of Free Church views, except for a certain number of MPs briefly in 1931, the Labour Party was generally closer to the Nonconformist than to the Catholic position on education.

The raising of the school-leaving age envisaged in 1936 was curtailed by the outbreak of war in 1939. It was only raised to fifteen under the 1944 Education Act, subsequently implemented by Ellen Wilkinson and George Tomlinson as the ministers responsible in the post-war Attlee government. Since Chuter Ede played a substantial part in the negotiations that led to the framing of the Act, Free Church Labour MPs clearly made a significant contribution to both the terms and application of this legislation. Nonconformist leaders were nevertheless unhappy with what they saw as overgenerous building grants and the continuing religious tests on teachers. Despite these objections, they came to share Labour's view that the religious aspects of the 1944 Act offered a workable compromise.[196] The ideals sketched out by Ayles and others in the 1920s, however, remained a long way off.

Disestablishment

A party of the Left, whatever its religious sensibilities, might be expected to share Nonconformist antipathies towards an established and privileged Church. The Church of England's landed wealth and power and relations with the squirearchy as much as its ecclesiastical pre-eminence had always been part of the disestablishmentarians' case. With many of its pioneers interested in land nationalization, disestablishment therefore won considerable sympathy from the early Labour Party. This sympathy was greatest where the power of the established Church was most overt. George Edwards's demand that 'the Privilege and monoply [*sic*] now enjoyed by a Church that have [*sic*] always proved itself a bigoted and tolerant Church be abolished', reflected the extent to which opposition to the continuing economic power of the Church of England merged with Methodist objections to its prejudices in areas like Norfolk.[197] Objections could, however, be equally strong in urban areas. Pronouncing itself uninterested in the contemporary debate on the new Prayer Book, the *Bradford Pioneer* in 1928 declared the sooner the Church of England was disestablished the better.[198]

At the beginning of the interwar period, Liberals like T. T. Broad were still those most conspicuously working for this eventuality. The Liberation Society remained virtually a Liberal preserve, although most of that party were far from fervent supporters of its cause. Few Liberal MPs backed Broad's 1919 disestablishment and disendowment amendment. Even Nonconformist Liberals mostly voted against.

Labour proved no more willing to support disestablishment. The only Labour MPs to speak (Waterson and Wedgwood) in the debate both strongly supported Broad. The PLP, however, largely abstained. A motion which, when last debated in 1907, had been carried by 198 votes to 90, accordingly failed by 304 votes to 16.[199]

Disestablishment nevertheless had its advocates within the party. Ramsay MacDonald delighted his friend John Clifford, in whose church he regularly worshipped, with a speech at the Liberation Society's annual meeting in 1923 in which he declared that the life of the Christian is liberty and that he therefore should not submit himself to anything except the bonds of the Infinite.[200] As prime minister the following year, he found his responsibilities for ecclesiastical patronage most distasteful, commenting in his diary, 'Why I, a Presbyterian, should be bothered with Bishops, I know not. A self-respecting Church would not allow me to interfere.'[201]

Many of his fellow Labour MPs in the course of the Prayer Book debates – Nonconformists, Anglicans and non-Christians – for varying reasons, pronounced themselves in favour of disestablishment. This did not mean that the party was prepared to do much corporately to further this cause. As Lansbury told the Commons during the 1928 Prayer Book debate, 'There is no party in this House, neither the party I belong to, nor what remains of the party below the Gangway [the Liberals], that proposes to put disestablishment of the English church on its programme.'[202] The debate in 1919 proved to be the last occasion during the interwar period when Parliament gave serious consideration to the question of disestablishment. Free Church Labour MPs like Morgan Jones, nevertheless, became as active on the Liberation Society's executive committee in the 1930s as some of his Liberal counterparts, while C. H. Wilson was the Society's parliamentary spokesman during the 1936 Tithe Bill debate.[203] It was on this issue of tithes, rather than disestablishment, that the Liberation Society came to the fore during the interwar years.

Lloyd George's Coalition in 1920 introduced the Tithes Rentcharge (Rates) Bill. Although Thetford Free Church Council urged the minister responsible, their

Liberal MP Sir Richard Winfrey (a Congregationalist), that this 'is a grave injustice under which Free Churchmen in all parts of the country are suffering', Liberal disestablishmentarians at the time let it pass as it was only a temporary measure.[204] The linkage of tithe rentcharge to rates that this established, rather than to cereal prices – as had been the case since payment in kind was commuted in 1836 – was, however, made permanent by the 1925 Tithe Act introduced by the Conservative government. Labour and Liberals were united in regarding this as unfair both to tithe-holders and Nonconformists. C. H. Wilson argued that clerical stipends should be maintained by the congregation, not supplemented by the nation. He complained that in requiring Nonconformists to contribute to something they do not believe in, the 1925 Tithes Bill was 'simply perpetuating an injustice which it ought to be our object to endeavour to remove'.[205]

After 1925, tithes remained high, while cereal prices plummeted, gravely affecting the ability of many farmers to pay this charge.[206] E. J. Butler of the Suffolk Tithepayers Association wrote to the *Christian World* in 1931, 'The Nonconformist ... has by law to pay an excessive charge, often several times more than the original one-tenth of his income to the support of a Church to which he does not belong.'[207] Passive resistance to tithes became increasingly common, as did a tendency to default on their payment. The result was the setting up of a Royal Commission in 1934. The substance of the Tithes Bill which the National government subsequently introduced in 1936 – the passing of responsibility for the collection of tithes to the government, the payment of compensation to the Church and the aim to redeem the tithe completely within a number of years – received all-party support.[208] However, both Liberals and Labour felt that the compensation of £70 million was too much and the period of redemption, at sixty years, was too long. The measure nevertheless survived largely unamended, despite Ammon's claim that it satisfied virtually no one.[209] Tithes were only finally abolished in England (having been abolished in Wales at disestablishment) by the Labour government in 1977.

As with many Nonconformist causes there were a number of Free Church Labour MPs who actively bore witness to their disestablishmentarian convictions and came to rival or surpass their Liberal counterparts both in terms of influence on bodies like the Liberation Society and in its parliamentary representation. Though there seems to have been a considerable body of opinion within the party which shared these convictions, few seem to have been prepared to do more than give voice to them. Lansbury was right; Labour showed little desire to take up this Nonconformist crusade.

Conclusion

As an institution, Labour did not become Nonconformist in attitude. It was individuals within the party who bore witness to Nonconformist causes and became active in the bodies that promoted them. In practice, however, they were not that different from the Nonconformist Liberal MPs of 1906, only a core of whom actively pursued Nonconformist causes in Parliament.[210] By the 1930s it was Labour MPs who supplied that active core. Quaker Labour MPs like Hudson and Wilson certainly became far more prominent than Liberals in both the parliamentary representation and the counsels of the Society of Friends. Others were equally active in the affairs of their denominations. Ernest Winterton, the first Socialist president of the UKA, was probably the most regular of Labour contributors to the Free Church press. Will John became president of the Welsh Baptist Union. Arthur Henderson was the first Labour figure to be elected to the executive committee of the NCEFC. Nevertheless, his obituary in the *Methodist Times* commented that he had been one of the few Labour laymen at the Wesleyan Conference.[211] By 1938–9 there were still only two Labour MPs (and one ex-MP), and as many Liberal MPs on the NCEFC executive.[212]

The first Labour government was a defining moment when the party established its distance from Nonconformity. To an outsider like the Tory MP Duff Cooper its 1924 victory rally had a distinctly Nonconformist flavour.[213] The policies actually pursued, not least in the fields of temperance and defence, made clear, however, that the party – while colonizing Nonconformity's rhetoric of conscience – would make its own pragmatic decisions in office. This was despite the apparent assumptions of the Free Churches that the party might be susceptible to their influence and criticism. Outside influences were resisted, after 1929 with all-party agreement. Nonconformist causes such as anti-gambling were simply the preserve of small groups of usually the same committed individuals within Labour, while the generality of Labour Nonconformists largely accepted the wider direction of the party. After 1924, this focused less on moral regeneration, not least for electoral reasons.

For all classes, Labour nevertheless retained Nonconformist overtones of moral seriousness very much in keeping with the rhetoric of Morgan Phillips. Patrick Leigh Fermor recalled the attitudes towards the party among his contemporaries in the mid-1930s in the ancient public school of King's Canterbury: 'Labour MPs conjured up visions of steelrimmed spectacles, homespun cloth, cocoa and seed-cake and long killjoy faces bent on dismantling – what? ... Why, the Empire, for a start! The Fleet! The Army! Established religion – "except Methodist chapels".'[214] The same unpatriotic and puritanical associations put off the masses of working-class Tories whose support Labour needed to acquire.[215] They also, as Ammon pointed out during the Prayer Book debates, distracted from the main cause of elevating the condition of the people. As the young Harold Wilson complained in 1938, the Free Churches were nevertheless still inclined to concentrate excessively on issues such as drink, rather than the low wages and unemployment which undermined the quality of life for so many.[216] It was to the addressing of these latter issues that Labour had adapted the rhetorical flourishes of the Nonconformist Conscience.

7

Nonconformity, Labour and Class Consciousness

If we live exclusively in a middle-class world and view every question from a middle-class point of view, we shall not influence a world that is revolting against certain assumptions of our class. The Christian Church is too often stamped with our image instead of that of Christ.

Dorothea Price Hughes[1]

The theory of a class war is not only anti-religious but anti-human.

T. Rhondda Williams[2]

Nonconformity in the interwar years was depicted by commentators such as the journalist Harry Jeffs as the historic cradle of the Labour movement in the eighteenth century because 'Wesley was converted to the belief that Christ called to the ministry of the pulpit not only ordained ministers who had received college training, but men of all classes, including farm labourers, miners, potters and fishermen'. This idea of Nonconformity as a vehicle for the aspirations of the working classes remained part of its self-image. It was, as Jeffs implied, seen as the Free Churches' legacy to Labour.[3] However, class-based politics, particularly of a more left-wing kind, could be seen both as a challenge and a rebuke to Nonconformity. It also complicated mission in two ways. First, shifting debate onto divisive economic issues was an obvious problem for churches which often relied upon their wealthier members to underwrite their activities. Second, sin was seen all too readily as committed by the possessing classes against the poor, rather than inherent in the human condition. This suggested that salvation lay in political rather than spiritual activity.

The working classes and Nonconformity

Notwithstanding their self-image as the churches that nurtured the labouring poor, there was also an acute awareness of the often middle-class nature of Nonconformist congregations. The claim that F. W. Newland's Claremont Mission 'has done much to redeem Congregationalism from the reproach of being a middle class religion' indicates sensitivity on this point. In 1926, the *Methodist Times* acknowledged the predominantly middle-class character of Methodism. The following year the Society of Friends was described by one of its adherents as almost exclusively middle class. Social surveys of the time tended to confirm this picture.[4]

The extensive Victorian and Edwardian analyses of church attendance in cities like London and Liverpool were disappearing before 1914, yet they left a picture of middle-class predominance and working-class indifference which the more limited studies of the interwar years did little to dispel. The disproportionately middle-class nature of Dissent on predominantly working-class Merseyside was reflected in D. Caradog Jones's social survey in 1934.[5] Furthermore, the disastrous effect on attendance in inner urban areas of middle-class flight to the suburbs was confirmed by Arthur Black's 1927–28 survey in South West London.[6]

Attempts to draw attention to working-class enclaves within Nonconformity, in Wales, in the coalfields, in agricultural Somerset, or in the slum churches of popular ministers like William Dick of Poplar, were nevertheless not without validity.[7] Though the working classes were nowhere predominantly Nonconformist, there were some areas where Nonconformists were predominantly working class. This is not just the case with the missions and settlements planted in the late nineteenth century, which though drawing working-class congregations were substantially middle-class both in terms of staff and inspiration.[8] The deacons' benches and leadership of South Wales' chapels, which T. Rhondda Williams remembered from the nineteenth century as being substantially working class, seem to have become in the twentieth century noticeably more middle class in character.[9] In rural Norfolk, however, it is clear from the lists of the occupations of chapel trustees that the leadership of many of these causes remained mainly working class.[10] The chapel was not everywhere alien territory for the working classes, or merely a centre of charity for people in slum areas who otherwise never entered its doors. There was a working-class presence in most congregations.

The bulk of the working class was, however, otherwise engaged on Sundays. The churches nevertheless maintained residual connections to belief and allegiance. To some extent, this was encouraged and instrumentalized by the growing reliance upon associational culture. For the poor, the annual treats and seaside trips could prove a great lure. There is evidence that these led some to move promiscuously among local places of worship, depending on the varying attractions. This was hardly a way of nurturing a robust Christianity. It also tended to undermine rather than develop any sense of denominational identity. Instead, there was a tendency to identify with a particular local fane, even if attendance there proved sparing. This could reflect propinquity, connections through more observant neighbours, or links established through associational activities or Sunday School.[11] As noted in Chapter 3, until well into the twentieth century the vast majority of the working classes had attended Sunday School, however briefly. Most may not have kept up their religious connections. Nonetheless, a sense of respect could clearly still be felt and expressed. Thousands of them lined the streets in 1921 for the funeral cortege of Samuel Collier, the founding superintendent of the Manchester Methodist

Mission. There was mourning on a similar scale in the East End for the funeral of F. W. Chudleigh in the 1930s.[12]

Overt hostility to religion could certainly be found among the poor. For example, her drunken brute of a father had tried to beat her faith out of one of Walter Spencer's Sunday School teachers at the Wesleyans' South London Mission.[13] This and similar stories, however, are as much about identities and activities as about faith. It reflects hostility to the challenges Christianity was felt to pose to those identities, in this case by moving the Sunday School teacher out of her parents' social sphere and class. Similarly, by enjoining temperance, the South London Mission implied (if accurately in this case) their failings as people and as parents. Such stories thus reflect rejection of Christianity as a value system, rather than a conscious atheism. This hostility was, as Horace Mann had noted in his report on the 1851 religious census, primarily for social reasons. His description of this group as 'unconscious secularists' thus still seems apt.[14] Conscious secularism, in contrast, was more the preserve of the middle classes and the autodidacts amongst whom the chapels also found their working-class leaders.[15] Despite Nonconformist anxiety during the Edwardian years about the likely consequences of the materialist popular science of Ernst Haeckel, the activities of the Rationalist Press Association, and the atheistic propaganda of the eminent Socialist journalist Robert Blatchford, the impact upon the beliefs and practices of the working classes of these various efforts seems to have been even more limited than that of the chapels themselves.[16] These secularist forces certainly seem to have had little or no effect upon the largely working-class and unchurched armies of the Great War. Cairns's report found belief among the soldiers to be almost universal. There was a pervasive 'dim and instinctive theism'. Unbelief was also extremely rare among the armies of the Second World War.[17] Even where anti-religious positions were adopted they often seem to have been ex post facto rationalizations of a falling-out with the vicar or minister, rather than the cause of non-attendance. Oral histories - and anecdotal accounts by ministers - meanwhile suggest that those members of the working class who were most active in chapel society were also the most likely to remain so.[18] The working classes were accordingly characterized not so much by irreligion as by the widespread - but by no means universal - absence of formal and regular religious practice.

The problem was seen by many observers as being one, not so much of unbelief, as irrelevance. F. H. Stead commented in 1911:

> Probably no Englishman now believes that if he does not go to church in this life he will certainly go to hell in the next. So the men who a generation ago went to church to avoid going later to a destination still more unagreeable now consider themselves excused from putting in an appearance at either place. They spend Sunday 'as they please'.[19]

The rise of Darwinism was seen as having similar effects. The fact 'that the religious conception of sin, implying individual responsibility and accountability to God, had been softened to the natural imperfection of an evolving being', did not assist in making the case for Christian witness more compelling.[20] The importance of declining belief in Hell and related intellectual doubts should not, however, be overstated.[21]

Of more significance in explaining low levels of working-class church attendance is the fact that the value of Christian observance was not widely appreciated. Though there was much respect and reverence for Jesus in the army, 'of Jesus as the Son of God, and as the Atoning Sacrifice for the world, they have little or no knowledge at all'.[22] The annual drift of large numbers from the Sunday Schools was ample evidence of this failure to make God real for the vast majority of their scholars. The significance of this lack of vital faith should not be underestimated, not least at a time when alternatives to church attendance and to the community fostered by the chapel were increasingly available.

By the end of the nineteenth century, an alternative explanation for working-class non-attendance popular among the churches was the prevalence of pew rents. This method of raising revenue was heavily emphasized in a *Methodist Times* competition in the 1890s as a principal factor in causing this problematic phenomenon.[23] Working-class resentment at the invidious class distinctions which the pew rent system fostered and the exclusion of the working classes from all but the poorer seats that it involved is often cited in analyses of this period. There was, however, rarely much empirical basis for such claims.[24] Such analyses merely provided a well-used explanation for what was already the habitual absence of the working classes from the churches. They were also echoed by and lent credence to Labour criticisms of the churches.

W. E. Orchard contended that pandering to such critics through adopting left-wing politics in the pulpit would not attract 'Labour enthusiasts'. This, however, was not entirely correct.[25] Vint Laughland undeniably succeeded in drawing many, mostly unemployed, people into membership at Pembroke Chapel, Liverpool for a time in the early 1920s.[26] A series of industrial conferences in South Wales later in that decade by S. E. Keeble led to packed congregations.[27] Certainly, the adoption of a sympathetic approach towards social issues affecting the working class and the eschewing of a rather middle-class identity removed major disincentives to working-class church attendance. Whether the actual preaching of left-wing politics was necessarily successful in gaining the allegiance of a working class not always marked by left-wing sympathies, or was indeed any more successful in most areas than the efforts of popular preachers of Liberal political persuasions, like William Paxton, W. H. Lax or F. W. Newland, is however open to doubt.

Furthermore, there remained much respect for Christian ethics. Elizabeth Roberts's oral histories in the Lancashire towns of Barrow, Lancaster and Preston illustrate the pervasive influence of such ethics and of loose contact with the churches among working-class women.[28] This was combined with ample regard for Christ, if not as the Son of God, then as a great teacher. Familiarity with evangelical rhetoric, with its compelling appeal both for better men and a better world, through the influence of Sunday School and the open-air evangelism that though declining remained common in this period, helped to nurture this respect. Indeed, part of the virtue of Snowden, Simmons or Sorensen as itinerant Labour lecturers was their ability to tap into this respect with perorations modelled on evangelical appeals.[29]

Accordingly, working-class indifference to the best efforts of the churches does not necessarily indicate indifference to Christianity per se. Outright working-class hostility to overt irreligion could be equally apparent. Robert Williams, Labour's atheist candidate for Aberdare in 1918, was met on polling day by crowds of children booing and shouting at 'the man who don't love Jesus!'[30] This attitude may have been declining: certainly the Conservatives proved less inclined to use the charge of atheist with telling effect against Labour candidates after the First World War. Nevertheless, Communists in Aberdare in the 1950s were still careful to avoid appearing anti-religious for fear of losing support and members.[31] Instead, even the most bitter disputes served to illustrate the pervasive influence of Christianity in the South Wales valleys, despite assiduous Marxist propaganda and the faith-shattering hardships that followed the miners' defeat in 1926. Hymn-singing, interdenominational services and prayer meetings were facets of the hunger marches and stay-down strikes of the 1930s.[32]

A similar religiosity of tone was also apparent elsewhere during the General Strike. Some of the strongest centres of the strike were indeed also the most religious. Strikers at Wigan were enjoined to 'remember the Sabbath Day to keep it holy' and to remember Christ's commandments. Services and intercessions were included in the strike timetable at Shrewsbury.[33] Such practices built upon ecumenical celebrations of Labour (or industrial) Sunday with the official participation of the local trades council in places like Bradford in the immediate aftermath of the Great War. They were, however, already in decline by the time of the General Strike. Although, for instance, Bradford Trades Council sent delegates to the regional version of the COPEC conference in 1924 thereafter they regularly turned down invitations to participate in similar events.[34]

Working-class pleasures, Nonconformity and Labour

Labour Sunday, and successor concepts such as Housing Sunday, were attempts to bridge a perceived cultural gulf between the churches and the local working classes that they sought to serve, through finding a common ground of concern. These events sought to undermine perceptions of churches as alien (and unmasculine) institutions, speaking an alien language, condemning working-class interests and pastimes and operating in a class-biased way. One man told J. W. James, 'Every blessed thing that we really enjoy doing is condemned by you Church folk.'[35]

Attempts to steer working-class recreation into more desirable directions were often doomed to failure. Henry Solly, the Unitarian minister who established what became the CIU in 1862, was an ardent teetotaller. Four years later he decided that beer had to be available in the clubs, having found 'by sad experience that the men whom we specially wanted to attract from the public-house would not come to clubs where they could get only the drinks which they did *not* want.'[36] By 1924, only 36 of the 2,401 clubs affiliated to the CIU did not serve alcohol.[37] Their dramatic growth in the early twentieth century was fuelled by cheap liquor and licensing laws which affected on-licences but not the clubs, much to the chagrin of temperance reformers. Alfred Salter accordingly saw them 'as the greatest possible centres of injury to working people as a whole', unsuccessfully attempting in 1933 to make their hours of operation the same as licensed premises.[38] His fellow Quaker Seebohm Rowntree, however, recognized that they were places of fellowship and entertainment as well as drink.[39] In contrast to the churches, as well, these clubs were growing. This did not mean they were anti-religious. Though none of the men at his local club were churchgoers, J. W. James was allowed to conduct a monthly service there.[40] Nevertheless, their attendance at the clubs and the still very much more numerous, if less exclusively working class and declining, public houses indicated a rejection, in some measure, by many of the working classes of the chapel and its values.

There were regional differences in such attitudes. With local plebiscites in Manchester and Nottingham in the late 1920s heavily rejecting Sunday entertainments, the enthusiasm for Sunday cinema in the East End was clearly not ubiquitous.[41] Gambling, in contrast, seems to have been very widespread among the working classes. A survey by Benson Perkins in the 1920s suggested that some 80 per cent of the working class gambled to some extent.[42] Reformed gamblers like Jack Lawson were certainly well aware of the popularity of street-betting and gambling in mining communities, though his fellow Free Church Labour MP David Grenfell was horrified when he learnt of its prevalence in his native South Wales.[43] A Congregationalist who first went down the pit aged twelve, Grenfell was himself of impeccable working-class origins. Indeed, as a body, and despite a number of former middle-class Liberals amid their ranks, Free Church Labour MPs overall were no less working-class in composition and origin than the generality of the PLP. Grenfell's ascent to be the miners' agent and thence through the rungs of the Labour movement arguably moved him socially from those he represented. Culturally as well, as with many Nonconformist Labour MPs, there was a certain distance between him and his working-class constituents. Colleagues like the Anglican Robert Richardson, who in the 1920s acted as the parliamentary mouthpiece of the CIU, were perhaps closer to the typical attitudes of the electorate they represented.

Although George Thomas later warned that Labour MPs who joined him in expressing their conscience on matters such as alcohol were unlikely to escape criticism from their constituency parties, tension between the MP and his rather less chapel-orientated supporters did not necessarily result.[44] Undoubtedly some constituency parties and trades councils were as unhappy about the temperance activities of their MPs as were the CIU. Snowden, one of the most fervent of teetotallers, was nevertheless able to report, 'some of the most energetic of my workers are members of clubs and they respect me for my attitude'.[45] As noted in Chapter 6, not all Free Church Labour MPs were willing to put this to the test by openly opposing the will of the clubs. In other areas, however, Nonconformists were disproportionately strong among the active party membership and, in some places, predominated on constituency party executives into the post-war years.[46] These factors might explain the limited evidence of difficult local relationships for temperance MPs. Apart from the example of J. H. Hudson, there is little sign of it in the NEC minutes. Nor is it suggested by the large numbers of Free Churchmen who were nevertheless selected as parliamentary candidates.

Nonconformists, however, were not always seen as the right sort of candidates for the electors the party ought to be aiming at. This was at least the opinion of the president of the Cardiganshire party, the Baptist minister D. M. Jones – curiously enough, considering that 46 per cent of the county's population, according to the 1905 survey, were Nonconformist – who stood in the 1932 by-election.[47] Against this, however, can be set the selection of a London Methodist like J. R. Leslie, a member of the NCEFC executive, for the Durham mining/agricultural constituency of Sedgefield, where Nonconformity was virtually non-existent according to Kinnear's figures.[48] Free Churchmanship did not necessarily prove much of a liability for Labour MPs.

Class conflict in industry

Arguably more of a challenge was the growth of class antagonism apparent by the end of the Great War. This was not so much as a result of changes to the political environment by the extension of the franchise and the rise of a Labour Party identified with working-class interests, as because of the effects of wartime production controls and inflation on the respective sides of industry. The controls were blamed by employers for distorting production and increasing their costs. Wartime scarcity of labour meanwhile increased its bargaining power, though not enough to ensure that wage levels kept up with inflation rates, which more than doubled between 1914 and 1920. The result was a flurry of wage claims during the brief post-war boom.[49] For example, a motion put to the Lancashire and Cheshire Miners' Federation in 1920 argued,

> Seeing that when the war was on Lloyd George said that never again must the working classes of this country go back to the pre-war standard of living and that he would make this country a place fit for heroes to live in, we move that our officials do all in their power to secure an increase in wages that will put us on the pre-war level with 30 per cent increases in wages added.[50]

The brief post-war boom that encouraged such inflationary wage claims was choked off by a credit squeeze from 1921. Thereafter, it was pressure to reduce wages that was more conspicuous. Addressing the need to reduce the selling price of British goods to more competitive levels, a Federation of British Industries lecturer in 1922 was quoted as claiming:

> It cannot be denied that by far the greatest element in cost of production is the wages cost, since we must include in this not only the direct wage cost, but the wages involved in the production of fuel, power, materials and machinery, and in transport. We must, therefore, face the fact that to secure a substantial reduction in prices we must effect a substantial reduction in wage costs.[51]

Efforts to do so however did little for industrial peace. The attack upon working-class conditions and living standards they came to symbolize was, once the post-war boom was over, a major element in most of the industrial disputes of the period.

Few Free Churchmen were enthusiasts for class conflict. It did nothing, the *Christian World* pointed out, to address the structural problems of British industry.[52] Nonconformist leaders, being themselves often of marginal social status on the fringes of the middle classes and conscious of their relatively recent wider acceptance within British society, tended to find class conflict difficult to address. The response of the Brotherhood president F. D. Laptham to the industrial conflagration of 1926 – that in any struggle whichever side won, both lost – was typical of the Nonconformist reaction to most of the industrial disputes of the period.[53] Such conflicts were seen as divisive and destructive. This remained broadly the case even for figures such as F. H. Stead. He portrayed Christ as standing 'for the sway of the proletariat' and preaching, through parables such as that of Dives and Lazarus, a vehement class consciousness. Nevertheless, Stead also urged:

> Let us overcome not by class-conflict, but by class co-operation; not by deepening antagonisms until social explosion and social wreck result, but by strengthening amongst all men the spirit of Brotherhood based upon the common Fatherhood.[54]

Nonconformist trade union leaders were not necessarily any more convinced of the virtues of class conflict. Resort to strike action was often regarded as evidence of failure to achieve a settlement, not as a means of forcing one. Strikes were after all not only risky, but costly both to the union and its membership. Men like John Hodge (Wesleyan) and Arthur Pugh (undenominational) of the Iron and Steel Union took pride instead in their general success in achieving peaceful and amicable settlements.[55] Nonconformists were accordingly heavily involved in the attempt through the Mond-Turner talks to promote industrial conciliation in the aftermath of the General Strike.

Class conflict was regarded with particular hostility by some Nonconformist trade union leaders, notably J. H. Thomas.[56] The use of the coercive power of the strike, as opposed to the legitimacy of the ballot box, was to be deprecated.[57] Nonconformists were indeed prominently involved in the establishment of non-confrontational company labour organizations, such as the 'Spencer' unions (named after George Spencer, the Wesleyan miners' leader), which arose in the Nottinghamshire coalfield in the aftermath of the 1926 lockout.

Class consciousness and Nonconformity, however, should not be seen as irreconcilable strangers. Working-class Methodists like Jack Lawson or Ellen Wilkinson clearly had a strong sense of class identity.[58] Even among those not drawn to Communism, class conflict could be seen as unavoidable. Salter told an election meeting in 1924 that it was a necessary and defensive reaction against exploitation.[59] Workers themselves were frequently depicted as lamentably unaware of the attacks they were subject to. H. E. Rose complained in Pembroke chapel's magazine in 1921, in the face of massive unemployment on Merseyside, 'when are the workers going to learn the lesson of class consciousness which the possessing classes have learnt so well and with so much advantage to themselves?'[60] There had always been class war, Morgan Jones told the NCEFC Assembly in the run-up to the General Strike. Clearly intent on reprimanding by implication the predispositions of his audience, he argued that conciliation and co-partnership were mere phrases to beguile the working class.[61]

In this, however, Morgan Jones may have reflected the heightened emotions of that strained period between the submission of the Samuel Report and the launch of the strike itself, pre-emptively seeking to justify the impending clash. In the aftermath of those May days, it was instead the concept of the general strike and the usefulness of the industrial militancy that had built up since 1918 that was called into question. Some, albeit a minority, of the leaders of the triple industrial alliance of miners, railwaymen and transport workers after the war, seem to have fervently believed that in industrial action lay the road to power. Robert Williams declared in 1921, 'Before the General Strike the general election pales into insignificance.'[62] Five years later in his chairman's address to the TUC he surveyed the wreckage of such delusions, concluding 'While the Communist Party and the Minority Movement still believed in the General Strike, the Labour Party would look forward with confidence to the General Election.'[63]

This shift in emphasis from industrial to political action was not without justification. The Hammersmith by-election victory of May 1926 was the start of what seemed to be a marked increase in class-conscious voting in the wake of the General Strike.[64] Local elections later in the year were certainly interpreted in this fashion.[65] At the same time, impoverished unions were turning their backs on industrial conflict. Will Lawther in retrospect considered, 'We got more by arbitration than we ever got by all the strikes we had. That is my firm conviction.'[66] Many of those who, like Fred Jowett, were unable to join Ramsay MacDonald in seeing the General Strike as wrong in principle nevertheless came with hindsight to regard it as a tactical mistake.[67] There was wide acceptance of the view put forward by one of Bolton's strike leaders that, 'The General Strike was not a success, except as a generous gesture to help the miners. There will never be another.'[68] The industrial militancy of the early 1920s was largely discredited.

The emphasis then shifted to ways of avoiding such conflict, a welcome development to the Free Churches. They had long been concerned about the need to develop conciliation machinery and a more consensual form of industrial modus vivendi. Indeed, few Free Churchmen, even of the most militant variety, relished industrial confrontation. The most class conscious of them could join A. J. Cook in declaring after the bitter 1926 lockout: 'I hate strikes ... My life has been spent in trying to prevent strikes, not in making them.'[69]

It was in order to prevent them that in the 1890s men like Arthur Henderson took the initiative in setting up conciliation boards.[70] From the other side of industry, Nonconformist manufacturers – particularly Quaker employers like the Cadburys – organized works councils which encompassed both arbitration and consultation, while the Congregational businessman Sir Malcolm Stewart (son of Sir Halley) continued to promote joint consultation, profit-sharing and model villages for his workers in the 1930s and 1940s. A conference of Quaker manufacturers in 1918 even urged that workers should share fully in both the administration and prosperity of industry.[71]

The need for industrial harmony during the First World War prompted such considerations. In October 1916, an inquiry was set up into relations between employers and their workers under the Congregationalist J. H. Whitley, Liberal MP for Halifax.[72] The resulting Whitley Councils – to negotiate pay rates, terms and conditions in specific industries – met with much Free Church enthusiasm. They, however, proved largely toothless, as did the great National Industrial Conference of 1919. Its main recommendations were a maximum working week of forty-eight hours, a statutory minimum wage, and the setting up of a National Industrial Council. Henderson led for the labour side, but he did not have the united support of the unions. The unwillingness of the government to take a lead or establish an industrial rival meanwhile ensured the failure of these initiatives. The 'Magna Carta of Industry' hoped for by the *Methodist Times* did not emerge.[73]

'In view of the serious injury to human welfare – industrial, financial, social and moral – inflicted by the repeated conflicts between Capital and Labour', the Congregational Union welcomed renewed efforts towards similar ends in the aftermath of the General Strike.[74] These, however, were on an altogether more informal basis. Those responsible for these moves were, on the Labour side at least, responding to the same pressures on working-class living standards that prompted the 'living wage' proposals contained in the ILP policy document of early 1926, *Socialism in Our Time*. Whereas this sought to safeguard them by paying higher wages and thus hopefully securing higher production – then an unorthodox notion – the solution propounded by Snowden in his 1927 Clifford lecture to the Brotherhood conference in Hastings hinged on less innovative and thus more widely accepted ideas of the need for better organization of industry and industrial relations.[75] He later declared, 'It is obviously to the interests of both employers and workmen that the enterprise in which they are jointly concerned should be efficient and prosperous.'[76]

The rationalization of industry was criticized by Brockway as strengthening Capitalism and endangering jobs.[77] It was, however, a more positive response to the problems of British industry than simply cutting labour costs. According to Walter Citrine, rationalization meant the maximization of efficiency, facilitation of the design, manufacture, use and replacement of standardized parts, the simplification of distribution and the financial restructuring of industry. Indeed, 'Rationalisation can be made a step towards Socialism … [in] that it would be easier publicly to control and nationalise a comparatively few big undertakings than thousands of small and inefficient ones.' Since rationalization was clearly going to happen anyway, he argued that the unions had nothing to lose and everything to gain from responding positively to any opportunity to influence the manner in which it was introduced. Among the benefits that he expected were greatly improved job security (the absence of which was commonly identified as a source of labour unrest) and higher rates of pay.[78] Ben Turner declared in 1928 that it was the employers' desire for this rationalization, together with workers' need of security, that brought renewed efforts to secure better industrial relations.[79]

The scene for these efforts had been set by speeches like that of Snowden, and that of George Hicks as chairman of the 1927 TUC conference. In response to Snowden's speech, the Lord Mayor of London Sir Rowland Blades convened a conference on industrial peace in October 1927.[80] Similar gatherings had in fact been promoted by others active in the Brotherhood movement, such as the Congregational businessman Sir R. Murray Hyslop, since 1926.[81] At the same time, industrialists, such as the Scottish engineering manufacturer Lord Weir, had been making contact with union leaders like Ernest Bevin. These activities culminated in the letter sent by Sir Alfred Mond of Imperial Chemical Industries to the TUC General Council which led to the setting up of the Mond-Turner talks.[82]

The group of employers that coalesced around Mond for the purpose of these negotiations made proposals for the rationalization of industry and the enhancement of labour's position within it, the institution of company pensions and the creation of that ill-fated objective of 1919, a National Industrial Council.[83] The Left viewed the ensuing discussions with distaste. A. J. Cook and the Scottish ILP chairman James Maxton produced a manifesto in 1928 that was very much a response to the betrayal of the working-class cause they felt the talks represented. The vote at the 1928 TUC conference nevertheless clearly indicated that the talks were supported by the bulk of the Labour movement. Discussions, however, never passed the preliminary stage and the National Industrial Council was once again stillborn. The reluctance and divided counsels of employer organizations contributed to this failure. So did the changing economic climate. The prosperous conditions of 1927–28 were replaced by the Slump and rising unemployment. Pressure on labour costs was accordingly renewed, with ensuing industrial disputes.[84] The hopes which the Free Churches and particularly the Brotherhood movement had of the Mond-Turner talks were accordingly disappointed. The talks were nevertheless not entirely futile. Some rationalization proceeded with government sanction in the 1930s. Strikes and lockouts were no longer waged with the ferocity often exhibited between 1918 and 1926. Nor did the sense of class confrontation continue with the same intensity. Although the circumstances of the early 1920s to some extent returned after the Mond-Turner talks, the mood did not.

The Free Churches and Communism

There was more Free Church concern about Communism than about class conflict during the 1930s. This reflected the fashionableness of Communism, particularly among intellectuals, as a result of the CPGB's emergence as the focus of implacable opposition to Fascism. Marxist theories and Communist activity had hitherto provoked only limited responses from the Nonconformist leadership outside the areas most affected by Marxist propaganda, such as South Wales or London's East End. Some concern was voiced about the atheism of Soviet Russia.[85] Yet individual congregations collected for Russian famine relief in the early 1920s. Various figures shaped by Nonconformity also joined the Communist Party formed in 1920, including Ellen Wilkinson, Walton Newbold and the former Churches of Christ lay preacher and conscientious objector from South Wales, Arthur Horner.[86]

There was certainly awareness in the Free Church press of the challenge Communism could pose. In 1922, the *Methodist Times* even carried an interview with a former Methodist turned Communist in which he denounced both the message and the relief dispensed by the churches as dope, which duped, 'the workless into acquiescence with hunger and unemployment and led them to hope for a better state of affairs. Dope and hope are poor substitutes for vigorous action.'[87] Such views were widely shared and propagated by those under the influence of the unequivocally Marxist National Council of Labour Colleges.[88] The challenge thus posed was not, however, a matter of wide concern. Few Nonconformists in the 1920s felt, like W. E. Orchard, the necessity for detailed refutation of the theories and practises of Marx and Lenin.[89]

Of the factors changing this in the 1930s, the electoral performance of the Communists cannot be said to be one. Only in a few areas, most notably South Wales, did Communists achieve political success. The position they won in parts of this region by virtue of their identification with vigorous action in the face of the coalfield's various interwar crises encouraged ministers like R. J. Barker to define the differences between Marxism and Christianity:

> The one stands for the working class only; the other for all mankind. The one believes in violence; the other in the way of the Cross. The one has no faith in conversion; the other believes in the transforming power of the Spirit of Christ. The one believes that matter is the only reality; the other conceives of the universe as fundamentally spiritual and material.[90]

Even in South Wales, the one area where the depression worked unequivocally in favour of the Communists, they remained however a minority party. In most parts of the country their electoral record was no less dismal than it had been in the 1920s.

Maldwyn Edwards, who ran a centre for the unemployed at his Methodist church in Gateshead in the 1930s, noted that the circumstances were not necessarily propitious for revolutionaries: 'short unemployment produces resentment, but long unemployment produces despair'.[91] Nevertheless, by 1935, W. F. Lofthouse could write: 'Most people have become familiar in the last ten years with the idea that the two great antagonists in the modern world are Christianity and Communism.'[92] This sense of an ideological and theological challenge was very much a response to Communism's intellectual appeal at the time in the light of Webbian enthusiasm for Soviet Russia, and as a bastion against Fascism.[93] There was a spate of books and articles on the relationship between Christianity and Communism in the 1930s. John Lewis, for instance, pointed out in his Left Book Club text that Marxism shared the teleology, apocalyptic faith and bias to the poor that were attributes of Christianity.[94] Its rise, Lofthouse argued, served as a telling indictment of the inadequacy of Christian social activism.[95] Even far from revolutionary figures like Angus Watson accepted that Communism contained much of value. He told the Congregational Union in 1935: 'Christianity dogmatically asserts that with some error many of the claims advanced by the communistic viewpoint are true.'[96] Free Churchmen, though not always as admiring of Communists as A. Herbert Gray, were far from condemning them.[97]

What they did disapprove of was the view of man presented in Marxist theory and the rather sanguinary attitude to the process of political change taken by many of its followers. Arguing that 'Marxism attributes practically all ills from which the human flesh suffers to the capitalistic social order, and promises every type of redemption in a new society in which the productive process is socially owned', the influential American theologian Reinhold Niebuhr concluded in his piece in Lewis's volume for the Left Book Club that it was a 'faulty religion with its mistaken analysis of the problem of human sin'.[98] Changing the system was not enough. Marx's analysis of the problem of man, as essentially the soon-to-be-solved alienation of the proletariat from the ownership of the means of production, ignored the more intractable difficulties presented by the individual's moral shortcomings. It did not, argued the Quaker theologian H. G. Wood, recognize the importance of a sense of individual responsibility for social welfare.[99] Nor, pointed out A. Herbert Gray, did it see any need for the love and goodwill upon which the Kingdom of God was to be founded.[100]

An awareness of such omissions perhaps explains why Labour MPs like Willie Brooke, although Marxist in economics, remained Free Churchmen.[101] These omissions did not, however, prevent some Free Churchmen from supporting the Communist Party or becoming involved in its activities. Although R. J. Barker warned during the 1935 general election that Communist hostility to Christianity made Christian support for Communism impossible, he found several of the Tonypandy churches enthusiastically behind the Communist candidate.[102] They were attracted, as was P. N. Harker, a member of the Unitarian Pioneer Preachers Movement and the leader of the Bolton NUWM in the early 1930s, not by the ideology so much as the activism of the CPGB.[103] Few Free Churchmen elsewhere, however, became as involved with Communism.

The extremes of class consciousness Communism represented appealed to few of their fellow Nonconformists. The continuing role these Nonconformists played in the trade union movement into the interwar years, meanwhile helped to ensure that Communist penetration therein was very limited, forcing the CPGB instead to set up their own alternative Minority Movement. This seems to have been a key factor in excluding Marxists from key roles in the Labour movement.

Marxists also lacked rhetorical space, even without the introduction of the 1934 black circular excluding Communists from leading roles in trade unions and councils.[104] As Wertheimer noted, the alienation to which it appealed never gained sufficient purchase. Whereas the structured political exclusion of the SPD in Germany had led to endless theoretical disputation, the relatively weak Labour Party had, from its inception, been absorbed in practical parliamentary politics. Labour accordingly did not need 'a constructive theoretical explanation of their movement'. Nor, Wertheimer argued, did they require political analysis derived from a dialectical materialism which was dubiously foreign, when the quasi-religious idealism derived from Nonconformity was readily to hand.[105] Marxism made little headway either within or without the Labour Party. Indeed, the CPGB was not to grow significantly until the late 1930s, when the threat of Fascism elsewhere in Europe could be used to mobilize support.[106]

Voting issues and class consciousness

It has nevertheless been argued that class and class consciousness assumed unprecedented importance in the political landscape of the early twentieth century. Historians in the 1970s indeed tried to locate a transition from what they saw as the status-related issues of the political world of the nineteenth century – such as civil equality, land, temperance and education, upon which aggressive Nonconformist politics thrived – to the supremacy of class-related issues during the general elections of the Edwardian era.[107] There are clearly problems with this class-based voting hypothesis given estimates that about 50 per cent of the working classes supported the Tories in the 1930s and 30 per cent of the middle classes voted Labour in 1945. Class may have become a more important source of identity, but it did not necessarily eradicate other identities or interests. Indeed, class is often simply an (often unconscious) rationalization of instrumental attitudes. Ross McKibbin's attempt to relocate a shift to class-based voting from the First World War to the Second World War thus breaks down due to lack of clarity over whether shifts in voting behaviour are occurring because of class or instead as a result of instrumental responses to the idea of the welfare state.[108]

Shifts in voting behaviour after 1918 may similarly reflect instrumental responses to changes in political issues as much as class-based voting. Such change was undoubtedly occurring. The problems to which nineteenth-century political issues were addressed such as franchise reform, Irish Home Rule or Welsh disestablishment were either in the process of being solved or becoming less intractable. Instead, the breakdown of the political economy of the nineteenth century, paralleled by growing unemployment and labour unrest, helped to bring to the fore issues where class and economic interest aligned and created at least the appearance of increased class-based voting. So did the changing nature of industry, with deskilling from the late nineteenth century in many trades arguably creating a greater sense of common interests among the working classes. The resulting apparent rise of class identities was indeed noted by Nonconformist newspapers by the end of the 1920s.[109]

An important aspect of this shift was the acceptance of the principle of ameliorative intervention by both local and central government on issues such as housing, pensions and unemployment. Voting thus became more a matter of determining how, and how far, State action should distribute such social goods.

This shift was encouraged by a number of factors. First, Gladstonian inhibitions about extending the range of government activity were gradually disappearing in the late Victorian era. The breakdown of classical political economy undermined their ideological basis. The emphasis slowly shifted away from laissez-faire towards vouchsafing minimum standards to the people. Secondly, this partly reflected growing awareness of social conditions thanks to various reports and surveys of the late nineteenth century. Thirdly, it also reflected changes in the analysis of the problems of poverty or of health. There was growing awareness of the inadequacy, for instance, of the Victorian Poor Law. The assumption on which it was based: that poverty is the result of personal failings rather than economic circumstances, was increasingly untenable in the face of mass unemployment. Finally, Nonconformist campaigning for temperance and other social causes drew attention to the potentialities of State action to protect the weak from their own weaknesses.[110] A positive view of the State and its social role was thus emerging by the late nineteenth century regardless of any shift towards class-based voting.

As a result, Victorian scruples about the demoralizing effects of charity were slowly disappearing. The financial and administrative capacity to discharge this obligation was meanwhile gradually increasing. The social reforms of the Liberal governments of 1906–14 would not have been possible on the smaller revenue of twenty years earlier. Increasing taxation and prosperity thus financed social reform. At the same time, the changes in local government in the late nineteenth century created local authorities that were better equipped to implement it. By the interwar period, both central and local governments were at least expected to address social conditions, even if they could not always do much about them. With unemployment and economic difficulties of major importance throughout the period, political issues came to revolve more around the question of living standards or the management of the economy. These developments, together with the significance of issues such as the legal position of the trade unions, certainly reconfigured political interests and encouraged voting patterns that appeared to be more class-based.

By changing the nature and grounds of political debate, the rise of new issues also had an effect on the survival of other determinants of political behaviour. The sense of political contest between chapel and church or chapel and public house was not as intense as in the Edwardian period, when church bells could greet a Tory election victory or a chapel service a Liberal.[111] Many Nonconformists clearly remained aware of divisions in politics and social status between themselves and those attending the parish church. However, with the virtual disappearance of the local power of the churchwardens and vestry in the late nineteenth century, such sentiments, often bearing some relationship to class feeling, no longer shaped local politics. Meanwhile, rationalization and new corporate business structures eclipsed the great Anglican and Nonconformist families which had once dominated towns like Glossop and done so much, in their rivalry, to lend substance to the political contest between church and chapel.[112] Only in areas with few alternative means of mobilizing politicization, such as rural Norfolk, did the church-chapel divide remain an important means of enforcing identity in local politics, at least until the 1960s.[113]

The diminishing importance of local politics in the interwar years also undermined the political influence of major and rival institutions which had hitherto operated within it, like the chapel or the public house. In the early 1920s, however, their contest remained an important part of the political landscape. This was partly because the possibility of tightening the licensing laws remained a live issue. As the *Christian World* pointed out, Sunday drinking was virtually the only issue in the Tory triumph in the Newport by-election of 1922 that led indirectly to the fall of Lloyd George's Coalition.[114]

The Drink Trade in the 1880s and 1890s had begun mobilizing publicans locally to support Conservatives opposing the temperance reformers largely in Labour and Liberal ranks. It has not always been recognized that this 'beer-barrel politics', as Jon Lawrence designated it,[115] continued into the 1920s. This is readily apparent from the endorsements of general election candidates in the trade newspaper of the licensed victuallers, the *Morning Advertiser*. Of the 140 candidates endorsed in 1923, apart from four Liberals, all were Conservatives.[116] Indeed, the Liberal success in Bethnal Green was partly attributed to their control of the largest local working men's club.[117]

In contrast, the Congregational minister who stood as a Liberal in Central Bradford in 1922 and 1923 complained that children were taught to sing 'Paxton will rob you of your beer'.[118] Morgan Jones faced similar opposition from the Trade when securing re-election in Caerphilly in 1923. Indeed, he was opposed by one of the six Tory clubmen candidates whose campaigns in working-class constituencies were endorsed by the Trade.[119] This opposition from the Drink Trade persisted throughout the 1920s. It was not until 1929 that the *Morning Advertiser* featured Labour figures among the general election candidates it endorsed. Even then, these were five out of 153 endorsed candidates, 145 of whom were Tories.[120]

By then, however, changes were occurring which would ensure that the 1929 election was the last in which alcohol was a significant issue. With the advent of a mass electorate following the 1918 Representation of the People Act, increasingly professionalized parties were concerned to strictly control the way in which their message and image was conveyed to the public, in the process reducing the influence of intermediary bodies between them and the electorate. As noted in Chapter 6, the three main parties agreed in 1929 not to respond to lobbying from outside particular constituencies. This helped to ensure that by the time of the 1935 election, drink was no longer a political issue. The *Morning Advertiser* by then was also happy to endorse considerable numbers of Labour candidates.[121]

Meanwhile, their publican readership was becoming more concerned about competition from the steadily growing clubs than the threat from chapel-going temperance reformers.[122] Claiming that they had done more for temperance through their activities than any of their opponents, the CIU had, by the 1930s, become a significant force within Labour. In the process, it brought the beer-barrel politics which had hitherto aided the Tories into the Labour Party. As clubs run by their own members, these organizations represented an amalgamation of Liberal ideas of self-help, Tory working-class drinking culture and a labourist, class-based political milieu. By deliberately marginalizing the politics of alcohol in the later 1920s, Labour had not just found a way of managing its internal conflict on the issue, but also embedded itself in a working-class culture suspicious of chapel-based moralizing and of statist social (as opposed to economic) controls. These suspicions had limited Labour's electoral advance in the 1920s.[123] Containing them helped to extend the party's appeal into working-class Tory as well as working-class Liberal culture. It was also a piece of statecraft whereby Labour's place within a reconfigured two-party system was cemented and the Liberals displaced, not in the early 1920s as suggested by Maurice Cowling,[124] but in the early 1930s. This cleared the way for a straightforward fight with the Conservatives around economic rather than morality issues.

As noted in Chapter 4, the electoral politics of the interwar years can broadly be explored through four principal prisms:

(a) **High Politics**: focusing upon the role of the parties in structuring the political marketplace and the resulting forced choice offered to voters;
(b) **Electoral Geography**: analysing how local characteristics and boundaries can embed distinctive voting cultures;
(c) **Contingent Events and/or Trends**: such as strikes, economic circumstances or international crises;
(d) **Electoral Sociology**: including class identities and generational changes.

The apparent rise in the significance of the latter was partly the result of the way in which parties structured other factors, including morality issues like the drink question, out of the political marketplace by the end of the 1920s. Accordingly, that electoral behaviour appears more class-based in the 1930s does not necessarily reflect rising class consciousness any more than it does the role of parties in restructuring political issues or the contingent effects of the Budget crisis of 1931.

Instead, it seems likely that the ensuing Slump led to a closer alignment of economic interests and class identities. This was not least the case with women voters. In the 1920s they had been heavily and apparently successfully targeted by the Tories. Conservative electoral propaganda played upon assumptions that women would be put off by Labour's masculine emphases on the world of work and production, rather than domestic consumption. The efforts of the Labour women's organization led by the Congregationalist Marion Phillips, to counter this targeting of female voters by the Tories had only limited success. Furthermore, if anything, Labour's image was even more male-dominated in the 1930s. Nevertheless, the realignment of *issues* during the Slump brought more consumerist concerns to the fore. Meanwhile, the reduction of Labour's revenue after the 1927 Trade Union Act ended contracting-in by an anyway shrinking union membership, forcing it to look elsewhere for funds. These factors pushed Labour to move beyond its trade union basis, building an organization which could also appeal to the interests of women and consumers.[125] An apparent restructuring of electoral behaviour around class was thus driven primarily by economic factors and the needs of party finance.

Before then, outside particular working-class monocultures like the mining districts, there was certainly no guarantee that the working classes would vote Labour. The slums down by the canal in Blackburn were unpropitious territory for Mary Agnes Hamilton in the early 1920s.[126] In late 1930s Bolton, Joseph Hale still found: 'Rumworth ward consisted of solid working class houses, not of the best type a lot of them … in fact during the election campaign … Joseph Street more or less collapsed … yet, in wards such as this the Conservatives consistently won the seat.'[127]

Labour, class and nation

Labour may have developed as a party resting financially, and to some extent organizationally and electorally, on the trade unions. It was, however, careful to try to avoid an exclusively working-class identity, particularly in the 1920s. Class war was left to a Communist Party that Labour was at pains to keep at arm's length. 'Our work', J. R. Clynes pointed out, is 'the work of conversion and not coercion. We must advance by consent'.[128] Labour's association with the sort of class consciousness peddled by the advocates of Direct Action was, Arthur Henderson argued in 1921, doing great damage to its electoral prospects.[129] He steered the party away from such associations and from appearing to be an exclusively working-class party. One of the objects of the reorganization of 1918 that he led, particularly the introduction of individual membership, was to remove that stigma. Henderson told the *Christian World* that:

> The basis of membership in the party has been deliberately broadened in order to allow any man or woman in sympathy with its aims to join … Without ceasing to be the party of the workers, its basis has been widened … and its character as a federation of trade unions, Socialist societies, trades councils and local Labour parties has been transformed by the adoption of the principle of individual membership. It has become a real national party.[130]

Not least, this emphasis sought to appeal to the conventional patriotism widespread among the working classes, for whom national loyalties remained important, as was ruefully acknowledged by one Nonconformist Socialist commenting on the impact of the Zinoviev letter.[131]

Sorensen tried to suggest instead that Socialists were the true patriots because they love their fellows most of all.[132] Free Churchmen in the party were generally happier emphasizing love, goodwill, and common humanity rather than class or nation. This was not least true of Independent Methodists like Wellock or Rennie Smith. The latter's comments in 1934 that 'neither "blood" nor "class" categories are good enough as a foundation for a Socialist way of thinking and a Socialist way of action' provoked a storm of protest from Marxist subscribers to the *New Nation*, the organ of the Labour League of Youth.[133] These Marxists were, however, in the minority. Labour showed little inclination to appear to be preaching class consciousness, particularly of the revolutionary variety, not least because of the lack of class consciousness among the working classes themselves.[134]

For most of the time, except when industrial or political conflict were very real issues, the working classes were as inclined to absent themselves from Labour and trade union meetings as from the chapels. Indeed, voluntary working-class attendance at church and chapel was probably considerably greater than at meetings of trade union branches or Labour constituency parties. It was not these but the clubs and pubs that were working-class rivals to the chapels. Even Labour activists were not immune to these attractions: as Salter ruefully reflected in 1927, 'There are generally more people hanging around the bar than will trouble to attend the meeting upstairs.'[135] Furthermore, the clubs certainly had the highest working-class attendance.[136]

Beer therefore cannot be ignored in any list of working-class political interests. That the Labour Party had to appeal to and embed itself in the leisure interests of the working classes was clearly grasped by some of those who came into the party from more Tory backgrounds: as Hugh Dalton noted, Labour would only win power 'with the votes of the football crowds'.[137] Class consciousness per se was not so conspicuous. Changing social and political issues, structured by party behaviour, gave the impression of a shift towards class-based voting. It was the developments which brought this about – including the acceptance of the possibility and even duty of government intervention in the social and economic spheres and the simultaneous decline in the importance of local policies – rather than class consciousness, which proved more significant elements in the politics of the interwar years.

8

The Kingdom, the State and Socialism

Of course the great social problems cannot be solved by any individual or any Mission. There must be an appropriate division of labour between Church and State. The Church may, in a few instances, set an example and teach the State how to do its duty; but the social aspect of the problem must be grappled by the State itself.

Hugh Price Hughes[1]

The State can never satisfy all the needs of men. It can provide security on the basis of brotherhood but it cannot make men live as brothers. Fellowship depends, not on Parliament, but on ourselves.

George Thomas[2]

Nonconformity and the State

Christians are enjoined to feed the hungry, clothe the naked and care for those who are ill or in prison (Matthew 25.24–40). Nonconformists, however, were not always ready to see the State as the agency whereby these tasks are performed. In 1847 the Congregational proprietor of the *Leeds Mercury*, Edward Baines Jr, wrote:

> It is *not* the duty of the Government to feed the people, to clothe them, to build houses for them, to direct their industry or their commerce, to superintend their families, to cultivate their minds, to shape their opinions or to supply them with religious teachers, physicians, schoolmasters, books or newspapers.[3]

His attitude clearly reflected the suspicion, born of Nonconformist disabilities, of the coercive power of an Erastian State. Any extension of its power in these directions was also seen as liable to undermine individual responsibility and self-reliance.[4]

At the time, the State was broadly incapable of fulfilling these functions anyway. This, however, was to change with growing tax revenues and the gradual extension of the administrative competences of central and local government in the second half of the nineteenth century. Growing taxes, by reducing the scope of paternalistic philanthropy, were significant factors in the declining adequacy of the voluntaristic welfare, often run by the churches, that supplemented the Poor Law.[5] Meanwhile, Nonconformist attitudes towards the State also underwent a thorough transformation.

Even by the time of Baines's remarks, Nonconformist views of the best means of promoting public welfare were changing. Early nineteenth-century efforts had focused upon tackling, at the individual level, the improvident habits or intemperance which were then seen as prime causes of want. A growing awareness of the needs of the young and the vulnerable evident from the establishment of the Ragged School Union in 1844 was to encourage a shift in emphasis. Rather than stressing the rescue of the fallen, Nonconformist charitable work moved towards trying to protect such groups from falling in the first place. As the Unitarian educationalist Mary Carpenter observed in 1861: 'the low moral, intellectual and often physical conditions' of the working classes were unlikely to be alleviated 'unless a helping hand is held out to the children to aid them to rise to a higher and better life'.[6] Similar concerns in 1873 led the Congregationalist minister Benjamin Waugh to urge the creation of juvenile courts and detention centres to prevent the Poor Law and criminal justice system from institutionalizing children, trapping them in criminality.[7] Ten years later Waugh was to found the National Society for the Prevention of Cruelty to Children. Stress was thus placed increasingly on preventative intervention.

Such developments led Nonconformity to a shift of focus away from concentrating on the moral responsibility of the individual. Three factors particularly shaped this development. First, following the 1851 religious census, there was growing awareness of Nonconformity's national importance and responsibility to speak to the needs of wider society rather than simply those gathered in its chapels. Secondly, temperance campaigning familiarized Nonconformists with the idea of ameliorative State action to protect the vulnerable from their own weaknesses. Most significant, however, was the effect of the campaigns against the Contagious Diseases Acts of the 1860s. Through this legislation the State turned prostitutes from fallen women, to be redeemed individually by tracts and calls to repentance, instead into a stigmatized social category. Nonconformists were thus led to think about society as a whole, rather than the failings of individuals within society. At the same time, the Contagious Diseases Acts also impacted on their views of the State. Involvement in the campaign to get them repealed led figures like Hugh Price Hughes to become aware that, if the State could make things worse by ill-conceived interventions, it might also ameliorate them, and that the State had far more resources with which to do so than the churches.[8]

The campaign against the Contagious Diseases Acts, which culminated in their repeal in 1886, thus led to a refocusing on moral problems as social rather than simply individual failings. It was in this charged atmosphere that *The Bitter Cry of Outcast London* in 1883 drew attention to the way in which squalid housing fostered illicit sexual relations. Its subjects were thus not only sinners but also victims, both of poorly conceived housing legislation that had led to more overcrowding and of rapacious capitalists making 'a richer harvest of their misery, buying up property condemned as unfit for habitation, and turning it into a gold-mine because the poor must have shelter somewhere'. *The Bitter Cry* emphasized that the State 'must make short work of this iniquitous traffic, and secure for the poorest the rights of citizenship'.[9] This call was endorsed by *The Congregationalist* in November 1883.

Interestingly, it noted that 'we are not advocates of any revolutionary Socialism'. Socialism for them was not a new system of political economy to replace Capitalist modes of production, though it considered that 'there is a certain Socialism which Christianity sanctions'. This was the socialization of welfare through State action: 'The State may lawfully be called upon to deal with a mass of evil which is … beyond the capacity of private benevolence'.[10] Such interventions could also be seen as using the State to advance rather than curb liberties already trammelled by the privations imposed by poverty.[11] They could thus serve, as R. W. Thompson stressed in his 1939 Congregational Union assembly address, as natural developments from traditional Free Church witness.[12]

The voluntary principle of self-reliance and individual responsibility was increasingly untenable as it became clearer that need was not necessarily the product of moral failings. The feeding of schoolchildren was a case in point. Liberals on Bradford Council shrank from taking on this obligation when it was first mooted in 1904, fearing that it would undermine parental responsibility, family life, and self-respect. The feeding of children they regarded as the duty of the family, not the municipality. As the Labour councillor Fred Jowett pointed out, too many families were, however, incapable of discharging this function. The school meals legislation he helped to promote after his election as one of the city's MPs in 1906 reflected his dictum: 'It is the duty of the community to see that all children are sufficiently fed.'[13] The responsibility of the community was replacing the voluntary principle.

Socialist ministers like C. Ensor Walters were by 1905 declaring the necessity of State intervention: 'Soup kitchens, wood-chopping and cheap lodging houses will not of themselves solve the social problem.'[14] The failings of such voluntaristic welfare were powerfully indicted by Revis Barber, secretary of Bradford Trades Council, in his 1932 Annual Report. Of the National government he wrote:

> The only gesture which has been made to the unemployed has been the grant of the munificent sum of £10,000 to the National Council for Social Service, to which body has been handed over the care of the unemployed, who are to be catered for on the lines of Sainted Sunday School scholars who, if they are good, will be allowed to go to the bun-field at Whitsuntide.[15]

Barber was the son of a Methodist trade unionist and clearly felt such welfare gestures and moral judgements to be wholly inadequate. For such figures, who abandoned faith for belief in socialistic welfare based on needs rather than moral deserts, this passage shows church-based welfare being held up to ridicule.

Barber's criticism was, however, an unfair reflection on the efforts made by the Free Churches to introduce more effective welfare services. The institutional churches, settlements, and central halls set up from the 1880s onwards sought to offer a wide range of innovative services in response to the spiritual and social difficulties of the period. Common examples included maternity care; the provision of job registries and employment as well as relief for the unemployed; the running of dispensaries and clinics and a system of health visiting; convalescent home treatment and the 'poor man's lawyer' service introduced by Frank Tillyard at Mansfield House in 1891.

Various leading figures in the Labour movement were well aware of such developments. Mansfield House, established in Canning Town in 1891, was regularly visited in its early years by Ramsay MacDonald, Keir Hardie, Ben Tillett, Tom Mann and Will Crooks.[16] Such institutions also acted as foci of agitation for public welfare provision. Mansfield House and F. H. Stead's Browning Settlement played leading roles in the campaigns for the provision of public baths, adequate sanitation and old age pensions.[17] Furthermore, future Labour politicians were introduced to such welfare services through working in these institutions. For instance, F. W. Pethick-Lawrence was a poor man's lawyer at Mansfield House, where Percy Alden served as warden, as was the Tory MP Kingsley Wood for various Methodist missions. Somerville Hastings and Alfred Salter were similarly active on the medical side at Whitefield's Tabernacle and the Bermondsey Settlement respectively.[18]

These activities sketched out areas where responsibility would eventually be shouldered by local or central government. In some cases government not only imitated the function but took it over wholesale. Thus in 1900 the local borough council – established the previous year under the London Government Act – began to absorb the educational institute created at John Clifford's Westbourne Park chapel.[19] Men like Clifford were indeed more than ready to regard the State which took over such capacities as an institution every bit as divinely ordained as the Church.[20]

There was clearly a preparedness to regard the municipality in the same light. Reviewing the achievements of Bradford corporation, the city's first Labour mayor, the Primitive Methodist Joseph Hayhurst, declared in 1918: 'When we quietly subject our municipal activities to a calm examination and contemplate what the future will be, we can only come to one conclusion – that to-day we are assembled in the greatest temple of God in our city.' As a result, he claimed, 'Christ's injunction of "feed my lambs" has been transformed from precept into practice.'[21]

Local government, of course, had historically provided support for the indigent in the form of the Poor Law. The moral economy that it expressed, however, continued to reflect that of the early nineteenth century. Seeing poverty as a by-product of improvidence and indolence, the Poor Law attached to the payment of relief both deterrence and stigma. This analysis was harder to sustain in the face of the mass unemployment of the interwar years. As Percy Alden pointed out in 1930, it was now 'proved conclusively that the main cause of unemployment is maladjustment of our industrial organization. It is true that personal defects whether physical or moral have a bearing on the problem, but no one now contends that it will account for more than a very small percentage of the 2,200,000 unemployed'.[22]

Accordingly, Nonconformist reluctance to sanction what would at one time have been regarded as demoralizing charity and unwarranted State interference was disappearing. In 1921, a Quaker conference on Industry for Service argued that a worker when unemployed must be supported either by industry or by the State.[23] Despite a considerable expansion of the unemployment benefit the previous year (admittedly at scales which Seebohm Rowntree denounced as 'totally inadequate'),[24] recourse to the locally elected Guardians who administered the Poor Law was nevertheless still necessary on a massive scale during the recession that set in at this time. The peak figure of 1,837,980 on poor relief was reached on 17 June 1922.[25] This placed a colossal burden on local ratepayers. In 1921, the NCEFC accordingly urged: 'unemployment is a national, and not a local evil, to be dealt with, therefore, by the Government of the country and not only through the limited powers and straitened resources of local authorities.'[26] The extralegal exigencies to which rebellious Labour councillors in Poplar felt driven by the burden of local unemployment made much the same point rather more forcefully. Although the Guardians were replaced in 1930, the Exchequer only slowly assumed full responsibility for the unemployed. It was not until the creation of the Unemployment Assistance Board in 1934 and with agricultural workers at last eligible for unemployment benefit from November 1936 that this responsibility could be said to have effectively passed to central government.

Nonconformity and Socialism

For Nonconformist Labour MPs these defects of poor housing, food, health, pay and employment marred the image of God in man and undermined his dignity. They thus reflected a Nonconformist sense of the unlimited value of each child of God. After visiting one slum-ridden area of Northampton, Margaret Bondfield wrote of 'such poor feeble children with little withered faces that were all of them of infinite worth in the eyes of the Father of us all'.[27]

This infinite worth was, however, hardly reflected in their living standards. These were not noticeably improved by the great increase in the wealth and productive capacity of the nation that was apparent by the late nineteenth century. A Socialist Quaker Society tract in 1901 emphasized that the fruits of industry were far from being distributed as if all were of equal and infinite worth.[28] Remedying such defects, for Nonconformist Socialists, required more thoroughgoing intervention into the social and economic systems, rather than simply extending the range of the State. As Wilfred Wellock put it:

> Surely there is a better way, a nobler motive in industry than greed, a right above that of the few to amass huge fortunes whilst others starve! Is it beyond our dreams that society can function as a great brotherhood, can co-operate as fellow citizens instead of exploiters and exploited? What say you who profess Christianity?[29]

E. R. Hartley's years of professing Christianity in Sunday Schools, Adult Schools and Bands of Hope taught him that all should be able to lead happy and healthy lives. He, however, came to find that:

> [T]here was a vast army of people who never were happy and never had a chance to be healthy. A little enquiry showed this was not because there was not the means to make them happy, but because they had not yet the means. Further enquiry showed the only way to get the means to the people is production for use instead of profit, and that brings Socialism.[30]

Many interwar Nonconformists indeed enthusiastically subscribed to the idea of production for use not profit, including Liberal businessmen like Angus Watson.[31] Such Liberals could share with Socialists a sense of the importance of a more ample and equitable provision of goods and services for the community. What distinguished Socialists was the view that social organization and ownership of the means of production, distribution and exchange were necessary in order to distribute its fruits. This was the view enshrined in Clause IV of the Labour Party's constitution. Capitalism, indicted both for its inefficient use of resources, labour and productive capacity and for failing to provide the necessities of life, had to be replaced. J. H. Hudson's election literature of 1922 argued:

> Not until the land of England, the mines, the railways and all the highly organised and monopolised means of production are possessed by the community, and managed and controlled for the community by the hand workers and brain workers can we stamp out the poverty of the unemployed and the low paid worker.[32]

This was not the woolly ethical Socialism often associated with the infusion of Labour politics by chapel rhetoric in the later historiography mentioned in the Introduction. Instead, in Hudson's formulation, the process of nationalization was a means to the end of enlarging the life and opportunities of the workers. In the process, argued his fellow Quaker and Labour MP George Benson, this would replace the competition and waste of the present system with one based upon more efficient co-operation: 'Industry, instead of being run on a basis of haphazard anarchism, split into a thousand hostile units, would be organised for the sole purpose of rendering to the community service.'[33] Clause IV of the 1918 Labour Party constitution, far from marking a break with pre-war ethical Socialism, was thus a natural development of its themes. Nationalization, through which class and industrial conflict would be replaced by production for the good of the whole community, was a means to achieve the ethical society which Nonconformists in the Labour Party envisaged.

This effectively reflected a moral order against which to measure the shortcomings of the world every bit as absolute as that of Marxism. For instance, it was to this moral order that Ben Turner appealed in introducing his 1924 Bill to nationalize natural resources with quotations from Psalm 24, Ecclesiastes and Leviticus.[34] As this example shows, such language was entirely compatible with the increased emphasis on nationalization within the party after 1918. The Great War was not the fundamental caesura in religiosity of tone within the party it has sometimes been portrayed.

A similar continuity into the 1920s can be seen in attitudes towards municipal Socialism. The first cohorts of Labour activists had grown up deeply conscious of the fruits of the 'gas and water' Socialism of the late nineteenth century. Even in a rural county like Norfolk, by 1914, the local authority was responsible for provision of care for the blind, mothers and babies, the mentally ill, and tuberculosis sufferers.[35] Liverpool Labour Party was by no means alone in 1919 in aspiring towards a massive extension of municipalization into fields such as milk, coal, gas, lighting and heating supply, washhouses, laundries, restaurants, theatres, opera-houses and halls, 'so that the social and intellectual life of the workers may be encouraged and developed'.[36]

The nationalization of policy

In the 1930s, the party's emphasis shifted towards national rather than municipal action.[37] The aftermath of the financial crisis of 1931 drew attention to the way in which national financial problems could stymie Labour's aspirations. This need for national solutions also reflected a response to the Slump that began in 1929 and to the unemployment it brought in its train. The TUC shifted rapidly to the view that this required planning as well as the control of the economy. A resolution at its 1931 conference stated:

> Having regard to the seriousness of the economic situation, Congress explicitly expresses the view that only by a comprehensive planning of our economic development and regulated trade relations can the needs of the present day be met.[38]

Such views increasingly shaped Labour's policies during the 1930s. This was not least because the variable regional impact of the economic travails of the decade made it clear that local solutions and local funding of them would not prove adequate to meet such challenges. Staple industrial areas were now in long-term decline. In response, the National government in 1934 created four Special Areas, departing from the policy used in the 1920s of merely encouraging the unemployed to move in search of jobs.[39] However, it provided insufficient funds and incentives to achieve its object of attracting investment and industry to these areas. Complaining of this and of Whitehall interference, the commissioner for the Special Areas created by the 1934 legislation, Sir Malcolm Stewart, resigned in 1936, to be succeeded by the Quaker and former Labour MP turned National Government supporter Sir George Gillett.[40] Labour was equally critical, with the 1935 manifesto referring to tackling 'the problem of the distressed areas by … a vigorous policy of national planning'.[41]

A shift towards policy being controlled at national rather than local level was as evident in the 1930s in social as well as economic affairs. One example is that, with the passing of legislation such as the Poor Prisoners' Defence Act 1930, much of the work of the poor man's lawyers was now increasingly undertaken by the State. Another is that the probation work of police court missionaries, like Tom Holmes of the Claremont Mission, was in 1938 transferred to the direct control of the Home Office.[42] Where missions innovated, as with the experiments with evacuation conducted by the Wesleyans' South London Mission during the German air raids of the Great War, the State later provided the resources to manage such schemes on a much larger scale.[43]

In the interwar years, there nevertheless remained many welfare issues which were only gradually coming to be addressed by State provision. The far from generous unemployment assistance scales did not prevent cases of malnutrition in the more depressed areas of the country, while half of the population was still not covered by health insurance by the end of the period.[44] In the 1920s some central halls and missions accordingly continued to extend their provision. The West London Mission moved into providing hostels, a maternity hospital and systematic prison visiting, while in Poplar, W. H. Lax established dental, chiropody, physiotherapy, optical and cancer clinics.[45] He was nevertheless clear about the crucial role of the State in securing better social conditions. Reflecting on the social improvements he had observed during a career which had commenced at the West London Mission in the 1890s, Lax recorded in his memoirs in 1936: 'If we seek a reason we shall probably find it in the ameliorative legislation of the last thirty-five years, in the pushing back of the frontiers of liberty and in the recognition of the fact that the well-being of one is the well-being of all.'[46] Meanwhile, the churches were increasingly becoming ancillary in the provision of social welfare.[47]

The rationale for this process was well expressed by W. F. Lofthouse in 1957. Of the State, he noted:

> It must take the place of the careless parent, check the heartless employer, and generally secure a reasonable measure of comfort for all its citizens. It is doing today far more than the founders of the Settlement movement ever hoped to accomplish by their modest technique.[48]

Much of the public clearly agreed. For instance, in 1948, as the West Ham Central Mission opened a new care home for boys in Essex, an opinion poll found that 90 per cent felt that there was no longer a need for such charitable activity.[49] By that point, Lax's medical services – except chiropody and a new psychotherapy unit introduced during the Blitz – were also being subsumed into the National Health Service newly created by the post-war Labour government.[50]

This process of nationalizing social welfare had two important consequences. For the churches, it compounded the difficulties which they were already experiencing as social institutions during the interwar years. The provision of social services, just like the late Victorian move into associational culture, ran the risk of creating an instrumental nexus between church and community. Churches faced the danger of being seen merely as socially rather than spiritually useful. This reduced their overall societal relevance. It also made them vulnerable to loss of function, as indeed occurred as the State moved into providing such services directly.

The nationalization of religion

A further consequence was that the State, as Lofthouse implied, came to be invested with the role of moral and social guardian. There is an irony in the major role played by Nonconformity – once so apt to condemn it – in investing the twentieth-century State with moral values and presenting its assumption of welfare functions from the churches as the discharge of sacred communal duties. Religious values, and the religious responsibility of caring for one another came to be seen as exercised through the State.

As Durkheim pointed out, the collectivity of society effectively functions as a religion, enforcing values and duties.[51] By the end of the interwar years this mantle was, in practical terms, falling upon the State. Its welfare activities, in particular, became central to the moral economy of the nation and were invested with a quasi-Christian glow.

This nationalization of religion was also occurring at the level of public doctrine. Arguably, this was always likely to happen as a result of democratization. The advent of democracy means that authority tends to become socially defined through collectivities, rather than externally defined through, for instance, the exposition of eternal truths contained in sacred texts which are in turn interpreted by religious institutions. Democratization also affects churches as social organizations, as well as sources of authority. Social authority becomes centralized in democratically elected institutions, weakening in the process the autonomous elements of civil society. As de Tocqueville pointed out in the preface to his *Democracy in America*: 'it is the government alone that has inherited all the privilege of which families, guilds and individuals have been deprived', and he might well have added churches as among the social institutions which stood to lose status.[52] Ironically, in the American system, where government was deliberately checked by a formal separation of powers, in practice this loss of status happened far less than in Britain, where instead democracy simply adapted itself to the existing strong central State apparatus.[53]

This erosion of the autonomous social significance of the churches can be illustrated by reference to the central warfare function of the State. It was this, especially in response to the challenges of external threats from the 1880s, which led to the elaboration not of a welfare, but of a warfare state in Britain in the early twentieth century, as required to meet the demands upon it unleashed by the outbreak of total war in 1914.[54] The one area that was relatively neglected in the Edwardian war-book preparations was manpower.[55] Social institutions such as churches became necessarily supplementary recruiting sergeants at least until conscription was introduced in 1916, a role fulfilled with particular gusto by Nonconformists such as A. T. Guttery. In the Second World War, however, the State had no corresponding need for the churches to play a public role, other than the supplementary one of helping to maintain domestic morale. Instead, it was primarily politicians who gave voice to the values being defended in the struggle against Nazi Germany. There is an irony here, as neither Churchill nor his Labour deputy Attlee had a Christian faith. Both, however, espoused Christian values and it was these they invoked as national leaders during that conflict.[56]

Archbishop William Temple may have aspired to articulate a vision of a Christian social order worth defending in his wartime writings, but his invocation of a welfare state in *Citizen and Churchman* (1941) made clear the role that the State had to play in delivering that order.[57] A Christian social order accordingly became dependent upon State action. The nationalization of religion in the welfare state Attlee went on to create during his post-war government of 1945–51 thus followed on from the nationalization of religion in the warfare state, in which Attlee played a leading part as deputy prime minister in 1940–45.

The post-war Attlee government sought to tackle the perennial difficulties of social distress and economic insecurity by utilizing the power of the State to institute the National Health Service and attempting to create conditions of full employment. The

State thus assumed a much greater responsibility for the well-being of the community. In the process, it reduced the social services of the chapels and missions to very much a supplementary role.

By then, however, Free Churchmen, concerned that this responsibility should nevertheless be borne as effectively as possible, were far more inclined to greet such developments with enthusiasm than had been their co-religionists of a hundred years earlier. Indeed, they had helped to set examples for State action through the social services offered in the settlements, while also acting as cheerleaders for the national assumption of such responsibilities. Ammon's comments from the late 1940s: 'I am sure the Brotherhood Movement has not had the credit due for its share in the work of paving the way to the welfare state by its teaching of the exercise of Christian citizenship' could apply more broadly to the whole of Nonconformity.[58]

The assumption of these responsibilities by the State had long been an article of faith for Free Church Socialists. Ammon, for instance, told an Industrial Christian Fellowship conference in 1921 that he wanted the end of competition, to be replaced by a political economy of co-operation, with the State as guardian and custodian.[59] It was not, however, enough. 'Paradoxical as it seems', he warned in a lecture in the 1940s, 'as the Party gained in parliamentary representation and office … so its moral influence in the country waned.' This was not just because Labour ceased to be a crusade and became a political organization. It was also, for Ammon, because 'material success can be disastrous to ideals'.[60] As W. Emrys Davies reflected, writing in 1956 of his father, Rhys Davies:

> We would be wise … to remind ourselves that the pioneers of the Movement sought what is now called the Welfare State not as an end in itself but as a means of providing people with opportunities for greater happiness. Happiness is not the automatic product of some social and economic system; it lies within the people themselves. Thus it was that towards the end of his political life my father felt increasingly that the Movement should strive not only to preserve and augment the material gains, but also to discover ways by which people might find true happiness. Such happiness, that is satisfaction in living, he believed lay in self-realisation, a sense of community responsibility, a readiness to render service for the common good, a willingness to co-operate with others in worthwhile endeavour and in such personal and social virtues as honesty, trustworthiness, truthfulness and courtesy.[61]

This view reflected three facets of Rhys Davies's Nonconformist Socialism. First, though a champion of the welfare state, he had no illusions that the social justice and economic security which it endeavoured to provide would inevitably, of themselves, create a happier society. This was not least because this improved social order had itself to be sustained by the moral vision that had brought it into being. Otherwise it ran the risk of merely becoming an end in itself.

Secondly, it reflected a Nonconformist respect for the value of the individual. A better life for each individual was what the welfare state was designed to secure. For the Free Church Socialist, self-improvement and self-fulfilment were not merely facets of this better life that were good in themselves to achieve, but sources of a more responsible attitude towards society. This meant, as Ammon told the NCEFC Assembly in 1923 that:

> The object of work should be for the Community, rather than for the profit of one man, or a limited liability company. It should include the development of education, craftsmanship and citizenship. Freedom and self-respect are the most important steps towards social consciousness.[62]

Thirdly, the well-being of the community, and of the individual within that community was not secured simply by an improvement in living standards but by the development of such attitudes. This linked Nonconformist Socialists to a traditional Free Church emphasis on individual improvement. Typical of such views was Henderson's comment in 1922 that 'improved social conditions should have their counterpart in the elevation of the individual'.[63] For, as Alfred Salter pointed out at the inaugural meeting of the Christian Socialist Crusade in 1931, 'If we are going to create a new social order wherein dwelleth righteousness, we can only create such a state through the agency of righteous men and women.'[64] Free Church Socialists were far from sharing the view of their Marxist counterparts that 'the way to make people "good" is not to ask them to be good or to exhort them to be good, but to give them social conditions which will enable them to be good'.[65] As Walter Spencer of the South London Mission noted:

> A man cannot overcome habits of sin and degradation … by the exercise of his own will power … It has been so undermined and weakened as to be almost extinct. It is necessary for Another with a sharper will to take possession of the erring soul and cleanse the heart.[66]

Notwithstanding George Bernard Shaw's view that poverty is the only sin,[67] simply abolishing the resulting social evils would not put an end to the equally intransigent ones born of the greed, selfishness and pride reflected in but not exclusive to the Capitalist system.

In the vision of a future Socialist society drawn up by Samuel Keeble in 1936, such social evils had been eradicated by new social and economic mechanisms: 'distribution of the products of joint industry is scientific and universal. The new political economy … has made [of] distribution as careful a study as that of the nineteenth century did production for profit'. In Keeble's vision, people live in well-planned residential districts. 'Each one is well-educated'. There is no army and no war. There is no crime. 'Everyone controls himself'. The distribution of goods and services is 'scientifically organised by cheerful consent'. This has been achieved by ensuring that 'the motive … is not self but service'. Accordingly, 'each one has his or her allocated and congenial or socially necessary post'.[68]

The well-being of the community in Keeble's vision thus depended not so much on the assumption of responsibility by the State as on the consent, motive of service and acceptance of personal responsibility and agency before God of and by the people. Indeed, through the exercise of that responsibility the need for the State was gradually minimized. Keeble, one of Marx's earliest English readers, thus went further than Marx himself ever did in trying to offer a vision of a social order following the withering away of the State.

In practice, however, the State was extending its reach into all aspects of social life to an extent hitherto undreamt of. The demoralizing effects of this on moral character were among the major reasons why nineteenth-century Nonconformists had such scruples about its activities. Their twentieth-century successors reconciled themselves to the growth of public welfare systems in the hope that the State would prove an enabler, rather than the great provider. Otherwise, as George Thomas warned in 1959:

> Our peril now is that what was established for Christian motives has to be maintained by an increasingly secular society. Social security is treated as an end in itself, rather than as a means to enable men to give greater service to their fellows.[69]

Or, as his fellow Methodist Socialist Maldwyn Edwards put it the following year: 'The welfare state is only properly so called when men freely work in voluntary or statutory bodies for the welfare of the whole. Deny this and the State becomes a bureaucratic machine in which civil servants and public officials become the true masters and the rest an army of recipients.'[70]

This sort of stress was not necessarily peculiar to Nonconformist Socialists, but it was certainly characteristic of them. An emphasis on the importance of changing people's attitudes in order to create a society in which, mirroring the mutuality of the Body of Christ as drawn by St Paul, all are servants of the well-being of each other indeed seems to have been expected of them. For example, in 1944 the Keighley Baptist Young People's Fellowship, where Stanley Bell was a member, was challenged to debate against the local Labour League of Youth the view that the future of man depends upon a change of heart rather than circumstances. The Labour League of Youth were so impressed by Bell's contribution that a year later they made him their president.[71] For Nonconformist Socialists it was not enough to change social conditions and structures. It was not enough to make the State responsible for the provision of social welfare. These changes had to be sustained by a sense of responsibility and a moral vision of their purpose. They were furthermore a means to an end; the fulfilment within society and greater happiness of each individual, and the mutual service of all.

Conclusion

> *Now it is commonly supposed that Christian theology is so remote from practical life that it has little or no bearing upon the political fortunes of this or any nation. So far from this being true, however, we believe it may be shown that the rapid emergence of the social conscience of which organised Labour is a symbol, owes not a little to Methodist teaching.*
>
> A. Gordon James[1]

> *We may thus visualise the Socialist ideal, each industry working in unison for the common good, each individual finding his good linked with the good of all. All will be members one of another, for Socialism, in its structure and organisation, is the economic parallel of Christ's spiritual teaching.*
>
> George Benson[2]

Shortly before the 1929 election Ammon addressed the Wesleyan social services committee on the subject of unemployment. 'The discussion', he concluded, 'was quite worthwhile, but for all practical purposes much like sowing the wind.'[3] It is easy to see this observation from so committed a Methodist as a damning indictment of the declining political and social relevance of Nonconformity after 1918. The issues which the Free Churches had highlighted were, like temperance, no longer significant after the 1920s.[4] In the economic and class conflict of that decade, Free Church commentators meanwhile feared that Nonconformity had become irrelevant, the victim of the rise of new issues with the enfranchisement of the largely unchurched working classes.[5]

Ammon's diary note might thus suggest a simple conclusion to the investigation of the first of the four prisms through which this study has sought to explore the interaction between Labour and Nonconformity. The Free Church leadership, it seemed, failed to respond. The reality, however, is more complex. Even Ammon's observation reveals that the Free Churches did try to respond to such issues, as well as that there was regular and informal contact between Nonconformity at official levels and leading Nonconformists in the Labour Party. Sketching out the circumstances in which such contacts emerged began in Chapter 1 with analysis of the theological ferment of the late nineteenth century. This helped to create the intellectual setting in which the socialistic ideas developed that would shape the early Labour movement from the 1880s. Notwithstanding the work of Pope and Smith,[6] it was not just through the emergence of theological modernism that this occurred. Indeed, the range of ways – from modernism to sacramentalism – in which these theological changes helped to ensure a receptivity among the Free Churches' ministry to the rise of Labour politics, arguably deprived them at the same time of a singular and coherent message in response.

There is an irony here. The creation of bodies like the Wesleyan Social Services Committee in the early twentieth century was supposed to allow each Nonconformist denomination to pronounce authoritatively on social issues. The need for such guidance at the level of principles rather than mere policies had been acknowledged by Labour's general secretary Arthur Henderson, when he wrote in 1919: 'The Church is the one institution left in the world to-day that must not be allowed to take sides, but must stand "above the battle" and interpret the secular struggle in terms of moral progress and spiritual visions.'[7] There is polling evidence from the Second World War that suggests that the public also wanted to see the churches take such a lead on social questions and values.[8]

Doing so, however, could prove easier said than done. In practice, the new bodies of the early twentieth century proved less authoritative than the charismatic pulpit policy entrepreneurs of the late Victorian and Edwardian eras such as Price Hughes, Dale or Horne. All too often, apart from when addressing well-worn themes around matters of personal morality, the pronouncements of these committees were overly consensual and cautious. They sought more often to express the spirit in which solutions should be pursued, rather than their form. Instead, particularly during the Second World War, it was politicians like Henderson's successor as leader of the Labour Party Clement Attlee, who came to speak increasingly for Christian values, and to associate them with a political order which, through the creation of the welfare state, effectively nationalized the articulation of those values.[9]

It would nevertheless be wrong to argue that Nonconformist social concerns disappeared during the interwar years. Chapter 2 shows not only that some traditional Nonconformist concerns, such as anti-gambling, continued to be pressed, but also that the Free Churches attempted to respond positively to the social challenges presented by housing issues, unemployment, and industrial conflict. As J. D. Jones pointed out in 1938, these complex issues did not readily offer simple moral equations.[10] The result was the disappearance of the aggressive moral certitude of the fight against evil that had characterized the Nonconformist Conscience in its heyday. This had involved a pugnacious confrontation with all that undermined righteous living. However, as John Clifford put it, this was about more than 'working for one's personal good. Rather it is working with God for the regeneration of the world'.[11] Shorn of the latter, however, particularly for those who abandoned a faith in God simply for a faith in Socialism, it could become a form of secular self-righteousness. As noted in Chapter 8, for them, in contrast to Clifford, it did not require working with God as, by definition, to be Socialist was to be personally good. The pursuit of righteousness, accordingly, did not involve the improvement of the self so much as the denunciation of others identified as blocking the way to the better society.

In the process, some of the techniques and tone of the Nonconformist Conscience were adopted by Labour. For instance, the Passive Resistance pioneered by Nonconformity against the 1902 Education Act arguably came to be used in more secular settings by wartime Conscientious Objectors or the strikers of 1926.

This assimilation of practices borrowed from Nonconformity is apparent from the rhetorical uses frequently made of religiously inflected language within the movement. One use was defensive, to rebut charges that Socialism was merely an aggressive materialism aimed at the overthrow of the established order. More common, however, was the use of such rhetoric in terms of truth. Both religion and politics are knowledge systems resting upon understood truths about the human condition. While the absoluteness of the truths expressed by Christianity are tempered by awareness of human need for grace and salvation and, in Protestantism, by emphases on the individual's relationship to God,[12] Protestant Nonconformity still expressed 'truths' about social values, social conduct and liberty of conscience. Growing up among the chapels, the men and women born in the second half of the nineteenth century, who went on to shape the values and politics of the Labour movement until well into the twentieth, necessarily responded to those truths. Politics, after all, also expresses 'truths' about social order and social potentialities. It is noteworthy how often those truths for the early Labour movement were expressed in a competitive way, to claim that Labour expressed a purer version of them than the churches. This was not least in response to the continuing political tensions within particular chapels over the rise of the new party. In this way Labour both rebuked the churches and imbued itself with religious values. A typical example is the comment in the *Bradford Pioneer* that 'the fellow who would suggest consulting the Church when you want to get something done in the year 1919 ought to be taken to see a doctor at once'.[13] The discarded mantle, such statements implied, had fallen instead upon Labour. In other words, the Nonconformist Conscience had not so much disappeared as relocated. This was marked by the way in which the Nonconformist habit of identifying themselves as an outsider group working for righteousness in national affairs against the self-interested resistance of the established order was, as noted in Chapter 6, readily adopted by Labour ministers. As the Wesleyan Labour MP Ernest Winterton put it in 1929, Labour saw itself as 'the expression of a modern Nonconformist conscience or a devout Anglicanism which regards the working of modern capitalism as alien both to the spirit and teaching of Jesus of Nazareth'.[14] Sometimes in the process, the tropes of that same Nonconformist Conscience were now used to beat the Free Churches themselves and suggest thereby the contrasting righteousness of Labour's cause. Even figures like Henderson could adopt such rhetoric.[15]

Labour was thus shaped by Nonconformity at the level of systems of truth and of rhetoric. It is less clear that there was a relationship at an institutional level. In terms of the Free Church leaders, the old alliance with Liberalism lingered. Nonconformity was to help to supply additional Liberal candidates in the free trade election of 1923, as it had in the election of 1906. Thereafter the decline of free trade as an issue weakened Nonconformity's alignment with Liberalism. So did concerns over Liberal education policy. Among younger ministers, meanwhile, there was a clear movement towards Labour. Labour leaders, however, were less assiduous at courting Nonconformity than the Tory leader Stanley Baldwin. Reassured by the appearance of national unity after the social and industrial conflicts of the 1920s, much of the Nonconformist leadership ended up as supporters of the National government in which Baldwin was a central figure throughout the 1930s.

There is little evidence that, except in certain areas, the chapels were any more ready to support the Labour Party. The disappearance of Nonconformist disabilities weakened the ties that had bound them to the Liberals. The chapels diminishing commitment to the Liberal Party certainly did not assist the latter's survival. This was not, however, replaced by a similar commitment to Labour. Inferential evidence suggests some shift towards both Labour and Tories, with only small groups like the Quakers swinging significantly to Labour. The key point is that most Labour-held seats were in urban working-class areas with a limited Nonconformist presence. This does not demonstrate that Nonconformists did not vote Labour, but instead that they were not central to Labour's ability to win in such constituencies. Nor did the party generally court them as zealously as it did Catholic voters. Apart from in certain areas such as Norfolk, the chapels were not a decisive factor in Labour's electoral advance.

Meanwhile, chapels themselves became less central social institutions, less well-equipped to inculcate values and ideals in their adherents. This process should not be exaggerated. Even small rural causes could feature thriving LNU or Christian Citizenship societies in the 1930s.[16] Nonetheless, cash-strapped institutions which had been built in too great numbers in the wrong places during the population movements of the late nineteenth century began to reflect these financial pressures. If anything, these pressures became even greater with the proliferating new housing estates of the interwar years. In order to embed themselves in these new communities, an emphasis on experiential religion was gradually replaced by an associational culture of fraternals, sports and pastimes. This helped to maintain the chapels' social relevance into the interwar years, albeit at a diminishing level,[17] but undermined their spiritual relevance and distinctiveness. Allied with the theological changes outlined in Chapter 1, the result was a loss of sense, even among their own members, of what Free Churchmanship meant.[18]

At the same time, the declining importance of local politics and the more socially homogenous constituency boundaries after 1918 contributed to an impression of rising class-based voting and undermined the position of cross-class institutions like the chapels. Prominence in the chapel was therefore less likely to be reflected in prominence in the local community. It could still definitely help to make lay preachers well-known local figures. In general, however, chapel membership was ceasing to confer status. This was not least because the distinction between the rough and the respectable, so very noticeable in the late nineteenth century and a key factor in the tendency for unchurched working men to elect chapel men to responsible offices in trade unions, was also slowly becoming less apparent by the 1930s.[19] The erosion of such distinctions undermined both the appeal and the vitality of the chapel. In the process, this also meant that those activities, such as debating and mutual improvement societies, which had helped to train the Nonconformists of the early Labour movement, steadily disappeared. In particular, the Brotherhood was hit hard by the Great War. It was probably the most significant attempt to link the Labour movement to religious organizations. Something like a third of interwar Labour MPs were active in the Brotherhood movement (see Table 9), which continued to serve as a forum for debate about principles and politics. However, although it retained a membership running to six figures during the interwar years and was to play a role in the attempts at industrial conciliation of 1927–28, it was no longer as large, vital or influential as during its Edwardian heyday. This was another sign that the chapels were not only weakening as spiritual and social institutions, but also proving less of a schooling-ground for those who went on to serve the Labour movement.

Throughout the interwar years, however, Labour was differentially likely to run Nonconformist candidates for both local and parliamentary elections, including in areas where Nonconformity was itself thin on the ground. Indeed, by the 1930s, the bulk of Nonconformist parliamentary candidates were standing in the Labour interest. This, however, was essentially reflective of the declining number of Liberal candidates. As a proportion of total candidates, Nonconformists remained most noticeable in the Liberal and Liberal National ranks, while also steadily increasing their (tiny) presence among the Tories (see Appendix).

The large numbers of interwar Labour candidates shaped to a greater or lesser degree by Nonconformity were born in the 1860s onwards. Many had risen to leading positions in the trade unions by the late nineteenth century and acted as pioneers of the Labour movement. An intergenerational diminution in the role of Nonconformity in providing leading personnel for the movement is apparent from the Appendix and Table 9. The latter shows that of the Labour MPs first elected between 1918 and 1929, some 47 per cent were Nonconformists, a figure which fell to 26 per cent for those first elected to Parliament in the following decade. Even this latter figure is, however, still substantial, far in excess of Nonconformity's weight within the overall population. Together with the other tables presented in Chapter 5, it suggests that Bullock's commonplace about the role of Nonconformity in shaping many Labour activists continued to have considerable force during the interwar years. After all, Free Churchmen were to remain well represented within the generations who formed the party leadership into the post-war years. For instance, Harold Wilson, a man born fifty-three years after Arthur Henderson in 1916 and who therefore only came to maturity at the end of the interwar years, described himself as 'the first radical Nonconformist Prime Minister'.[20]

With the exception of the ILP, where a hostility towards organized religion was increasingly marked in the 1930s, a statistically significant presence of Nonconformists remained apparent between the wars in many parts of the Labour movement, from the TUC General Council to the personnel of the affiliated Co-operative Party. Not least important was the significant role played by Nonconformists such as Charlie Simmons or Reg Sorensen as itinerant lecturers for the party. As Simmons noted, these meetings often developed a revivalist character that maintained a Nonconformist religiosity of tone in the party's language and outreach activities. Labour, contrary to some accounts, did not cease to have the attributes of an ethical crusade after 1918. Instead, Simmons preached individual responsibility for seeking and maintaining social justice. For Nonconformists like Simmons, Socialism was not only a materialistic process to secure better living standards, but remained a moral imperative, a great crusade in which all should find fulfilment through mutual service. It was not only that the community had a responsibility for the well-being of the individual, but also that the individual had a responsibility for the well-being of the community.

The importance of such thought-worlds has largely gone unacknowledged in Labour histories,[21] especially since the 1970s. Even biographers of so devout a figure as Henderson have treated his religion almost as a compartmentalized optional extra.[22] Both in his personal and his political life, however, Henderson was clearly shaped by principles influenced by the distinctive religious setting Nonconformity supplied in England and Wales, as were most of his fellow Nonconformists in the party.

After 1922 there were more of these Free Churchmen and women among Labour rather than Liberal MPs (see Appendix). Apart from briefly in 1931 they did not, however, attempt to act together as Nonconformists, as had happened with the Nonconformist parliamentary committee of the Edwardian era chaired by Robert Perks and George White. With the decimation of Labour in the election that autumn and the subsequent cooling of the arguments over denominational education which scarred that Parliament, this initiative lapsed, never to be revived. It was through the values that they espoused, rather than their adherence to traditional Free Church causes, that Nonconformists most shaped the ideas and tone of the developing Labour Party.

Labour, founded as it was upon an alliance between the trade unions and various Socialist organizations, proved much less susceptible to outside influences than the Liberals had been. Where it was susceptible to such influences on, for instance, the drink question, it was not Nonconformity which won out. Not least for electoral reasons, the CIU proved to be rather more significant in shaping party policy in this area, certainly by the 1930s. Even the shift of Labour Nonconformists to concentrating on issues like drink-driving rather than local option could not determine wider party policy. Instead, the party moved to neutralize the drink question, a process which enabled it to tap into the beer-barrel politics which had continued to give the Conservatives a role in working-class culture. This was not just an important means for Labour to widen its electoral appeal to the working classes it sought to represent.[23] It also meant that, although the leading temperance advocates in Parliament by the outbreak of the Second World War were now on the Labour benches, they had no discernible influence on the policies pursued by their party.

It was a similar story in terms of Labour's attitude towards gambling. By the 1930s, for Free Church leaders like E. Benson Perkins, this had become an even bigger menace than alcohol. A number of mainly Nonconformist Labour MPs strongly sympathized with this view. In general, however, Labour moved towards accepting gambling, like drink, as part of working-class culture. In these areas of policy, generally small groups of Nonconformist MPs, reckless of the likely responses of working-class Labour voters of a Catholic or CIU persuasion, maintained a witness. As a whole, however, the party was not shaped by their views. At the policy level, Nonconformity had but limited influence on Labour.

On the other hand, Free Churchmanship does not seem to have been much of a liability for Labour candidates. This is despite, as Chapter 7 shows, a certain cultural distance from the attitudes and mores of the working classes. Instead, Nonconformists continued to act differentially as leaders of working-class organizations. This was likely a major factor in the limited headway made by Marxism in Britain. Until the post-war years, trade unions proved difficult for Communists to take over. Marxists were also denied rhetorical space, Wertheimer pointing out how this reflected the influence of the distinctive religious situation in Britain upon its left-wing politics.

Furthermore, the kind of radical alienation from the State that bred Communism elsewhere only briefly obtained during the increasing controls brought in under DORA towards the end of the Great War.[24] Some Nonconformists such as Horner or A. J. Cook, who were imprisoned for their conscientious objection to conscription in this period, shifted towards Communism thereafter. In general, however, organizations like the NUWM ended up campaigning in a reformist way for the State to be more generous with welfare. Chapter 7 argues that the emergence of this positive view of the State and State welfare, one shaped in part by Nonconformist rhetoric, was more important than any shift towards class consciousness in explaining the politics of the interwar years. It also, in the process, helped to contain the rise of Communism.

Class consciousness could nevertheless be expressed with vehemence by Nonconformist Socialists, some of whom also became Marxist in their economics. This did not necessarily translate into enthusiasm for class conflict. When it did occur, as all too often in the 1920s, Nonconformist trade unionists could see it as essentially defensive, protecting working-class living standards against attack. A concern instead to promote more conciliatory industrial management is apparent from the major role played by the Brotherhood, behind the scenes, in prompting what became the Mond-Turner talks following the 1926 General Strike.

This reflected Nonconformist sensibilities. Conflict, certainly as an end in itself, was to be eschewed. As *Ploughshare*, the journal of the Socialist Quaker Society, put it in 1919, 'the methods of Marxian Socialism, which puts such emphasis on the means, that the end to be attained is lost sight of' were better avoided.[25] Finding means of avoiding class conflict in the first place, and instead replacing the competitive waste of the present system with one based upon co-operative production for service not profit seemed a better way forward. This was marked by the emphasis placed by Nonconformist Socialists upon rationalizing and nationalizing industry, especially after 1926.[26] This was seen as a more acceptable means than those of Marxists for achieving the production for the good of all that was the end Nonconformist Socialists sought.

A growing emphasis on nationalization has often been portrayed as marking a caesura from what has been depicted as a woolly, religiously infused pre-war ethicalism to a more practical interwar politics. As is shown in Chapter 8, however, the one was a means to achieve the ends of the other. The dichotomy is thus false. Nationalization may have become more fully delineated during the 1920s, but its function was as a means to ethical ends which continued to be clearly and frequently articulated – though not necessarily along the corporatist lines that emerged during the 1930s as the way to achieve it.

The other theme of Chapter 8 is the rise of the State. Traditionally an object of well-founded suspicion among Nonconformists, in the early twentieth century they instead came to see the State as the means of achieving welfare ends that the churches could not adequately deliver. Its apparent ability to operate practical Christianity through social-democratic transfer mechanisms thus imbued the State with quasi-religious values. Therein, however, warned Nonconformist Socialists, lay a risk which rested upon the tendency to confuse means and ends.

A fairer economic system, or the exercise of social obligations towards the well-being of others through the State, were for them means, not ends. The object of such an exercise was not to improve an abstraction called society, but the lives of the men and women who composed that society. Socialism as a rational system of organizing and owning the means of production and a complementary system of administration, was seen as the necessary solution. For Nonconformist Socialists, however, it was not enough to aim to achieve this and eradicate the various problems that confronted early twentieth-century Britain by changing economic and social structures and ownership. It was not enough to give the State responsibility for the provision of social welfare. The growing responsibility of the community for the well-being of society had to be complemented by an awareness of personal responsibility and a moral vision of their purpose.

It was the exercise of duties in mutual service that secured the benefits and rights of the better society for all that Free Church Socialists aimed at. For them, if not always for all their colleagues in the Labour Party, Socialism was thus to be achieved not just by changing people's circumstances, but by changing their attitude to these circumstances, and to each other. Ideals, such as the mutual work of all in the service of the community, so beloved of early Socialists, will after all only work if all involved are committed to them. If Socialism is about giving greater power to and encouraging the fulfilment of the individual within society, as Nonconformist Socialists maintained, this emphasis on a heightened sense of personal responsibility was essential. Indeed, Wellock argued, if individuals could be improved in this way, there would be no need for the State as the organizing mechanism for a more just society, for 'if you can only get men with the right spirit in them you will have no need for Socialism, but will then proceed on the more simple lines of co-operation'.[27]

This study thus suggests, through investigation of the four prisms through which Labour's relationship with Nonconformity has been explored, a different approach both to the politics of the interwar years and to the understanding of public policy. In terms of the former, Chapter 4 shows that the apparent shift to class-based voting is more an artifice of restructured electoral boundaries, policy issues and party behaviour, offering a model for explaining where and why Nonconformist voting remained important. There was otherwise much more continuity into the 1920s of the social and political characteristics of the Edwardian period than has hitherto generally been acknowledged. In the Labour movement, for instance, it was only by the end of that decade that there was a decisive shift away from temperance politics, from municipal to national politics, and towards nationalization and planning rather than the industrial confrontations that marked the period between 1911 and 1913 and culminated in 1926. As discussed in Chapters 1 and 6, this was part of a general shift towards a more professionalized politics shared with the other parties. Party behaviour and changing issues, explored in Chapter 7, were more significant than class in determining voting behaviour throughout the period.

PRINCIPLES:
A society in which people's talents are not wasted and all are able to fulfil their potential in mutual service.

AIMS:
Tackling the scourge of unemployment.

POLICIES:
The overall design of the methods and devices used to do this, taking into account externalities and constraints such as finance, legal powers and so on.

PROCESSES:
The mechanisms (legal powers, administrative structures, communications) through which the policies are implemented.

OUTCOMES:
Measurable improvements in the quality of life and opportunities enjoyed by people.

Figure 1 A framework for the relationship between religious principles and politics.

These changing issues posed public policy challenges to which Labour and the Free Churches tried to respond. Public policy development processes are usually understood in terms of a cycle of actions from investigation, through formulation and decision to implementation and review. Instead, Henderson's point about the role of the churches in politics suggests a different framework. An attempt to sketch this out appears in Figure 1. This uses Ammon's complaint about discussion on unemployment as a starting point. Ammon may indeed have found that his ministerial colleagues in the Wesleyan social services committee had only limited practical suggestions of means to address this problem. However, their job, according to Henderson, was not to focus upon the third stage and beyond in this framework, but upon the first and the fifth. The risk otherwise, as the Anglican, Labour peer and political scientist Raymond Plant has pointed out more recently, is that the churches get drawn into sometimes simplistic policy suggestions.[28]

This is problematic for a number of reasons. While it is impossible to know all the likely ramifications of a policy sufficiently to always avoid producing perverse incentives or unintended outcomes, the churches' knowledge base may be more limited in particular areas, not least given the growing complexity of policy in the twentieth century. Secondly, and more significantly, the churches, unlike political parties, do not bear the responsibility and democratic accountability for the implementation of policies. Churches loudly proclaiming that this or that policy is fundamentally right are in danger of exercising what Baldwin decried, when referring instead to the press, as the harlot's prerogative of power without responsibility.[29] They also run the risk of damaging their own credibility through becoming overly identified with particular policies, as arguably proved the case with moral crusades such as temperance. Thirdly, such an approach risks investing policies with the appurtenances of truth and making them central when – like the State's role in the promotion of welfare for interwar Nonconformist Socialists – they are only ever the means and never the ends. Emphasizing policy without making clear its relationship to the core principles and values that should shape it is thus a classic example of a category error. Fourthly, as the Free Churches found in the interwar years, a focus on social issues can distract from and obscure their spiritual message.[30] Finally, the circumstances in which policies are appropriate will change anyway. Public policy is a Sisyphean task, one which never ends. The circumstances in which it is articulated, however, are always changing. For instance, take Harold Wilson's attempts to maintain full employment in the 1960s and 1970s. Prices and incomes policy may or may not have been the most appropriate method to achieve this, but it was the one adopted. The Social Contract which Wilson tried to implement with the trade unions, however, ended in demarcation disputes, competitive wage-bargaining and the collapse of the policy in the 'Winter of Discontent' of 1978–79. Being reasonable in the interests of a wider whole proved very difficult to achieve in practice. In such circumstances the churches' role, Henderson implied, was to maintain a sense of what that vision was, rather than attempting detailed policy formulation.

In the end, however, the churches did play a part during the interwar years in elevating a very particular policy device called the State. The State historically can perhaps most usefully be understood – in the best possible construction of the phrase – as a protection racket. It took tax revenues in order to protect against external and internal enemies (and at times numbered Nonconformists among the latter). From the late nineteenth century, culminating in the Attleean welfare state, it also became a risk pool to protect citizens in social need. This process was positively encouraged by Nonconformity. It invested the State with religious values, turning it into the provider of practical Christianity. The State's delivery mechanisms, instead of being understood simply as means to an end, became good in and of themselves, elevated into quasi-religious truths. For Nonconformist Socialists, however, State welfarism was only ever a means not an end, and one which, to be effective, had to be maintained by the elevation of righteous individuals, both in the pursuit of their own lives and in their dealing with each other. Otherwise there was a risk that the State would become merely a paternalistic mechanism.

In addition to drawing attention to changing concepts of the State, as noted above this study also draws attention to the adoption within Labour, of some of the tone, if not the tenets, of the Nonconformist Conscience. As an exhortation to improving both society and the individual, the nineteenth-century Nonconformist Conscience had been a call for national righteousness. Shorn of the principles and faith that animated it, not to mention the focus on the elevation of the individual as well as of society, however, it could too easily simply become a self-righteous shopping list of supposedly self-evident 'goods'. Righteousness, nonetheless, is not maintained just by espousing particular policies and values. Furthermore, supporting those does not, in itself, make an individual 'good'. They could instead, Mary Agnes Hamilton found, lead to being an apologist for Hitler. She was not alone in discovering that the eventual need to confront evil in the ensuing Second World War tested her optimistic humanism to destruction. Long after she ceased to be a Labour MP she eventually found her faith, noting in 1944: 'I now see that a Socialism which leaves unexplained the question of whence values originate leaves out the essential element.'[31] To this, Nonconformist Socialists added a sense of individual responsibility for social improvement. Otherwise, as Ammon warned four years later, 'A people may be assured of all the essentials of material life and live under the most perfect social system and yet the nation hurtle to destruction. It is right that such things be sought and gained; but by themselves they are not enough.'[32]

Appendix: Nonconformist Candidates in England and Wales in the General Elections, 1918–35

These tables are based on lists of Nonconformist candidates given in the Free Church press and local newspapers, Franz Linden's analysis, memoirs and biographies. These tables thus derive from a wider range of sources than those in provided in the appendices of Stephen Koss's *Nonconformity in Modern British Politics* (London: Batsford, 1975) which were essentially derived from the lists published at the time of each election in the *Christian World*.

A.1. 1918

	LAB candidates	LAB MPs	LIB candidates	LIB MPs	CoL/NDP candidates	CoL/NDP MPs	CON candidates	CON MPs	IND candidates	Total candidates	Total MPs
Baptist	17	4	15	1	9	9				41	14
Presbyterian	5		1				1	1	1	8	1
Congregational	22	8	28	3	20	19	1	1	3	74	31
Quaker	5		5		1	1				11	1
Unitarian	5		9	2	6	5	3	3		23	10
Wesleyan	32	7	29	3	14	11	7	7		82	28
Primitive	16	8	5	1	1	1				22	10
United Methodist	8	5	8	3	5	5				21	13
Independent Methodist					1	1				1	1
Calvinistic Methodist	6	3	5	2	5	4				16	9
Moravian			1							1	
Undesignated	6	1								6	1
TOTAL	122	36	106	15	62	56	12	12	4	306	119
Candidates/MPs per party	343	53	248	29	142	113	367	325			528
% Nonconformist	35.57	67.92	42.74	51.72	43.66	49.56	3.27	3.69			22.54

Note: The abbreviations along the top of the table represent respectively: LAB = Labour Party; LIB = Liberal Party; CoL = Coalition Liberal; NDP = National Democratic Party; CON = Conservative Party; IND = Independent.

A.2. 1922

	LAB candidates	LAB MPs	LIB candidates	LIB MPs	NAT LIB candidates	NAT LIB MPs	CON candidates	CON MPs	IND candidates	Total candidates	Total MPs
Baptist	16	8	14	2	7	5				37	15
Presbyterian	3	3	2	1			1	1		6	5
Congregational	30	16	39	5	16	6	2	2	1	88	29
Quaker	9	2	7		1		1			18	2
Unitarian	5	1	11	2	3	1	3	3	1	23	7
Wesleyan	39	17	30	3	9	3	11	7		89	30
Primitive	23	7	11	2	2					36	9
United Methodist	9	5	5	2	1				2	17	7
Wesleyan Reform Union			1							1	
Independent Methodist					1	1				1	1
Calvinistic Methodist	8	5	5	3	7	4	1			21	12
Salvation Army	1									1	
Moravian	1									1	
Churches of Christ	1		1							2	
Undesignated	6	4			1					7	4
TOTAL	151	69	126	20	48	20	19	13	4	347	122
Candidates/MPs per party	371	114	286	46	116	41	430	318			528
% Nonconformist	40.70	60.53	44.06	43.48	41.38	48.78	4.42	4.09			23.11

Note: The abbreviations along the top of the table represent respectively: LAB = Labour Party; LIB = Liberal Party; NAT LIB = National Liberal; CON = Conservative Party; IND = Independent.

A.3. 1923

	LAB candidates	LAB MPs	LIB candidates	LIB MPs	CON candidates	CON MPs	IND candidates	IND MPs	Total candidates	Total MPs
Baptist	15	11	23	7					38	18
Presbyterian	5	4	5	2	1	1			11	7
Congregational	27	16	54	22	4	2	1	1	86	41
Quaker	14	4	6	3	1				21	7
Unitarian	8	3	12	6	3	3			23	12
Wesleyan	39	23	42	18	9	3			90	44
Primitive	17	8	13	2					30	10
United Methodist	6	6	7	2					13	8
Wesleyan Reform Union			2						2	
Independent Methodist	2		1	1					3	1
Calvinistic Methodist	8	5	14	9	1				23	14
Salvation Army	1								1	
Moravian	1								1	
Churches of Christ			1	1					1	1
Undesignated	7	5	2	1					9	6
TOTAL	150	85	182	74	19	9	1	1	352	169
Candidates/MPs per party	380	158	397	135	469	231				528
% Nonconformist	39.47	53.80	45.84	53.81	4.05	3.90				32.01

Note: The abbreviations along the top of the table represent respectively: LAB = Labour Party; LIB = Liberal Party; CON = Conservative Party; IND = Independent.

A.4. 1924

	LAB candidates	LAB MPs	LIB candidates	LIB MPs[a]	CON candidates	CON MPs	Total candidates	Total MPs
Baptist	15	9	9	3			24	12
Presbyterian	8	3	4				12	3
Congregational	24	12	49	7	3	2	76	21
Quaker	21	3	7		1	1	29	4
Unitarian	10	2	14	1	5	5	29	8
Wesleyan	37	16	32	3	6	6	75	25
Primitive	18	6	11	2	1	1	30	9
United Methodist	6	5	6				12	5
Wesleyan Reform Union			1				1	
Independent Methodist	3	1	1	1			4	2
Calvinistic Methodist	12	4	9	5	1		22	9
Moravian	1						1	
Churches of Christ			1				1	
Undesignated	10	4	1				11	4
TOTAL	165	65	145	22	17	15	327	102
Candidates/MPs per party	450	125	317	38	464	361		528
% Nonconformist	36.67	52.00	45.74	57.89	3.66	4.16		19.32

Note: The abbreviations along the top of the table represent respectively: LAB = Labour Party; LIB = Liberal Party; CON = Conservative Party.

[a] In addition, W. M. Wiggins (the son of a Baptist minister) was elected as Liberal MP for Oldham at a by-election in 1925 but stood down in 1929.

A.5. 1929

	LAB candidates	LAB MPs	LIB candidates	LIB MPs	CON candidates	CON MPs	IND candidates	IND MPs	Plaid Cymru candidates	Total candidates	Total MPs
Baptist	18	12	21	2					1	40	14
Presbyterian	8	5	5	1	2		1			16	6
Congregational	31	26	54	8	1	1				86	35
Quaker	22	10	9		1	1				32	11
Unitarian	11	7	10	1	5	5	1	1		27	14
Wesleyan	44	35	53	13	15	2	1			113	50
Primitive	13	10	16	1	1	1				30	12
United Methodist	7	6	7		1					15	6
Wesleyan Reform Union			1							1	
Independent Methodist	3	2					1	1		4	3
Calvinistic Methodist	8	4	12	7	1					21	11
Salvation Army	1									1	
Moravian	1	1								1	1
Undesignated	12	4	1							13	4
TOTAL	179	122	189	33	27	10	4	2	1	400	167
Candidates/MPs per party	502	251	461	45	512	227			1		528
% Nonconformist	35.66	48.61	41.00	73.33	5.27	4.41			100.00		31.63

Note: The abbreviations along the top of the table represent respectively: LAB = Labour Party; LIB = Liberal Party; CON = Conservative Party; IND = Independent.

A.6. 1931

	LAB candidates	LAB MPs	LIB candidates	LIB MPs	LN candidates	LN MPS	NAT LAB candidates	NAT LAB MPs	CON candidates	CON MPs	IND/PROT candidates	IND/PROT MPs	Plaid Cymru candidates	Total candidates	Total MPs
Baptist	16	4	6	2	1	1	1	1			2			26	8
Presbyterian	5	1	1	1	1	1	2	2	1	1	1			11	6
Congregational	29	5	15	6	5	3	1	1	3	3			1	54	18
Quaker	19	1	3				1	1	1	1				24	3
Unitarian	11	1	3	1					6	5	1	1		21	8
Wesleyan	40	5	9	1	11	10			12	12	1			73	28
Primitive	13	3	1	1	1	1			1	1				16	6
United Methodist	8	2	3	1										12	3
Wesleyan Reform Union			1								1			1	
Independent Methodist	2													2	
Calvinistic Methodist	5	3	7	5	3	3								15	11
Salvation Army	1													1	
Moravian	1													1	
Undesignated	12													12	
TOTAL	162	25	49	18	22	19	5	5	24	23	6	1	1	269	91
Candidates/MPs per party	454	44	103	29	35	29	19	12	449	410			2		528
% Nonconformist	35.68	56.82	47.57	62.07	62.86	65.52	26.32	41.67	5.35	5.61			50.00		17.23

Note: The abbreviations along the top of the table represent respectively: LAB = Labour Party; LIB = Liberal Party; LN = Liberal National; NAT LAB = National Labour; CON = Conservative Party; IND = Independent; PROT = Protestant Party.

A.7. 1935

	LAB candidates	LAB MPs	LIB candidates	LIB MPs	LN candidates	LN MPs	NAT LAB candidates	NAT LAB MPs	CON candidates	CON MPs	IND/ PROT candidates	IND/ PROT MPs	ILP candidates	Plaid Cymru candidates	Total candidates	Total MPs
Baptist	14	9	4	2	1	1	2	1			1				22	13
Presbyterian	5	2			1	1	2		2	1					10	4
Congregational	22	13	13	2	4	4			2	2				1	43	21
Quaker	17	3	4				1		1	1	1				24	4
Unitarian	12	6	3		1				5	5	1	1			22	12
Methodist	50	24	21		12	9			12	8	1		1		97	41
Independent Methodist	1														1	
Calvinistic Methodist	7	1	8	5	2	2			1	1					18	9
Salvation Army	1	1													1	1
Moravian	1	1													1	1
Undesignated	7	2													7	2
TOTAL	137	62	53	9	21	17	5	1	23	18	4	1	1	1	246	108
Candidates/MPs per party	490	134	143	18	34	25	19	7	442	339			6	1		528
% Nonconformist	27.96	46.27	37.06	50.00	61.76	68.00	26.32	14.29	5.20	5.31			16.66	100.00		20.45

Note: The abbreviations along the top of the table represent respectively: LAB = Labour Party; LIB = Liberal Party; LN = Liberal National; NAT LAB = National Labour; CON = Conservative Party; IND = Independent; PROT = Protestant Party; ILP = Independent Labour Party.

Notes

Introduction

1 Cited in *British Weekly*, 10 January, 1924.
2 J. Keir Hardie, from his Brotherhood speaking tour of France and Belgium in 1910, cited in Harry Jeffs, *Press, Preachers and Politicians: Reminiscences 1874 to 1932* (London: Independent Press, 1938), p. 97.
3 Alan Bullock, *The Life and Times of Ernest Bevin: Volume 1, Trade Union Leader, 1881–1940* (London: Heinemann, 1960), p. 9; Alan Bullock, *Building Jerusalem: A Portrait of My Father* (London: Allen Lane, 2000).
4 Herbert Tracey (ed.), *The Book of the Labour Party*, vol. 2 (London: Caxton, 1925), p. 83; Clement Attlee, *The Labour Party in Perspective* (London: Gollancz, 1937), p. 27; G. D. H. Cole, *A Guide to the Elements of Socialism* (London: Labour Party, 1947), p. 2.
5 Harold Wilson, *The Relevance of British Socialism* (London: Weidenfeld and Nicolson, 1964), p. 1.
6 See Hugh McLeod, 'Dissent and the Peculiarities of the English, c.1870–1914', in Jane Shaw and Alan Kreider (eds), *Culture and the Nonconformist Tradition* (Cardiff: University of Wales Press, 1999), pp. 117–41; Peter Catterall, 'The Distinctiveness of British Socialism?: Religion and the Rise of Labour, c.1900–39' in Matthew Worley (ed.), *The Foundations of the British Labour Party: Identities, Cultures and Perspectives, 1900–39* (Farnham: Ashgate, 2009), p. 133.
7 J. T. Walton Newbold, 'The ILP: A Marxist Study', *Socialist Review* 17 (1920), pp. 77–86.
8 John Kent, *William Temple: Church, State and Society in Britain, 1880–1950* (Cambridge: Cambridge University Press, 1992), pp. 145–96.
9 Clive D. Field, 'The Faith Society? Clarifying Religious Belonging in Edwardian Britain 1901–1914', *Journal of Religious History*, 37/1 (2013), pp. 39–63.
10 Ernest A. Payne, *The Free Church Tradition in the Life of England* (London: SCM Press, 1944), p. 151.
11 C. G. Ammon et al., *Labour's Dynamic* (London: Labour Publishing, 1922), p. 17; G. N. Barnes et al., *Religion and the Labour Movement* (London: Holborn Press, 1919); Catterall, 'Distinctiveness', p. 138.
12 See James Hinton, *Labour and Socialism: A History of the British Labour Movement, 1867–1974* (Brighton: Wheatsheaf, 1983).
13 David Redvaldsen, *The Labour Party in Britain and Norway: Elections and the Pursuit of Power between the World Wars* (London: I. B. Tauris, 2011), pp. 9–10.
14 See David Hempton, *Methodism and Politics in British Society 1750–1850* (London: Hutchinson, 1984).
15 See Stephen Yeo, *Religion and Voluntary Organisations in Crisis* (London: Croom Helm, 1976); Stanley Pierson, *British Socialism: The Journey from Fantasy to Politics*

(London: Harvard University Press, 1979); Leonard Smith, *Religion and the Rise of Labour: Nonconformity and the Independent Labour Movement in Lancashire and the West Riding 1880–1914* (Keele: Ryburn, 1993).

16 S. H. Mayor, *The Churches and the Labour Movement* (London: Independent Press, 1967); Kenneth D. Brown 'English Nonconformity and the British Labour Movement: A Study', *Journal of Social History* 9/2 (1975): 113–20; David E. Martin, 'The Instrument of the People? The Parliamentary Labour Party in 1906', in David E. Martin and David Rubinstein (eds), *Ideology and the Labour Movement* (London: Croom Helm, 1979), pp. 125–46; Robert Moore, *Pitmen, Preachers and Politics: The Effects of Methodism in a Durham Mining Community* (Cambridge: Cambridge University Press, 1974).

17 Franz Linden, *Sozialismus und Religion: Konfessionsoziologische Untersuchung der Labour Party 1929–1931* (Leipzig: Kölner anglistische Arbeiten, Bande.17, 1932).

18 Stefan Berger, *The Labour Party and the German Social Democrats, 1900–1931* (Oxford: Oxford University Press, 1994), pp. 196–206.

19 *Christian World*, 23 October 1924.

20 James Dingley, *Nationalism, Social Theory and Durkheim* (Basingstoke: Palgrave Macmillan, 2008).

21 Robert Pope, *Building Jerusalem: Nonconformity, Labour and the Social Question in Wales, 1906–1939* (Cardiff: University of Wales Press, 1998), pp. 62–5.

22 Catterall, 'Distinctiveness', p. 149.

23 *Christian World*, 14 December 1922.

24 Stephen Koss, *Nonconformity in Modern British Politics* (London: Batsford, 1975); Michael Bentley, *The Liberal Mind, 1914–1929* (Cambridge: Cambridge University Press, 1977), pp. 191–204; John F. Glaser, 'English Nonconformity and the Decline of Liberalism', *American Historical Review* 63/2 (1958), pp. 352–63.

25 Kenneth D. Brown, 'The Baptist Ministry of England and Wales: A Social Profile', *Baptist Quarterly* 32/3 (1987), p. 117; Sir Geoffrey Shakespeare, *Let Candles Be Brought In* (London: Macdonald, 1949), p. 343; J. D. Jones, *Three Score Years and Ten* (London: Hodder & Stoughton, 1940), pp. 97–124.

26 *Christian World*, 28 October 1918; Norfolk Record Office (henceforward NRO): Norfolk Congregational Union minutes, 9 April 1919.

27 Jeffs, *Press, Preachers and Politicians*, p. 239; Arthur Porritt, *More and More of Memories* (London: Allen & Unwin, 1947), p. 77.

28 *Congregational Year Book* (henceforward *CYB*) (1919), pp. xii, 7–8; A. C. Underwood, *A History of the English Baptists* (London: Baptist Union, 1947), pp. 248–9; R. Tudur Jones, *Congregationalism in England 1662–1962* (London: Independent Press, 1962), pp. 395–6.

29 John Dolan, *The Independent Methodists: A History* (Cambridge: James Clarke, 2005), p. 156.

30 John D. Gay, *The Geography of Religion in England* (London: Duckworth, 1971), pp. 127–33, 180; Dolan, *Independent Methodists*, pp. 66, 124, 193.

31 David Bebbington, *Evangelicalism in Modern Britain: A History from the 1730s to the 1980s* (London: Unwin Hyman, 1989), pp. 16–17.

32 Dorothea Price Hughes, *The Life of Hugh Price Hughes* (London: Hodder & Stoughton, 1905), p. 457; E. K. H. Jordan, *Free Church Unity: History of the Free Church Council Movement 1896–1941* (London: Lutterworth, 1956), p. 50.

33 Cited in Jordan, *Free Church Unity*, pp. 47–8.

34 *War Cry*, 2 November 1935.

35 Peter Ackers, *Labour and Capital in the Wigan Churches of Christ c1845–1945* (Loughborough University Business School Research Paper 4, 1994), p. 14; Michael W. Casey, 'The Overlooked Pacifist Tradition of the Old Paths Churches of Christ, Part II', *Journal of the United Reformed Church History Society* [*JURCHS*] 6/7 (2000), pp. 517–28.
36 Noel Edwards, *Ploughboy's Progress: The Life of Sir George Edwards* (Norwich: Centre for East Anglian Studies, University of East Anglia, 1998), chaps. 2–4.
37 *Bradford Pioneer*, 11 January 1929.
38 Travis L. Crosby, *The Unknown Lloyd George: A Statesman in Conflict* (London: I. B. Tauris, 2014), pp. 171, 173, 201, 421.
39 Porritt, *Memories*, pp. 73–7; Jones, *Three Score Years*, pp. 232–3; Koss, *Nonconformity*, pp. 132–6.
40 David Bebbington, *The Nonconformist Conscience: Chapel and Politics, c.1870–1914* (London: Allen & Unwin, 1982); Robert Pope, 'The Nonconformist Conscience' in Robert Pope (ed.), *Companion to Nonconformity* (London: Bloomsbury, 2013), pp. 437–58.
41 Philip Williamson, *National Crisis and National Government: British Politics, the Economy and Empire 1926–1932* (Cambridge: Cambridge University Press, 1991); Michael John Law, '"The Car Indispensable": The Hidden Influence of the Car in Inter-War Suburban London', *Journal of Historical Geography* 38/4 (2013), pp. 424–33.
42 Ross McKibbin, 'Why Was There No Marxism in Great Britain?', *English Historical Review* 99/391 (1984), pp. 297–331 focuses on divisions in the workplace and economic reformism.
43 Chris Cook, *The Age of Alignment: Electoral Politics in Britain, 1922–1929* (London: Macmillan, 1975), pp. 56–8. In 1937, Labour in Bolton, in the face of reversals at the municipal polls and the entrenched power of the Tories, even contemplated an expedient electoral arrangement with the Liberals (*Bolton Citizen*, November 1937).
44 P. J. Waller, *Democracy and Sectarianism: A Political and Social History of Liverpool 1868–1939* (Liverpool: Liverpool University Press, 1981); Sam Davies, *Liverpool Labour: Social and Political Influences on the Development of the Labour Party in Liverpool 1900–39* (Keele: Keele University Press, 1996).
45 Nigel Scotland, *Methodism and the Revolt of the Field* (Gloucester: Sutton, 1981); Edwards, *Ploughboy's Progress*, chap. 4; Clare V. J. Griffiths, *Labour and the Countryside: The Politics of Rural Britain 1918–1939* (Oxford: Oxford University Press, 2007), p. 159.
46 The exceptions are J. W. Tuffley, *The Sowers* (London: Brotherhood Movement, 1937); A. Gregory, *Romance and Revolution: The Story of the Brotherhood Movement* (London: Grammer, 1975); David Killingray, 'The Pleasant Sunday Afternoon Movement: Revival in the West Midlands 1875–1900?', in Kate Cooper and Jeremy Gregory (eds), *Studies in Church History Volume 44: Revival and Resurgence in Christian History* (Woodbridge: Boydell, 2008), pp. 262–74.
47 Hull History Centre, Ammon Papers (henceforward AP): U DMN/9/1, C. G. Ammon, 'Building the New World', undated lecture, c.1940s.

Chapter 1

1 G. O. Griffith, 'Political Liberalism and Evangelical Faith', *Congregational Quarterly* (1937), p. 317.

2 Arthur Porritt, *The Best I Remember* (London: Cassell, 1922), p. 143.
3 W. T. Davidson, 'The Religion of Tomorrow', *London Quarterly Review* (1926), p. 14.
4 Cited in Alan D. Gilbert, *The Making of Post-Christian Britain* (London: Longman, 1980), p. 107.
5 *CYB* (1939), p. 75.
6 Roger Tomes, '"Learning a New Technique": The Reception of Biblical Criticism in the Nonconformist Colleges', *JURCHS* 7/5 (2004), pp. 288–314; Tudur Jones, *Congregationalism in England*, pp. 254–6.
7 Jones, *Three Score Years*, p. 30.
8 J. K. Mozley, *The Doctrine of the Atonement* (London: Duckworth, 1915), p. 167; Robert Pope, *Building Jerusalem: Nonconformity, Labour and the Social Question in Wales 1906–1939* (Cardiff: University of Wales Press, 1998), p. 68; Dolan, *Independent Methodists*, p. 171.
9 Dale A. Johnson, *The Changing Shape of English Nonconformity, 1825–1925* (Oxford: Oxford University Press, 1999), pp. 178–9; David Bebbington, 'The Baptist Colleges in the Mid-Nineteenth Century', *Baptist Quarterly* 46/2 (2015), pp. 49–68.
10 The reflections on the challenge of Muslim missions stressing brotherhood and equality in James Johnston's *A Century of Protestant Mission and the Increase of the Heathen during the Last Hundred Years* (London: Nisbet, 1886) seem to have been influential.
11 Frank Lenwood, *Jesus: Lord or Leader?* (London: Constable, 1930), p. 13.
12 John Williamson, 'Half a Century of Theological Change', *Congregational Quarterly* (1924), p. 357.
13 Kenneth D. Brown, 'Nineteenth-Century Methodist Theological College Principals', *Proceedings of the Wesley Historical Society* [*PWHS*] 44/4 (1984), p. 101.
14 John Kent, *From Darwin to Blatchford: The Role of Darwinism in Christian Apologetic 1875–1910* (London: Dr Williams's Trust, 1966), pp. 12–13.
15 Kent, *From Darwin to Blatchford*, pp. 1–2.
16 Jones, *Three Score Years*, p. 312 (original italics).
17 Jones, *Three Score Years*, p. 312.
18 *Christian World*, 16 July 1925.
19 Johnson, *English Nonconformity*, p. 114.
20 Cited in Johnson, *English Nonconformity*, p. 141.
21 Johnson, *English Nonconformity*, pp. 138–9, 154–5.
22 Pope, *Building Jerusalem*, pp. 155–62.
23 Christopher Oldstone-Moore, *Hugh Price Hughes: Founder of a New Methodism, Conscience of a New Nonconformity* (Cardiff: University of Wales Press, 1999), pp. 89–111; Peter Catterall, 'Slums and Salvation', in Lesley Husselbee and Paul Ballard (eds), *Free Churches and Society: The Nonconformist Contribution to Social Welfare 1800–2010* (London: Continuum, 2012), pp. 117–18.
24 Cited in T. Rhondda Williams, *How I Found My Faith: A Religious Pilgrimage* (London: Cassell, 1938), pp. 127–8.
25 Cited in Oldstone-Moore, *Hugh Price Hughes*, p. 111.
26 John Beasley, *The Bitter Cry Heard and Heeded: The Story of the South London Mission* (London: South London Mission, 1990), pp. 14–15.
27 Seth Koven, *Slumming: Sexual and Social Politics in Victorian London* (London: Princeton University Press, 2004), pp. 8–15.
28 Disputed between Andrew Mearns and William C. Preston: see Beasley, *The Bitter Cry Heard and Heeded*, pp. 217–19.

29 Andrew Mearns, *The Bitter Cry of Outcast London* (London: London Congregational Union, 1883), pp. 11–13.
30 Mearns, *Bitter Cry*, p. 24.
31 Cited in David M. Thompson, 'R. W. Dale and the "Civic Gospel"', in Alan P. F. Sell (ed.), *Protestant Nonconformists and the West Midlands of England* (Keele: Keele University Press, 1996), p. 103.
32 Crosby, *The Unknown Lloyd George*, pp. 14–15.
33 Norman Wallwork, 'Developments in Liturgy and Worship in Twentieth Century Protestant Nonconformity', in Alan P. F. Sell and Anthony R. Cross (eds), *Protestant Nonconformity in the Twentieth Century* (Carlisle: Paternoster, 2003), p. 118.
34 Thompson, 'Dale and the Civic Gospel', pp. 111–12.
35 Jeffs, *Press, Preachers and Politicians*, pp. 34–5.
36 Richenda C. Scott, *Elizabeth Cadbury 1858–1951* (London: Harrap, 1955), pp. 70–1.
37 *British Quarterly Review*, 35/69 (1862), pp. 220–1, cited in Timothy Larsen, *Friends of Religious Equality: Nonconformist Politics in Mid-Victorian England* (Woodbridge: Boydell Press, 1999), p. 38.
38 K. G. Brownell, 'Voluntary Saints: English Congregationalism and the Voluntary Principle 1825–62', unpub. St Andrews PhD Thesis (1982), cited in Larsen, p. 10; Dolan, *Independent Methodists*, p. 177.
39 Richard Helmstadter, 'The Nonconformist Conscience', in Peter Marsh (ed.), *The Conscience of the Victorian State* (Brighton: Harvester, 1979), pp. 135–72.
40 David Hempton, *Methodism and Politics in British Society 1750–1850* (London: Hutchinson, 1987), p. 235; see also Richard D. Floyd, *Church, Chapel and Party: Religious Dissent and Political Modernisation in Nineteenth Century England* (Basingstoke: Palgrave, 2008), pp. 174–8; Larsen, chap. 8.
41 See Larsen, chap. 7.
42 John F. Glaser, 'Parnell's Fall and the Nonconformist Conscience', *Irish Historical Studies* 12/46 (1960), pp. 119–38; Oldstone-Moore, *Hugh Price Hughes*, pp. 213–18. See also Bebbington, *Nonconformist Conscience*, pp. 100–1. The term first appeared in *The Times*, 26 December 1890.
43 Jones, *Three Score Years*, pp. 42, 51, 224–5; Bebbington, *Nonconformist Conscience*, chap. 5.
44 Jeffs, *Press, Preachers and Politicians*, pp. 87, 90, 125. Despite this, Guinness Rogers claimed in 1899 that middle-class Dissent was solidly Liberal: see Alex Windscheffel, *Popular Conservatism in Imperial London 1868–1906* (Woodbridge: Boydell, 2007), p. 9.
45 Hugh Gault, *Making the Heavens Hum: Kingsley Wood and the Art of the Possible 1881–1924* (Cambridge: Gretton Books, 2014), p. 56; Bebbington *Nonconformist Conscience*, pp. 92–6. Wesleyans seem to have been particularly concerned at the threat to their Irish co-religionists in a future Catholic Ireland.
46 Matthew Roberts, '"Villa Toryism" and Popular Conservatism in Leeds, 1885–1902', *Historical Journal* 49/1 (2006), pp. 217–46.
47 Price Hughes's *Methodist Times* complained on 27 September 1894 of Nonconformist desertions to the 'party of privilege'.
48 Clyde Binfield, 'Victorian Values and Industrious Connexions' *PWHS* 55/4 (2006), p. 165.
49 Cited in Oldstone-Moore, *Hugh Price Hughes*, p. 114.
50 J. W. Wolfenden, 'English Nonconformity and the Social Conscience 1880–1906', unpub. Yale PhD Thesis (1954), p. 67. See also Peter Catterall, 'Nonconformity

and the Labour Movement', in Robert Pope (ed.), *Companion to Nonconformity* (London: Bloomsbury T&T Clark, 2013), p. 463.

51 Peter d'A. Jones, *The Christian Socialist Revival 1877–1914: Religion, Class and Social Conscience in Late Victorian England* (Princeton, NJ: Princeton University Press, 1968), pp. 455–6.

52 Jones, *Christian Socialist Revival*, pp. 348–9, 367.

53 Smith, *Religion and the Rise of Labour*, chap. 6; David James, *Class and Politics in a Northern Industrial Town: Keighley 1890–1914* (Keele: Ryburn, 1995), p. 71.

54 Keith Laybourn and John Reynolds, *Liberalism and the Rise of Labour 1890–1914* (London: Croom Helm, 1984), pp. 34, 80.

55 B. S. Diggle, 'Illingworthism: Alfred Illingworth and Independent Labour politics', unpub. Huddersfield MA Thesis (1984), pp. 30–1.

56 H. F. Lovell Cocks, *The Nonconformist Conscience* (London: Independent Press, 1943), pp. 30–1; Wolfenden, p. 27.

57 James E. Cronin, *The Politics of State Expansion: War, State and Society in Twentieth-Century Britain* (London: Routledge, 1991), p. 26; Moore, *Pitmen, Preachers and Politics*, pp. 154–8.

58 *Christian World*, letter from Theodore Cooke Taylor, 16 July 1925; Catterall, 'Nonconformity and the Labour Movement', p. 462.

59 S. G. Hobson, *Pilgrim to the Left: Memoirs of a Modern Revolutionist* (London: Arnold, 1938), pp. 38–9.

60 Pope, *Building Jerusalem*, esp. chap. 3.

61 Jones, *Three Score Years*, p. 225. See also James Munson, *The Nonconformists: In Search of a Lost Culture* (London: SPCK, 1991), chap. 9.

62 David Carter, 'Joseph Agar Beet and the Eschatological Crisis', *PWHS* 51/6 (1998), p. 207.

63 Jones, *Three Score Years*, p. 213.

64 Porritt, *The Best I Remember*, p. 51.

65 Jones, *Three Score Years*, p. 230.

66 *Christian World*, 1 February 1906. A recent recalculation (David Bebbington, 'The Free Church MPs of the 1906 Parliament', in Stephen Taylor and David L. Wykes (eds), *Parliament and Dissent* (Edinburgh: Edinburgh University Press, 2005), pp. 140–4) suggests 179 Nonconformist MPs, plus 29 more who were associated with Nonconformity. Of the new MPs, 25 were Passive Resisters.

67 David E. Martin, 'The Instruments of the People? The Parliamentary Labour Party in 1906', in David E. Martin and David Rubenstein (eds), *Ideology and the Labour Movement* (London: Croom Helm, 1979), p. 131. Bebbington, 'Free Church MPs', p. 143, gives a much lower figure of seven, with two also associated with Nonconformity.

68 *Christian World*, 5 August 1926.

69 *Christian World*, 26 December 1918.

70 *CYB* (1918), p. 36.

71 *CYB* (1919), p. 36.

72 *CYB* (1919), pp. 36–7.

73 *Christian World*, 18 September 1924.

74 D. S. Cairns (ed.), *The Army and Religion* (London: Macmillan, 1919), esp. p. 127; *Christian World*, 24 October 1918; Sue Morgan, '"Iron Strength and Infinite Tenderness": Herbert Gray and the Making of Christian Masculinities at War and at Home, 1900–40', in Lucy Delap and Sue Morgan (eds), *Men, Masculinities and*

Religious Change in Twentieth-Century Britain (Basingstoke: Palgrave Macmillan, 2013), pp. 176–80; *CYB* (1918), p. 35.

75 Cairns, *Army and Religion*, p. 65; see also Clyde Binfield, *Pastors and People: The Biography of a Baptist Church, Queens Road, Coventry* (Coventry: Queen's Road Baptist Church, 1984), p. 173.

76 *Christian World*, 25 April 1918.

77 *Minutes and Proceedings of the London Yearly Meeting of the Society of Friends* [henceforward *LYM*] (1918), pp. 75–8.

78 *LYM* (1919), pp. 159–70.

79 Bebbington, *Evangelicalism*, pp. 155–6.

80 *The Friend*, 22 May 1925. The term had a much less formal meaning among Quakers and Independent Methodists than it did by the early twentieth century more generally within Nonconformity.

81 *The Friend*, 11 December 1931, 15 February 1935; Scott, *Elizabeth Cadbury*, pp. 159–60.

82 *CYB* (1919), p. 26.

83 Jones, *Three Score Years*, p. 71.

84 Rhondda Williams, *How I Found My Faith*, pp. 48, 74.

85 *British Weekly* 9 May 1929; Elisabeth J. Neale, 'Thomas Rhondda Williams (1860–1945) and Brighton', *JURCHS* 6/8 (2001), p. 615.

86 Pope, *Building Jerusalem*, pp. 161–2.

87 The Unitarian *Christian Reformer* in 1840 claimed some Congregational theologians only envisaged salvation for about 1 per cent of humanity: cited in Geoffrey Rowell, *Hell and the Victorians* (Oxford: Clarendon, 1974), p. 16n.

88 Robert Pope, 'The Rise and Fall of the Calvinist Consensus in Wales', *JURCHS* 8/7 (2010), p. 379.

89 Johnson, *English Nonconformity*, pp. 126–38. For similar processes in Wales see Pope, 'Calvinist Consensus', p. 383.

90 Mozley, *Doctrine of the Atonement*, p. 165; Henry Rack, 'A. S. Peake – Liberal Evangelical', *Epworth Review* 31/3 (2004), p. 51.

91 C. H. Spurgeon, 'Another Word concerning the Down-Grade', *The Sword and the Trowel* (August 1887), p. 399.

92 See Mark Hopkins, *Nonconformity's Romantic Generation: Evangelical and Liberal Theologies in Victorian England* (Carlisle: Paternoster, 2004), chap. 7.

93 Gerald Parsons, 'From Dissenters to Free Churchmen: The Transitions of Victorian Nonconformity', in Gerald Parsons (ed.), *Religion in Victorian Britain: I Traditions* (Manchester: Manchester University Press, 1988), pp. 106–7.

94 H. G. Wood, *Terrot Reaveley Glover* (Cambridge: Cambridge University Press, 1953), pp. 155–61; E. A. Payne, *The Baptist Union: A Short History* (London: Carey Kingsgate, 1959), pp. 205–6.

95 Carter, 'Joseph Agar Beet', pp. 197–216; Martin Camroux, 'Liberalism Preached – Leslie Weatherhead', *Epworth Review* 26/1 (1999), p. 74.

96 Johnson, *English Nonconformity*, pp. 152, 155.

97 John Kent, *Holding the Fort: Studies in Victorian Revivalism* (London: Epworth, 1978), p. 188.

98 Ian M. Randall, 'Southport and Swanwick: Contrasting Movements of Methodist Spirituality in Inter-War England', *PWHS* 50/1 (1995), pp. 2, 5, 12.

99 David H. Howarth, *How Great a Flame: The Story of Samuel Chadwick* (Ilkeston: Moorley's, 1983), pp. 21–2, 29.

100 *Christian World*, 1 August 1929.
101 W. F. Lofthouse, *Ethics and Atonement* (London: Methuen, 1906), p. 179, cited in Johnson, *English Nonconformity*, pp. 156–7.
102 *Methodist Times*, 29 July 1926.
103 A. D. Belden, 'The Atonement and Democracy', *Baptist Quarterly* (1926–7), p. 11.
104 W. E. Orchard, 'Hell: A Theological Exposition', in W. R. Inge (ed.), *What Is the Real Hell?* (London: Cassell, 1930), pp. 117–18. Orchard and Norwood were the only Nonconformists to contribute to this mainly Anglican collection of essays. See also Geoffrey Rowell, 'Heaven and Hell', *Epworth Review* 19/3 (1992), p. 17.
105 *Methodist Times*, 29 July 1926.
106 Randall, 'Southport and Swanwick', pp. 4, 8.
107 *British Weekly*, 12 April 1928; Lenwood, *Jesus*, p. 25.
108 J. W. Grant, *Free Churchmanship in England 1870–1914* (London: Independent Press, 1955), p. 303.
109 Henry Escott, 'A Few Thoughts on Modern Trends', *Congregational Quarterly* (1937), pp. 489–92. Similar developments occurred in Independent Methodism: Dolan, *Independent Methodists*, p. 210.
110 *Christian World*, 21 October 1926; Albert Peel and Sir John Marriott, *Robert Forman Horton* (London: Allen & Unwin, 1937), pp. 229, 240.
111 H. Bulcock, letter to *Christian World*, 24 November 1938.
112 Pope, *Building Jerusalem*, pp. 137, 208–12.
113 Joseph Maland, 'The Religion of Tomorrow', *Holborn Review* (April 1918), pp. 213–23; Rev. R. G. Parsons, 'Democracy and Religion', *Contemporary Review* (September 1918), pp. 322–8.
114 P. T. Forsyth, 'Some Effects of the War on Belief', *Holborn Review* (January 1918), pp. 16–26; see also John Huxtable, 'P. T. Forsyth 1848–1921', *JURCHS* 4/1 (1987), pp. 72–8.
115 Nathaniel Micklem, *The Box and the Puppets* (London: Geoffrey Bles, 1957), pp. 78–99; D. Elton Trueblood, 'Quakerism and Original Sin', *Friends Quarterly Examiner* (1934), pp. 68–74; J. Hugh Stafford, 'Modern Pelagianism', *Congregational Quarterly* (1937), pp. 363–5; Markus Barth, 'P. T. Forsyth: The Theologian for the Practical Man', *Congregational Quarterly* (1939), pp. 436–42; Huxtable, 'Forsyth', p. 77; Alan Argent, 'The Pilot on the Bridge: John Daniel Jones (1865–1942)', *JURCHS* 5/10 (1997), p. 618.
116 Alan Wilkinson, *Dissent or Conform? War, Peace and the English Churches 1900–1945* (London: SCM Press, 1986), p. 331.
117 W. F. Lofthouse, 'The Warden of the Bermondsey Settlement', in Rupert E. Davies (ed.), *John Scott Lidgett: A Symposium* (London: Epworth, 1957), p. 69.
118 Wilkinson, *Dissent or Conform?*, p. 39; Michael Moynihan (ed.), *God on Our Side: The British Padre in World War I* (London: Secker & Warburg. 1983), p. 12.
119 R. J. Barker, *Christ in the Valley of Unemployment* (London: Hodder & Stoughton, 1936), pp. 75–6; see also David Milner, *Twice Happy Place: A History of Zion Baptist Church, Mirfield* (Mirfield: Zion Baptist, 1973), p. 51.
120 Wilkinson, *Dissent or Conform?*, pp. 38–42; Thomas Tiplady, *Social Christianity in the New Era* (New York: F. H. Revell, 1919), pp. 9–11, 30–42; Kingsley Weatherhead *Leslie Weatherhead: A Personal Portrait* (London: Hodder & Stoughton, 1975), p. 48.
121 Barker, *Christ in the Valley*, p. 76.
122 *Free Churchman*, May 1936.

123 David M. Thompson, *Let Sects and Parties Fall: A Short History of the Association of Churches of Christ in Great Britain and Ireland* (Birmingham: Berean Press, 1980), pp. 150–1; Grant, *Free Churchmanship*, p. 254; J. C. Carlile, *My Life's Little Day* (London: Blackie, 1935), pp. 174–5; Porritt, *Memories*, p. 79.
124 J. H. Shakespeare, *The Churches at the Cross-Roads: A Study in Church Unity* (London: Williams & Norgate, 1918), p. 146; David M. Thompson, 'Edinburgh 1910: Myths, Mission and Unity', *JURCHS* 8/7 (2010), pp. 386–99.
125 Shakespeare, *Churches at the Cross-Roads*, pp. 32, 94–5, 146; Payne, *The Baptist Union*, p. 185.
126 Robert Currie, *Methodism Divided: A Study in the Sociology of Ecumenicalism* (London: Faber, 1968), chap. 5.
127 Wilkinson, *Dissent or Conform?*, p. 41; Tiplady, *Social Christianity*, pp. 39–47; Cairns, *Army and Religion*; Shakespeare, *Churches at the Cross-Roads*, p. 172; Michael Snape, *Revisiting Religion and the British Soldier in the First World War* (London: Dr Williams's Trust, 2015), pp. 18–22.
128 *British Weekly*, 8 March 1928, 15 August 1940; *Christian World*, 25 May 1939.
129 Underwood, *English Baptists*, p. 269; *LYM* (1920), pp. 116–19; *Christian World*, 20 September 1923; *CYB* (1937), pp. 94–5.
130 W. Gordon Robinson, *A History of the Lancashire Congregational Union 1806–1956* (Manchester: Lancashire Congregational Union, 1955), p. 104.
131 Thomas Tiplady, *Spiritual Adventure: The Story of 'the Ideal' Film Service* (London: United Society for Christian Literature, 1935), p. 35.
132 Donald Soper, *Calling for Action: An Autobiographical Enquiry* (London: Robson, 1984), p. 79.
133 Fred Smith, 'The Sacramental Trend in Modern Protestantism', *Congregational Quarterly* (1925), p. 220.
134 *Socialist Christian*, September 1929.
135 Barker, *Christ in the Valley*, pp. 34–48, 93–112.
136 Elaine Kaye and Ross Mackenzie, *W. E. Orchard: A Study in Christian Exploration* (Oxford: Education Services, 1990), chap. 7; Norman Wallwork, *The Gospel Church Secure: The Official History of the Methodist Sacramental Fellowship* (London: Church in the Marketplace Publications, 2013).
137 K. S. Inglis, *Churches and the Working Class in Victorian England* (London: Routledge & Kegan Paul, 1963), pp. 291–2; Smith, *Religion and the Rise of Labour*, pp. 33–56, 170.
138 Rev. W. Major Scott (a Congregationalist like Lees-Smith), 'Nonconformist Churches and Labour', in H. B. Lees-Smith (ed.), *The Encyclopaedia of the Labour Movement*, vol.2 (London: Caxton, 1928), p. 302.
139 *Socialist Christian*, August 1929.
140 *British Weekly*, 19 July 1928.
141 Binfield, *Pastors and People*, p. 237.
142 Henry Carter (ed.), *For Christ and Humanity* (London: Epworth, 1935), pp. 13–25, 42.
143 W. H. Armstrong, 'The Secret of a New World', *Bolton Congregationalist*, September 1919.
144 *Bradford Congregational Yearbook* (1937), p. 11.
145 John Lewis, 'Communism the Heir to the Christian Tradition', in John Lewis (ed.), *Christianity and the Social Revolution* (London: Gollancz, 1935), p. 485.
146 Soper, *Calling for Action*, p. 81.

147 Jones, *Three Score Years*, p. 226.
148 *Bradford Pioneer*, 29 December 1922.
149 *Christian World*, 14 December 1922.
150 Rev. B. C. Shildrick to the author, February 1986, writing of his father, a Baptist minister of the interwar years.
151 *Christian World*, 29 November 1923; Stephen Koss, 'Lloyd George and Nonconformity: The Last Rally', *English Historical Review* 89 (1974), p. 87.
152 *British Weekly*, 22 March 1928; Quo-Usque (F. A. Atkins), letter to *British Weekly*, 5 April 1928.
153 *Liverpool Daily Post*, 10 March 1912.
154 *Methodist Times*, 6 March 1919.
155 *Christian World*, 2 April 1936; *Methodist Times*, 26 March 1936.
156 J. Graham Jones, 'Welsh Politics between the Wars: The Personnel of Labour', *Transactions of the Honourable Society of Cymmorodorion* (1983), p. 179; *Christian World*, 23 November 1922.
157 C. Silvester Horne, *A Popular History of the Free Churches, with an Additional Chapter 1903–1926 by Albert Peel* (London: Congregational Union, 1926), p. 429.
158 *Free Church Year Book* [henceforward *FCYB*] (1926), p. 55.
159 B. Cozens-Hardy, letter to *Christian World*, 15 July 1926.
160 A Nonconformist Minister, *Nonconformity and Politics* (London: Pitman, 1909).
161 Jordan, *Free Church Unity*, p. 225.
162 H. B. Kendall, *History of the Primitive Methodist Church*, vol. 2 (London: Dalton, 1919), p. 172.
163 Wilkinson, *Dissent or Conform?*, p. 54.
164 *Christian World*, 29 January 1931.
165 Cited in E. J. Dukes, 'Memories of London and London Congregationalism Sixty Years Ago', *Congregational Quarterly* (1927), pp. 201–2; see also Horne, *Popular History*, pp. 427–9.
166 *British Weekly*, 29 November 1923.
167 *Christian World*, 7 January 1926.
168 Alan Turberfield, *John Scott Lidgett: Archbishop of British Methodism* (Peterborough: Epworth, 2003), pp. 165–80.
169 Duncan Tanner, *Political Change and the Labour Party 1900–1918* (Cambridge: Cambridge University Press, 1990), pp. 402–3.
170 Brock Millman, *Managing Domestic Dissent in First World War Britain* (London: Cass, 2000), p. 209.
171 Stephen White, 'Soviets in Britain: The Leeds Convention of 1917', *International Review of Social History* 19/2 (1974), pp. 165–93.
172 AP: U DMN/9/6, draft autobiography, chap. 6, p. 3.
173 *The Ploughshare*, August 1917, pp. 195–7; June 1919, pp. 125–6.
174 John Rylands Library, Manchester, Ramsay MacDonald Papers: RMD/1/15/176, Newbold to MacDonald, 30 May 1937.
175 *Baptist Times*, 15 February 1918; *Methodist Times*, 7 March 1918; *The Friend*, 24 May 1918; *Christian World*, 29 August 1918.
176 *Christian World*, 21 March 1918, 18 April 1918.
177 Arthur Henderson, 'The Outlook for Labour', *Contemporary Review* (February 1918), pp. 121–30; *Methodist Times*, 31 January 1918. Lidgett was the co-editor of the *Contemporary Review*: Turberfield, *Lidgett*, p. 2.
178 *Methodist Times*, 14 March 1918.

179 Porritt, *The Best I Remember*, pp. 26, 98.
180 *Free Church Chronicle*, April 1918.
181 *Labour Leader*, 21 March 1918; *Bradford Pioneer*, 29 March 1918.
182 *Labour Leader*, 8 August 1918.
183 *Christian World*, 12 December 1918.
184 A. E. Garvie, *Memories and Meanings of My Life* (London: Allen & Unwin, 1938), p. 171.
185 *Christian World*, 19 December 1918.
186 Koss, *Nonconformity in Modern British Politics*, pp. 140–41; *Baptist Times*, 6 December 1918.
187 *Primitive Methodist Leader*, 5 December 1918, 2 January 1919; *Methodist Times*, 12 December 1918; *Christian World*, 12 December 1918.
188 Michael Hughes, *Conscience and Conflict: Methodism, Peace and War in the Twentieth Century* (Peterborough: Epworth, 2008), pp. 30, 72; *Labour Leader*, 20 March 1919.
189 *The Crusader*, 18 March 1921; 1 July 1921; Koss, 'Lloyd George and Nonconformity', p. 81.
190 *Brotherhood Outlook*, May 1921.
191 *CYB* (1922), p. 52.
192 S. E. Keeble, *Christian Responsibility for the Social Order* (London: Fernley Lecture Trust, 1922); Michael S. Edwards, *S. E. Keeble: The Rejected Prophet* (Chester: Wesley Historical Society, 1977), pp. 12, 45.
193 *The Crusader*, 22 July 1921; 2 June 1922.
194 *The Crusader*, 28 July 1922; Bolton Metropolitan Archives [henceforward BMA]: Bolton & District Evangelical Free Church Council [BDFCC] minute book (1902–26), pp. 440–1; Liverpool City Archives [henceforward LCA]: Liverpool Free Church Council [LFCC] minutes 31 May 1922, 16 June 1922.
195 Andrew Rigby, *A Life in Peace: A Biography of Wilfrid Wellock* (Bridport: Prism Press, 1988), pp. 21, 37; Martin Ceadel, *Pacifism in Britain 1914–1945: The Defining of a Faith* (Oxford: Clarendon, 1980), p. 50; Dolan, *Independent Methodists*, p. 157.
196 *Baptist Times*, 27 December 1918; *Methodist Times*, 13 February 1919.
197 *The Crusader*, 7 October 1921.
198 *The Crusader*, 9 March 1923.
199 Kenneth O. Morgan, 'Twilight of Welsh Liberalism: Lloyd George and the Wee Frees 1918–1935', *Bulletin of the Board of Celtic Studies* 22 (1968), pp. 391, 396, 401–2; *The Friend*, 27 October 1922, 3 November 1922.
200 *Christian World*, 23 November 1922.
201 A. E. Garvie, *The Fatherly Rule of God: A Study of Society, State and Church* (London: Hodder & Stoughton, 1935), p. 232.
202 However, see J. P. W. Mallalieu, *On Larkhill* (London: Allison & Busby, 1983), p. 62.
203 *Christian World*, 25 December 1924.
204 Cited in Philip Snowden, *An Autobiography: Volume Two, 1919–1934* (London: Nicholson & Watson, 1934), pp. 591–2.
205 Sir Henry Lunn, *Nearing Harbour* (London: Nicholson & Watson, 1934), pp. 191–2.
206 Garry Tregidga, *The Liberal Party in South-West Britain since 1918: Political Decline, Dormancy and Rebirth* (Exeter: University of Exeter Press, 2000), pp. 34–5; Michael Kinnear, *The British Voter: An Atlas and Survey since 1885* (London: Batsford, 1981), pp. 43–4.

207 W. M. R. Pringle, ‘The General Election’, *Contemporary Review* (January 1924), p. 9.
208 Isaac Foot, ‘Liberals and Labour in the House’, *Contemporary Review* (June 1924), p. 724.
209 *British Weekly*, 10 January 1924; 17 January 1924.
210 *Baptist Times*, 10 October 1924.
211 *Methodist Times*, 10 April 1924; *Christian World*, 10 April 1924.
212 People’s History Museum, Manchester: Labour Party Archives [henceforward LPA]: J. S. Middleton Papers: JSM/TEM/1; *Christian World*, 23 October 1924.
213 *Methodist Times*, 30 October 1924; *Christian World*, 23 October 1924; Koss, *Nonconformity in Modern British Politics*, p. 171.
214 *Baptist Times*, 24 October 1924; *Christian World*, 13 November 1924; Cook, *Age of Alignment*, pp. 285–7.
215 Peel and Marriott, *Robert Forman Horton*, p. 277.
216 *United Methodist*, 27 November 1924.
217 *British Weekly*, 30 July 1925.
218 *Methodist Recorder*, 10 April 1924.
219 Jones, *Three Score Years*, pp. 241–3.
220 Stanley Baldwin, *On England* (London: Hodder & Stoughton, 1938), p. 215.
221 *Christian World*, 7 February 1929. John Clifford died in 1923.
222 Jones had briefly trained for the ministry. *Christian World*, 21 May 1931; Keith Middlemas (ed.), *Thomas Jones: The Whitehall Diary, Volume II 1926–1930* (London: Oxford University Press, 1969), p. 11.
223 *Christian World*, 7 February 1929; *CYB* (1930), p. 66; Peel and Marriott, *Robert Forman Horton*, p. 357.
224 Lambeth Palace Library, London: Randall Davidson [henceforward Davidson] MSS 15, fol. 2–10, diary, 11 January 1925.
225 Porritt, *The Best I Remember*, p. 228; *FCYB* (1928), p. 114.
226 Henry Townsend, *Robert Wilson Black* (London: Carey Kingsgate, 1954), p. 34.
227 *Baptist Times*, 18 April 1929, 25 April 1929, 16 May 1929; *Christian World*, 9 May 1929, 16 May 1929, 23 May 1929.
228 Bentley, *Liberal Mind*, p. 204.
229 Lofthouse’s forebears had all been ‘staunch Tories’: *Methodist Recorder*, 15 May 1930.
230 *The Crusader*, 15 February 1924.
231 Letter to *The Crusader*, 17 October 1924.
232 LPA: NEC minutes, 26 September 1925.
233 *Liverpool Daily Post*, 8 December 1926, 9 December 1926, 10 December 1926, 13 December 1926, 14 December 1926.
234 Pope, *Building Jerusalem*, chap. 6; Rev James Fraser, letter to *New Leader*, 5 July 1929.
235 Letter to *Christian World*, 25 November 1926.
236 *Methodist Times*, 22 October 1931.
237 *Methodist Times*, 10 September 1931; *Baptist Times*, 27 August 1931, 29 October 1931; *Christian World*, 27 August 1931; *British Weekly*, 22 October 1931.
238 Morgan Phillips Price, *My Three Revolutions* (London: Allen & Unwin, 1969), p. 268.
239 *Christian World*, 17 September 1931.
240 Letter to *Christian World*, 12 November 1931.
241 *The Inquirer*, 29 August 1931.
242 *Christian World*, 8 October 1931.
243 *British Weekly*, 15 October 1931.
244 *Christian World*, 15 October 1931.

245 *Baptist Times*, 24 September 1931, 15 October 1931.
246 *Baptist Times*, 29 January 1931.
247 *Baptist Times*, 5 March 1931, 12 March 1931; *School Child and Juvenile Worker*, April 1931.
248 *Christian World*, 5 November 1931.
249 *Christian World*, 25 March 1937.
250 *Christian World*, 21 November 1935.
251 Shakespeare, *Candles*, p. 125.
252 Letter to *Baptist Times*, 18 July 1935.
253 Porritt, *Memories*, p. 127; *Christian World*, 4 July 1935; Dr Williams's Library, London; NCEFC papers [henceforward NCEFCP]: executive committee minutes, 21 June 1935; Jordan, *Free Church Unity*, p. 161.
254 The National Archives, London [henceforward TNA]: PREM1/183, Lloyd George to Baldwin, 14 March 1935; 'Statement by His Majesty's Government on Certain Proposals submitted to them by Mr Lloyd George', 18 July 1935.
255 *Baptist Times*, 24 January 1935, 4 July 1935.
256 Koss, 'Lloyd George and Nonconformity', pp. 98–100; LCA: LFCC minutes 17 October 1935.
257 Koss, 'Lloyd George and Nonconformity', pp. 85–91; *Christian World*, 20 June 1935.
258 *Baptist Times*, 27 June 1935, 4 July 1935.
259 *Christian World*, 11 April 1935.
260 Parliamentary Record Office, London [henceforward PROL]: David Lloyd George Papers [henceforward DLGP], G141/27/1, Scott Lidgett to Lloyd George, 11 November 1935.
261 Koss, *Nonconformity in Modern British Politics*, pp. 210–1.
262 F. W. Atkin, letter to *Methodist Times*, 21 November 1935.
263 *Methodist Times*, 5 December 1935; NCEFCP: executive committee minutes, 6 December 1935.
264 *Christian World*, 15 January 1931; Stanley Evans, *Christian Socialism* (London: Christian Socialist Movement, 1962), p. 22.
265 *Free Churchman*, July 1931.
266 Letter to *Christian World*, 11 July 1935.
267 Jones, *Three Score Years*, p. 240. His older brother, Henry Haydn Jones, was Liberal MP for Merioneth 1910–45.
268 David M. Thompson, 'The Older Free Churches', in Rupert E. Davies (ed.) *The Testing of the Churches 1932–1982* (London: Epworth, 1982), p. 109.

Chapter 2

1 Presidential address to the Wesleyan conference, *Methodist Times*, 18 July 1929.
2 Chairman's address to the Congregational Union, *CYB* (1939), p. 74.
3 *Free Churchman*, September 1936.
4 Cited in Kingsley Weatherhead, *Leslie Weatherhead*, p. 110; Hughes, *Conscience and Conflict*, pp. 10, 18–21.
5 Cited in *New Leader*, 22 August 1924.
6 Bebbington, *Nonconformist Conscience*, p. 11.
7 C. Silvester Horne, 'A New Protestantism', *Brotherhood Year Book* (1913–14), p. 33.

8 Stanley Mellor, *Liberation* (London: Constable, 1929), p. 91. His son was William Mellor who, after he lost his faith, became a Socialist journalist and organizer and a founder member of the CPGB in 1920.
9 Noel J. Richards, 'The Education Bill of 1906 and the Decline of Political Nonconformity', *Journal of Ecclesiastical History* 23/1 (1972), pp. 49–64.
10 Milner, *Twice Happy Place*, pp. 46–8.
11 Cited in Koss, 'Lloyd George and Nonconformity', p. 87.
12 M. E. Aubrey, *The Free Churches in our National Life* (London: Carey Kingsgate, 1936), p. 14.
13 *Christian World*, 1 April 1926.
14 Hobson, *Pilgrim to the Left*, p. 12.
15 *Methodist Times*, 9 January 1919.
16 *Free Churchman*, December 1934.
17 AP: U DMN/9/6: draft autobiography, chap. 3, p. 35.
18 George Thomas, *The Christian Heritage in Politics* (London: Epworth, 1959), p. 34.
19 Catterall, 'Slums and Salvation', pp. 114–19.
20 Sir Josiah Stamp, *The Christian Ethic as an Economic Factor* (London: Epworth, 1926), p. 66; Olinthus Gregory (ed.), *The Works of Robert Hall A.M.* vol 6 (New York: J & J Harper, 1832), p. 458.
21 *CYB* (1936), p. 75.
22 H. Bodell Smith, *Christ and the Political Economists* (London: Daniel, 1926), p. 8. On his early career see Leonard Smith, *Religion and the Rise of Labour*, chap. 6.
23 *Labour Leader*, 5 June 1919; similar views can be found among the alumni of the more Marxist Social Democratic Federation founded in 1884; see W. Stephen Sanders, *Early Socialist Days* (London: L&V Woolf, 1927), p. 12.
24 W. T. Carter, 'Is It possible to be in business and Remain a Christian?', *Congregational Quarterly* (1924), p. 138.
25 Barry M. Doyle, 'Modernity or Morality? George White, Liberalism and the Nonconformist Conscience in Edwardian England', *Historical Research* 71/176 (1998), p. 336.
26 *CYB* (1918), p. 34.
27 Garvie, *Fatherly Rule*, pp. 165–6.
28 C. Ellis Lloyd, *Scarlet Nest* (London: Hodder & Stoughton, 1919), p. 312. Ellis Lloyd was listed as an undenominational Nonconformist by Linden.
29 Cairns, *Army and Religion*, p. 315.
30 Cairns, *Army and Religion*, p. 206; Charles Rudy, 'Concerning Tommy', *Contemporary Review* (November 1918), pp. 545–52.
31 As one Home Office agent warned: 'For the first time in history, the rioters will be better trained than the troops': Stephen R. Ward, 'Intelligence Surveillance of British Ex-Servicemen 1918–20', *Historical Journal* 16/1 (1973), p. 179.
32 Stephen R. Ward, 'The British Veterans' Ticket of 1918', *Journal of British Studies* 8/1 (1968), pp. 155–69; Barry M. Doyle, 'A Conflict of Interests? The Local and National Dimensions of Middle Class Liberalism 1900–1935', *Parliamentary History* 17/1 (2008), p. 137.
33 Cited in Nicholas Mansfield, 'Farmworkers and Local Conservatism in South-West Shropshire, 1916–23', in Stuart Ball and Ian Holliday (eds), *Mass Conservatism: The Conservatives and the Public since the 1880s* (London: Cass, 2002), p. 49; John H. Millett, 'British Interest-Group Tactics: A Case Study', *Political Science Quarterly* 72/1 (1957), p. 78.

34 Kenneth O. Morgan, *Rebirth of a Nation: Wales 1880–1980* (Oxford: Oxford University Press, 1981), pp. 212–13; W. R. Garside, *The Durham Miners 1919–1960* (London: Allen & Unwin, 1971), pp. 31–7.
35 *Christian World*, 17 July 1937.
36 George Thomas, *Mr Speaker* (London: Century, 1985), p. 31.
37 BMA: Bolton and District Operative Cotton Spinners' Provincial Association [henceforward BOCSPA], *Annual Report* (1920), p. 5.
38 BOCSPA, *Annual Report* (1934), p. 8; Marguerite Dupree, 'Foreign Competition and the Interwar Period', in Mary B. Rose (ed.), *The Lancashire Cotton Industry: A History since 1700* (Preston: Lancashire County Books, 1996), p. 283.
39 *Bolton Evening News*, 16 July 1931; BOCSPA, *Annual Report* (1931), p. 3, (1933), pp. 6–7; George Birtill, *The Changing Years: Chorley and District between the Wars* (Chorley: Guardian Press, 1976), pp. 19–20; Dupree, 'Foreign Competition', pp. 272–3.
40 BOCSPA, *Annual Report* (1933), pp. 8–9; J. Percival Davies, *The Politics of a Socialist Employer* (Skipton-in-Craven: Maurice Webb, 1929), pp. 79–80; P. A. Harris, 'Social Leadership and Social Attitudes in Bolton 1919–1939', unpub. Lancaster PhD Thesis (1973), pp. 151–65; Dupree, 'Foreign Competition', pp. 275, 281, 292.
41 John Singleton, *Lancashire on the Scrapheap: The Cotton Industry 1945–1970* (Oxford: Oxford University Press, 1991), pp. 11–22.
42 For instance, Lancashire weavers were asked to tend more looms in 1932, prompting a strike: see Dupree, 'Foreign Competition', p. 280; Jeffrey Hill, *Nelson: Politics, Economy, Community* (Edinburgh: Keele University Press, 1997), pp. 76–82.
43 *Industrial Review*, April 1931.
44 BMA: Bolton and District Card, Blowing, Ring and Throstle Room Operatives' Association [henceforward BCBRTOA], *Rules* (1906), p. 1.
45 BMA: BCBRTOA, minute book 1920–29, General Secretary's report, August 1929.
46 BOCSPA, *Annual Report* (1919), p. 5.
47 Harris, 'Social Leadership', pp. 25–33, 261–2; A. H. Birch, *Small Town Politics: A Study of Political Life in Glossop* (London: Oxford University Press, 1959), pp. 28–30; Angus Watson, 'The Human Factor in Industrial Rationalisation', *Congregational Quarterly* (1931), pp. 266–7.
48 *FCYB* (1923), pp. 47, 53.
49 Cited in Stuart McIntyre, *Little Moscows* (London: Croom Helm, 1980), p. 115; see also Hywel Francis, 'The Anthracite Strike and Disturbances of 1925', *Llafur* 1/2 (1973), p. 17.
50 *House of Commons Debates*, 5th ser., vol. 166, col.1921, 16 July 1923: J. R. Clynes speaking to the 'Capitalist System – Motion'.
51 Wil Jon Edwards, *From the Valley I Came* (London: Angus & Robertson, 1956), pp. 181–2; see also Moore, *Pitmen, Preachers and Politics*, pp. 29, 154–6.
52 Catterall, 'Slums and Salvation', pp. 119–20.
53 AP: U DMN/2/5, diary entry, 29 May 1933.
54 *Methodist Times*, 24 April 1924.
55 Andrew Thorpe, *A History of the British Labour Party* 2nd ed. (Basingstoke: Palgrave, 2001), p. 42.
56 *CYB* (1921), pp. 19–20.
57 *FCYB* (1919), p. 46.
58 The first woman to be ordained to Nonconformist ministry was Gertrud von Petzold, as a Unitarian in Leicester in 1904: see Elaine Kaye, 'From "Woman Minister" to "Minister": One Hundred Congregational Ministers Ordained

between 1917 and 1972 in England and Wales', *JURCHS* 6/10 (2002), pp. 762–4. A small proportion of the preachers in the various branches of Methodism in the interwar years were women: see Dolan, *Independent Methodists*, p.143; Dorothy Graham, *Women Local Preachers in the British Isles* (Christchurch: Wesley Historical Society (NZ), 1998), pp. 21–30.

59 Kaye and Mackenzie, *W. E. Orchard*, pp. 68–70; Tudur Jones, *Congregationalism in England*, pp. 408–9.

60 Rupert E. Davies, 'The Ordination of Women: A Personal Account', *PWHS* 48 (1992), pp. 105–6.

61 Gerard de Groot, *Blighty: British Society in the Era of the Great War* (Harlow: Longman, 1996), pp. 113–14.

62 Thorpe, *British Labour Party*, p. 88.

63 de Groot, *Blighty*, p. 306; Susan R. Grayzel, *Women and the First World War* (Harlow: Longman, 2002), pp. 106–7; Cathy Hunt, 'Sex versus Class in Two British Trade Unions in the Early Twentieth Century', *Journal of Women's History* 24/1 (2012), pp. 86–110.

64 Frank Ballard, *The Rational Way to Spiritual Revival* (London: Kelly, 1917), pp. 11–12.

65 *CYB* (1925), pp. 60–83.

66 *CYB* (1921), p. 68; Garvie, *Memories and Meanings*, p. 183.

67 *The Inquirer* (Unitarian Union of Social Service supplement), 16 October 1926; *CYB* (1922), p. 24 (1925), pp. 20–1.

68 *Primitive Methodist Leader*, 31 January 1924.

69 Fenner Brockway, *Towards Tomorrow: The Autobiography of Fenner Brockway* (London: Hart-Davis MacGibbon, 1977), p. 101.

70 *Methodist Times*, 4 April 1935, 11 April 1935.

71 Henry Carter, 'The Youth and Christian Citizenship Movement', in Carter (ed.), *For Christ and Humanity* (London: Epworth, 1935), p. 13.

72 *The Crusader*, 4 March 1921.

73 *Methodist Times*, 29 April 1924.

74 Garvie, *Fatherly Rule*, p. 173.

75 Arthur Henderson, *At the Cross-Roads* (London: National Brotherhood Council, 1919), p. 6.

76 Hughes, *Conscience and Conflict*, pp. 18–28; David Bebbington, 'Conscience and Politics', in Lesley Husselbee and Paul Ballard (eds), *Free Churches and Society: The Nonconformist Contribution to Social Welfare 1800–2010* (London: Continuum, 2012), p. 57.

77 Peel and Marriott, *Robert Forman Horton*, pp. 257–8.

78 Keith Robbins, *The Abolition of War: The 'Peace Movement' in Britain 1914–1919* (Cardiff: University of Wales Press, 1976), p. 18.

79 Wilkinson, *Dissent or Conform?*, pp. 22–35; Hughes, *Conscience and Conflict*, pp. 49–51.

80 Keeble, *Christian Responsibility*, p. 277; Catriona Pennell, *A Kingdom United: Popular Responses to the Outbreak of the First World War in Britain and Ireland* (Oxford: Oxford University Press, 2012), p. 63.

81 *Bradford and District Baptist Magazine*, April 1938; Kingsley Weatherhead, *Leslie Weatherhead*, p. 81.

82 *Bradford Pioneer*, 11 January 1918.

83 *Labour Leader*, 4 April 1918.

84 Hughes, *Conscience and Conflict*, pp. 53–4.

85 Millman, *Managing Domestic Dissent*, pp. 194, 203–4.
86 *The Crusader*, 21 February 1919.
87 Letter to *Christian World*, 5 November 1936.
88 Jones, *Three Score Years* p. 234.
89 Tudur Jones, *Congregationalism in England*, p. 359.
90 Wilkinson, *Dissent or Conform?*, p. 52.
91 *Bradford Pioneer*, 6 February 1925.
92 LFCC, *Official Handbook* (1919), p. 5; *CYB* (1921), p. 65.
93 Wilkinson, *Dissent or Conform?*, p. 42; Hughes, *Conscience and Conflict*, pp. 58–9.
94 Peel and Marriott, *Robert Forman Horton*, p. 260.
95 NCEFCP: executive committee minutes, 3 December 1915, 24 March 1916, 23 June 1916, 22 June 1917, 7 December 1917, 10 March 1919.
96 NCEFCP: 23 June 1916; Garvie, *Memories and Meanings*, p. 169.
97 Tudur Jones, *Congregationalism in England*, p. 359; Wilkinson, *Dissent or Conform?*, pp. 49–50.
98 *LYM* (1918), pp. 8–10; Brockway, *Towards Tomorrow*, pp. 43–4; Millman, *Managing Domestic Dissent*, 60–1.
99 *Labour Leader*, 30 May 1918.
100 *FCYB* (1929), Part II, p. 13.
101 *Primitive Methodist Leader*, 5 December 1918; *United Methodist*, 5 December 1918.
102 *Methodist Times*, 5 December 1918, 12 December 1918.
103 *Primitive Methodist Leader*, 9 November 1922.
104 *British Weekly*, 9 November 1922.
105 *Methodist Times*, 9 November 1922.
106 NCEFCP: minutes, 21 November 1923.
107 *Methodist Times*, 6 March 1924; *Free Church Chronicle*, October 1924.
108 NCEFCP: minutes, 11 March 1929; *Baptist Times*, 7 March 1929.
109 *The Highroad*, May 1929.
110 *CYB* (1936), pp. 117–19; *Methodist Times*, 4 July 1935; *Yorkshire Observer*, 22 October 1935.
111 Kenneth D. Brown, 'Ministerial Recruitment and Training: An Aspect of the Crisis of Victorian Nonconformity', *Victorian Studies* 30/3 (1987), pp. 377–8; Kenneth D. Brown, 'Methodist Theological College Principals', p. 100.
112 Tiplady, *Spiritual Adventure*, p. 17.
113 Kenneth D. Brown, 'College Principals – A Cause of Nonconformist Decay?', *Journal of Ecclesiastical History* 38/2 (1987), p. 252.
114 J. Keir Hardie, *Can a Man Be a Christian on a Pound a Week?* (London: Independent Labour Party, 1906), pp. 8–9. Hardie's churchmanship was eclectic, but he is usually regarded primarily as Congregationalist.
115 Kenneth D. Brown, 'The Baptist Ministry of Victorian England and Wales: A Social Profile', *Baptist Quarterly* (1987), pp. 111–12.
116 Keeble, *Christian Responsibility*, p. 284.
117 Brown, 'College Principals', p. 242; Keeble, *Christian Responsibility*, p. 284.
118 Soper, *Calling for Action*, p. 83.
119 Ammon, *Labour's Dynamic*, p.20.
120 F. W. Newland, *Now, Now, Not Forty Years On* (London: Congregational Union of England and Wales, 1926), p. 7.
121 *Methodist Times*, 30 July 1936.
122 Horne, *Popular History*, p. 443.

123 http://www.methodist.org.uk/prayer-and-worship/theology/the-beckly-lectures [accessed 24 August 2015].
124 *Bradford Pioneer*, 2 May 1924.
125 S. E. Keeble, *COPEC: An Account of the Christian Conference on Politics, Economics and Citizenship* (London: Epworth, 1924), pp. 6–10.
126 *The Crusader*, 25 April 1924.
127 *The Crusader*, 1 August 1924; Jeffery Cox, *English Churches in a Secular Society: Lambeth 1870–1930* (Oxford: Oxford University Press, 1982), p. 263.
128 LCA: Liverpool COPEC regional committee minute book 1924–25.
129 *The Crusader*, 4 March 1921.
130 NCEFC, *The England of Tomorrow* (London: NCEFC, 1921), pp. 74–9.
131 *British Weekly*, 13 September 1928.
132 *Christian World*, 26 January 1922, 9 July 1925; William S. Rowntree, 'Democracy, Liberty and State Socialism', *Friends Quarterly Examiner* (1918), p. 113.
133 *Primitive Methodist Leader*, 27 September 1923.
134 E. B. Storr, 'Socialism', *Baptist Quarterly*, June 1929, p.62.
135 Atkinson Lee, 'Property', *Holborn Review*, April 1923, p.213.
136 *LYM* (1919), p. 118.
137 C. R. Attlee, 'Guild versus Municipal Socialism', *Socialist Review* 21 (1923), pp. 213–18.
138 Cited in Frank Matthews, 'The Building Guilds', in Asa Briggs and John Savile (eds), *Essays in Labour History 1886–1923* (London: Macmillan, 1971), p. 305.
139 *LYM* (1921), pp. 117–18.
140 *Bradford Pioneer*, 8 April 1921; *CYB* (1922), p. 25.
141 *Minutes of the Methodist Conference* (1934), pp. 391–400.
142 *The Crusader*, 23 May 1919, 3 June 1921; John Pease Fry, 'The Function of the Society of Friends', *Friends Quarterly Examiner* (1927), p. 274.
143 George Thompson Brake, *Policy and Politics in British Methodism 1932–1982* (London: Edsall, 1984), pp. 481–4 provides an effective critique.
144 David J. Jeremy, *Capitalists and Christians: Business Leaders and the Churches in Britain 1900–1960* (Oxford: Clarendon, 1990), pp. 177–8.
145 *Minutes of the Methodist Conference* (1934), p. 399.
146 *FCYB* (1923), p. 35.
147 For example, *House of Commons Debates*, 5th ser., vol. 222, cols. 91–99, 7 November 1928; vol. 226, cols. 1443–58, 15 March 1929.
148 Joan Fry cited in James Power, 'Aspects of Working-Class Leisure during the Depression Years: Bolton in the 1930s', unpub. Warwick MA Thesis (1980), p. 76; Barrie Naylor, *Quakers in the Rhondda 1926–1986* (Chepstow: Maes-yr-haf Educational Trust, 1986), p. 42.
149 *Brotherhood Outlook*, December 1931.
150 S. E. Keeble, 'What the Church Is doing: Social Activities', in Percy Dearmer (ed.), *Christianity and the Crisis* (London: Gollancz, 1933), p. 295; Catterall, 'Slums and Salvation', pp. 126–7.
151 Cited in G. M. Lloyd Davies, 'Work among the Unemployed', *Contemporary Review*, (April 1935), p. 478.
152 Naylor, *Quakers in the Rhondda*, pp. 20–51.
153 Margaret R. Pitt, *Our Unemployed: Can the Past Teach the Present?* (Harrow: privately printed, 1982), pp. 6–8, 20.
154 Pitt, *Our Unemployed*, pp.24–25; *LYM* (1930), pp. 155–6; Naylor, *Quakers in the Rhondda*, p. 43.

155 *LYM* (1936), p. 157.
156 *LYM* (1931), pp. 161–2.
157 *LYM* (1936), p. 154.
158 Bebbington, *The Nonconformist Conscience*, pp. 43–4.
159 Tiplady, *Social Christianity*, p. 104.
160 Ian Packer, *Lloyd George, Liberalism and the Land: The Land Issue and Party Politics 1906–1914* (Woodbridge: Boydell, 2001), pp. 65, 90; *Labour Year Book* [*LYB*], (1919), pp. 207–8, 217; de Groot, *Blighty*, p. 198.
161 Cited in P. Dickens and P. Gilbert, 'Inter-war Housing Policy: A Study of Brighton' *Southern History* 3 (1981), p. 210.
162 Mark Freeman, *Social Investigation and Rural England 1870–1914* (Woodbridge: Boydell, 2003), pp. 159–60.
163 Gault, *Kingsley Wood*, p. 194; George Hicks, 'More and Better Houses', in Herbert Tracey (ed.), *The Book of the Labour Party* vol.2 (London: Caxton, 1925), p. 208. Hicks addressed Brotherhood meetings but otherwise had no known religious affiliations.
164 Newland, *Now, Now, Not Forty Years On*, p. 4.
165 *Methodist Times*, 20 June 1929.
166 Ross McKibbin, *Classes and Cultures: England 1918–1951* (Oxford: Oxford University Press, 2000), pp. 96–100, 110–11, 189.
167 Mearns, *The Bitter Cry of Outcast London*, pp. 12–13.
168 Scott, *Elizabeth Cadbury*, p. 94.
169 Keeble, 'Social Activities', pp. 297–8.
170 Clyde Binfield, 'Industry, Philanthropy and Citizenship: Pioneers in Paternalism', in Lesley Husselbee and Paul Ballard (eds), *Free Churches and Society: The Nonconformist Contribution to Social Welfare 1800–2010* (London: Continuum, 2012), pp. 87–8, 107.
171 Bebbington, *The Nonconformist Conscience*, p. 57.
172 Catterall, 'Slums and Salvation', p. 125.
173 A. Fenner Brockway, *Bermondsey Story: The Life of Alfred Salter* (London: Allen & Unwin, 1949), pp. 87–96.
174 *Daily Herald*, 20 March 1933.
175 Shakespeare, *Candles*, pp. 144, 148.
176 Shakespeare, *Candles*, pp. 144–59.
177 Dickens and Gilbert, 'Inter-war Housing Policy', p. 224.
178 Rowntree, *Poverty and Progress: A Second Social Survey of York* (London: Longmans, 1941), pp. 462–5 referring back to B. Seebohm Rowntree, *Poverty: A Study in Town Life* (London: Nelson, 1901).
179 *Bolton Congregationalist*, June 1926.
180 *Wesleyan Methodist Conference Official Handbook, Eastbrook Hall, Bradford* (1927), pp. 93–100.
181 Naylor, *Quakers in the Rhondda*, p. 30.
182 *Christian World*, 6 February 1919.
183 *The Inquirer*, 18 October 1919; *Free Church Chronicle*, November 1919.
184 Arthur Henderson, 'The Industrial Unrest: A New Policy Required', *Contemporary Review* (April 1919), p. 361.
185 *Christian World*, 27 February 1919.
186 *CYB* (1922), pp. 3–4. His resolution on the dispute was unanimously supported by the assembly.
187 Merseyside Free Church Federation, *Report for the Year* (1926), p. 6.
188 *Methodist Times*, 29 July 1926.

189 *Christian World*, 15 July 1926.
190 *British Weekly*, 28 February 1924.
191 *British Weekly*, 6 March 1924.
192 *British Weekly*, 13 March 1924.
193 *Christian World*, 7 May 1925, 16 July 1925.
194 *Methodist Times*, 30 July 1925; Viscount (Herbert) Samuel, *Memoirs* (London: Cresset, 1950), p. 185.
195 *The Friend*, 31 July 1925.
196 *Christian World*, 9 July 1925. *The Inquirer*, 8 August 1925, instead described the subsidies as 'a dangerous precedent'.
197 Churchill College, Cambridge, Sir Winston Churchill papers [henceforward WSC]: CHAR 22/142/49, Churchill draft letter, c.4 May 1926.
198 Howard Hodgkin and R. J. Mounsey, letter to *The Friend*, 4 June 1926.
199 *Baptist Times*, 8 April 1926, 29 April 1926.
200 A. Adamson, letter to *The Inquirer*, 29 May 1926.
201 Cited in Brockway, *Bermondsey Story*, p. 129.
202 *Textile Workers' Record*, June 1926.
203 *Methodist Times*, 20 May 1926; *British Weekly*, 20 May 1926.
204 *TUC Strike Bulletin*, no. 6, 9 May 1926.
205 *LYM* (1926), p. 84; *Christian World*, 20 May 1926, 17 June 1926; *Methodist Times*, 22 July 1926; *Liverpool Daily Post*, 8 December 1926.
206 Davidson: vol. 6 fol. 107, Davidson to Bishop John Talbot, 25 May 1926.
207 G. I. T. Machin, *Churches and Social Issues in Twentieth-Century Britain* (Oxford: Oxford University Press, 1998), pp. 38–9.
208 Davidson: vol. 10, Davidson diary, 8 May 1926.
209 Walter Citrine, *Men and Work* (London: Hutchinson, 1964), pp. 188–204.
210 *LYM* (1926), p. 230.
211 *The Friend*, 6 August 1926.
212 *Christian World*, 12 August 1926.
213 *Christian World*, 22 July 1926; Philip Williamson (ed.), *The Modernisation of Conservative Politics: The Diaries and Letters of William Bridgeman 1904–1935* (London: Historians' Press, 1988), p. 199.
214 Tudur Jones, *Congregationalism in England*, pp. 342–3.
215 *Methodist Times*, 23 July 1936.
216 *Methodist Times*, 24 January 1935.
217 NCEFC, *Annual Report* (1935–36), p. 6; (1936–37), p. 5.
218 *Christian World*, 12 November 1936.
219 James Nicholls, *The Politics of Alcohol: A History of the Drink Question in England* (Manchester: Manchester University Press, 2009), pp. 90–100.
220 Bebbington, *The Nonconformist Conscience*, p. 46; *Alliance Year Book and Temperance Reformer's Handbook* [henceforward *AYB*], (1936), pp. 62–74.
221 *LYM* (1931), p. 283.
222 Mass Observation, *The Pub and the People* (London: Gollancz, 1943), p. 324.
223 *Primitive Methodist Leader*, 23 October 1924.
224 Ian Sellers, 'Nonconformist Attitudes in Late Nineteenth Century Liverpool' *Transactions of the Historic Society of Lancashire and Cheshire* 114 (1962), p. 232.
225 *AYB* (1930), p. 188.
226 NRO: Sir George Edwards Papers [henceforward GEP]: George Edwards, 'Religion and Labour', undated and unpaginated broadsheet, c.1920.

227 *Labour Leader*, 20 July 1922.
228 *AYB* (1927), p. 54; Walter Spencer, *The Glory in the Garret* (London: Epworth, 1932), p.118.
229 See Mark Freeman, 'Seebohm Rowntree and Secondary Poverty, 1899–1954', *Economic History Review* 64/4 (2011), pp. 1175–94.
230 *Methodist Times*, 29 November 1923; *AYB* (1930), p. 112; (1931), p. 170; *Alliance News*, January 1939.
231 NRO: GEP, temperance sermon.
232 *The Inquirer* (Unitarian Union of Social Service Supplement), 16 October 1926; Peter Catterall, *Labour and the Politics of Alcohol: The Decline of a Cause* (London: Institute of Alcohol Studies, 2014), p. 27.
233 Royal Commission on Licensing 1929–31, *Report*, pp.19–20 Cmnd 3988, *Parliamentary Papers* 1931–32, xi, 573.
234 *Bolton Evening News*, 29 January 1920.
235 David Lloyd George, *War Memoirs* vol. 1, 2nd ed. (London: Odhams, 1934), pp. 194, 202; E. C. Urwin, *Henry Carter CBE* (London: Epworth, 1951), p. 41.
236 Bebbington, *The Nonconformist Conscience*, p. 49; Nicholls, *The Politics of Alcohol*, pp.139, 158; Philip Snowden, *Socialism and the Drink Question* (London: Independent Labour Party, 1908), pp.142, 174.
237 Lloyd George, *War Memoirs* vol. 1, pp. 196–7; Philip Snowden, *Autobiography* vol. 1 (London: Nicholson and Watson, 1934), chap. 26; *AYB* (1921), pp. 120–6; (1931), pp. 203–5.
238 G. P. Williams and George Thompson Brake, *Drink in Great Britain 1900–1979* (London: Edsall, 1980), pp.104–6; Nicholls, *The Politics of Alcohol*, p. 156.
239 George B. Wilson, *Alcohol and the Nation* (London: Nicholson & Watson, 1940), p. 192; Snowden, *Autobiography*, vol. 1, pp. 380–5; Nicholls, *The Politics of Alcohol*, pp. 155–7, 180.
240 F. W. Newland, *Newland of Claremont and Canning Town* (London: Epworth, 1932), pp. 154, 183.
241 Ernest Selley, *The English Public House as It Is* (London: Longmans Green, 1927), p. 141; Rowntree, *Poverty and Progress*, pp. 370–2; FTU, *Annual Report* (1925–6), p. 3.
242 W. G. Hall, *Let the People Decide: Some Notes on the Drink Problem* (London: Liquor (Popular Control) Bill Committee, 1928), foreword.
243 *Morning Advertiser*, 6 August 1923; T. R. Gourvish and R. G. Wilson, *The British Brewing Industry 1830–1980* (Cambridge: Cambridge University Press, 1994), p. 419.
244 Sir Edgar Sanders cited in *Alliance News*, September 1933.
245 Institute of Alcohol Studies, London [henceforward IAS]: GP Box, Dr Alfred Salter MP, *A Message to Labour*, speech delivered to the United Kingdom Alliance, 19 October 1927, p. 4.
246 IAS: GP Box, Alfred Salter, *The Prospect before the Temperance Movement in This Country* (1939 handbill), p. 3.
247 *LYM* (1936), p. 303; (1937), pp. 128–30; *Christian World*, 15 October 1931.
248 Micklem, p. 101; Interview: Rev. Howard Williams, 29 October 1986.
249 *AYB* (1936), pp. 17–27. Black's son Cyril was the Conservative MP for Wimbledon 1950–70.
250 *The Times*, 18 September 1954.

251 Andrew Davies, 'The Police and the People: Gambling in Salford 1900–1939', *Historical Journal* 34/1 (1991), pp. 90–1.
252 Power, 'Bolton in the 1930s', p. 38.
253 *FCYB* (1920), p. 35; *Christian World*, 4 December 1919. They were eventually introduced in 1956.
254 WSC: CHAR18/79/80–85, 'Betting Duty Evasion' memorandum, 30 May 1928.
255 Cecil H. Rose, 'Gambling and the Community', *Liverpool Quarterly* (April 1936), p. 70.
256 E. Benson Perkins, 'Money and Gambling', in Carter (ed.), *For Christ and Humanity* (London: Epworth, 1935), pp. 83–6.
257 *FCYB* (1924), pp. 36–40.
258 *Methodist Times*, 9 November 1922.
259 *Free Churchman*, January 1934.
260 *FCYB* (1924), p. 39.
261 *Liverpool Daily Post*, 14 March 1934, 15 March 1934.
262 *House of Commons Debates*, 5th ser., vol. 310, cols. 2326–8. Betting (No. 1) Bill, 2nd Reading, 3 April 1936.
263 Mark Clapson, *A Bit of a Flutter: Popular Gambling and English Society c1823–1961* (Manchester: Manchester University Press, 1992), pp. 162–6.
264 H. Allen Job, letter to *Christian World*, 12 March 1936.
265 NCEFCP: NCEFC minutes, 12 March 1934.
266 *House of Commons Debates*, 5th ser., vol. 267, col. 1916. The Presbyterian and Liberal National MP J A. Leckie speaking on the Sunday Entertainments Bill, 2nd reading, 29 June 1932.
267 Charlie Chaplin, *My Autobiography* (London: Bodley Head, 1964), pp. 12, 53.
268 *Christian World*, 21 March 1929.
269 *House of Commons Debates*, 5th ser., vol. 267, cols. 1956–7, 29 June 1932.
270 H. Harding, letter to *Christian World*, 25 April 1935.
271 W. H. Lax, *Lax His Book: The Autobiography of Lax of Poplar* (London: Epworth, 1937), p. 61.
272 Morgan, *Rebirth of a Nation*, p. 201.
273 Edwards, *Ploughboy's Progress*, p. 83; *Methodist Times*, 23 October 1924; Interview: Howard Williams, 29 October 1986; Griffiths, *Labour and the Countryside*, p. 152. Bevan was raised a Baptist and, shortly before his death, gave the speech at the inaugural meeting of the Christian Socialist Movement in 1960: Soper, *Calling for Action*, p. 137.
274 BMA: Bolton Nonconformist Ministers' Association minutes, 12 December 1922.
275 *Brotherhood Outlook*, June 1923.
276 *LYM* (1935), p. 115; Machin, *Churches and Social Issues*, p. 58.
277 Frank Hall, 'For Sunday Games'; T. T. James, 'Against Sunday Games'; Halley Stewart, 'Summing Up Sunday Games', *Congregational Quarterly* (1923), pp. 188–97.
278 Harold Murray, *Press, Pulpit and Pew* (London: Epworth, 1934), pp. 142–3.
279 Urwin, *Henry Carter*, p. 62.
280 Clive D. Field, 'Gradualist or Revolutionary Secularisation? A Case Study of Religious Belonging in Inter-War Britain 1918–1939', *Church History and Culture* 93 (2013), p. 69.

281 Mel Johnson, 'Primitive Parliamentarians, the Great War, and its Aftermath', *PWHS*, 59/4 (2014), p. 130.
282 Millman, *Managing Domestic Dissent*, pp. 20–2; Helen McCarthy, *The British People and the League of Nations: Democracy, Citizenship and Internationalism, c.1918–45* (Manchester: Manchester University Press, 2011), pp. 2, 63, 87–8.
283 *CYB* (1924), p. 6.
284 McCarthy, *British People*, p. 89.
285 G. Stanley Russell citing a ministerial colleague in a letter to *Christian World*, 26 April 1923.
286 NCEFCP: NCEFC minutes, 22 September 1922.
287 BMA: BDFCC minute book (1903–26), p. 413; NRO: Thetford Free Church Council minutes, 12 March 1920; Peel and Marriott, *Robert Forman Horton*, p. 276; Lunn, *Nearing Harbour*, pp. 211–19.
288 George A. Barton, 'The Official Quaker Testimony against War Re-examined', *Friends Quarterly Examiner* (1918), pp.13–32; Edward Grubb, 'A Rejoinder', *Friends Quarterly Examiner* (1918), pp. 33–8; J. B. Braithwaite, 'The Society of Friends and the Limitations of Its Peace Testimony', *Friends Quarterly Examiner* (1918), pp. 202–20; Margaret E. Hirst, 'The Society of Friends and the Limitations of Its Peace Testimony', *Friends Quarterly Examiner* (1918), pp. 297–311; Clement Leon, 'From a Volunteer to His Extreme Pacifist Friends', *Friends Quarterly Examiner* (1919), pp. 60–8.
289 *The Friend*, 13 September 1918; R. B. Hey, letter to *The Friend*, 18 October 1918.
290 Tudur Jones, *Congregationalism in England*, p. 415.
291 *Bradford Pioneer*, 17 February 1928.
292 Michael W. Casey, 'The Overlooked Pacifist Tradition of the Old Paths Churches of Christ, Part I', *JURCHS* 6/6 (2000), pp. 446–59.
293 *LYM* (1919), pp. 64–5; W. R. Davies (ed.), *The United Nations at Fifty: The Welsh Contribution* (Cardiff: University of Wales Press, 1995).
294 A. E. Garvie, 'COPEC and After', *Contemporary Review* (May 1924), pp. 574–5.
295 *CYB* (1934), p. 71. Methodists passed a similar declaration on peace and war in 1933: Thompson Brake, *Policy and Politics*, pp. 444–5.
296 Hughes, *Conscience and Conflict*, p. 91.
297 Urwin, *Henry Carter*, pp. 79–81.
298 *Christian World*, 11 April 1929.
299 *CYB* (1933), p. 65.
300 *Liverpool Daily Post*, 15 March 1934.
301 *Christian World*, 29 April 1937.
302 *Christian World*, 10 October 1935.
303 Letter to *Christian World*, 16 April 1936.
304 *The Inquirer*, 16 May 1936; 13 June 1936.
305 Frederick Hale, 'English Congregational Responses to the Spanish Civil War, 1936–1939', *JURCHS* 7/3 (2003), pp. 166–79; Frederick Hale, 'A Methodist Pacifist and the Spanish Civil War', *PWHS* 54/5 (2004), p. 151.
306 Kingsley Weatherhead, *Leslie Weatherhead*, pp. 83, 118; Jean C. Greaves, *Corder Catchpool* (London: Friends Home Service Committee, 1953), p. 31.
307 *LYM* (1937), p. 41.
308 Ceadel, *Pacifism in Britain*, p. 212; Keith Robbins, 'Free Churchmen and the Twenty Year Crisis' in Keith Robbins, *History, Religion and Identity in Modern Britain* (London: Hambledon, 1993), pp. 149–60.

309 Cited in Wilkinson, *Dissent or Conform?*, p. 178.
310 PROL: DLGP: G/6/9/1, Chuter Ede to Lloyd George, 29 October 1938.
311 Stephen Orchard, 'Providers and Protagonists in the Nation's Education' in Lesley Husselbee and Paul Ballard (eds), *Free Churches and Society: The Nonconformist Contribution to Social Welfare 1800–2010* (London: Continuum, 2012), pp. 70–5.
312 *CYB* (1936), p. 113.
313 David Thompson, 'John Clifford's Social Gospel', *Baptist Quarterly* 31/5 (1986), p. 203.
314 Cited in Milner, *Twice Happy Place*, p. 46.
315 London Metropolitan Archives [henceforward LMA]: Liberation Society management committee minutes, 23 October 1918.
316 John Saville and Joyce Bellamy (eds), *Dictionary of Labour Biography* vol.5 (London: Macmillan, 1979), p. 203; Jordan, *Free Church Unity*, p. 117; Adrian Hastings, *A History of English Christianity 1920–1990* (London: SCM Press, 1991), p. 130.
317 *The Inquirer*, 26 April 1919.
318 *CYB* (1919), p. 9.
319 Scott, *Elizabeth Cadbury*, pp. 110–11; Asa Briggs, *Social Thought and Social Action: A Study of the Work of Seebohm Rowntree 1871–1954* (London: Longmans, 1961), pp. 100–2.
320 *Christian World*, 16 February 1922.
321 Board of Education, *Report of the Consultative Committee on The Education of the Adolescent* (London: HMSO, 1927).
322 Ernest Green, 'Education for Citizenship', in Herbert Tracey (ed.), *The British Labour Party: Its History, Growth, Policy and Leaders* vol. 2 (London: Caxton, 1948), p. 157.
323 Rowntree, *Poverty and Progress*, p. 466.
324 *Parliamentary Papers* (1936–37) X 39, Board of Education, *Education in 1936*, Cmd. 5564, p. 85; *School Child and Juvenile Worker*, July–August 1931.
325 *British Weekly*, 8 May 1930; Joseph King, 'The School-Leaving Age Raised', *Contemporary Review* (September 1939), p. 348.
326 John T. Smith, *Methodism and Education 1849–1902: J. H. Rigg, Romanism and Wesleyan Schools* (Oxford: Clarendon Press, 1998); *Methodist Times*, 11 July 1929.
327 John Coventry, 'Roman Catholicism' in Rupert E. Davies (ed.), *The Testing of the Churches 1932–1982* (London: Epworth, 1982), p. 7.
328 LPA: NEC minutes, 20 February 1929, 22 February 1929, 26 February 1929; *The Times*, 7 October 1930.
329 *Birkenhead Advertiser*, 5 October 1927.
330 *CYB* (1930), pp. 69–70.
331 LPA: NEC minutes, 18 March 1929; Neil Riddell, 'The Catholic Church and the Labour Party 1918–31', *Twentieth Century British History* 8/2 (1997), pp. 165–93.
332 Jones, *Three Score Years*, pp. 243–6; *Liberation Society Bulletin*, May 1930.
333 *School Child and Juvenile Worker*, September 1930.
334 *Christian World*, 22 January 1931.
335 *Christian World*, 19 February 1931. The bill was eventually defeated in the Lords.
336 *CYB* (1936), p. 202.
337 NCEFC, *Annual Report* (1934–35), p. 9.
338 *CYB* (1936), pp. 112–13; *Christian World*, 10 October 1935.
339 *CYB* (1937), pp. 204–8.
340 *Christian World*, 25 March 1937.

341 *Baptist Times*, 26 March 1936.
342 NCEFC, *Annual Report* (1938–39), pp. 5, 34, 58; *CYB* (1939), pp. 231–3.
343 J. Scott Lidgett, 'Religious Education', *Contemporary Review* (February 1939), pp. 149–51.
344 Wilfred J. Rowland, *The Free Churches and the People: A Report of the Work of the Free Churches of Liverpool* (Liverpool: Arthur Black, 1908), p. 90.
345 Catterall, 'Slums and Salvation', pp. 115–18; Frank Prochaska, *Women and Philanthropy in Nineteenth-Century England* (Oxford: Clarendon, 1980), pp. 188–90.
346 Cited in Oldstone-Moore, *Hugh Price Hughes*, p. 147.
347 Tiplady, *Social Christianity*, pp. 137, 141; *Methodist Times*, 29 May 1924, 5 June 1924.
348 Philip S. Bagwell, *Outcast London: A Christian Response* (London: Epworth, 1987), p. 32; Charles Ogden, *The History of Bradford* (Bradford: Bradford & District Newspaper Co., 1934), p. 42.
349 NCEFCP: minutes, 11 March 1918.
350 *Brotherhood Journal*, July 1918.
351 *Free Church Chronicle*, May 1918, August 1918; Grayzel, *Women and the First World War*, p. 71; *House of Commons Debates*, 5th ser., vol. 106, cols. 1731–2, 6 June 1918.
352 Cairns, *Army and Religion*, pp. 374–9.
353 Morgan, 'Herbert Gray', pp. 168–96.
354 Stephen Brooke, *Sexual Politics: Sexuality, Family Planning and the British Left from the 1880s to the Present Day* (Oxford: Oxford University Press, 2011), pp. 40, 46.
355 Lenwood, *Jesus*, p. 338.
356 Machin, *Churches and Social Issues*, p. 19; Keeble, *COPEC*, p. 11; *Christian World*, 22 May 1924; Stephen Orchard, 'The Free Churches and Their Nation' in Lesley Husselbee and Paul Ballard (eds), *Free Churches and Society: The Nonconformist Contribution to Social Welfare 1800–2010* (London: Continuum, 2012), p. 12.
357 W. F. Lofthouse, 'COPEC and the Relationship of the Sexes', *The Review of the Churches* (1924), pp. 350–5.
358 *Free Churchman*, March 1932.
359 W. H. Lax, *Lax*, p. 225.
360 Wilkinson, *Dissent or Conform?*, p. 61.
361 Bullock, *Building Jerusalem*, pp. 16, 26–8.
362 *House of Commons Debates*, 5th ser., vol. 264, col. 850. Sunday Performances (Regulation) Bill, 2nd Reading, 13 April 1932.
363 Jeffery Richards, *The Age of the Dream Palace: Cinema and Society in 1930s Britain* (London: Routledge, 1984), pp. 59–60.
364 *Methodist Times*, 30 July 1936.
365 Cited in Richards, *Dream Palace*, p. 50.
366 Daniel Tomkins, *Mission Accomplished: The Story of the First One Hundred Years of the Bolton Methodist Mission* (Bolton: Bolton Methodist Mission, 1997), pp. 55–7; Brian Frost, *Pioneers of Social Passion: London's Cosmopolitan Methodism* (Peterborough: Epworth, 2006), p. 21.
367 Tiplady, *Spiritual Adventure*, pp. 20, 26–7.
368 Tiplady, *Spiritual Adventure*, pp. 22–3, 43; Richards, *Dream Palace*, pp. 50, 82.
369 Tiplady, *Spiritual Adventure*, preface, p. 45.
370 Richards, *Dream Palace*, pp. 42–3; Frost, *Pioneers*, p. 23; Michael Wakelin, *J. Arthur Rank: The Man Behind the Gong* (Oxford: Lion, 1996), pp. 42–8.
371 Edward Carpenter, *Cantuar: The Archbishops in their Office* (Oxford: Mowbray, 1988), pp. 426–7; Hastings, *A History of English Christianity*, pp. 62–3.

372 *House of Commons Debates*, 5th ser., vol. 120, col. 1831, 7 November 1919.
373 *Free Church Chronicle*, July 1919.
374 *FCYB* (1920), pp. 31–2.
375 *Christian World*, 2 April 1936.
376 *Liberation Society Bulletin*, April 1929.
377 G. R. Thorne, a Baptist and Liberal MP, speaking on the Prayer Book Measure, *House of Commons Debates*, 5th ser., vol. 218, cols. 1224–9, 14 June 1928.
378 Garvie, *Fatherly Rule*, p. 206.
379 LMA: Liberation Society executive committee minutes, 24 November 1938.
380 Cited in Wilkinson, *Dissent or Conform?*, p. 178.
381 Keeble, 'Social Activities', p. 305.

Chapter 3

1 *Wesleyan Methodist Conference Handbook, Bradford* (1927), pp. 74–5.
2 *Methodist Conference Handbook, Liverpool* (1939), p. 72.
3 George Green, *Central Hall, Bradford Centenary Souvenir Handbook 1821–1921* (Bradford: Central Hall, 1922), pp. 21–5.
4 *The Story of a Great Achievement 1904–1954* (Bradford: Eastbrook Hall, 1954), pp. 4–6.
5 John Banks, *The Story So Far: The First Hundred Years of the Manchester and Salford Methodist Mission* (Manchester: Manchester and Salford Methodist Mission, 1986), p. 21; Cox, *Lambeth*, p. 31.
6 Christopher French, 'Slums and Suburbs' *The Local Historian* 47/2 (2013), p. 161.
7 Spencer, *Glory in the Garret*, p. 48.
8 *Methodist Times*, 6 June 1924.
9 Catterall, 'Slums and Salvation', pp. 112–14.
10 Charles F. G. Masterman, 'The Problem of South London', in R. W. Mudie-Smith (ed.), *The Religious Life of London* (London: Hodder & Stoughton, 1904), pp. 202–3; Cox, *Lambeth*, pp. 25, 43, 45; Bagwell, *Outcast London*, pp. 17–20.
11 Clive D. Field, 'Zion's People: Who Were the English Nonconformists? Part 2: Occupation (Quakers, Baptists, Congregationalists)', *The Local Historian* 40/3 (2010), p. 217; Clive D. Field, 'Zion's People: Who Were the English Nonconformists? Part 3: Occupation (Methodists) and Conclusions', *The Local Historian* 40/4 (2010), pp. 294–300.
12 *Methodist Times*, 1 May 1924.
13 Ian Sellers, *Salute to Pembroke: Pembroke Chapel, Liverpool 1838–1931* (Liverpool: privately printed, 1960); Bradford Congregational Association [henceforward BCA], *Report of the Commission Set Up to Inquire into the Condition of the Churches of the Bradford Congregational Association*, 13 July 1936, p. 3; Clyde Binfield, 'True to Stereotype? Vivian and Dorothy Pomeroy and the Patch in Lumb Lane', in Stuart Mews (ed.) *Modern Religious Rebels* (London: Epworth, 1993), pp. 185–205.
14 West Yorkshire Archives, Bradford [henceforward WYAB]: Stourbridge Road United Methodist Church leaders' minutes, 6 April 1934.
15 Cited in Banks, *The Story So Far*, p. 38.
16 Green, *Central Hall*, p. 38.

17 Philip Snowden, *The Christ That Is to Be* (London: Independent Labour Party, 1904), pp. 4–5.
18 R. G. Burnett, *Through the Mill: The Life of Joseph Rank* (London: Epworth, 1945), pp. 148–50.
19 *Bradford Worker*, 13 May 1926.
20 *Bradford Pioneer*, 13 August 1920, 10 September 1920, 11 April 1924.
21 Beasley, *The Bitter Cry Heard and Heeded*, chap. 6.
22 Paul Rowntree Clifford, *Venture in Faith: The Story of the West Ham Central Mission* (London: Carey Kingsgate, 1950), pp. 87–90.
23 Bagwell, *Outcast London*, pp. 16–23; Lax, *Lax*, chap. 16.
24 Frost, *Pioneers*, pp. 119–20.
25 Sir James Marchant, *Dr John Clifford CH: Life, Letters and Reminiscences* (London: Cassell, 1924), pp. 44, 62–4; Robert Pope, 'Congregations and Community', in Lesley Husselbee and Paul Ballard (eds), *Free Churches and Society: The Nonconformist Contribution to Social Welfare 1800–2010* (London: Continuum, 2012), pp. 37, 39.
26 Lofthouse, 'The Warden', p. 51.
27 Percy Alden, 'That Reminds Me', *Congregational Quarterly* 11 (1933), pp. 197–200; *Mansfield House Settlement* (London: Mansfield House University Settlement, 1932), pp. 22–3.
28 Seth Koven, *The Match Girl and the Heiress* (London: Princeton University Press, 2015).
29 Interview: Frank Waddington, 8 August 1986.
30 Lax, *Lax*, p. 103.
31 Clive D. Field, 'A Sociological Profile of English Methodism 1900-1932', *Oral History* 4/1 (1976), p. 91.
32 Maggie Newbery, *Reminiscences of a Bradford Mill Girl* (Bradford: Bradford Metropolitan Council Libraries Division, 1980), p. 32.
33 Merfyn Jones, 'Welsh Immigrants in the Cities of North West England 1890–1930: Some Oral Testimony', *Oral History* 9/2 (1981), pp. 36–7.
34 Ernest Armstrong MP, letter to author, November 1986.
35 Harold Miller, *Growing Up with Primitive Methodism*, 5th Chapel Aid lecture (Alderley Edge: privately printed, 1995).
36 *Methodist Recorder*, 21 April 1966.
37 *Free Churchman*, December 1933.
38 NRO: GEP, George Edwards pamphlet, *The Agricultural Labourer: His Life during the Past Half Century* (1919), p. 3.
39 G. Rowland Owen and G. G. Stammers, *A Century and a Quarter 1822 to 1947: St Michael's Methodist Church, Banham, Norfolk* (Norwich: privately printed, 1947), unpaginated.
40 Robin Gill, *Competing Convictions* (London: SCM Press, 1989), chap. 6; Robin Gill, *The Myth of the Empty Church* (London: SPCK, 1993), chap. 3.
41 *FCYB* (1927), pp. 51–5.
42 Currie, *Methodism Divided*, pp. 188–9; *CYB* (1939), p. 741.
43 Moore, *Pitmen, Preachers and Politics*, p. 126.
44 Rupert E. Davies, 'Methodism', in Rupert E. Davies (ed.), *The Testing of the Churches 1932–1982* (London: Epworth, 1982), p. 204; interview: Robert Allison, 27 August 1986; Benjamin Drewery, 'Methodist Union in Theory and Practice', *Wesley Historical Society Yorkshire Branch Bulletin* 42 (1983), p. 3.

45 C. J. Simmons, *Soap-Box Evangelist* (Chichester: Janay, 1972), p. 58.
46 *Methodist Recorder*, 26 April 1951.
47 Bradford Museums: Bradford Heritage Recording Unit [henceforward BHRU]: M0057.
48 R. G. Milne, 'County Road: The Story of a Methodist Church in North Liverpool' (unpublished 1980 typescript in LCA), p. 13.
49 Moore, *Pitmen, Preachers and Politics*, p. 148.
50 Hugh McLeod, 'New Perspectives on Victorian Working-Class Religion: The Oral Evidence', *Oral History* 14/1 (1986), p. 45.
51 Bradford Town Mission, *Annual Report* (1923–24); (1927–28), unpaginated; Banks, *The Story So Far*, pp. 84–6; Moore, *Pitmen, Preachers and Politics*, p. 146.
52 Sir R. Murray Hyslop, *The Centenary of the Temperance Movement 1832–1932* (London: Independent Press, 1931), p. 31.
53 *Alliance News*, August 1939.
54 Cited in Cox, *Lambeth*, p. 41.
55 LCA: LFCC advisory board minutes, 16 June 1911.
56 *Methodist Times*, 7 March 1918.
57 *Baptist Times*, 14 May 1931.
58 Banks, *The Story So Far*, pp. 64, 70; C. A. Piper, *A Century of Service: The Story of Liverpool North End Domestic Mission Society's First Hundred Years 1859–1959* (Liverpool: privately printed, 1959), p. 56.
59 Banks, *The Story So Far*, p. 150.
60 Phil J. Fisher, 'The Army and Religion', *Holborn Review* (January 1920), p. 63.
61 Tiplady, *Social Christianity*, p. 77; Dorothy Entwistle, '"Hope, Colour, and Citizenship": Loyalty and Opportunism in Early Twentieth-Century Church Attendance', *Journal of Religious History* 25/1 (2001), p. 24.
62 Information provided by Eastbrook Hall, July 1986.
63 George Edwards, *From Crow-Scaring to Westminster* (London: Labour Publishing, 1922), p. 21.
64 *Punch*, 4 May 1921.
65 Field, 'Gradualist or Revolutionary Secularisation?', pp. 86–7.
66 Frank Morris, *Lord of the Years: The Story of Cannock URC* (Cannock: privately printed, 2006), p. 240; Letter to *Christian World*, 11 March 1937; see also *Farnworth Methodist Church, Widnes: One Hundred Years Remembered* (Widnes: privately printed, 1991), p. 17.
67 Cited in G. M. Ramsden, *A Responsible Society: The Life and Times of the Congregation of Bank Street Chapel, Bolton, Lancashire* (Bolton: privately printed, 1985), pp. 46–7.
68 *FCYB* (1927), p. 47.
69 Lord Morrison of Lambeth, *Herbert Morrison: An Autobiography* (London: Odhams, 1960), p. 22.
70 *British Weekly*, 23 February 1928. On the locations Black studied see Gill, *Myth*, pp. 78–9, 194.
71 Thompson, 'The Older Free Churches', p. 94.
72 WYAB: Great Horton Wesleyan leaders' meeting minutes, 17 May 1934.
73 *Christian World*, 1 October 1936.
74 Miller, *Growing Up with Primitive Methodism*, pp. 1–44; interviews: Norman Free, 24 July 1986; Noel Edwards, 2 September 1986; Moore, *Pitmen, Preachers and Politics*, p. 107.
75 Linden, *Socialismus und Religion*, p. 116.

76 *Daily Herald*, 26 February 1923.
77 J. Gwynfor Jones, 'Reflections on the Religious Revival in Wales 1904–05', *JURCHS* 7/7 (2005), pp. 427–45.
78 George Davy cited in C. E. Gwyther, 'Methodism and Syndicalism in the Rhondda Valley 1906–1926', unpub. Sheffield PhD Thesis (1967), p. 278.
79 Pope, *Building Jerusalem*, esp. chaps. 2 and 3.
80 Edwards, *From the Valley*, p. 183.
81 T. Brennan, E. W. Cooney and H. Pollins, *Social Change in South West Wales* (London: Watts, 1954), p. 105.
82 Steve Bruce, 'Methodism and Mining in County Durham 1881–1991', *Northern History* 48/2 (2011), pp. 340, 353.
83 Rosemary Crook, 'Tidy Women: Women in the Rhondda between the Wars' *Oral History* 10/2 (1982), pp. 40–6.
84 Ackers, *Labour and Capital*, p. 11.
85 S. J. D. Green, *Religion in the Age of Decline: Organisation and Experience in Industrial Yorkshire 1870–1920* (Cambridge: Cambridge University Press, 1996), pp. 206–7; Clive D. Field, 'Zion's People: Who Were the English Nonconformists? Part 1: Gender, Age and Ethnicity', *The Local Historian* 40/2 (2010), pp. 94–8; Barry M. Doyle, 'Gender, Class and Congregational Culture in Early Twentieth-Century Norwich', *JURCHS* 5/6 (1995), p. 335,
86 D. Ben Rees, *Chapels in the Valleys: A Study in the Sociology of Welsh Nonconformity* (Wirral: Ffynnon Press, 1975), pp. 72–80.
87 *Christian World*, 13 May 1937; Morgan, *Rebirth of a Nation*, p. 229; John Wearmouth, *This from That: The Story of 200 years of Methodism in the Area of Newton Aycliffe New Town in County Durham* (Darlington: privately published, 1980), pp. 21–2.
88 Letters to *Christian World*, 21 February 1929, 11 April 1929.
89 Kenneth D. Brown, 'An Unsettled Ministry? Some Aspects of Nineteenth Century British Nonconformity', *Church History* 56/2 (1987), p. 217; Clifford, *Venture in Faith*, pp. 20–32.
90 Green, *Religion in the Age of Decline*, pp. 152–64; Elisabeth J. Neale, 'A Type of Congregational Ministry: R. F. Horton (1855–1934) and Lyndhurst Road', *JURCHS* 5/4, (1994), pp. 222–3.
91 *Christian World*, 16 July 1925.
92 *Methodist Times*, 18 February 1926.
93 *FCYB* (1929), p. 61; Gill, *Myth*, p. 195.
94 *CYB* (1929), p. 114.
95 *CYB* (1927), p. 67.
96 *Heaton Review*, 2 (1928), p. 56.
97 *Christian World*, 9 July 1925.
98 *Christian World*, letter from J. W. Ewing, 16 July 1925; *British Weekly*, 8 March 1928.
99 *Merseyside Congregationalist*, March 1935, June 1938.
100 *Free Churchman*, July 1934.
101 John S. Morgan, 'The Progress of the New Estates Community Movement', *Liverpool Quarterly* (July 1937), pp. 137–41.
102 J. W. Overend, *Eccleshill United Methodist Church (1838) Now Victoria Road Methodist Church (1938)* (Bradford: privately printed, 1938), p. 13.
103 Ramsden, *Bank Street*, p. 40; Ian Sellers, 'The Methodist Chapels and Preaching Places of Liverpool and District 1750–1971' (unpublished 1971 typescript in LCA),

pp. 2–3; F. H. Stead in Barnes, *Religion in the Labour Movement* (London: Holborn Press, 1919), p. 118.

104 Interview: 15 February 1992.

105 Report by Horace Fleming, 25 November 1926, cited in Naylor, *Quakers in the Rhondda*, p. 27.

106 Moore, *Pitmen, Preachers and Politics*, p. 85.

107 John Jones, *A Century of Hope: A Short History of Hope Congregational Church* (Oldham: privately printed, 1966), p. 35.

108 *Report for the Year 1926* (Liverpool: Merseyside Free Church Federation, 1926), p. 11.

109 *Albert Spicer 1847–1934: A Man of His Time by One of His Family* (London: Simpkin & Marshall, 1938), pp. 20, 55.

110 Interview: Fred and Grace Wilkinson, 14 July 1986.

111 Fell Lane Wesleyans, Keighley, cited in Green, *Religion in the Age of Decline*, p. 348.

112 Hugh McLeod, 'Sport and the English Sunday School 1869–1939', in Stephen Orchard and John Briggs (eds), *The Sunday School Movement* (Milton Keynes: Paternoster, 2007), pp. 109–23; Dolan, *Independent Methodists*, p. 205.

113 T. A. Fairweather and Percy Ackroyd, *Fifty Years of Primitive Methodism in West Bowling* (Bradford: privately printed, 1928), p. 55.

114 W. Glyn Jones, *Trinity Methodist Church, Tonge Fold, Bolton* (Bolton: privately printed, 1987), p. 13; Field, 'Sociological Profile', p. 74.

115 *Bradford Pioneer*, 20 October 1920.

116 Alfred Green, *Growing up in Attercliffe* (Sheffield: New City Paperbacks, 1981), pp. 111–12.

117 J. J. Nott, *Music for the People: Popular Music and Dance in Interwar Britain* (Oxford: Oxford University Press, 2002).

118 Ackers, *Labour and Capital*, p. 23.

119 Interview: Harold Meadows, 2 August 1986; J. Basil Horsman, *A History of Hope Congregational Church, Wigan 1812–1962* (Wigan: Thomas Wall & Sons, 1962), p. 103; Pope, 'Congregations and Community', p. 37.

120 M. O. Paulden, 'How to Use a Downtown Church' *Congregational Quarterly* (1923), pp. 91–3.

121 Frank Pogson letter to author, 24 February 1986; *Christian World*, 25 April 1935.

122 *Fling Wide the Gates! Thirty-Fifth Anniversary* (Bradford: Bradford Methodist Mission, 1939), p. 7.

123 Gill, *Myth*, chap. 7.

124 Cited in *The Review of the Methodist London Mission and Extension Fund 1986*, p. 9.

125 Peter Catterall, 'Church Decline, Secularism and Ecumenism', *Contemporary Record* 5/2 (1991), pp. 286–7; Doyle, 'Gender, Class and Congregational Culture', p. 322.

126 Green, *Religion in the Age of Decline*, pp. 388–9; Michael Childs, 'Labour Grows Up: The Electoral System, Political Generations and British Politics 1890–1929', *Twentieth Century British History* 6 (1995), pp. 141–2.

127 *British Weekly*, 1 March 1928.

128 J. Ernest Rattenbury, *Evangelism: Its Shame and Glory* (London: Epworth, 1932), p. 95.

129 J. W. James, 'The Religious Apathy of the Masses', *Congregational Quarterly* (1932), p. 477.

130 Cairns, *Army and Religion*, p.33.

131 S. C. Williams, *Religious Belief and Popular Culture in Southwark c1880–1939* (Oxford: Oxford University Press, 1999), esp. pp. 67–8.
132 Cairns, *Army and Religion*, pp. 121–2, 448; Clive D. Field, 'Keeping the Spiritual Home Fires Burning: Religious Belonging in Britain during the First World War', *War and Society* 33/4 (2014), pp. 244–68; Field, 'The Faith Society?', p. 61.
133 Morgan, 'Herbert Gray', pp. 175–8.
134 Snape, *Revisiting Religion*, pp. 15–17.
135 Michael Snape, *God and the British Soldier: Religion and the British Army in the First and Second World Wars* (London: Routledge, 2005), p. 243; H. Marsden (Horwich), letter to *Christian World*, 4 April 1935.
136 Nicholas Farr, *At the Heart of the City: A Methodist Mission in the Twentieth Century* (Sheffield: Victoria Hall Methodist Church, 1991), p. 38.
137 D. Caradog Jones (ed.), *The Social Survey of Merseyside* vol. 3 (Liverpool: Liverpool University Press, 1934), pp. 333–5.
138 B. Seebohm Rowntree and George R. Lavers, *English Life and Leisure: A Social Study* (Harlow: Longmans, 1951), pp. 353–5.
139 Bruce, 'Methodism and Mining', p. 351 puts the ratio of adherents to members at 3:1 in the Durham coalfield. A similar ratio obtained at Rhondda Williams's Union Church, Brighton, perhaps – like Ramsay MacDonald on occasion – drawn by the preacher: Neale, 'Thomas Rhondda Williams', pp. 607, 612, 614. Field, 'Gradualist or Revolutionary Secularisation?' p. 85 suggests lower figures and overall decline.
140 *Baptist Times*, 31 March 1922.
141 *Methodist Times*, 2 May 1935.
142 Charles H. Goodwin, 'The Revival of Religion 1923–1926', *PWHS* 51/1 (1997), p. 11.
143 NRO: Attleborough Wesleyan circuit quarterly meeting minutes, 29 March 1922.
144 Harold Murray, *Sixty Years an Evangelist: An Intimate Study of Gipsy Smith* (London: Marshall, Morgan & Scott, 1937), pp. 40, 117–18.
145 *The Crusader*, 13 October 1922; Soper, *Calling for Action*, chap.17.
146 Porritt, *The Best I Remember*, p. 207; Murray, *Gipsy Smith*, pp. 57–8, 60–1.
147 Tiplady, *Spiritual Adventure*, p. 16.
148 *Christian World*, 10 December 1936.
149 Gwyther, 'Methodism and Syndicalism', p. 306.
150 *Methodist Times*, 11 November 1923.
151 *Brotherhood Outlook*, February 1924.
152 *Hope Street Monthly Calendar*, April–May 1922.
153 Sellers, *Salute to Pembroke*, pp. 30–31.
154 *CYB* (1934), p. 149.
155 *The Highroad*, February 1932; LCA: LFCC minutes, 21 January 1932.
156 Pitt, *Our Unemployed*, pp. 17–36; Naylor, *Quakers in the Rhondda*, chap. 1; Barker, *Christ in the Valley*, pp. 94–5.
157 Hywel Francis and David Smith, *The Fed: A History of the South Wales Miners in the Twentieth Century* (London: Lawrence & Wishart, 1980), p. 256; *Christian World*, 19 November 1936; Pope, 'Congregations and Community', p. 38.
158 *The Things We Do: The Means Test* (London: Quaker Industrial and Social Council, 1937), p. 8.
159 Cited in Pitt, *Our Unemployed*, p. 52.
160 *Baptist Times*, 30 July 1936; Stephanie Ward, '"The Workers Are in the Mood to Fight the Act": Protest against the Means Test 1931–1935', in Matthias Reiss and

Matt Perry (eds), *Unemployment Protest: New Perspectives on Two Centuries of Contention* (Oxford: Oxford University Press, 2011), p. 251.
161 *AYB* (1936), p. 26.
162 *The Friend*, 29 May 1925.
163 *United Kingdom Band of Hope Annual Report* [henceforward *UKBHAR*] (1932–33), p. 9.
164 *UKBHAR* (1914–15), p. 6. This figure includes Scottish societies.
165 *UKBHAR* (1939–40), p. 2.
166 Mass Observation, *The Pub and the People*, pp. 162–3.
167 McCarthy, *British People*, p. 84.
168 *The Inquirer*, 9 November 1929.
169 *The Crusader*, 20 April 1921.
170 *Christian World*, 15 October 1936; David Bebbington, 'Baptists and Politics since 1914' in K. W. Clements (ed.), *Baptists in the Twentieth Century* (London: Baptist Historical Society, 1983), p. 84.
171 Interview: 15 February 1992.
172 *Methodist Recorder*, 7 November 1935.
173 *Christian World*, 19 August 1937; Binfield, *Pastors and People*, p. 253.
174 Wilkinson, *Dissent or Conform?*, p. 136.
175 Wilkinson, *Dissent or Conform?*, p. 81; Interview: Noel Edwards, 2 September 1986.
176 Bebbington, *Nonconformist Conscience*, pp. 146–7.
177 *Christian World*, 17 December 1959.
178 Wilkinson, *Dissent or Conform?*, pp. 59–60.
179 *House of Commons Debates*, vol. 251, cols. 658, 653–4: Sunday Performances (Regulation) Bill, 2nd Reading, 20 April 1931.
180 George Bell, *Primitive Methodism in King's Lynn Circuit 1821–1900* (King's Lynn: Foster & Bird, 1904), p. 38; Green, *Religion in the Age of Decline*, pp. 162–324.
181 Mallalieu, *On Larkhill*, p. 8.
182 Interview: 6 August 1986.
183 Murray, *Gipsy Smith*, p. 56; Moore, *Pitmen, Preachers and Politics*, p. 117.
184 *Wesleyan Methodist Conference Handbook, Bradford* (1927), pp. 101–102.
185 *CYB* (1926), p. 91.
186 *Christian World*, 30 May 1929.
187 Milne, 'County Road', p. 21.
188 *Liverpool and District Congregationalist*, September 1930.
189 *Girlington Methodist*, March 1936.
190 Moore, *Pitmen, Preachers and Politics*, p. 132.
191 Field, 'Zion's People: Part 1', p. 101.
192 Rowland, *Free Churches and the People*, p. 75.
193 *British Weekly*, 24 February 1938.
194 BCA, p. 9.
195 Gilbert, *Post-Christian Britain*, pp. 111–12.

Chapter 4

1 *Christian World*, 5 August 1926.
2 *The Crusader*, 3 November 1922

3 D. W. Bebbington, 'Nonconformity and Electoral Sociology 1867–1918', *Historical Journal* 27/3 (1984), pp. 644–5, 648–53.
4 *The Liberator*, February 1909.
5 *Christian World*, 5 August 1926.
6 *Christian World*, 2 January 1919.
7 Childs, 'Labour Grows Up', pp. 126, 130.
8 Tanner, *Political Change and the Labour Party*, pp. 386–9.
9 Tanner, *Political Change and the Labour Party*, p. 388; John Ramsden, *A History of the Conservative Party Volume 3: The Age of Balfour and Baldwin* (London: Longman, 1978), p. 121.
10 Peter Catterall 'The Politics of Electoral Reform since 1885', in Peter Catterall, Wolfram Kaiser and Ulrike Walton-Jordan (eds), *Reforming the Constitution: Debates in Twentieth-Century Britain* (London: Cass, 2000), pp. 138–40.
11 Tanner, *Political Change and the Labour Party*, p. 392.
12 In particular, Peter Clarke, 'Electoral Sociology of Modern Britain', *History* 57 (1972), pp. 31–55; H. G. C. Matthew, R. I. McKibbin and J. A. Kay, 'The Franchise Factor in the Rise of the Labour Party', *English Historical Review* 91 (1976), pp. 723–52.
13 See Jean Blondel, *Voters, Parties and Leaders: The Social Fabric of British Politics* (Harmondsworth: Penguin, 1963); Peter Pulzer, *Political Representation and Elections in Britain* (London: Allen & Unwin, 1967); David Butler and Donald Stokes, *Political Change in Britain: Forces Shaping Electoral Choice* (Harmondsworth: Penguin, 1971).
14 Christopher Howard, 'Expectations Born to Death: Local Labour Party Expansion in the 1920s', in J. M. Winter (ed.), *The Working Class in Modern British History: Essays in Honour of Henry Pelling* (Cambridge: Cambridge University Press, 1983), pp. 65–81.
15 *Yorkshire Observer*, 1 November 1924.
16 Stuart Ball, *Portrait of a Party: The Conservative Party in Britain 1918–1945* (Oxford: Oxford University Press, 2013), p. 130.
17 Kinnear, *The British Voter*, pp. 43–4; Edith H. Whetham, *The Agrarian History of England and Wales: Volume 8, 1914–1939* (Cambridge: Cambridge University Press, 1978), pp. 140–8.
18 David Redvaldsen, '"Today is the Dawn": The Labour Party and the 1929 General Election', *Parliamentary History* 29/3 (2010), pp. 395–415.
19 Tregidga, *The Liberal Party in South-West Britain*, pp. 24–5.
20 Most recently in Laura Beers and Geraint Thomas (eds), *Brave New World: Imperial and Democratic Nation-Building in Britain between the Wars* (London: Institute of Historical Research, 2011), p.10.
21 Cited in Griffiths, *Labour and the Countryside*, p.159.
22 Robert Waller, 'Conservative Electoral Support and Social Class', in Anthony Seldon and Stuart Ball (eds), *Conservative Century: The Conservative Party since 1900* (Oxford: Oxford University Press, 1994), pp. 584, 594–5.
23 Jon Lawrence and Miles Taylor (eds), *Party, State and Society: Electoral Behaviour in Modern Britain* (Aldershot: Scolar, 1996), chaps. 1 and 3; Christopher Stevens, 'The Electoral Sociology of Britain Reconsidered', *Contemporary British History* 13/1 (1999), pp. 62–94.
24 Tregidga, *The Liberal Party in South-West Britain*, p. 31.

25 Interview: Stephen Mayor, 11 June 1985. See also Waller, 'Conservative Electoral Support', p. 581.
26 Richard Grayson, *Liberals, International Relations and Appeasement: The Liberal Party 1919–1939* (London: Cass, 2001); Tregidga, *The Liberal Party in South-West Britain*, p. 46.
27 Andrew Thorpe, 'J. H. Thomas and the Rise of Labour in Derby 1880–1945', *Midland History* 15 (1990), pp. 113–18.
28 Snowden, *Autobiography*, vol. 1, pp. 16–19; Peter Catterall and Joyce Howson, 'New Unionism', in Peter Catterall (ed.) *Britain 1867–1918* (Oxford: Heinemann Educational, 1994), pp. 93–100; Childs, 'Labour Grows Up', pp. 132, 140–2.
29 Childs, 'Labour Grows Up', pp. 132–7.
30 B. M. Doyle, 'Urban Liberalism and the "Lost Generation": Politics and Middle-class Culture in Norwich 1900–35', *Historical Journal* 38 (1995), pp. 617–34.
31 Thomas, *Mr Speaker*, p. 23.
32 *Bolton Evening News*, 29 October 1930.
33 Arthur Black, 'How the Churches Use Their Laymen', *The Review of the Churches* (1927), p. 212.
34 J. J. Lawson, *A Man's Life* (London: Hodder & Stoughton, 1932), p. 108.
35 Cited in Alun Howkins, *Poor Labouring Men: Rural Radicalism in Norfolk, 1870–1923* (London: Routledge & Kegan Paul, 1985), p. 53.
36 For instance, John Hodge, *Workman's Cottage to Windsor Castle* (London: Sampson Low, 1931), pp. 21–2.
37 Thomas, *Mr Speaker*, p. 40.
38 *Girlington Methodist*, September 1936.
39 Bebbington, 'Baptists and Politics', p. 82; Bullock, *Ernest Bevin: Volume1*, p. 9.
40 Rev. B. C. Shildrick, written communication, February 1986.
41 NRO: GEP, 'Religion and Labour'.
42 Wilfrid Wellock, *The Way Out, or the Road to the New World* (London: Labour Publishing, 1922), p. 41.
43 Margaret Bondfield, *A Life's Work* (London: Hutchinson, 1948), pp. 352–3.
44 *The Inquirer*, 15 March 1919.
45 In particular, Stanley Baldwin, *Service of Our Lives: Last Speeches as Prime Minister* (London: Hodder & Stoughton, 1937).
46 *Baptist Times*, 31 January 1935. See also Stanley Baldwin, *Looking Ahead: A Restatement of Unionist Principles and Aims* (London: National Union of Conservative and Constitutional Associations, 1924), pp. 38–9.
47 Peter Catterall, 'The Party and Religion', in Anthony Seldon and Stuart Ball (eds), *Conservative Century: The Conservative Party since 1900* (Oxford: Oxford University Press, 1994), p. 669.
48 Ammon, *Labour's Dynamic*, p. 5.
49 NCEFC, *The England of Tomorrow*, p. 83.
50 *Methodist Times*, 23 February 1933.
51 *The Times*, letter by Ammon, 7 September 1932.
52 *The Times*, letter by Cockerill, 10 September 1932. See also Ammon's response in *The Times*, 5 October 1932.
53 AP: U DMN/9/6, draft autobiography, chap. 6, p. 3.
54 *Daily Telegraph*, 11 February 1922.
55 *Liverpool Daily Post*, 14 December 1926.
56 Horsman, *Hope Congregational Church*, p. 103.

57 AP: U DLB/1/11.
58 Tudur Jones, *Congregationalism in England*, p. 317.
59 Rowland, *The Free Churches and the People*, pp. 22, 37–43; Hugh McLeod, *Class and Religion in the Late Victorian City* (London: Croom Helm, 1974), p. 66.
60 W. Forbes Gray (ed.), *Non-Church Going: Its Reasons and Remedies* (Edinburgh: Oliphant, Anderson & Ferrier, 1911), pp. 174–83.
61 A. Fenner Brockway, *Inside the Left* (London: Allen & Unwin, 1942), p. 15.
62 F. H. Stead, 'Keir Hardie: Politician or Labour Evangelist?', *London Quarterly Review* (1922), p. 211; Jeffs, *Press, Preachers and Politicians*, pp. 96–7.
63 *Brotherhood Year Book* (1913–14), p. 26. See also Smith, *Religion and the Rise of Labour*, pp. 68–9.
64 *The Inquirer*, 14 August 1919.
65 J. P. Perkins, letter to *Christian World*, 28 December 1922.
66 *Brotherhood Journal*, November 1918, August 1919; *Labour Leader*, 18 September 1919.
67 *Methodist Times*, 13 June 1935.
68 *Baptist Times*, 16 May 1919; see also John Stevenson, *British Society 1914–1945* (London: Allen Lane, 1984), p. 360.
69 *Christian World*, 2 July 1925; Tuffley, *The Sowers*, p. 45.
70 AP: U DMN/2/5, diary 1 January 1933.
71 *Brotherhood Year Book* (1930–31), p. 17.
72 Linden, *Sozialismus und Religion*, p. 77.
73 *Methodist Times*, 12 November 1931.
74 Doyle, 'Modernity or Morality?', p. 331.
75 Mark Freeman, 'The Decline of the Adult School Movement between the Wars', *History of Education* 39/4 (2010), pp. 483, 486.
76 Cited in W. Arnold Hall, *The Adult School Movement in the Twentieth Century* (Nottingham: Department of Adult Education, University of Nottingham, 1985), p. 151.
77 Freeman, 'Decline', pp. 503–4.
78 H. G. Wood and Arthur F. Ball, *Tom Bryan, First Warden of Fircroft: A Memoir* (London: Allen & Unwin, 1922), pp. 147–53.
79 James Dudley, 'Educational Settlements and the Society of Friends', *Friends Quarterly Examiner* (1937), pp. 15–21; Hall, *Adult School Movement*, pp. 50–2, 141; Freeman, 'Decline', pp. 482, 484–5, 491.
80 P. Ollerhead, 'Unitarianism in Crewe 1860–1940', *Unitarian Historical Society Transactions* 17 (1979), pp. 31–2.
81 *Socialist Christian*, October 1929.
82 Letter to *The Inquirer*, 22 November 1919.
83 *The Inquirer*, 2 February 1929, 2 November 1929.
84 *The Crusader*, 2 February 1923.
85 W. McLeod Girdwood, letter to *Christian World*, 8 July 1926.
86 Doyle, 'Gender, Class and Congregational Culture', p. 323; John Parker, *Father of the House: Fifty Years in Politics* (London: Routledge and Kegan Paul, 1982), pp. 9, 32.
87 John R. Hodgkins, *The History of Cliff Town Congregational Church, Southend-on-Sea 1799–1972* (Southend-on-Sea: Clifton Books, 1974), p. 35.
88 *Christian World*, 2 January 1919.
89 'Diary of a Forlorn Hope', *Socialist Review* July 1929, pp. 33–41.
90 *Bradford Pioneer*, 30 October 1931.

91 Letter to *Methodist Times*, 22 October 1931.
92 R. A. Davey, letter to *Christian World*, 29 September 1932: see Appendix.
93 Interview: Alan Brigg, 14 October 1985.
94 NRO: Wymondham Primitive Methodist circuit quarterly meeting minutes, 1 December 1920; Interview: Noel Edwards, 2 September 1986.
95 Cited in Howkins, *Poor Labouring Men*, p. 73.
96 Interview: F. A. Lord, 25 October 1985.
97 Letter from Frank Pogson, 24 February 1986.
98 A. Fenner Brockway, 'British Socialists and the Church', in Jerome Davis (ed.), *Labor Speaks for Itself on Religion* (New York: Macmillan, 1929), p. 152.
99 Lloyd, *Scarlet Nest*, p. 190.
100 BHRU: AO145/36–8; interview: Fred & Grace Wilkinson, 8 August 1986.
101 Porritt, *The Best I Remember*, p. 139.
102 *Christian World*, 13 March 1919.
103 *Bradford Pioneer*, 2 July 1920.
104 Letter to *Methodist Times*, 22 February 1923.
105 *Christian World*, 2 November 1922.
106 Letter to *Methodist Times*, 8 March 1923.
107 Kenneth Wood, *The Coal Pits of Chowbent* (Bolton: privately printed, 1984), pp. 43, 69–70, 81, 108–9; letters to *Baptist Times*, 11 April 1919, 2 May 1919, 10 June 1926.
108 *Primitive Methodist Leader*, 31 January 1924.
109 BOCSPA, *Annual Report* (1919), p. 4; B. Seebohm Rowntree, *Industrial Unrest: A Way Out* (London: Longmans, 1922), pp. 7–8.
110 *Christian World*, 21 July 1921.
111 Rowntree, *Industrial Unrest*, p. 12.
112 Theodore Cooke Taylor, 'The Labour Crisis', *Contemporary Review* (May 1922), p. 594.
113 *New Leader*, 22 February 1929.
114 T. C. Barker, *The Glassmakers, Pilkington: The Rise of an International Company 1826–1976* (London: Weidenfeld & Nicolson, 1977), pp. 97, 233.
115 Doyle, 'Urban Liberalism', pp. 617–34; similar evidence from Bolton is noted in Harris, 'Social Leadership', p. 23.
116 Doyle, 'A Conflict of Interests?' p. 131; Cook, *Age of Alignment*, pp. 56–8, 290.
117 *Bolton Congregationalist*, December 1920.
118 John Rowett, 'The Labour Party and Local Government: Theory and Practice in the Inter-War Years', unpub. Oxford DPhil Thesis (1979), pp. 233–4.
119 Doyle, 'A Conflict of Interests', pp. 133–40; Cook, *Age of Alignment*, p. 136.
120 Interview: Joan Riley, 2 July 1986.
121 AP: U DMN/2/2, diary, 9 January 1923.
122 Edwards, *Crow-Scaring*, pp. 201, 208.
123 *Methodist Times*, 26 October 1922, 23 November 1922. On this rising social status see Field, 'Zion's People Part 3', p. 298.
124 Interview: Dr Stanley Kennett, 3 February 1986.
125 WYAB: Kirkgate Wesleyan Chapel, Bradford leaders' meeting minute book, 22 February 1925; 23 March 1925; Trustees' minutes, 21 May 1935; Murray, *Press, Pulpit and Pew*, p. 161.
126 Interview: Norman Free, 24 July 1986.
127 Sellers, 'Nonconformist Attitudes', pp. 217, 234–7; *The Highroad*, October 1929; Merseyside Free Church Federation, *Report for the Year 1922*, p. 4.

128 David A. Roberts, 'Religion and Politics in Liverpool since 1900', unpub. London MSc Thesis (1965), p. 154.
129 Brennan, Cooney and Pollins, *Social Change in South West Wales*, pp. 84–6.
130 Ackers, *Labour and Capital*, pp. 14–17.
131 In Penistone, Yorkshire, where only 4.4 per cent of the population were Nonconformist in 1921, all three parties regularly selected Nonconformist candidates.
132 *British Weekly*, 6 November 1924.
133 Field, 'Sociological Profile', p. 91.
134 *Bradford Pioneer*, 28 March 1924.
135 Fred Blackburn, *George Tomlinson* (London: Heinemann, 1954), pp. 38–9.
136 *The Friend*, 25 May 1918.
137 Friends House Library, London [henceforward FHL]: Socialist Quaker Society minutes, 25 October 1910, 16 February 1911, 30 April 1912.
138 R. Dodds, letter to *Socialist Review*, September 1928, pp. 23–4.
139 Letter to *The Friend*, 18 January 1924.
140 *Socialist Review*, March 1926, pp. 50–1; *The Friend*, 2 April 1926.
141 Casey, 'The Overlooked Pacifist Tradition Part II', pp. 517–28.
142 Laurence A. Kotler-Berkowitz, 'Religion and Voting Behaviour in Great Britain: A Reassessment', *British Journal of Political Science* 31/3 (2001), p. 537.

Chapter 5

1 Arthur Henderson, 'British Labour and Religion', in Jerome Davis (ed.), *Labor Speaks for Itself on Religion* (New York: Macmillan, 1929), pp. 144–5.
2 Ammon, *Labour's Dynamic*, p. 31. Carter was a Wesleyan and Labour MP.
3 F. H. Stead, *The Proletarian Gospel of Galilee in Some of Its Phases* (London: Labour Publishing, 1922), p. viii; J. Ramsay MacDonald, preface to A. D. Belden, *George Whitefield the Awakener: A Modern Study of the Evangelical Revival* (London: Sampson Law, 1930), p. xi.
4 Bruce, 'Methodism and Mining', p. 340.
5 R. F. Wearmouth, *Methodism and the Working-Class Movements of England 1800–1850* (London: Epworth, 1937); R. F. Wearmouth, *Some Working-Class Movements of the Nineteenth Century; Methodism and the Struggle of the Working Classes 1850–1900* (London: Epworth, 1954); R. F. Wearmouth, *The Social and Political Influence of Methodism in the Twentieth Century* (London: Epworth, 1957); R. F. Wearmouth, *Methodism and Trade Unions* (London: Epworth, 1959).
6 *British Weekly*, 29 September 1949.
7 *Christian World*, 26 March 1931.
8 *The Inquirer*, 8 June 1929.
9 David Bebbington, 'Baptist Members of Parliament in the Twentieth Century', *Baptist Quarterly* (April 1986), p. 252; S. V. Bracher, *The Herald Book of Labour Members* (London: Labour Publishing, 1924), p. 76; *Yorkshire Observer Budget*, 7 November 1936.
10 Bebbington, 'Baptist Members', p. 279.
11 Pope, *Building Jerusalem*, p. 122; Mary Agnes Hamilton, *Remembering My Good Friends* (London: Cape, 1944), p. 44.

12 See Paul Mulvey, *The Political Life of Josiah C. Wedgwood: Land, Liberty and Empire 1872–1943* (Woodbridge: Boydell, 2010), p. 20.
13 Martin, 'The Instruments of the People?', p. 131.
14 Cyril Pearce, 'An Interview with Wilfrid Whiteley', *Bulletin of the Society for the Study of Labour History* [*BSSLH*], 18 (1969), p. 16.
15 Ben Turner, *About Myself* (London: Cayme Press, 1930), pp. 176, 242–5.
16 *Methodist Times*, 17 March 1919.
17 Ammon, *Labour's Dynamic*, p. 64.
18 Linden, *Sozialismus und Religion*, p. 86.
19 Dorothy Entwistle, '"Hope, Colour, and Citizenship": Loyalty and Opportunism in Early Twentieth-Century Church Attendance', *Journal of Religious History* 25/1 (2001), pp. 20–38.
20 Fenner Brockway, 'The Church and World Problems', *Congregational Quarterly* (1931), pp. 12–18.
21 Barnes, *Religion and the Labour Movement*, p. 111.
22 *British Weekly*, 17 January 1924.
23 They were, for instance, well represented on the 1923 strike committee: Reg Groves, *Sharpen the Sickle! The History of the Farm Workers' Union* (London: Merlin, 1981), p. 180.
24 Bruce, 'Methodism and Mining', pp. 337–55.
25 Wolfenden, 'English Nonconformity', p. 70.
26 Frank Hodges, *My Adventures as a Labour Leader* (London: Newnes, 1925), p. 18.
27 Herbert Smith, Peter Lee and Joseph Jones. Tom Richardson was a Congregationalist. Robert Smillie was of Presbyterian background though, despite the frequency and fervour with which he quoted scripture, his links with the church seem rather tenuous. Will Lawther, who became president in 1939, was also of Methodist stock.
28 Matthew Worley, *Labour inside the Gate: A History of the British Labour Party between the Wars* (London: I. B. Tauris, 2005), pp. 10–12.
29 Wilfrid Winterton, *Harvest of the Years* (Birmingham: Templar Press, 1969), pp. 94–5.
30 Eric Taylor, 'An Interview with Wesley Perrins', *Bulletin of the Society for the Study of Labour History* 21 (1970), pp. 18–19.
31 Interview: Alan Brigg, 14 October 1985; *Methodist Times*, 13 June 1929, 7 November 1935; Wood and Ball, *Tom Bryan*, pp. 22–3; *United Methodist*, 20 November 1924; *Methodist Recorder*, 6 June 1929; Ackers, *Labour and Capital*, p. 14; Dolan, *Independent Methodists*, p. 219.
32 *Methodist Times*, 30 July 1936.
33 For instance, *Bolton Evening News*, 30 October 1925.
34 Underwood, *English Baptists*, p. 255.
35 A. Fenner Brockway, *Socialism over Sixty Years: The Life of Jowett of Bradford* (London: Allen & Unwin, 1946), p. 31; *Girlington Methodist*, October 1935; *Bradford Pioneer*, 2 November 1925, 15 November 1929.
36 Small Centre Parties formed by disgruntled Catholics nevertheless emerged in the 1930s in both Liverpool and Glasgow (see Riddell, 'The Catholic Church', pp. 167, 170).
37 *The Liverpolitan*, October 1938.
38 Letters to *Yorkshire Evening Argus*, 28 November 1924.

39 *The Times*, 14 February 1924 cited in Chris Cook, 'By-elections of the First Labour Government', in Chris Cook and John Ramsden (eds), *By-Elections in British Politics* (London: UCL Press, 1997), pp. 42–3.
40 Hugh Dalton, *Call Back Yesterday: Memoirs 1887–1931* (London: Frederick Muller, 1953), p. 172.
41 Andrew Thorpe, *A History of the British Labour Party* 2nd ed (Basingstoke: Palgrave, 2001), pp. 69–73.
42 Catterall, 'Distinctiveness', pp. 140–3; Christopher Howard, 'Henderson, MacDonald and Leadership in the Labour Party 1914–1922', unpub. Cambridge PhD Thesis (1978), pp. 255–7; Michael Hornsby-Smith, *Roman Catholics in England* (Cambridge: Cambridge University Press, 1987).
43 Roberts, 'Religion and Politics', p. 117.
44 Because of his position on the education issue, Ammon was told he would not get the Catholic vote: AP: U DMN.2/3, diary 27 May 1929.
45 *The Liverpolitan*, December 1934, May 1935.
46 LCA: Liverpool Trades Council and Labour Party papers, 331 TRA 14/2; 331 TRA 18/1; 331 TRA 18/2; 331 TRA 18/3; 331 TRA 18/4; 331 TRA 18/11.
47 Waller, *Democracy and Sectarianism*, pp. 341–2; Robert Baxter, 'The Liverpool Labour Party 1918–1963', unpub. Oxford D.Phil Thesis (1969), pp. 82–5.
48 Interview: Arthur Amis, 10 September 1986.
49 Griffiths, *Labour and the Countryside*, p. 316; Groves, *Sharpen the Sickle!*, p. 129.
50 Josiah Sage, *Memoirs of Josiah Sage* (London: Lawrence & Wishart, 1951), p. 27. See also M. F. Serpell, *History of the Lophams* (London: Phillimore, 1980), pp. 248–56; Edwards, *Crow-Scaring*, pp. 35–6.
51 Griffiths, *Labour and the Countryside*, p. 159.
52 R. W. Johnson, 'The Nationalisation of English Rural Politics: Norfolk South West 1945–1970', *Parliamentary Affairs* 26/1 (1972/73), pp. 8–55.
53 Griffiths, *Labour and the Countryside*, pp. 326, 339; Redvaldsen, 'The Labour Party and the 1929 Election', pp. 395–415.
54 Winterton, *Harvest of the Years*, p. 96; Mansfield, 'Farmworkers and Local Conservatism', p. 52.
55 FHL: Box V, 1/3, Glenvil Hall to A. Neave Brayshaw, 17 November 1922.
56 Johnson, 'The Nationalisation of English Rural Politics', p. 18.
57 Peter Catterall, 'Preface' in Stuart Ball and Ian Holliday (eds), *Mass Conservatism: The Conservatives and the Public since the 1880s* (London: Cass, 2002), pp. xii–xiii; Mansfield, 'Farmworkers and Local Conservatism', pp. 36–57.
58 Scotland, *Methodism and the Revolt of the Field*, p. 51.
59 Blackburn, *Tomlinson*, p. 51.
60 Interview: Arthur Amis, 10 September 1986.
61 Johnson, 'The Nationalisation of English Rural Politics', p. 22.
62 Interview: Arthur Amis, 10 September 1986.
63 A. L. Rowse, *Autobiography of a Cornishman: A Cornish Childhood* (London: Cape, 1942), p. 128.
64 Cited in Linden, *Sozialismus und Religion*, p. 123.
65 Brennan, Cooney and Pollins, *Social Change in South West Wales*, pp. 80–1; David Berry, *The Sociology of Grass Roots Politics: A Study of Party Membership* (London: Macmillan, 1970), pp. 50–1.
66 *Christian World*, 12 November 1931.

67 *Great Thoughts*, 16 November 1907.
68 Smith, *Religion and the Rise of Labour*, pp. 166–8.
69 Brockway, *Bermondsey Story*, p. 33; AP: U DLB/1/11.
70 Egon Wertheimer, 'The Crisis in the ILP: An Attack', *Socialist Review* (July 1929), p. 13.
71 *New Leader*, 23 May 1924, 5 March 1926; *Bradford Pioneer*, 30 December 1927.
72 See *New Leader*, 1 October 1926.
73 *New Leader*, 15 June 1928.
74 Clifford Allen, 'The ILP and Revolution', *Socialist Review*, October 1925, p. 150.
75 Pierson, *British Socialists*, p. 155.
76 *New Leader*, 25 January 1929.
77 *New Leader*, 11 January 1929.
78 Janet Chance, 'The Spinster-Minded in Politics and Marriage', *Socialist Review*, January 1930, p. 157.
79 John Radcliff, 'Sex Reform and the Christ-Ideal', *Socialist Review*, July 1930, pp. 145–51, 'The Religious Instinct', *Socialist Review*, July/September 1931, pp. 307–11. The first of these was sufficiently controversial for the printers to refuse to be responsible for the article's publication.
80 Letter to *New Leader*, 10 January 1930.
81 AP: U DMN/2/6, diary 17 March 1934.
82 Morgan, 'Herbert Gray', pp. 180–5.
83 *New Leader*, 27 December 1929.
84 Laurence Thompson, *The Enthusiasts: A Biography of John and Katherine Bruce Glasier* (London: Gollancz, 1971), p. 237.
85 *Methodist Times*, 7 November 1935.
86 *Christian World*, 4 June 1931.
87 A. J. Marriott, letter to *Labour Leader*, 20 April 1922.
88 *Bolton Citizen*, August 1937.
89 Attlee, *The Labour Party in Perspective*, p.27.
90 *Liverpool's Labour Voice*, 30 September 1927.
91 J. R. B. McBride, diary cited in *Daily Telegraph*, 5 November 1986.
92 E. P. Thompson, 'Homage to Tom Maguire', in Asa Briggs and John Savile (eds), *Essays in Labour History 1886–1923* (London: Macmillan, 1971), p. 200.
93 See *Bolton Citizen*, October 1932; Bondfield, *A Life's Work*, p. 352.
94 *Bradford Pioneer*, 30 January 1920.
95 Keir Hardie, 'Christ and the Modern Movement', in Ammon, *Christ and Labour* (London: Jarrold, 1912), p. 87.
96 Jack and Bessie Braddock, *The Braddocks* (London: Macdonald, 1963), p. 33.
97 *Bolton Journal and Guardian*, 30 July 1926.
98 Cited in Linden, *Sozialismus und Religion*, p. 161.
99 Scotland, *Methodism and the Revolt of the Field*, pp. 87–99.
100 George Benson, *Socialism and the Teaching of Jesus* (London: Independent Labour Party, 1925), p. 6.
101 *House of Commons Debates*, 5th ser., vol. 166, col. 1984, 16 July 1923.
102 Katherine Bruce Glasier, *Socialism for Beginners* (London: ILP Publication Department, 1929), p. 1.
103 Simmons, *Soap-Box Evangelist*, p. 101.
104 *Christian World*, 31 October 1935.
105 Casey, 'The Overlooked Pacifist Tradition Part II', p. 517.

Chapter 6

1 *Club and Institute Union Report* (1923), cited in *AYB* (1926), p. 87.
2 *FCYB* (1927), p. 89.
3 *House of Commons Debates*, 5th ser., vol. 144, cols. 2618–19: Licensing (No. 2) Bill, 2nd Reading, 22 July 1921.
4 F. C. Thornborough, letter to *Christian World*, 28 December 1922.
5 LMA: Liberation Society management committee minutes, 23 March 1920.
6 R. E. Dowse, *Left in the Centre: The Independent Labour Party 1893–1940* (London: Longmans, 1966), pp. 177–80.
7 Koss, 'Lloyd George and Nonconformity', p. 105.
8 LPA: NEC minutes, 22 January 1936.
9 H. B. Lees-Smith, 'The General Election and After', *Contemporary Review* (January 1936), p. 12.
10 LPA: NEC minutes, 7 February 1928.
11 Gregg McClymont, 'The Labour Party's Attitude to Gambling, 1918–1970', unpub. Oxford D.Phil thesis 2006, p. 95.
12 *Bradford Pioneer*, 2 January 1925.
13 *Washington Labour News*, 24 August 1923.
14 Edwards, *Crow-Scaring*, p. 82.
15 *Bradford Socialist Vanguard*, August 1920.
16 Pope, *Building Jerusalem*, pp. 78–9.
17 Robert Taylor, 'John Robert Clynes and the Making of Labour Socialism, 1890–1918' in Matthew Worley (ed.), *The Foundations of the British Labour Party: Identities, Cultures and Perspectives, 1900–39* (Farnham: Ashgate, 2009), p. 21.
18 J. R. Clynes, *Memoirs, 1924–37* (London: Hutchinson, 1937), p. 294.
19 Simmons, *Soap-Box Evangelist*, p. 10.
20 Wellock, *The Way Out*, p. 56.
21 *Christian World*, 6 March 1924.
22 *Methodist Times*, 10 April 1924.
23 Thomas, *Mr Speaker*, p. 56.
24 *LYM* (1923), p. 329.
25 *The Friend*, 1 May 1925; *LYM* (1926), p. 119.
26 *FCYB* (1929), Part II, p. 13.
27 Ingli James, letter to *Baptist Times*, 18 April 1924.
28 Henderson (Wesleyan), Clynes (Congregationalist) and Chuter Ede (Unitarian).
29 F. M. Leventhal, *Arthur Henderson* (Manchester: Manchester University Press, 1989), p. 126.
30 *House of Commons Debates*, 5th ser., vol. 231, cols. 241–93, Capital Punishment motion, 30 October 1929.
31 *LYM* (1931), p. 112.
32 *New Leader*, 19 June 1931.
33 Thomas, *Mr Speaker*, pp. 59–61.
34 C. R. Attlee, *As It Happened* (London: Heinemann, 1954), p. 88.
35 J. C. Wedgwood, *Memoirs of a Fighting Life* (London: Hutchinson, 1940), p. 198.
36 *Socialist Christian*, January 1929.
37 Porritt, *Memories*, pp. 89, 131.

38 *House of Commons Debates*, 5th ser., vol. 218, cols. 1044–5, Prayer Book Measure, 14 June 1928; Ernest Thurtle, *Time's Winged Chariot: Memories and Comments* (London: Chaterson, 1946), p. 99.
39 *House of Commons Debates*, 5th ser., vol. 218, col. 1228, 14 June 1928.
40 *House of Commons Debates*, 5th ser., vol. 211, col. 2560, Prayer Book Measure, 15 December 1927.
41 *Baptist Times*, 2 May 1924.
42 *Primitive Methodist Leader*, 9 November 1922.
43 *Baptist Times*, 24 November 1922.
44 BMA: BDFCC, p. 449 (3 March 1924).
45 Catterall, *Labour and the Politics of Alcohol*, pp. 15–29.
46 *House of Commons Debates*, 5th ser., vol. 169, col. 1255, David Lloyd George speaking on the Wales (Temperance) Bill, 2nd Reading, 15 February 1924.
47 LPA: NEC minutes, 9 March 1920; Catterall, *Labour and the Politics of Alcohol*, pp. 7–13.
48 Philip Snowden, *Socialism and the Drink Question* (London: Independent Labour Party, 1908), pp. 142, 174.
49 *AYB* (1920), p. 75.
50 *Sussex Daily News*, 24 June 1921.
51 Sidney Webb (chairman), *Labour and the Liquor Trade* (London: Labour Party, 1923), pp. 6–7.
52 Webb, *Labour and the Liquor Trade*, pp. 20–1. This lack of firm conclusions reflected the divisions within the committee.
53 J. Ramsay MacDonald, 'Foreword' in Sidney Webb, *Labour and the Liquor Trade* (London: Labour Party, 1923), pp. 2–3.
54 *Morning Advertiser*, 25 November 1923.
55 Hall, *Let the People Decide*, foreword.
56 *Alliance News*, June 1929.
57 *AYB* (1921), p. 67.
58 LPA: LP/LIQ/22.
59 Webb, *Labour and the Liquor Trade*, pp. 15–16.
60 *House of Commons Debates*, 5th ser., vol. 169, col. 1238, Wales (Temperance) Bill, 2nd Reading, 5 February 1924.
61 *AYB* (1926), p. 87.
62 Cited in *Primitive Methodist Leader*, 23 October 1924.
63 *Methodist Times*, 23 February 1922.
64 Webb, *Labour and the Liquor Trade*, p. 16; *Club and Institute Journal*, January 1922.
65 Johnson, 'Primitive Parliamentarians', p. 133.
66 IAS: GP Box, Dr Alfred Salter MP, *A Message to Labour*, speech delivered to the UKA, 19 October 1927, p. 2.
67 LPA: LP/LIQ/22, Nicholson to Middleton, 13 February 1923.
68 *Alliance News*, May 1929.
69 LPA: NEC minutes, 21 December 1927; Dalton, *Call Back Yesterday*, p.172.
70 *Methodist Times*, 23 October 1924.
71 *Alliance News*, January 1936. These figures include Scottish MPs.
72 Cited in Rowett, 'Labour Party and Local Government', pp. 81–2.
73 *Alliance News*, January 1936.
74 *AYB* (1929), p. 70.
75 *Alliance News*, May 1929.

76 LPA: NEC minutes, 26 March 1929.
77 LPA: NEC minutes, 24 January 1934.
78 *Alliance News*, July 1932. A similar organization, the Labour Temperance Fellowship, had existed before 1914.
79 *House of Commons Debates*, 5th ser., vol. 282, cols. 2013–14, 8 December 1933.
80 *House of Commons Debates*, 5th ser., vol. 309, col. 1699, 6 March 1936.
81 *Christian World*, 7 November 1935.
82 *Morning Advertiser*, 4 May 1929.
83 *Methodist Times*, 10 October 1935.
84 *AYB* (1937), p. 17.
85 *House of Commons Debates*, 5th ser., vol. 291, col. 1231, Betting and Lotteries Bill, 2nd Reading, 27 June 1934.
86 *House of Commons Debates*, 5th ser., vol. 217, col. 570, J. H. Thomas speaking on the Dog Track Racing Bill, 2nd Reading, 11 May 1928.
87 *House of Commons Debates*, 5th ser., vol. 194, cols. 1706–8, Budget Statement, 26 April 1926.
88 Porritt, *Memories*, pp. 102–4.
89 Peter Catterall, 'Chancellor of the Exchequer and the Return to the Gold Standard', in Richard Toye (ed.), *Winston Churchill: Politics, Strategy and Statecraft in the Twentieth Century* (London: Bloomsbury, 2017), chap. 4.
90 *House of Commons Debates*, 5th ser., vol. 220, cols. 722–31, Racecourse Betting Bill, 3rd Reading, 19 July 1928.
91 *Methodist Times*, 22 November 1923, 23 October 1924; *House of Commons Debates*, 5th ser., vol. 214, cols. 2311–12, Racecourse Betting Bill, 2nd Reading, 16 March 1928.
92 *House of Commons Debates*, 5th ser., vol. 220, col. 663, Racecourse Betting Bill, 3rd Reading, 19 July 1928.
93 McClymont, 'Labour Party's Attitude to Gambling', p. 59.
94 *New Leader*, 20 July 1928.
95 *New Leader*, 3 August 1928. See also McClymont, 'Labour Party's Attitude to Gambling', chap. 1.
96 *House of Commons Debates*, 5th ser., vol. 293, cols. 1849–50, John McGovern speaking on the Betting and Lotteries Bill, 3rd Reading, 13 November 1934; McClymont, 'Labour Party's Attitude to Gambling', p. 84.
97 LPA: NEC minutes, 25 September 1923, 26 June 1933.
98 Interview: Arthur Amis, 10 September 1986.
99 McClymont, 'Labour Party's Attitude to Gambling', p. 98. On widespread working-class gambling see Rowntree, *Poverty and Progress*, pp. 401–6.
100 McClymont, 'Labour Party's Attitude to Gambling', pp. 51, 93–8.
101 Marie Coleman, *The Irish Sweep: A History of the Irish Hospitals Sweepstake 1930–87* (Dublin: University College Dublin Press, 2009), pp. 90, 107–8; *House of Commons Debates*, 5th ser., vol. 252, col. 1781–2, Hospital Lotteries Bill, 1st Reading, 19 May 1931.
102 *House of Commons Debates*, 5th ser., vol. 252, col. 1786, Hospital Lotteries Bill, 1st Reading, 19 May 1931. Davidson's Bill got past the second reading after the 1931 election, though with half a greatly shrunken PLP opposed to it: McClymont, 'Labour Party's Attitude to Gambling', p. 83.
103 *Christian World*, 9 April 1936.
104 Snowden, *Autobiography*, vol. 2, p. 855.

105 Coleman, *The Irish Sweep*, pp. 98–102; *House of Commons Debates*, 5th ser., vol. 291, col. 1137–51, Sir John Gilmour speaking on the Betting and Lotteries Bill, 2nd Reading, 27 June 1934.
106 *House of Commons Debates*, 5th ser., vol. 293, cols. 1627, 1654, Betting and Lotteries Bill, 3rd Reading, 13 November 1934; McClymont, 'Labour Party's Attitude to Gambling', pp. 104–5.
107 McClymont, 'Labour Party's Attitude to Gambling', p. 112.
108 McClymont, 'Labour Party's Attitude to Gambling', pp. 114–15.
109 *House of Commons Debates*, 5th ser., vol. 293, col. 1254, Betting and Lotteries Bill, 3rd Reading, 13 November 1934.
110 *House of Commons Debates*, 5th ser., vol. 293, col. 1160, Betting and Lotteries Bill, 3rd Reading, 13 November 1934.
111 *House of Commons Debates*, 5th ser., vol. 293, col. 1155, Betting and Lotteries Bill, 3rd Reading, 13 November 1934.
112 *House of Commons Debates*, 5th ser., vol. 310, col.2353, Betting (No. 1) Bill, 2nd Reading, 3 April 1936.
113 McClymont, 'Labour Party's Attitude to Gambling', pp. 85–92.
114 *House of Commons Debates*, 5th ser., vol. 310, col. 2348, Betting (No. 1) Bill, 2nd Reading, 3 April 1936.
115 McClymont, 'Labour Party's Attitude to Gambling', pp. 110–20.
116 Stockport Archives: B/X/7/12: Jacqueline Turner, 'Labour's Lost Soul? Recovering the Labour Church', in Worley (ed.), *The Foundations of the Labour Party: Identities, Cultures and Perspectives, 1900–39* (Farnham: Ashgate, 2009), p. 168.
117 F. Reid, 'Socialist Sunday Schools in Britain 1892–1939', *International Review of Social History* 11/1 (1966), pp. 18–47.
118 Tudur Jones, *Congregationalism in Wales*, p. 228.
119 *Bradford Pioneer*, 30 October 1931.
120 *Baptist Times*, 9 May 1929.
121 *Co-operative News*, 30 March 1929.
122 *Methodist Times*, 27 November 1924.
123 D. J. Vaughan, letter to *Methodist Times*, 20 December 1923.
124 Bebbington, *The Nonconformist Conscience*, p. 12.
125 Winterton, *Harvest of the Years*, p. 54.
126 *Bradford Pioneer*, 18 August 1926. See also Simmons, *Soap-Box Evangelist*, pp. 58, 64.
127 G. Alcock, letter to *Primitive Methodist Leader*, 18 September 1924.
128 NRO: Docking Primitive Methodist circuit quarterly meeting minutes, 4 June 1924; Edwards, *Ploughboy's Progress*, p. 98.
129 WYAB: 66D 83/7/1/d, Edward Siddle, municipal election handbill, 1924.
130 *Bradford Pioneer*, 21 September 1928.
131 PROL: LGP, G/4/6/1, Clynes to Lloyd George, 18 February 1931.
132 *House of Commons Debates*, 5th ser., vol. 251, col. 691, 20 April 1931. See also Sir John Simon in the same debate at col. 669 and *Christian World*, 9 April 1931.
133 *Daily Herald*, 25 January 1923.
134 *House of Commons Debates*, 5th ser., vol. 267, col. 1955, 29 June 1932.
135 *House of Commons Debates*, 5th ser., vol. 264, cols. 930–3, 13 April 1932.
136 *House of Commons Debates*, 5th ser., vol. 267, col. 1889, 29 June 1932.
137 Edward Gillett and Kenneth A. MacMahon, *A History of Hull* (London: Oxford University Press, 1980), p. 383; *House of Commons Debates*, 5th ser., vol. 326, cols. 356–9, 7 July 1937.

138 *Portsmouth Evening News*, 14 February 1933; *House of Commons Debates*, 5th ser., vol. 264, col. 689, 13 April 1932.
139 *House of Commons Debates*, 5th ser., vol. 264, col. 943, 13 April 1932.
140 LCA: LFCC minutes, 29 July 1922.
141 Marvin Swartz, *The Union of Democratic Control in British Politics during the First World War* (Oxford: Clarendon, 1971), p. 42.
142 David Marquand, *Ramsay MacDonald* (London: Cape, 1977), p. 221.
143 Marquand, *MacDonald*, pp. 250–2.
144 *The Crusader*, 23 May 1919.
145 *Labour and the Nation* (London: Labour Party, 1928), pp. 54–5.
146 *Methodist Times*, 10 April 1924.
147 *House of Commons Debates*, 5th ser., vol. 171, col. 193, 17 March 1924.
148 *House of Commons Debates*, 5th ser., vol. 171, col. 400, 18 March 1924.
149 *New Leader*, 14 March 1924.
150 *House of Commons Debates*, 5th ser., vol. 171, col. 359, 18 March 1924.
151 *House of Commons Debates*, 5th ser., vol. 171, cols. 142–3, 160–1, 164, 166, 17 March 1924. Haden Guest was a Theosophist according to the *Labour Leader*, 13 March 1919.
152 *House of Commons Debates*, 5th ser., vol. 171, cols. 83–196, 17 March 1924.
153 *LYM* (1924), p. 61.
154 *Ploughshare*, August 1917.
155 Ceadel, *Pacifism in Britain*, p. 80.
156 Ceadel, *Pacifism in Britain*, p. 82; Raymond A. Jones, *Arthur Ponsonby: The Politics of Life* (Bromley: Christopher Helm, 1989), chap. 5.
157 *Methodist Times*, 1 January 1931.
158 Davies, *Socialist Employer*, p. 26.
159 F. W. Pethick-Lawrence, *Fate Has Been Kind* (London: Hutchinson, 1943), p. 185.
160 Michael R. Gordon, *Conflict and Consensus in Labour's Foreign Policy 1914–1965* (Stanford, CA: Stanford University Press, 1969), p. 74.
161 Brockway, *Bermondsey Story*, p. 188.
162 Pethick-Lawrence, *Fate*, p. 188.
163 Bullock, *Ernest Bevin: Volume1*, pp. 562–71.
164 Ceadel, *Pacifism in Britain*, p. 275.
165 Thurtle, *Time's Winged Chariot*, p. 121.
166 See George Lansbury, *My Quest for Peace* (London: Michael Joseph, 1938).
167 Brockway, *Bermondsey Story*, p. 221.
168 *Liverpool Red Book* (1936), pp. 592–3; WYAB: BTC minutes, 19 September 1935; *Bradford Trades Council Year Book* [*BTCYB*] (1939), p. 3; LPA: NEC minutes file, August 1935.
169 *House of Commons Debates*, 5th ser., vol. 318, col. 425, oral answers, 25 November 1936.
170 Jerry H. Brookshire, '"Speak for England", Act for England: Labour's Leadership and British National Security under the Threat of War in the Late 1930s', *European History Quarterly* 29/2 (1999), p. 256; *House of Commons Debates*, 5th ser., vol. 320, cols. 2226–35, 25 February 1937.
171 Wilfrid Wellock, *Destruction or Construction: An Open Letter to Members of the Labour Party* (London: Peace Pledge Union, 1938), pp. 2–6; *South London Press*, 23 September 1938.
172 *South London Press*, 19 May 1939.

173 Phillips Price, *My Three Revolutions*, p. 274.
174 Blackburn, *Tomlinson*, p. 28.
175 Pethick-Lawrence, *Fate*, p. 200.
176 Attlee, *As It Happened*, pp. 106–8.
177 Brockway, *Socialism over Sixty Years*, p. 88.
178 Snowden, *Autobiography*, vol. 1, p. 134.
179 Cited in Elizabeth Bradburn, *Margaret McMillan: Framework and Expansion of Nursery Education* (Redhill: Denholm House Press, 1976), p. 26. See also Brockway, *Socialism over Sixty Years*, pp. 54–60; *Christian World*, 9 April 1931.
180 WYAB: Federated Trades Councils of Yorkshire minutes, 24 June 1929.
181 Green, 'Education for Citizenship', p. 154.
182 FHL: Box V, 1/3.
183 *Brotherhood Outlook*, November 1922.
184 *Labour and the Nation*, p. 54.
185 LPA: NEC minutes, 18 March 1929.
186 *Christian World*, 1 February 1906.
187 Jones, *Three Score Years*, pp. 243–6.
188 A. J. A. Morris, *C. P. Trevelyan 1870–1958* (Belfast: Blackstaff, 1977), p. 176.
189 *House of Commons Debates*, 5th ser., vol. 247, col. 200, 21 January 1931.
190 *School Child and Juvenile Worker*, November 1931.
191 *Christian World*, 19 February 1931; *Baptist Times*, 29 January 1931, 5 March 1931.
192 *School Child and Juvenile Worker*, July-August 1931.
193 *School Child and Juvenile Worker*, March 1931.
194 LPA: NEC minutes, 'Memorandum on Denominational Education', April 1935.
195 Waller, *Democracy and Sectarianism*, pp. 341–2.
196 Thompson, 'The Older Free Churches', p. 109.
197 NRO: GEP, Address, 'The History and Place of Lay-Preaching' (n.d.).
198 *Bradford Pioneer*, 22 June 1928.
199 Bebbington, *The Nonconformist Conscience*, p. 35; *House of Commons Debates*, 5th ser., vol. 120, col. 1823–97, 7 November 1919.
200 *Christian World*, 17 May 1923; Porritt, *Memories*, p. 132.
201 Marquand, *MacDonald*, p. 307.
202 *House of Commons Debates*, 5th ser., vol. 218, col. 1277, 14 June 1928.
203 LMA: Liberation Society executive committee minutes, 18 May 1936.
204 Sir Beddoe Rees explained this in the 2nd Reading debate on the Tithe Bill in *House of Commons Debates*, 5th ser., vol. 185, col. 866, 18 June 1925. See also NRO: Thetford Free Church Council minutes, 14 February 1921.
205 *House of Commons Debates*, 5th ser., vol. 185, col. 860, 18 June 1925.
206 W. C. Elliott speaking on the Tithe Bill, 2nd Reading, *House of Commons Debates*, 5th ser., vol. 312, col. 407, 13 May 1936.
207 Letter to *Christian World*, 1 October 1931.
208 James Cameron, *Yesterday's Witness* (London: BBC, 1979), pp. 71–4; Whetham, *Agrarian History*, p. 263.
209 *House of Commons Debates*, 5th ser., vol. 314, col. 56, 29 June 1936.
210 Bebbington, 'Free Church MPs of the 1906 Parliament', pp. 136–50.
211 *Methodist Times*, 24 October 1935.
212 NCEFC, *Annual Report* (1938–39), p. 2.
213 J. J. Norwich (ed.), *The Duff Cooper Diaries 1915–1951* (London: Orion, 2005), p. 188 (8 January 1924).

214 Patrick Leigh Fermor, *A Time of Gifts* (London: John Murray, 2004 [1977]), p. 109.
215 Catterall, *Labour and the Politics of Alcohol*, pp. 23, 33; Martin Pugh, *Speak for Britain! A New History of the Labour Party* (London: Vintage, 2011), pp. 154–5.
216 Letter to *Christian World*, 1 December 1938.

Chapter 7

1 *Methodist Times*, 10 October 1918.
2 T. Rhondda Williams, *Making the Better World* (London: Independent Press, 1929), p. 2.
3 *Brotherhood Outlook*, September 1928; Belden, *George Whitefield*, pp. 247–51; Payne, *Free Church Tradition*, pp. 116–28; F. H. Stead, *The Story of Social Christianity*, vol.2 (London: Clarke, 1922), p. 177; *Christian World*, 25 August 1932.
4 *Christian World*, 2 November 1922; *Methodist Times*, 4 February 1926; C. E. Stansfield, 'Social Responsibility and the Teacher', *Friends Quarterly Examiner* (1927), pp. 6–7; see also Field, 'Zion's People', Parts 1–3.
5 Caradog Jones, *Social Survey*, vol. 3, pp. 334–40.
6 *British Weekly*, 23 February 1928, 1 March 1928, 8 March 1928. See also Gill, *Myth*, pp. 78–79.
7 Hugh Jenkins, letter to *Christian World*, 27 February 1936.
8 George Haw (ed.), *Christianity and the Working Classes* (London: Macmillan, 1906), p. 26; interview: Joyce Jewson, 4 September 1986; Lofthouse, 'The Warden', p. 57.
9 Bradford Central Library: Memoirs of T. Rhondda Williams (newscuttings); Brennan, Cooney and Pollins, *Social Change in South West Wales*, p. 85.
10 See, for instance, NRO: FC18/45, Fakenham Primitive Methodist circuit trustees 1879–1932.
11 Williams, *Religious Belief and Popular Culture*, chaps. 4 and 6; Entwistle, '"Hope, Colour, and Citizenship"', pp. 20–38.
12 Banks, *The Story So Far*, pp. 43, 103–4; Harold Murray, *Twixt Aldgate Pump and Poplar: The Story of Fifty Years of Adventure in East London* (London: Epworth, 1935), p. 131.
13 Spencer, *Glory in the Garret*, pp. 165–7; Lax, *Lax*, p. 94; Field, 'Sociological Profile', p. 91.
14 James Walvin, *English Urban Life 1776-1851*(London: Routledge, 2013), pp. 105–6.
15 For example, Hamilton, *Remembering*, pp. 20–1; Harry Snell, *Men, Movements and Myself* (London: Dent, 1938).
16 Kent, *From Darwin to Blatchford*, pp. 28–33; Owen Chadwick, *The Secularization of the European Mind in the Nineteenth Century* (Cambridge: Cambridge University Press, 1975), chap. 4; Frank Ballard in W. Forbes Gray (ed.), *Non-Church Going: Its Reasons and Remedies* (Edinburgh: Oliphant, Anderson & Ferrier, 1911), pp. 137–40; Field, 'Gradualist or Revolutionary Secularisation?', p. 88.
17 Cairns, *Army and Religion*, pp. 2,7, 30, 274; Snape, *Revisiting Religion*, p. 35.
18 Entwistle, '"Hope, Colour, and Citizenship"', pp. 20–38; Spencer, *Glory in the Garret*, chaps. 6 and 11.
19 F. Herbert Stead in W. Forbes Gray (ed.), *Non-Church Going: Its Reasons and Remedies* (Edinburgh: Oliphant, Anderson & Ferrier, 1911), p. 86.
20 James, 'Religious Apathy', p. 478; W. H. Marshall, letter to *Christian World*, 25 June 1931.

21 Cox, *Lambeth*, pp. 105–7; Williams, *Religious Belief and Popular Culture*, chaps. 4 and 6.
22 Cairns, *Army and Religion*, p. 33; Cox, *Lambeth*, p. 91.
23 Milne, 'County Road', p. 14.
24 Green, *Religion in the Age of Decline*, pp. 152–64.
25 *The Crusader*, May/June 1928.
26 Sellers, *Salute to Pembroke*, p. 31.
27 Barker, *Christ in the Valley*, p. 77; see also Pope, *Building Jerusalem*, p. 242.
28 Elizabeth Roberts, *A Woman's Place: An Oral History of Working-Class Women 1890–1940* (Oxford: Blackwell, 1984), pp. 5–6.
29 See also Morgan Jones in C. G. Ammon (ed.), *Labour's Dynamic* (London: Labour Publishing, 1922), p. 39.
30 Marquand, *MacDonald*, p. 280.
31 Brennan, Cooney and Pollins, *Social Change in South West Wales*, p. 98.
32 Francis and Smith, *The Fed*, pp. 272, 286, 291.
33 R. W. Postgate, Ellen Wilkinson and J. F. Horrabin, *A Worker's History of the Great Strike* (London: Plebs League, 1927), pp. 41–3.
34 WYAB: Bradford Trades Council minutes 28 September 1922, 17 April 1924, 31 July 1924, 16 April 1925, 18 March 1926, 15 April 1926.
35 J. W. James, 'The Working Man's Criticism of the Churches', *Congregational Quarterly* (1932), pp. 66–7; Ballard in W. Forbes Gray (ed.), *Non-Church Going: Its Reasons and Remedies* (Edinburgh: Oliphant, Anderson & Ferrier, 1911), p. 143; Cairns, *Army and Religion*, pp. 65, 205; Morgan, 'Herbert Gray and the Making of Christian Masculinities', p. 175.
36 Henry Solly, *These Eighty Years* (London: Simpkin & Marshall, 1893) cited in George Tremlett, *Clubmen* (London: Secker & Warburg, 1987), p. 22.
37 *AYB* (1926), p.74.
38 *House of Commons Debates*, 5th ser., vol. 283, col. 1999, 8 December 1933.
39 Rowntree, *Poverty and Progress*, p. 333.
40 Letter to *Christian World*, 2 July 1931.
41 *British Weekly*, 1 March 1928.
42 Ross McKibbin, 'Working-Class Gambling in Britain 1880–1939', *Past & Present* 82 (1979), p. 154.
43 Lawson, *A Man's Life*, pp. 76–80; Morgan, *Rebirth of a Nation*, p.198.
44 Thomas, *Christian Heritage*, p. 59.
45 *House of Commons Debates*, 5th ser., vol. 169, col. 1270, 15 February 1924.
46 Interview, Arthur Amis, 10 September 1986; written communications, Peter Archer, Ernest Armstrong, November 1986.
47 Kinnear, *The British Voter*, p. 134; Howard C. Jones, 'The Labour Party in Cardiganshire', *Ceredigion* 9 (1980–84), p. 56.
48 Kinnear, *The British Voter*, p. 126.
49 Whetham, *Agrarian History*, pp. 130–6; S. N. Broadberry and A Ritschl, 'Real Wages, Productivity and Unemployment in Britain and Germany during the 1920s', *Explorations in Economic History* 32 (1995), pp. 327–49.
50 BMA: Lancashire and Cheshire Miners' Federation minutes, 22 May 1920.
51 Cited by A Backbench MP, 'Thoughts on Our Present Discontents', *Socialist Review* 25 (1925), p. 68.
52 *Christian World*, 4 September 1924.
53 *Brotherhood Outlook*, June 1926.

54 Stead, *Proletarian Gospel*, pp. 68–74.
55 G. W. McDonald and Howard F. Gospel, 'The Mond-Turner Talks 1927–1933: A Study in Industrial Co-operation', *Historical Journal* 16/4 (1973), p. 809; Hodge, *Workman's Cottage*, p. 72.
56 J. H. Thomas, *My Story* (London: Hutchinson, 1937), pp. 82–3.
57 *Bolton Journal*, March 1919.
58 Lawson, *A Man's Life*, p. 261; Betty D. Vernon, *Ellen Wilkinson* (London: Croom Helm, 1982), p. 1.
59 *Daily Chronicle*, 15 November 1924.
60 *Justice for All*, 15 October 1921.
61 *Christian World*, 1 April 1926.
62 Philip S. Bagwell, 'The Triple Industrial Alliance 1913–1922', in Asa Briggs and John Savile (eds), *Essays in Labour History 1886–1923* (London: Macmillan, 1971), p. 103.
63 *LYB* (1927), p. 13.
64 Thurtle, *Time's Winged Chariot*, pp. 96–7; Herbert Tracey, 'From Industrial to Political Action', in Herbert Tracey (ed.), *The British Labour Party*, vol. 2, p. 158; M. Phillips Price, 'The General Strike and a Labour Majority', *Socialist Review* (July 1926), pp. 9–15; Michael Savage, *The Dynamics of Working-Class Politics: The Labour Movement in Preston, 1880–1940* (Cambridge: Cambridge University Press, 1987), pp. 177–90.
65 *Bradford Daily Telegraph*, 2 November 1926.
66 J. F. Clarke, 'An Interview with Sir Will Lawther', *BSSLH* 18 (1969), p. 14.
67 J. Ramsay MacDonald, 'The Outlook', *Socialist Review* (June 1926), p. 8; *BTCYB* (1927), p. 25.
68 Cited in *Bolton Journal and Guardian*, 5 May 1933.
69 Cited in *Bolton Evening News*, 31 October 1927.
70 Mary Agnes Hamilton, *Arthur Henderson* (London: Heinemann, 1938), pp. 24–6.
71 Charles Dellheim,'The Creation of a Company Culture: Cadbury's 1861–1931', *American Historical Review* 92/1 (1987), p. 38; Rowntree, *Industrial Unrest*, pp. 37–8; G. H. Shakespeare (revised by Chris Pickford), 'Sir (Percy) Malcolm Stewart (1872–1951)', ODNB, http://www.oxforddnb.com/view/article/36297 [accessed 27 August 2015]; Clyde Binfield, 'Industry, Philanthropy and Christian Citizenship: Pioneers in Paternalism', in Lesley Husselbee and Paul Ballard (eds), *Free Churches and Society: The Nonconformist Contribution to Social Welfare 1800–2010* (London: Continuum, 2012), pp. 107–9; Horace B. Pointing, *Political Thought in the Society of Friends* (London: Friends Book Centre, 1939), p. 24.
72 Other Free Churchmen to serve on Whitley's committee included Arthur Greenwood and Malcolm Sparkes.
73 Rodney Lowe, 'The Failure of Consensus in Britain: The National Industrial Conference, 1919–1921', *Historical Journal* 21/3 (1978), pp. 649–75; *Methodist Times*, 24 April 1919; *Christian World*, 8 May 1919.
74 *CYB*, (1928), pp. 5–6.
75 *Brotherhood Outlook*, July 1927.
76 *Brotherhood Outlook*, December 1927.
77 Brockway, *Socialism over Sixty Years*, pp. 247–8.
78 *Daily Herald*, 24 August 1928.
79 *Brotherhood Outlook*, May 1928.
80 *Financial Times*, 18 October 1927; *Brotherhood Outlook*, November 1927. Hicks and Blades were both active in the Brotherhood movement.
81 *Brotherhood Outlook*, May 1928.

82 *Brotherhood Outlook*, December 1927.
83 Bullock, *Ernest Bevin: Volume 1*, pp. 399–403; *New Leader*, 20 January 1928.
84 'Spotter', 'The Mond–Turner Conversations', *Socialist Review* (Sept 1929), pp. 10–14.
85 *British Weekly*, 10 January 1924;Newland, *Newland of Claremont*, p. 182.
86 Casey, 'The Overlooked Pacifist Tradition, Part II', pp. 518–20.
87 *Methodist Times*, 21 December 1922.
88 Edwards, *From the Valley*, p.170; BHRU AOO12/10.
89 *The Crusader*, 2 February 1923.
90 Barker, *Christ in the Valley*, pp. 44–5, 57; Francis and Smith, *The Fed*, pp. 267–70.
91 Cited in Pitt, *Our Unemployed*, p. 52. See also Pilgrim Trust, *Men without Work* (Cambridge: Cambridge University Press, 1938).
92 *Methodist Recorder*, 28 November 1935.
93 Sidney Webb and Beatrice Webb, *Soviet Russia: A New Civilisation?* 2v. (London: Longmans Green, 1935).
94 John Lewis, 'The Jesus of History', in John Lewis (ed.), *Christianity and the Social Revolution* (London: Gollancz, 1935), pp. 86–102.
95 W. F. Lofthouse, *Christianity in the Social State* (London: John Heritage, 1936), pp. 125–9; *Christian World*, 9 April 1936.
96 *CYB* (1936), p. 125.
97 A. Herbert Gray, 'Christ's Conception of the Kingdom of God', in Percy Dearmer (ed.), *Christianity and the Crisis* (London: Gollancz, 1933), p. 195
98 Reinhold Niebuhr, 'Christian Politics and Communist Religion' in John Lewis (ed.), *Christianity and the Social Revolution* (London: Gollancz, 1935), p. 464.
99 H. G. Wood, *The Truth and Error of Communism* (London: SCM Press, 1933), p. 7.
100 Gray, 'Christ's Conception', p. 195.
101 *Batley Reporter*, 24 December 1932. Brooke was a Methodist.
102 Barker, *Christ in the Valley*, p. 60.
103 *Bolton Evening News*, 2 November 1932. On the Pioneer Preachers see Smith, *Religion and the Rise of Labour*, pp. 42–3.
104 The notorious Circular No.16 (1934) and related correspondence can be found in Modern Records Centre, University of Warwick: TUC papers, MSS, 292/777/1 and 292/777/2.
105 Egon Wertheimer, *Portrait of the Labour Party* (London: Putnam, 1929), pp. xi, 196–7.
106 Willie Thompson, *The Good Old Cause: British Communism 1920–1991* (London: Pluto, 1992), pp. 15, 37, 51–64; Matthew Worley, *Class versus Class: The Communist Party in Britain between the Wars* (London: I. B. Tauris, 2002), pp. 315–20.
107 Peter Clarke, *Lancashire and the New Liberalism* (Cambridge: Cambridge, 1971); Clarke, 'Electoral Sociology', pp. 31–55; Peter Clarke, 'The Progressive Movement in England', *Transactions of the Royal Historical Society* 5th ser., vol. 24 (1974), pp. 154–82 ; E. V. Emy, *Liberals, Radicals and Social Politics 1892–1914* (Cambridge: Cambridge University Press, 1973); A. J. A. Morris (ed.), *Edwardian Radicalism 1900–1914* (London: Routledge and Kegan Paul, 1974).
108 Ross McKibbin, *Parties and People: England 1914–1951* (Oxford: Oxford University Press, 2010), esp. pp. 95–6, 186; Stevens, 'Electoral Sociology', pp. 62–94.
109 *British Weekly*, 23 February 1928; Andrew August, *The British Working Class 1832–1940* (Harlow: Longman, 2007), p. 113.
110 Catterall, 'Slums and Salvation', pp. 114–16.

111 Robbins, 'Free Churchmen and the Twenty Years Crisis', p. 348.
112 Birch, *Small Town Politics*, pp. 18–29, 178–86.
113 Johnson, 'The Nationalisation of English Rural Politics', p. 23.
114 *Christian World*, 26 October 1922; John Ramsden, 'Newport and the Fall of the Coalition', in Chris Cook and John Ramsden (eds), *By-Elections in British Politics* (London: UCL Press, 1997), pp. 35–7.
115 Jon Lawrence, 'Class and Gender in the Making of Urban Toryism 1880–1914', *English Historical Review* 108/428 (1993), pp. 629–52.
116 Catterall, *Labour and the Politics of Alcohol*, pp. 6, 20.
117 Cook, *Age of Alignment*, p. 78.
118 *Christian World*, 23 November 1922.
119 *House of Commons Debates*, 5th ser., vol. 169, col. 1260, 15 February 1924; *Morning Advertiser*, 29 November 1923.
120 *Morning Advertiser*, 29 May 1929.
121 *Morning Advertiser*, 6 November 1935.
122 IAS: *Some Club Problems* (London: Licensed Victuallers' Central Protection Society of London, 1932).
123 Martin Pugh, 'The Rise of Labour and the Political Culture of Conservatism 1890–1945', *History* 87/288 (2002), pp. 514–37.
124 Maurice Cowling, *The Impact of Labour: The Beginning of Modern British Politics* (Cambridge: Cambridge University Press, 1971).
125 Pamela M. Graves, *Labour Women: Women in British Working-Class Politics 1918–1939* (Cambridge: Cambridge University Press, 1994), pp. 181–3; Savage, *The Dynamics of Working-Class Politics*, pp. 177–80; Worley, *Labour inside the Gate*, pp. 119–20, 188–9; Ball, *Portrait of a Party*, pp. 82–90.
126 Hamilton, *Remembering*, p. 175.
127 BMA: Bolton Oral History Project Tape 14c.
128 *New Leader*, 21 November 1924.
129 LPA: NEC minutes, May 1921.
130 *Christian World*, 21 March 1918; Williamson, *National Crisis*, p. 37.
131 A Nonconformist, 'Reflections on the Election', *Socialist Review* 24 (1924), p. 225.
132 Reg Sorensen, *The 'Red Flag' and Patriotism* (Southampton: Hobbs, n.d. c1925), p. 6.
133 *New Nation*, February 1934, March 1934, April 1934; Rigby, *Wellock*, p. 52.
134 See, for instance, Norman McCord, *North East England: An Economic and Social History* (London: Batsford, 1979), p. 203.
135 Salter, *A Message to Labour*, p. 2.
136 Cox, *Lambeth*, pp. 23–4.
137 Cited in Martin Pugh, *Speak for Britain!*, p. 3.

Chapter 8

1 West London Mission, *Annual Report* (1899), cited in Bagwell, *Outcast London*, p. 47.
2 Thomas, *Christian Heritage*, pp. 76–7.
3 Cited in Wolfenden, 'English Nonconformity', p. 19.
4 See John Briggs and Ian Sellers (eds), *Victorian Nonconformity* (London: Arnold, 1973), pp. 131–4.
5 Piper, *Century of Service*, pp. 56–7.

6 Cited in Catterall, 'Slums and Salvation', pp. 117–18.
7 Benjamin Waugh, *The Gaol Cradle, Who Rocks It?* (London: Strahan, 1873).
8 Catterall, 'Slums and Salvation', pp. 116–18.
9 Mearns, *Bitter Cry*, p. 24.
10 Cited in Wolfenden, 'English Nonconformity', p. 53.
11 Bebbington, 'Conscience and Politics', p. 57.
12 *CYB* (1939), pp. 71–2.
13 Brockway, *Socialism over Sixty Years*, p. 55.
14 *Methodist Recorder*, 30 March 1905.
15 *BTCYB* (1933), p. 3.
16 Percy Alden, 'That Reminds Me', *Congregational Quarterly* (1933), pp. 197–200.
17 Alden, 'That Reminds Me', p. 198; Wood and Ball, *Tom Bryan*, pp. 26–30; Thomas Phillips, 'The Evangel and "The Prayers"', *The Review of the Churches* (1925), p. 84.
18 Alden, 'That Reminds Me', p. 196; Pethick-Lawrence, *Fate*, p. 49; *Christian World*, 29 November 1923; Turberfield, *Lidgett*, p. 87;Gault, *Kingsley Wood*, p. 26.
19 Thompson, 'Clifford's Social Gospel', p. 203.
20 Cox, *Lambeth*, pp. 241–2.
21 *BTCYB* (1919), pp. 29–31.
22 Percy Alden, 'Post-War Unemployment', *Contemporary Review* (December 1930), p. 721.
23 Pointing, *Social Thought in the Society of Friends*, p. 18.
24 Rowntree, *Industrial Unrest*, p. 25.
25 C. M. Lloyd, 'The Poor Law', in Herbert Tracey (ed.), *The Book of the Labour Party* vol. 3, (London: Caxton, 1925), p. 13.
26 NCEFCP: NCEFC minutes, 23 September 1921.
27 Bondfield, *A Life's Work*, p. 249.
28 Alfred Tuke Priestman, *Socialism an Essentially Christian Movement* (London: West, 1901), p. 2.
29 *New Leader*, 27 April 1928.
30 E. R. Hartley, *Rounds with the Socialists* (London: Independent Labour Party, 1914), p. 8.
31 *CYB* (1936), pp. 70–81.
32 FHL: Box V, 1/3, J. H. Hudson 'General Election Handbill' (1922).
33 George Benson, *Socialism and the Teaching of Jesus* (London: Independent Labour Party, 1925), p. 8.
34 *House of Commons Debates*, 5th series, vol. 174, cols. 221–5, 27 May 1924.
35 *Norfolk County Council 1889–1974* (Norwich: Norfolk County Council, 1974), p. 12.
36 LCA: 331, TRA 6/8, Liverpool Labour Party, draft copy of 1919 municipal election manifesto.
37 Rowett, 'Labour Party and Local Government', chap. 6.
38 *LYB* (1932), p. 4.
39 H. A. Marquand, 'The Depressed Areas – A Problem of Regional Development', *Liverpool Quarterly* (April 1936), p. 80.
40 Morgan, *Rebirth of a Nation*, pp. 226–7.
41 http://labourmanifesto.com/1935/1935-labour-manifesto.shtml [accessed 18 August 2015].
42 Newland, *Newland of Claremont*, pp. 82–7.
43 Spencer, *Glory in the Garret*, pp. 33–4.

44 Commission of Inquiry into the Distressed Areas, *Labour and the Distressed Areas: A Programme of Immediate Action* (London: Labour Party, 1937), p. 15; Bagwell, *Outcast London*, p. 98.
45 Frost, *Pioneers* pp. 25–6.
46 Bagwell, *Outcast London*, pp.102–6; Lax, *Lax*, p. 184. See also Murray, *Twixt*, pp. 154–5.
47 Cox, *Lambeth*, pp. 209, 273; Birch, *Small Town Politics*, p. 176.
48 Lofthouse, 'The Warden', p. 73.
49 Clifford, *Venture in Faith*, pp.155–9; Frank Prochaska, *Christianity and Social Service in Modern Britain* (Oxford: Oxford University Press, 2006), p. 149.
50 Frost, *Pioneers*, pp. 25–6.
51 Anthony Giddens (ed.), *Emile Durkheim: Selected Writings* (Cambridge: Cambridge University Press, 1972), p. 220.
52 Cited in Roger Boesche, *Tocqueville's Road Map: Methodology, Liberalism, Revolution and Despotism* (Lanham, MD: Lexington Books, 2006), p. 153.
53 Peter Catterall, '"Efficiency with Freedom"? Debates about the British Constitution in the Twentieth Century', in Catterall et al. (eds), *Reforming the Constitution: Debates in Twentieth Century Britain* (London: Cass, 2000), pp. 1–42.
54 Peter Catterall and Chris Brady, 'The Development and Role of Cabinet Committees in Britain' in R. A. W. Rhodes (ed.), *Transforming British Government: Volume 1, Changing Institutions* (Basingstoke: Macmillan, 2000), p. 160.
55 TNA: CAB 104/124, Sir Maurice Hankey, 'The Supreme Control in War', 24 May 1928, p. 4.
56 Philip Williamson, 'Christian Conservatism and the Totalitarian Challenge 1933–40', *English Historical Review* 115 (2000), p. 607; Keith Robbins, 'Britain, 1940 and "Christian Civilisation"', in Keith Robbins, *History, Religion and Identity in Modern Britain* (London: Hambledon, 1993), chap. 14.
57 Wilkinson, *Dissent or Conform?*, pp. 218, 283; S. J. D. Green, *The Passing of Protestant England: Secularisation and Social Change c.1920–1960* (Cambridge: Cambridge University Press, 2011), p. 53.
58 AP: U DMN/9/6, draft autobiography, chap. 3, p. 30.
59 *Church Times*, 14 January 1921.
60 AP: U DMN/9/1, 'The City Churches', undated lecture, c1940s.
61 W. Emrys Davies, 'The Late R. J. Davies', in *Ince and Westhoughton Constituencies and Parts of Wigan Souvenir Booklet 1906–1956* (Wigan: privately printed, 1956), pp. 16–18.
62 *FCYB* (1923), p. 56.
63 *Brotherhood Outlook*, October 1922.
64 *Christian World*, 15 January 1931.
65 Dan Griffiths, letter to *New Leader*, 28 June 1931.
66 Spencer, *Glory in the Garret*, p. 109.
67 See George Bernard Shaw's preface to *Major Barbara* (London: Methuen, [1907] 2008).
68 *Methodist Times*, 3 December 1936.
69 Thomas, *Christian Heritage*, p. 50.
70 Maldwyn Edwards, *The Christian Critique of the Welfare State* (London: Epworth, 1960), p. 8.
71 BHRU: H0010/01/028-9.

Conclusion

1 *Methodist Times*, 21 February 1924.
2 Benson, *Socialism and the Teaching of Jesus*, p. 8.
3 AP: U DMN/2/3, diary 21 February 1929.
4 Catterall, *Labour and the Politics of Alcohol*, pp. 28–30.
5 Horne, *Popular History*, pp. 427–9; *Christian World*, 5 August 1926.
6 Smith, *Religion and the Rise of Labour*, pp. 166–7; Pope, *Building Jerusalem*, chap. 2.
7 *Methodist Times*, 3 April 1919; Rigby, *Wellock*, p. 14.
8 Snape, *Revisiting Religion*, p. 35.
9 Keith Robbins, 'Britain, 1940, and "Christian Civilization"', in Keith Robbins, *History, Religion and Identity in Modern Britain* (London: Hambledon, 1993), pp. 195–214.
10 *British Weekly*, 24 February 1938.
11 Cited in Pope, 'Nonconformist Conscience', p. 454.
12 James Dingley, 'Sacred Communities: Religion and National Identities', *National Identities* 13/4 (2011), pp. 389–402.
13 *Bradford Pioneer*, 19 September 1919.
14 *Methodist Times*, 11 July 1929.
15 Henderson in Haw (ed.), *Christianity and the Working Classes*, p. 119.
16 Interview: Fred and Grace Wilkinson, 8 August 1986.
17 Rowntree, *Progress and Poverty*, pp. 425–6.
18 Harry Jeffs, *The Goodly Heritage of the Free Churches* (London: Independent Press, 1927), pp. 7–13.
19 Michael Home, *Winter Harvest: A Norfolk Boyhood* (London: Macdonald, 1967), p. 32.
20 Harold Wilson, *Memoirs: The Making of a Prime Minister, 1916–1964* (London: Weidenfeld & Nicolson, 1986), p. 34.
21 Though see Moore, *Pitmen, Preachers and Politics*, p. 172.
22 Leventhal, *Arthur Henderson*.
23 Pugh, 'The Rise of Labour', p. 522.
24 McKibbin, 'Marxism', pp. 328–30.
25 *Ploughshare*, June 1919.
26 See, for instance, Joseph Jones, *The Coal Scuttle* (London: Faber, 1936).
27 Cited in Rigby, *Wellock*, p. 16.
28 Raymond Plant, 'The Anglican Church and the Secular State', in George Moyser (ed.), *The Church and Politics Today: The Role of the Church of England in Contemporary Politics* (Edinburgh: T. & T. Clark, 1985), p. 328.
29 *The Times*, 18 March 1931.
30 Pope, *Building Jerusalem*, pp. 236–40.
31 Hamilton, *Remembering*, pp. 294, 307–10; see also Wilkinson, *Dissent or Conform?*, pp.197–8; R. H. S. Crossman (ed.), *New Fabian Essays* (London: Turnstile Press, 1952), p. 8.
32 AP: U DMN/9/1, 'Whither', draft article for the *Christian World*, c1948.

Bibliography

Primary unpublished sources

Private papers

Charles Ammon Papers (Hull History Centre)
Sir Winston Churchill Papers (Churchill College, Cambridge)
Randall Davidson Papers (Lambeth Palace Library, London)
Sir George Edwards Papers (Norfolk Record Office, Norwich)
Edwin Gooch Papers (Norfolk Record Office, Norwich)
James Hindle Hudson Papers (Institute of Alcohol Studies, London)
David Lloyd George Papers (Parliamentary Record Office, London)
J. Ramsay MacDonald Papers (John Rylands Library, Manchester)
J. S. Middleton Papers (People's History Museum, Manchester)
W. J. Rowland Papers (Dr Williams's Library, London)
Alfred Salter Papers (Institute of Alcohol Studies, London)

Major organizational records

Bolton Central Library

Lancashire and Cheshire Miners Federation minutes

Dr Williams's Library, London

Federal Council of the Evangelical Free Churches Papers
National Council of the Evangelical Free Churches Papers

Friends House Library

Quaker Election Handbills and Papers
Socialist Quaker Society Papers

Liverpool Record Office

Liverpool District Labour Party and Trades Council Papers
Merseyside Free Church Council Papers

London Metropolitan Archives

Liberation Society Papers

People's History Museum, Manchester

Labour Party National Executive Committee minutes and papers

West Yorkshire Archives, Bradford

Batley, Morley and Ossett Divisional Labour Party Papers
Bradford Labour Party Municipal and General Election Handbills and Papers
Bradford Trades Council Papers
Federated Trades Councils of Yorkshire Executive Committee minutes

Primary printed sources

Official publications

Board of Education, *Report of the Consultative Committee on the Education of the Adolescent* (London: HMSO, 1927).

Report of the Royal Commission on Licensing (England and Wales) 1929–1931 (Cmd. 3988 xi 573).

House of Commons Debates 5th series.

Newspapers

Alliance News
Band of Hope Chronicle
Baptist Times
Bolton Citizen
Bolton Evening News
Bolton Journal and Guardian
Bradford Daily Telegraph
Bradford Pioneer
Bradford Socialist Vanguard
Bradford Telegraph and Argus
Bradford Weekly Telegraph
Bradford Worker
British Weekly
British Worker
Brotherhood Journal
Brotherhood Outlook
Christian World
Club and Institute Journal
Co-operative News
Crusader
Daily Herald
Eastern Daily Press
Free Church Chronicle
Free Churchman
Friend
Highroad
Inquirer
Labour Leader
Liberation Society Bulletin

Liberator
Liverpool Daily Post
Liverpool Echo
Liverpool Evening Express
Liverpool's Labour Voice
Methodist Recorder
Methodist Times
Morning Advertiser
New Leader
New Nation
Ploughshare
Primitive Methodist Leader
School Child and Juvenile Worker
Socialist Christian
Textile Workers' Record
Times
United Methodist
Yorkshire Evening Argus
Yorkshire Observer

Periodicals

Baptist Quarterly
Bolton Congregationalist
Bradford and District Baptist Magazine
Congregational Quarterly
Contemporary Review
Friends Quarterly Examiner
Holborn Review
Industrial Review
Liverpolitan
Liverpool and District Congregationalist
Liverpool Quarterly
London Quarterly and Holborn Review
London Quarterly Review
Merseyside Congregationalist
Review of the Churches
Socialist Review

Yearbooks

Alliance Year Book and Temperance Reformers Handbook
Bolton and District Operative Cotton Spinners Provincial Association Annual Report
Bradford Congregational Year Book
Bradford Town Mission Annual Report
Bradford Trades Council Year Book
Brotherhood Year Book
Congregational Year Book

Free Church Year Book
Friends Temperance Union Annual Reports
Liverpool, Bootle, Birkenhead and Wallasey Official Red Book
Labour Year Book
Minutes and Proceedings of the London Yearly Meeting of the Society of Friends
Minutes of the Methodist Conference
United Kingdom Band of Hope Union Annual Report

Published diaries, memoirs and interviews of reminiscences

Attlee, C. R., *As It Happened* (London: Heinemann, 1954).
Barker, R. J., *Christ in the Valley of Unemployment* (London: Hodder & Stoughton, 1936).
Bondfield, Margaret, *A Life's Work* (London: Hutchinson, 1948).
Braddock, Jack, and Bessie Braddock, *The Braddocks* (London: Macdonald, 1963).
Brockway, A. Fenner, *Inside the Left* (London: Allen & Unwin, 1942).
Brockway, A. Fenner, *Towards Tomorrow: The Autobiography of Fenner Brockway* (London: Hart-Davis MacGibbon, 1977).
Carlile, J. C., *My Life's Little Day* (London: Blackie, 1935).
Citrine, Walter, *Men and Work* (London: Hutchinson, 1964).
Clarke, J. F., 'An Interview with Sir Will Lawther', *BSSLH* 19 (1969), 14–21.
Clynes, J. R., *Memoirs, 1924–37* (London: Hutchinson, 1937).
Dalton, Hugh, *Call Back Yesterday: Memoirs 1887–1931* (London: Frederick Muller, 1953).
Davies, J. Percival, *The Politics of a Socialist Employer* (Skipton-in-Craven: Maurice Webb, 1929).
Edwards, George, *From Crow-Scaring to Westminster* (London: Labour Publishing, 1922).
Edwards, Wil Jon, *From the Valley I Came* (London: Angus & Robertson, 1956).
Garvie, A. E., *Memories and Meanings of My Life* (London: Allen & Unwin, 1938).
Green, Alfred, *Growing Up in Attercliffe* (Sheffield: New City Paperbacks, 1981).
Hamilton, Mary Agnes, *Remembering My Good Friends* (London: Cape, 1944).
Hartley, E. R., *Rounds with the Socialists* (London: Independent Labour Party, 1914).
Hobson, S. G., *Pilgrim to the Left: Memoirs of a Modern Revolutionist* (London: Arnold, 1938).
Hodge, John, *Workman's Cottage to Windsor Castle* (London: Sampson Low, 1931).
Hodges, Frank, *My Adventures as a Labour Leader* (London: Newnes, 1925).
Home, Michael, *Winter Harvest: A Norfolk Boyhood* (London: Macdonald, 1967).
Jeffs, Harry, *Press, Preachers and Politicians: Reminiscences 1874 to 1932* (London: Independent Press, 1938).
Jones, J. D., *Three Score Years and Ten* (London: Hodder & Stoughton, 1940)
Lawson, J. J., *A Man's Life* (London: Hodder & Stoughton, 1932).
Lax, W. H., *Lax His Book: The Autobiography of Lax of Poplar* (London: Epworth, 1937).
Lloyd George, David, *War Memoirs* 2v. 2nd ed. (London: Odhams, 1934).
Lunn, Sir Henry, *Nearing Harbour* (London: Nicholson & Watson, 1934).
Mallalieu, J. P. W., *On Larkhill* (London: Allison & Busby, 1983).
Middlemas, Keith (ed.), *Thomas Jones: The Whitehall Diary, Volume II 1926–1930* (London: Oxford University Press, 1969).
Morrison, Herbert (Lord Morrison of Lambeth), *Herbert Morrison: An Autobiography* (London: Odhams, 1960).
Murray, Harold, *Press, Pulpit and Pew* (London: Epworth, 1934).

Newland, F. W., *Newland of Claremont and Canning Town* (London: Epworth, 1932).
Norwich, J. J. (ed.), *The Duff Cooper Diaries: 1915–1951* (London: Orion, 2005).
Parker, John, *Father of the House: Fifty Years in Politics* (London: Routledge and Kegan Paul, 1982).
Pearce, Cyril, 'An Interview with Wilfrid Whiteley', *BSSLH* 18 (1969), 14–21.
Pethick-Lawrence, F. W., *Fate Has Been Kind* (London: Hutchinson, 1943).
Phillips Price, Morgan, *My Three Revolutions* (London: Allen & Unwin, 1969).
Porritt, Arthur, *The Best I Remember* (London: Cassell, 1922).
Porritt, Arthur, *More and More of Memories* (London: Allen & Unwin, 1947).
Rowse, A. L., *Autobiography of a Cornishman: A Cornish Childhood* (London: Cape, 1942).
Sage, Josiah, *Memoirs of Josiah Sage* (London: Lawrence & Wishart, 1951).
Samuel, Herbert, *Memoirs* (London: Cresset, 1950).
Sanders, W. Stephen, *Early Socialist Days* (London: L&V Woolf, 1927).
Shakespeare, Geoffrey, *Let Candles Be Brought In* (London: Macdonald, 1949).
Simmons, C. J., *Soap-Box Evangelist* (Chichester: Janay, 1972).
Snowden, Philip, *An Autobiography* 2v. (London: Nicholson & Watson, 1934).
Soper, Donald, *Calling for Action: An Autobiographical Enquiry* (London: Robson, 1984).
Spencer, Walter, *The Glory in the Garret* (London: Epworth, 1932).
Taylor, Eric, 'An Interview with Wesley Perrins', *BSSLH* 21 (1970), 16–24.
Thomas, George, *Mr Speaker* (London: Century, 1985).
Thomas, J. H., *My Story* (London: Hutchinson, 1937).
Thurtle, Ernest, *Time's Winged Chariot: Memories and Comments* (London: Chaterson, 1946).
Turner, Ben, *About Myself* (London: Cayme Press, 1930).
Wedgwood, J. C., *Memoirs of a Fighting Life* (London: Hutchinson, 1940).
Williams, T. Rhondda, *How I Found My Faith: A Religious Pilgrimage* (London: Cassell, 1938).
Williamson, Philip (ed.), *The Modernisation of Conservative Politics: The Diaries and Letters of William Bridgeman 1904–1935* (London: Historians' Press, 1988).
Wilson, Harold, *Memoirs: The Making of a Prime Minister, 1916–1964* (London: Weidenfeld & Nicolson, 1986).
Winterton, Wilfrid, *Harvest of the Years* (Birmingham: Templar Press, 1969).

Contemporary works

Ammon, C. G. (ed.), *Christ and Labour* (London: Jarrold, 1912).
Ammon, C. G., *Labour's Dynamic* (London: Labour Publishing, 1922).
Attlee, Clement, *The Labour Party in Perspective* (London: Gollancz, 1937).
Aubrey, M. E., *The Free Churches in Our National Life* (London: Carey Kingsgate, 1936).
Ballard, Frank, *The Rational Way to Spiritual Revival* (London: Kelly, 1917).
Barnes, G. N., *Religion and the Labour Movement* (London: Holborn Press, 1919).
Benson, George, *Socialism and the Teaching of Jesus* (London: Independent Labour Party, 1925).
Bodell Smith, H., *Christ and the Political Economists* (London: Daniel, 1926).
Bracher, S. V., *The Herald Book of Labour Members* (London: Labour Publishing, 1924).
Cairns, D. S. (ed.), *The Army and Religion* (London: Macmillan, 1919).
Carter, Henry (ed.), *For Christ and Humanity* (London: Epworth, 1935).

Commission of Inquiry into the Distressed Areas, *Labour and the Distressed Areas: A Programme of Immediate Action* (London: Labour Party, 1937).
Davis, Jerome (ed.), *Labor Speaks for Itself on Religion* (New York: Macmillan, 1929).
Edwards, Maldwyn, *The Christian Critique of the Welfare State* (London: Epworth, 1960).
Garvie, A. E., *The Fatherly Rule of God: A Study of Society, State and Church* (London: Hodder & Stoughton, 1935).
Glasier, Katherine Bruce, *Socialism for Beginners* (London: ILP Publication Department, 1929).
Gray, W. Forbes (ed.), *Non-Church Going: Its Reasons and Remedies* (Edinburgh: Oliphant, Anderson & Ferrier, 1911).
Hardie, J. Keir, *Can a Man Be a Christian on a Pound a Week?* (London: Independent Labour Party, 1906).
Haw, George (ed.), *Christianity and the Working Classes* (London: Macmillan, 1906).
Henderson, Arthur, *At the Cross-Roads* (London: National Brotherhood Council, 1919).
Horne, C. Silvester, *A Popular History of the Free Churches, with an Additional Chapter 1903–1926 by Albert Peel* (London: Congregational Union, 1926).
Inge, W. R. (ed.), *What Is the Real Hell?* (London: Cassell, 1930).
Jeffs, Harry, *The Goodly Heritage of the Free Churches* (London: Independent Press, 1927).
Jones, D. Caradog (ed.) *The Social Survey of Merseyside* 3v. (London: Hodder & Stoughton, 1934).
Jones, Joseph, *The Coal Scuttle* (London: Faber, 1936).
Keeble, S. E., *Christian Responsibility for the Social Order* (London: Fernley Lecture Trust, 1922).
Keeble, S. E., *COPEC: An Account of the Christian Conference on Politics, Economics and Citizenship* (London: Epworth, 1924).
Keeble, S. E., 'What the Church Is doing: Social Activities', in Percy Dearmer (ed.), *Christianity and the Crisis* (London: Gollancz, 1933).
Lees-Smith, H. B. (ed.), *The Encyclopaedia of the Labour Movement* 3v. (London: Caxton, 1928).
Lenwood, Frank, *Jesus: Lord or Leader?* (London: Constable,1930).
Lewis, John (ed.), *Christianity and the Social Revolution* (London: Gollancz, 1935).
Linden, Franz, *Sozialismus und Religion: Konfessionsoziologische Untersuchung der Labour Party 1929–1931* (Leipzig: Kölner anglistische Arbeiten, Bande.17, 1932).
Lloyd, C. Ellis, *Scarlet Nest* (London: Hodder & Stoughton, 1919).
Lofthouse, W. F., *Christianity in the Social State* (London: John Heritage, 1936).
Lovell Cocks, H. F., *The Nonconformist Conscience* (London: Independent Press, 1943).
Mass Observation, *The Pub and the People* (London: Gollancz, 1943).
Mellor, Stanley, *Liberation* (London: Constable, 1929).
Murray Hyslop, R. *The Centenary of the Temperance Movement 1832–1932* (London: Independent Press, 1931).
Newland, F. W., *Now, Now, Not Forty Years On* (London: Congregational Union of England and Wales, 1926).
Payne, Ernest A., *The Free Church Tradition in the Life of England* (London: SCM Press, 1944).
Pointing, Horace B., *Political Thought in the Society of Friends* (London: Friends Book Centre, 1939).
Postgate, R. W., Ellen Wilkinson, and J. F. Horrabin, *A Worker's History of the Great Strike* (London: Plebs League, 1927).

Rowland, Wilfred J., *The Free Churches and the People: A Report of the Work of the Free Churches of Liverpool* (Liverpool: Arthur Black, 1908).
Rowntree, B. Seebohm, *Poverty and Progress: A Second Social Survey of York* (London: Longmans, 1941).
Rowntree, B. Seebohm and George R. Lavers, *English Life and Leisure: A Social Study* (Harlow: Longmans, 1951).
Selley, Ernest, *The English Public House as It Is* (London: Longmans Green, 1927).
Shakespeare, J. H., *The Churches at the Cross-Roads: A Study in Church Unity* (London: Williams & Norgate, 1918).
Snowden, Philip, *Socialism and the Drink Question* (London: Independent Labour Party, 1908).
Sorensen, Reg, *The 'Red Flag' and Patriotism* (Southampton: Hobbs, n.d. c1925).
Stamp, Josiah, *The Christian Ethic as an Economic Factor* (London: Epworth, 1926).
Stead, F. H., *The Proletarian Gospel of Galilee in Some of Its Phases* (London: Labour Publishing, 1922).
Thomas, George, *The Christian Heritage in Politics* (London: Epworth, 1959).
Tiplady, Thomas, *Social Christianity in the New Era* (New York: F. H. Revell, 1919).
Tiplady, Thomas, *Spiritual Adventure: The Story of 'the Ideal' Film Service* (London: United Society for Christian Literature, 1935).
Tracey, Herbert (ed.), *The Book of the Labour Party* 3v. (London: Caxton, 1925).
Tracey, Herbert (ed.), *The British Labour Party: Its History, Growth, Policy and Leaders* 3v. (London: Caxton, 1948).
Webb, Sidney, *Labour and the Liquor Trade* (London: Labour Party, 1923).
Wellock, Wilfrid, *The Way Out, or the Road to the New World* (London: Labour Publishing, 1922).
Wellock, Wilfrid, *Destruction or Construction: An Open Letter to Members of the Labour Party* (London: Peace Pledge Union, 1938).
Wertheimer, Egon, *Portrait of the Labour Party* (London: Putnam, 1929).
Williams, T. Rhondda, *Making the Better World* (London: Independent Press, 1929).
Wilson, George B., *Alcohol and the Nation* (London: Nicholson & Watson, 1940).
Wilson, Harold., *The Relevance of British Socialism* (London: Weidenfeld and Nicolson, 1964).

Secondary sources

Biographies

Blackburn, Fred, *George Tomlinson* (London: Heinemann, 1954).
Bradburn, Elizabeth, *Margaret McMillan: Framework and Expansion of Nursery Education* (Redhill: Denholm House Press, 1976).
Briggs, Asa, *Social Thought and Social Action: A Study of the Work of Seebohm Rowntree 1871–1954* (London: Longmans, 1961).
Brockway, A. Fenner, *Socialism over Sixty Years: The Life of Jowett of Bradford* (London: Allen & Unwin, 1946).
Brockway, A. Fenner, *Bermondsey Story: The Life of Alfred Salter* (London: Allen & Unwin, 1949).
Bullock, Alan, *The Life and Times of Ernest Bevin: Volume 1, Trade Union Leader, 1881–1940* (London: Heinemann, 1960).
Bullock, Alan, *Building Jerusalem: A Portrait of My Father* (London: Allen Lane, 2000).
Burnett, R. G., *Through the Mill: The Life of Joseph Rank* (London: Epworth, 1945).

Carter, David, 'Joseph Agar Beet and the Eschatological Crisis' *PWHS* 51/6 (1998), 197–216.
Davies, W. Emrys, 'The Late R. J. Davies', in *Ince and Westhoughton Constituencies and Parts of Wigan Souvenir Booklet 1906–1956* (Wigan: privately printed, 1956).
Edwards, Michael S., *S. E. Keeble: The Rejected Prophet* (Chester: Wesley Historical Society, 1977).
Edwards, Noel, *Ploughboy's Progress: The Life of Sir George Edwards* (Norwich: Centre for East Anglian Studies, University of East Anglia, 1998).
Gault, Hugh, *Making the Heavens Hum: Kingsley Wood and the Art of the Possible 1881–1924* (Cambridge: Gretton Books, 2014).
Hamilton, Mary Agnes, *Arthur Henderson* (London: Heinemann, 1938).
Howarth, David H., *How Great a Flame: The Story of Samuel Chadwick* (Ilkeston: Moorley's, 1983).
Kaye, Elaine, and Ross Mackenzie, *W. E. Orchard: A Study in Christian Exploration* (Oxford: Education Services, 1990).
Kent, John, *William Temple: Church, State and Society in Britain, 1880–1950* (Cambridge: Cambridge University Press, 1992).
Leventhal, F. M., *Arthur Henderson* (Manchester: Manchester University Press, 1989).
Lofthouse, W. F., 'The Warden of the Bermondsey Settlement', in Rupert E. Davies (ed.), *John Scott Lidgett: A Symposium* (London: Epworth, 1957).
Marchant, James, *Dr John Clifford CH: Life, Letters and Reminiscences* (London: Cassell, 1924).
Marquand, David, *Ramsay MacDonald* (London: Cape, 1977).
Morgan, Sue, '"Iron Strength and Infinite Tenderness": Herbert Gray and the Making of Christian Masculinities at War and at Home, 1900–40', in Lucy Delap and Sue Morgan (eds), *Men, Masculinities and Religious Change in Twentieth-Century Britain* (Basingstoke: Palgrave Macmillan, 2013).
Morris, A. J. A., *C. P. Trevelyan 1870–1958* (Belfast: Blackstaff, 1977)
Mulvey, Paul, *The Political Life of Josiah C. Wedgwood: Land, Liberty and Empire 1872–1943* (Woodbridge: Boydell, 2010).
Murray, Harold, *Sixty Years an Evangelist: An Intimate Study of Gipsy Smith* (London: Marshall, Morgan & Scott, 1937).
Neale, Elisabeth J., 'A Type of Congregational Ministry: R. F. Horton (1855–1934) and Lyndhurst Road', *JURCHS* 5/4 (1994), 215–31.
Neale, Elisabeth J., 'Thomas Rhondda Williams (1860–1945) and Brighton', *JURCHS* 6/8 (2001), 596–618.
Oldstone-Moore, Christopher, *Hugh Price Hughes: Founder of a New Methodism, Conscience of a New Nonconformity* (Cardiff: University of Wales Press, 1999).
Peel, Albert and John Marriott, *Robert Forman Horton* (London: Allen & Unwin, 1937).
Rigby, Andrew, *A Life in Peace: A Biography of Wilfrid Wellock* (Bridport: Prism Press, 1988).
Scott, Richenda C., *Elizabeth Cadbury 1858–1951* (London: Harrap, 1955).
Thompson, Laurence, *The Enthusiasts: A Biography of John and Katherine Bruce Glasier* (London: Gollancz, 1971).
Townsend, Henry, *Robert Wilson Black* (London: Carey Kingsgate, 1954).
Turberfield, Alan, *John Scott Lidgett: Archbishop of British Methodism* (Peterborough: Epworth, 2003).
Urwin, E. C., *Henry Carter CBE* (London: Epworth, 1951).
Wakelin, Michael, *J. Arthur Rank: The Man Behind the Gong* (Oxford: Lion, 1996).
Weatherhead, Kingsley, *Leslie Weatherhead: A Personal Portrait* (London: Hodder & Stoughton, 1975).

Wood, H. G., *Terrot Reaveley Glover* (Cambridge: Cambridge University Press, 1953).
Wood, H. G., and Arthur F. Ball, *Tom Bryan, First Warden of Fircroft: A Memoir* (London: Allen & Unwin, 1922).

Other published works

Ackers, Peter, *Labour and Capital in the Wigan Churches of Christ c1845–1945* (Loughborough University Business School Research Paper 4, 1994).
Bagwell, Philip S., 'The Triple Industrial Alliance 1913–1922', in Asa Briggs and John Savile (eds), *Essays in Labour History 1886–1923* (London: Macmillan, 1971).
Bagwell, Philip S., *Outcast London: A Christian Response* (London: Epworth, 1987).
Ball, Stuart, *Portrait of a Party: The Conservative Party in Britain 1918–1945* (Oxford: Oxford University Press, 2013).
Banks, John, *The Story So Far: The First Hundred Years of the Manchester and Salford Methodist Mission* (Manchester: Manchester and Salford Methodist Mission, 1986).
Barker, T. C., *The Glassmakers, Pilkington: The Rise of an International Company 1826–1976* (London: Weidenfeld & Nicolson, 1977).
Beasley, John, *The Bitter Cry Heard and Heeded: The Story of the South London Mission* (London: South London Mission, 1990).
Bebbington, David, *The Nonconformist Conscience: Chapel and Politics, c.1870–1914* (London: Allen & Unwin, 1982).
Bebbington, David, 'Baptists and Politics since 1914', in K. W. Clements (ed.), *Baptists in the Twentieth Century* (London: Baptist Historical Society, 1983).
Bebbington, David, 'Nonconformity and Electoral Sociology 1867–1918', *Historical Journal* 27/3 (1984), 633–56.
Bebbington, David, *Evangelicalism in Modern Britain: A History from the 1730s to the 1980s* (London: Unwin Hyman, 1989).
Bebbington, David, 'The Free Church MPs of the 1906 Parliament', in Stephen Taylor and David L. Wykes (eds), *Parliament and Dissent* (Edinburgh: Edinburgh University Press, 2005).
Bebbington, David, 'Conscience and Politics', in Lesley Husselbee and Paul Ballard (eds), *Free Churches and Society: The Nonconformist Contribution to Social Welfare 1800–2010* (London: Continuum, 2012).
Bebbington, David, 'The Baptist Colleges in the Mid-Nineteenth Century', *Baptist Quarterly* 46/2 (2015), 49–68.
Beers, Laura, and Geraint Thomas (eds), *Brave New World: Imperial and Democratic Nation-Building in Britain between the Wars* (London: Institute of Historical Research, 2011).
Bentley, Michael, *The Liberal Mind 1914–1929* (Cambridge: Cambridge University Press, 1977).
Berger, Stefan, *The Labour Party and the German Social Democrats 1900–1931* (Oxford: Oxford University Press, 1994).
Berry, David, *The Sociology of Grass Roots Politics: A Study of Party Membership* (London: Macmillan, 1970).
Binfield, Clyde, *Pastors and People: The Biography of a Baptist Church, Queens Road, Coventry* (Coventry: Queen's Road Baptist Church, 1984).
Binfield, Clyde, 'True to Stereotype? Vivian and Dorothy Pomeroy and the Patch in Lumb Lane', in Stuart Mews (ed.), *Modern Religious Rebels* (London: Epworth, 1993).

Binfield, Clyde, 'Victorian Values and Industrious Connexions', *PWHS* 55/4 (2006), 141–68.

Binfield, Clyde, 'Industry, Philanthropy and Citizenship: Pioneers in Paternalism', in Lesley Husselbee and Paul Ballard (eds), *Free Churches and Society: The Nonconformist Contribution to Social Welfare 1800–2010* (London: Continuum, 2012).

Birch, A. H., *Small Town Politics: A Study of Political Life in Glossop* (London: Oxford University Press, 1959).

Birtill, George, *The Changing Years: Chorley and District between the Wars* (Chorley, Guardian Press, 1976).

Brennan, T., E. W. Cooney and H. Pollins, *Social Change in South West Wales* (London: Watts, 1954).

Briggs, Asa, and John Savile (eds), *Essays in Labour History 1886–1923* (London: Macmillan, 1971).

Briggs, John, and Ian Sellers (eds), *Victorian Nonconformity* (London: Arnold, 1973).

Broadberry, S. N., and A. Ritschl, 'Real Wages, Productivity and Unemployment in Britain and Germany during the 1920s', *Explorations in Economic History* 32 (1995), 327–49.

Brooke, Stephen, *Sexual Politics: Sexuality, Family Planning and the British Left from the 1880s to the Present Day* (Oxford: Oxford University Press, 2011).

Brookshire, Jerry H., '"Speak for England", Act for England: Labour's Leadership and British National Security under the Threat of War in the Late 1930s', *European History Quarterly* 29/2 (1999), 251-87.

Brown, Kenneth D., 'English Nonconformity and the British Labour Movement: A Study', *Journal of Social History* 9/2 (1975), 113–20.

Brown, Kenneth D., 'Nineteenth-Century Methodist Theological College Principals', *PWHS* 44/4 (1984), 93–102.

Brown, Kenneth D., 'Ministerial Recruitment and Training: An Aspect of the Crisis of Victorian Nonconformity', *Victorian Studies*, 30/3 (1987), 365–84.

Brown, Kenneth D., 'The Baptist Ministry of England and Wales: A Social Profile', *Baptist Quarterly* 32/3 (1987), 105–20.

Brown, Kenneth D., 'College Principals – A Cause of Nonconformist Decay?', *Journal of Ecclesiastical History* 38/2 (1987), 236–53.

Brown, Kenneth D., 'An Unsettled Ministry? Some Aspects of Nineteenth Century British Nonconformity', *Church History* 56/2 (1987), 204–23.

Bruce, Steve, 'Methodism and Mining in County Durham 1881–1991', *Northern History* 48/2 (2011), 337–55.

Casey, Michael W., 'The Overlooked Pacifist Tradition of the Old Paths Churches of Christ, Part I', *JURCHS* 6/6 (2000), 446–59.

Casey, Michael W., 'The Overlooked Pacifist Tradition of the Old Paths Churches of Christ, Part II', *JURCHS* 6/7 (2000), 517–28.

Catterall, Peter, 'Church Decline, Secularism and Ecumenism', *Contemporary Record* 5/2 (1991), 276–90.

Catterall, Peter, 'The Party and Religion', in Anthony Seldon and Stuart Ball (eds), *Conservative Century: The Conservative Party in the Twentieth Century* (Oxford: Oxford University Press, 1994).

Catterall, Peter, '"Efficiency with Freedom"? Debates about the British Constitution in the Twentieth Century', in Peter Catterall, Wolfram Kaiser and Ulrike Walton-Jordan (eds), *Reforming the Constitution: Debates in Twentieth Century Britain* (London: Cass, 2000).

Catterall, Peter, 'The Politics of Electoral Reform since 1885', in Peter Catterall, Wolfram Kaiser and Ulrike Walton-Jordan (eds), *Reforming the Constitution: Debates in Twentieth-Century Britain* (London: Cass, 2000).

Catterall, Peter, 'The Distinctiveness of British Socialism? Religion and the Rise of Labour, c.1900–39', in Matthew Worley (ed.), *The Foundations of the British Labour Party: Identities, Cultures and Perspectives, 1900–39* (Farnham: Ashgate, 2009).

Catterall, Peter, 'Slums and Salvation', in Lesley Husselbee and Paul Ballard (eds), *Free Churches and Society: The Nonconformist Contribution to Social Welfare 1800–2010* (London: Continuum, 2012).

Catterall, Peter, 'Nonconformity and the Labour Movement', in Robert Pope (ed.), *Companion to Nonconformity* (London: Bloomsbury T&T Clark, 2013).

Catterall, Peter, *Labour and the Politics of Alcohol: The Decline of a Cause* (London: Institute of Alcohol Studies, 2014), online resource at http://www.ias.org.uk/uploads/pdf/IAS%20reports/Labour%20and%20the%20politics%20of%20alcohol%20-%20The%20decline%20of%20a%20cause.pdf.

Catterall, Peter, 'Chancellor of the Exchequer and the Return to the Gold Standard', in Richard Toye (ed.), *Winston Churchill: Politics, Strategy and Statecraft in the Twentieth Century* (London: Bloomsbury, 2017).

Catterall, Peter, and Chris Brady, 'The Development and Role of Cabinet Committees in Britain', in R. A. W. Rhodes (ed.), *Transforming British Government: Volume 1, Changing Institutions* (Basingstoke: Macmillan, 2000).

Catterall, Peter, and Joyce Howson, 'New Unionism', in Peter Catterall (ed.), *Britain 1867–1918* (Oxford: Heinemann Educational, 1994).

Ceadel, Martin, *Pacifism in Britain 1914–1945: The Defining of a Faith* (Oxford: Clarendon, 1980).

Childs, Michael, 'Labour Grows Up: The Electoral System, Political Generations and British Politics 1890–1929', *Twentieth Century British History* 6 (1995), 123–44.

Clapson, Mark, *A Bit of a Flutter: Popular Gambling and English Society c1823-1961* (Manchester: Manchester University Press, 1992).

Clarke, Peter, 'Electoral Sociology of Modern Britain', *History* 57 (1972), 31–55.

Coleman, Marie, *The Irish Sweep: A History of the Irish Hospitals Sweepstake 1930–87* (Dublin: University College Dublin Press, 2009).

Cook, Chris, *The Age of Alignment: Electoral Politics in Britain, 1922–1929* (London: Macmillan, 1975).

Cook, Chris, and John Ramsden (eds), *By-elections in British Politics*, 2nd ed. (London: UCL Press, 1997).

Cowling, Maurice, *The Impact of Labour: The Beginning of Modern British Politics* (Cambridge: Cambridge University Press, 1971).

Cox, Jeffery, *English Churches in a Secular Society: Lambeth 1870–1930* (Oxford: Oxford University Press, 1982).

Cronin, James E., *The Politics of State Expansion: War, State and Society in Twentieth-Century Britain* (London: Routledge, 1991).

Crook, Rosemary, 'Tidy Women: Women in the Rhondda between the Wars', *Oral History* 10/2 (1982), 40–6.

Currie, Robert, *Methodism Divided: A Study in the Sociology of Ecumenicalism* (London: Faber, 1968).

Currie, Robert, Alan Gilbert and Lee Horsley, *Churches and Churchgoers: Patterns of Church Growth in the British Isles since 1700* (Oxford: Clarendon, 1977).

Davies, Andrew, 'The Police and the People: Gambling in Salford 1900–1939', *Historical Journal* 34/1 (1991), 87–115.

Dickens, P., and P. Gilbert, 'Inter-war Housing Policy: A Study of Brighton', *Southern History* 3 (1981), 201–32.

Dingley, James, *Nationalism, Social Theory and Durkheim* (Basingstoke: Palgrave Macmillan, 2008).

Dingley, James, 'Sacred Communities: Religion and National Identities', *National Identities* 13/4 (2011), 389–402.

Dolan, John, *The Independent Methodists: A History* (Cambridge: James Clarke, 2005).

Doyle, Barry M., 'Gender, Class and Congregational Culture in Early Twentieth-Century Norwich', *JURCHS* 5/6 (1995), 317–35.

Doyle, Barry M., 'Urban Liberalism and the "Lost Generation": Politics and Middle-class Culture in Norwich 1900–35', *Historical Journal* 38 (1995), 617–34.

Doyle, Barry M., 'Modernity or Morality? George White, Liberalism and the Nonconformist Conscience in Edwardian England', *Historical Research* 71/176 (1998), 324–40.

Doyle, Barry M., 'A Conflict of Interests? The Local and National Dimensions of Middle Class Liberalism 1900–1935', *Parliamentary History* 17/1 (1998), 131–40.

Dowse, R. E., *Left in the Centre: The Independent Labour Party 1893–1940* (London: Longmans, 1966).

Dupree, Marguerite, 'Foreign Competition and the Interwar Period', in Mary B. Rose (ed.), *The Lancashire Cotton Industry: A History since 1700* (Preston: Lancashire County Books, 1996).

Entwistle, Dorothy, '"Hope, Colour, and Citizenship": Loyalty and Opportunism in Early Twentieth-Century Church Attendance', *Journal of Religious History* 25/1 (2001), 20–38.

Farr, Nicholas, *At the Heart of the City: A Methodist Mission in the Twentieth Century* (Sheffield: Victoria Hall Methodist Church, 1991).

Field, Clive D., 'A Sociological Profile of English Methodism 1900-1932', *Oral History* 4/1 (1976), 73–95.

Field, Clive D., 'Zion's People: who were the English Nonconformists? Part 1: Gender, Age and Ethnicity' *The Local Historian* 40/2 (2010), 91–112.

Field, Clive D., 'Zion's People: who were the English Nonconformists? Part 2: Occupation (Quakers, Baptists, Congregationalists)', *The Local Historian* 40/3 (2010), 208–23.

Field, Clive D., 'Zion's People: who were the English Nonconformists? Part 3: Occupation (Methodists) and Conclusions', *The Local Historian* 40/4 (2010), 292–308.

Field, Clive D., 'The Faith Society? Clarifying religious belonging in Edwardian Britain 1901–1914', *Journal of Religious History* 37/1 (2013), 39–63.

Field, Clive D., 'Gradualist or Revolutionary Secularisation? A Case Study of Religious Belonging in Inter-War Britain 1918–1939', *Church History and Culture* 93 (2013), 57–93.

Field, Clive D., 'Keeping the Spiritual Home Fires Burning: Religious Belonging in Britain during the First World War', *War and Society* 33/4 (2014), 244–68.

Francis, Hywel, 'The Anthracite Strike and Disturbances of 1925', *Llafur* 1/2 (1973), 15–28.

Francis, Hywel, and David Smith, *The Fed: A History of the South Wales Miners in the Twentieth Century* (London: Lawrence & Wishart, 1980).

Freeman, Mark, *Social Investigation and Rural England 1870–1914* (Woodbridge: Boydell, 2003).

Freeman, Mark, 'The Decline of the Adult School Movement between the Wars', *History of Education* 39/4 (2010), 481–506.

Freeman, Mark, 'Seebohm Rowntree and Secondary Poverty, 1899–1954', *Economic History Review* 64/4 (2011), 1175–94.
Frost, Brian, *Pioneers of Social Passion: London's Cosmopolitan Methodism* (Peterborough: Epworth, 2006).
Garside, W. R., *The Durham Miners 1919–1960* (London: Allen & Unwin, 1971).
Giddens, Anthony (ed.), *Emile Durkheim: Selected Writings* (Cambridge: Cambridge University Press, 1972).
Gilbert, A. D., *The Making of Post-Christian Britain: A History of the Secularization of Modern Society* (London: Longman, 1980).
Gill, Robin, *Competing Convictions* (London: SCM Press, 1989).
Gill, Robin, *The Myth of the Empty Church* (London: SPCK, 1993).
Glaser, John F., 'English Nonconformity and the Decline of Liberalism', *American Historical Review* 63/2 (1958), 352–63.
Glaser, John F., 'Parnell's Fall and the Nonconformist Conscience', *Irish Historical Studies* 12/46 (1960), 119–38.
Gourvish, T. R., and R. G. Wilson, *The British Brewing Industry 1830–1980* (Cambridge: Cambridge University Press, 1994).
Graham, Dorothy, *Women Local Preachers in the British Isles* (Christchurch: Wesley Historical Society (NZ), 1998).
Grant, J. W., *Free Churchmanship in England 1870–1914* (London: Independent Press, 1955).
Graves, Pamela M., *Labour Women: Women in British Working-Class Politics 1918–1939* (Cambridge: Cambridge University Press, 1994).
Grayson, Richard, *Liberals, International Relations and Appeasement* (London: Cass, 2001).
Grayzel, Susan R., *Women and the First World War* (Harlow: Longman, 2002).
Green, George, *Central Hall, Bradford Centenary Souvenir Handbook 1821–1921* (Bradford: Central Hall, 1922).
Green, S. J. D., *Religion in the Age of Decline: Organisation and Experience in Industrial Yorkshire 1870–1920* (Cambridge: Cambridge University Press, 1996).
Green, S. J. D., *The Passing of Protestant England: Secularisation and Social Change c.1920–1960* (Cambridge: Cambridge University Press, 2011).
Griffiths, Clare V. J., *Labour and the Countryside: The Politics of Rural Britain 1918–1939* (Oxford: Oxford University Press, 2007).
Groot, Gerard de, *Blighty: British Society in the Era of the Great War* (Harlow: Longman, 1996).
Groves, Reg, *Sharpen the Sickle! The History of the Farm Workers' Union* (London: Merlin, 1981).
Hall, W. Arnold, *The Adult School Movement in the Twentieth Century* (Nottingham: Department of Adult Education, University of Nottingham, 1985).
Hastings, Adrian, *A History of English Christianity 1920–1990* (London: SCM Press, 1991).
Helmstadter, Richard, 'The Nonconformist Conscience', in Peter Marsh (ed.), *The Conscience of the Victorian State* (Brighton: Harvester, 1979).
Hill, Jeffrey, *Nelson: Politics, Economy, Community* (Edinburgh: Keele University Press, 1997).
Howard, Christopher, 'Expectations born to death: local Labour party expansion in the 1920s', in J. M. Winter (ed.), *The Working Class in Modern British History: Essays in Honour of Henry Pelling* (Cambridge: Cambridge University Press, 1983).
Howkins, Alun, *Poor Labouring Men: Rural Radicalism in Norfolk 1870–1923* (London: Routledge & Kegan Paul, 1985).

Hughes, Michael, *Conscience and Conflict: Methodism, Peace and War in the Twentieth Century* (Peterborough: Epworth, 2008).

Hunt, Cathy, 'Sex versus Class in Two British Trade Unions in the Early Twentieth Century', *Journal of Women's History* 24/1 (2012), 86–110.

Husselbee, Lesley, and Paul Ballard (eds), *Free Churches and Society: The Nonconformist Contribution to Social Welfare 1800–2010* (London: Continuum, 2012).

Inglis, K. S., *Churches and the Working Class in Victorian England* (London: Routledge & Kegan Paul, 1963).

James, David, *Class and Politics in a Northern Industrial Town: Keighley 1890–1914* (Keele: Ryburn, 1995).

Jeremy, David J., *Capitalists and Christians: Business Leaders and the Churches in Britain 1900–1960* (Oxford: Clarendon, 1990).

Johnson, Dale A., *The Changing Shape of English Nonconformity 1825–1925* (Oxford: Oxford University Press, 1999).

Johnson, Mel, 'Primitive Parliamentarians, the Great War, and its Aftermath', *PWHS* 59/4 (2014), 125–35.

Johnson, R. W., 'The Nationalisation of English Rural Politics: Norfolk South West 1945–1970', *Parliamentary Affairs* 26/1 (1972/73), 8–55.

Jones, Peter d'A, *The Christian Socialist Revival 1877–1914: Religion, Class and Social Conscience in Late Victorian England* (Princeton, NJ: Princeton University Press, 1968).

Jordan, E. K. H., *Free Church Unity. History of the Free Church Council Movement 1896–1941* (London: Lutterworth, 1956).

Kent, John, *From Darwin to Blatchford: The Role of Darwinism in Christian Apologetic 1875–1910* (London: Dr Williams's Trust, 1966).

Kinnear, Michael, *The British Voter: An Atlas and Survey since 1885*, 2nd ed. (London: Batsford, 1981).

Koss, Stephen, 'Lloyd George and Nonconformity: The Last Rally', *English Historical Review* 89 (1974), 77–108.

Koss, Stephen, *Nonconformity in Modern British Politics* (London: Batsford, 1975).

Kotler-Berkowitz, Laurence A., 'Religion and Voting Behaviour in Great Britain: A Reassessment', *British Journal of Political Science* 31/3 (2001), 523–54.

Koven, Seth, *Slumming: Sexual and Social Politics in Victorian London* (London: Princeton University Press, 2004).

Koven, Seth, *The Match Girl and the Heiress* (London: Princeton University Press, 2015).

Larsen, Timothy, *Friends of Religious Equality: Nonconformist Politics in Mid-Victorian England* (Woodbridge: Boydell Press, 1999).

Law, Michael John, '"The Car Indispensable": The Hidden Influence of the Car in Inter-war Suburban London', *Journal of Historical Geography* 38/4 (2013), 424–33.

Lawrence, Jon, 'Class and Gender in the Making of Urban Toryism 1880–1914', *English Historical Review* 108/428 (1993), 629–52.

Lawrence, Jon, and Miles Taylor (eds), *Party, State and Society: Electoral Behaviour in Modern Britain* (Aldershot: Scolar, 1996).

Laybourn, Keith, and John Reynolds, *Liberalism and the Rise of Labour 1890–1914* (London: Croom Helm, 1984).

Lowe, Rodney, 'The Failure of Consensus in Britain: The National Industrial Conference, 1919–1921', *Historical Journal* 21/3 (1978), 649–75.

McCarthy, Helen, *The British People and the League of Nations: Democracy, Citizenship and Internationalism, c.1918–45* (Manchester: Manchester University Press, 2011).

McDonald, G. W., and Howard F. Gospel, 'The Mond-Turner Talks 1927–1933: A Study in Industrial Co-operation', *Historical Journal* 16/4 (1973), 807–29.
Machin, G. I. T., *Churches and Social Issues in Twentieth-Century Britain* (Oxford: Oxford University Press, 1998).
McIntyre, Stuart, *Little Moscows* (London: Croom Helm, 1980).
McKibbin, Ross, 'Working-Class Gambling in Britain 1880–1939', *Past & Present* 82 (1979), 147–78.
McKibbin, Ross, 'Why was there no Marxism in Great Britain?', *English Historical Review* 99/391 (1984), 297–331.
McKibbin, Ross, *Classes and Cultures: England 1918–1951* (Oxford: Oxford University Press, 2000).
McKibbin, Ross, *Parties and People: England 1914–1951* (Oxford: Oxford University Press, 2010).
McLeod, Hugh, *Class and Religion in the Late Victorian City* (London: Croom Helm, 1974).
McLeod, Hugh, 'New Perspectives on Victorian Working-Class Religion: The Oral Evidence', *Oral History* 14/1 (1986), 31–49.
McLeod, Hugh, 'Dissent and the Peculiarities of the English, c.1870–1914', in Jane Shaw and Alan Kreider (eds), *Culture and the Nonconformist Tradition* (Cardiff: University of Wales Press, 1999).
McLeod, Hugh, 'Sport and the English Sunday School 1869–1939', in Stephen Orchard and John Briggs (eds), *The Sunday School Movement* (Milton Keynes: Paternoster, 2007).
Mansfield, Nicholas, 'Farmworkers and Local Conservatism in South-West Shropshire, 1916–23', in Stuart Ball and Ian Holliday (eds) *Mass Conservatism: The Conservatives and the Public since the 1880s* (London: Cass, 2002).
Martin, David E., 'The Instruments of the People? The Parliamentary Labour Party in 1906', in David E. Martin and David Rubenstein (eds), *Ideology and the Labour Movement* (London: Croom Helm, 1979).
Matthew, H. G. C., R. I. McKibbin and J. A. Kay, 'The Franchise Factor in the Rise of the Labour Party', *English Historical Review* 91 (1976), 723–52.
Mayor, S. H., *The Churches and the Labour Movement* (London: Independent Press, 1967).
Millett, John H., 'British Interest-Group Tactics: A Case Study', *Political Science Quarterly* 72/1 (1957), 71-82.
Millman, Brock, *Managing Domestic Dissent in First World War Britain* (London: Cass, 2000).
Milner, David, *Twice Happy Place: A History of Zion Baptist Church, Mirfield* (Mirfield: Zion Baptist, 1973).
Moore, Robert, *Pitmen, Preachers and Politics: The Effects of Methodism in a Durham Mining Community* (Cambridge: Cambridge University Press, 1974)
Morgan, Kenneth O., 'Twilight of Welsh Liberalism: Lloyd George and the Wee Frees 1918–1935', *Bulletin of the Board of Celtic Studies* 22 (1968), 389-406.
Morgan, Kenneth O., *Rebirth of a Nation: Wales 1880–1980* (Oxford: Oxford University Press, 1981).
Moynihan, Michael (ed.), *God on Our Side: The British Padre in World War I* (London: Secker & Warburg. 1983).
Munson, James, *The Nonconformists: In Search of a Lost Culture* (London: SPCK, 1991).
Naylor, Barrie, *Quakers in the Rhondda 1926–1986* (Chepstow: Maes-yr-haf Educational Trust, 1986).

Nicholls, James, *The Politics of Alcohol: A History of the Drink Question in England* (Manchester: Manchester University Press, 2009).
Ollerhead, P., 'Unitarianism in Crewe 1860–1940', *Unitarian Historical Society Transactions* 17/1 (1979), 29–36.
Orchard, Stephen, 'The Free Churches and Their Nation', in Lesley Husselbee and Paul Ballard (eds), *Free Churches and Society: The Nonconformist Contribution to Social Welfare 1800–2010* (London: Continuum, 2012).
Orchard, Stephen, 'Providers and Protagonists in the Nation's Education', in Lesley Husselbee and Paul Ballard (eds), *Free Churches and Society: The Nonconformist Contribution to Social Welfare 1800–2010* (London: Continuum, 2012).
Packer, Ian, *Lloyd George, Liberalism and the Land: The Land Issue and Party Politics 1906–1914* (Woodbridge: Boydell, 2001).
Pennell, Catriona, *A Kingdom United: Popular Responses to the Outbreak of the First World War in Britain and Ireland* (Oxford: Oxford University Press, 2012).
Piper, C. A., *A Century of Service: The Story of Liverpool North End Domestic Mission Society's First Hundred Years 1859–1959* (Liverpool: privately printed, 1959).
Pitt, Margaret R., *Our Unemployed: Can the Past teach the present?* (Harrow: privately printed, 1982).
Plant, Raymond, 'The Anglican Church and the Secular State', in George Moyser (ed.), *The Church and Politics Today: The Role of the Church of England in Contemporary Politics* (Edinburgh: T. & T. Clark, 1985).
Pope, Robert, *Building Jerusalem: Nonconformity, Labour and the Social Question in Wales, 1906–1939* (Cardiff: University of Wales Press, 1998).
Pope, Robert, 'The Rise and Fall of the Calvinist Consensus in Wales', *JURCHS* 8/7 (2010), 369–85.
Pope, Robert, 'Congregations and Community', in Lesley Husselbee and Paul Ballard (eds), *Free Churches and Society: The Nonconformist Contribution to Social Welfare 1800–2010* (London: Continuum, 2012).
Pope, Robert, 'The Nonconformist Conscience', in Robert Pope (ed.), *Companion to Nonconformity* (London: Bloomsbury T&T Clark, 2013).
Prochaska, Frank, *Christianity and Social Service in Modern Britain* (Oxford: Oxford University Press, 2006).
Pugh, Martin, 'The Rise of Labour and the Political Culture of Conservatism 1890–1945', *History* 87/288 (2002), 514–37.
Pugh, Martin, *Speak for Britain! A New History of the Labour Party* (London: Vintage, 2011).
Ramsden, G. M., *A Responsible Society: The Life and Times of the Congregation of Bank Street Chapel, Bolton, Lancashire* (Bolton: privately printed, 1985).
Ramsden, John, *A History of the Conservative Party Volume 3: The Age of Balfour and Baldwin* (London: Longman, 1978).
Randall, Ian M., 'Southport and Swanwick: Contrasting Movements of Methodist Spirituality in Inter-War England', *PWHS* 50/1 (1995), 1–14.
Redvaldsen, David, '"Today is the Dawn": The Labour Party and the 1929 General Election', *Parliamentary History* 29/3 (2010), 395–415.
Redvaldsen, David *The Labour Party in Britain and Norway: Elections and the Pursuit of Power between the World Wars* (London: I. B. Tauris, 2011).
Rees, D. Ben, *Chapels in the Valleys: A Study in the Sociology of Welsh Nonconformity* (Wirral: Ffynnon Press, 1975).

Reid, F., 'Socialist Sunday Schools in Britain 1892–1939', *International Review of Social History* 11/1 (1966), 18–47.
Richards, Jeffery, *The Age of the Dream Palace: Cinema and Society in 1930s Britain* (London: Routledge, 1984).
Richards, Noel J., 'The Education Bill of 1906 and the Decline of Political Nonconformity', *Journal of Ecclesiastical History* 23/1 (1972), 49–64.
Riddell, Neil, 'The Catholic Church and the Labour Party 1918–31', *Twentieth Century British History* 8/2 (1997), 165–93.
Robbins, Keith, *The Abolition of War: The 'Peace Movement' in Britain 1914–1919* (Cardiff: University of Wales Press, 1976).
Robbins, Keith, *History, Religion and Identity in Modern Britain* (London: Hambledon, 1993).
Roberts, Elizabeth, *A Woman's Place: An Oral History of Working-Class Women 1890–1940* (Oxford: Blackwell, 1984).
Rowntree Clifford, Paul, *Venture in Faith: The Story of the West Ham Central Mission* (London: Carey Kingsgate, 1950).
Savage, Michael, *The Dynamics of Working-Class Politics: The Labour Movement in Preston, 1880–1940* (Cambridge: Cambridge University Press, 1987).
Scotland, Nigel, *Methodism and the Revolt of the Field* (Gloucester: Sutton, 1981).
Sell, Alan P. F., and Anthony R. Cross (eds), *Protestant Nonconformity in the Twentieth Century* (Carlisle: Paternoster, 2003).
Sellers, Ian, *Salute to Pembroke: Pembroke Chapel, Liverpool 1838–1931* (Liverpool: privately printed, 1960).
Sellers, Ian, 'Nonconformist Attitudes in Late Nineteenth Century Liverpool', *Transactions of the Historic Society of Lancashire and Cheshire* 114 (1962), 215–39.
Smith, Leonard, *Religion and the Rise of Labour: Nonconformity and the Independent Labour Movement in Lancashire and the West Riding 1880–1914* (Keele: Ryburn, 1993).
Snape, Michael, *God and the British Soldier: Religion and the British Army in the First and Second World Wars* (London: Routledge, 2005).
Snape, Michael, *Revisiting Religion and the British Soldier in the First World War* (London: Dr Williams's Trust, 2015).
Stenton, M., and S. Lees (eds), *Who's Who of British Members of Parliament* 4v. (Brighton: Harvester Press, 1978-81).
Stevens, Christopher, 'The Electoral Sociology of Britain Reconsidered', *Contemporary British History* 13/1 (1999), 62–94.
Stevenson, John, *British Society 1914–1945* (London: Allen Lane, 1984).
Swartz, Marvin, *The Union of Democratic Control in British Politics during the First World War* (Oxford: Clarendon, 1971).
Tanner, Duncan, *Political Change and the Labour Party 1900–1918* (Cambridge: Cambridge University Press, 1990).
Thompson, David M., *Let Sects and Parties Fall: A Short History of the Association of Churches of Christ in Great Britain and Ireland* (Birmingham: Berean Press, 1980).
Thompson, David M., 'The Older Free Churches', in Rupert E. Davies (ed.) *The Testing of the Churches 1932–1982* (London: Epworth, 1982).
Thompson, David M., 'John Clifford's Social Gospel' *Baptist Quarterly* 31/5 (1986), 199–217.
Thompson, David M., 'R. W. Dale and the "Civic Gospel"', in Alan P. F. Sell (ed.), *Protestant Nonconformists and the West Midlands of England* (Keele: Keele University Press, 1996).

Thompson, David M., 'Edinburgh 1910: Myths, Mission and Unity', *JURCHS* 8/7 (2010), 386–99.
Thompson, Willie, *The Good Old Cause: British Communism 1920–1991* (London: Pluto, 1992).
Thompson Brake, George, *Policy and Politics in British Methodism 1932–1982* (London: Edsall, 1984).
Thorpe, Andrew, 'J. H. Thomas and the rise of Labour in Derby 1880–1945', *Midland History* 15 (1990), 111–28.
Thorpe, Andrew, *A History of the British Labour Party*, 2nd ed. (Basingstoke: Palgrave, 2001).
Tomes, Roger, '"Learning a New Technique": The Reception of Biblical Criticism in the Nonconformist Colleges', *JURCHS* 7/5 (2004), 288–314.
Tomkins, Daniel, *Mission Accomplished: The Story of the First One Hundred Years of the Bolton Methodist Mission* (Bolton: Bolton Methodist Mission, 1997).
Tregidga, Garry, *The Liberal Party in South-West Britain since 1918: Political Decline, Dormancy and Rebirth* (Exeter: University of Exeter Press, 2000).
Tudur Jones, R., *Congregationalism in England 1662–1962* (London: Independent Press, 1962).
Underwood, A. C., *A History of the English Baptists* (London: Baptist Union, 1947).
Waller, P. J., *Democracy and Sectarianism: A Political and Social History of Liverpool 1868–1939* (Liverpool: Liverpool University Press, 1981).
Waller, Robert, 'Conservative Electoral Support and Social Class', in Anthony Seldon and Stuart Ball (eds), *Conservative Century: The Conservative Party since 1900* (Oxford: Oxford University Press, 1994).
Wallwork, Norman, *The Gospel Church Secure: The Official History of the Methodist Sacramental Fellowship* (London: Church in the Marketplace Publications, 2013).
Ward, Stephanie, '"The Workers Are in the Mood to Fight the Act": Protest against the Means Test 1931–1935', in Matthias Reiss and Matt Perry (eds), *Unemployment Protest: New Perspectives on Two Centuries of Contention* (Oxford: Oxford University Press, 2011).
Ward, Stephen R., 'The British Veterans' Ticket of 1918', *Journal of British Studies* 8/1 (1968), 155–69.
Ward, Stephen R., 'Intelligence Surveillance of British ex-servicemen 1918–20', *Historical Journal* 16/1 (1973), 179–88.
Whetham, Edith H., *The Agrarian History of England and Wales: vol.8, 1914–1939* (Cambridge: Cambridge University Press, 1978).
White, Stephen, 'Soviets in Britain: The Leeds Convention of 1917', *International Review of Social History* 19/2 (1974), 165–93.
Wilkinson, Alan, *Dissent or Conform? War, Peace and the English Churches 1900–1945* (London: SCM Press, 1986).
Williams, G. P., and George Thompson Brake, *Drink in Great Britain 1900–1979* (London: Edsall, 1980).
Williams, S. C., *Religious Belief and Popular Culture in Southwark c1880-1939* (Oxford: Oxford University Press, 1999).
Williamson, Philip, *National Crisis and National Government: British Politics, the Economy and Empire 1926–1932* (Cambridge: Cambridge University Press, 1991).
Williamson, Philip, 'Christian Conservatism and the Totalitarian Challenge 1933–40', *English Historical Review* 115 (2000), 607–42.
Wood, Kenneth, *The Coal Pits of Chowbent* (Bolton: privately printed, 1984).

Worley, Matthew, *Class versus Class: The Communist Party in Britain between the Wars* (London: I. B. Tauris, 2002).
Worley, Matthew *Labour inside the Gate: A History of the British Labour Party between the Wars* (London: I. B. Tauris, 2005).
Worley, Matthew (ed.), *The Foundations of the British Labour Party: Identities, Cultures and Perspectives, 1900–39* (Farnham: Ashgate, 2009).
Yeo, Stephen, *Religion and Voluntary Organisations in Crisis* (London: Croom Helm, 1976).

Unpublished theses and other manuscripts

Baxter, Robert, 'The Liverpool Labour Party 1918–1963', unpub. Oxford D.Phil Thesis (1969).
Diggle, B. S., 'Illingworthism: Alfred Illingworth and Independent Labour politics', unpub. Huddersfield MA Thesis (1984).
Gwyther, C. E., 'Methodism and Syndicalism in the Rhondda Valley 1906–1926', unpub. Sheffield PhD Thesis (1967).
Harris, P. A., 'Social Leadership and Social Attitudes in Bolton 1919–1939', unpub. Lancaster PhD Thesis (1973).
Howard, Christopher, 'Henderson, MacDonald and Leadership in the Labour Party 1914–1922', unpub. Cambridge PhD Thesis (1978).
McClymont, Gregg, 'The Labour Party's Attitude to Gambling, 1918–1970', unpub. Oxford D.Phil thesis (2006).
Milne, R. G., 'County Road: The Story of a Methodist Church in North Liverpool', unpub. typescript in LCA (1980).
Power, James, 'Aspects of working-class leisure during the depression years: Bolton in the 1930s', unpub. Warwick MA Thesis (1980).
Roberts, David A., 'Religion and Politics in Liverpool since 1900', unpub. London MSc Thesis (1965).
Rowett, John, 'The Labour Party and Local Government: Theory and Practice in the Inter-War Years', unpub. Oxford D.Phil Thesis (1979).
Sellers, Ian, 'The Methodist Chapels and Preaching Places of Liverpool and District 1750–1971', unpub. 1971 typescript in LCA.
Wolfenden, J. W., 'English Nonconformity and the Social Conscience 1880–1906', unpub. Yale PhD Thesis (1954).

Index

Lightning Source UK Ltd.
Milton Keynes UK
UKHW022138100919
349507UK00015B/146/P

9 781350 067264